"*Thank you for the opportunity to read your book, A Girl Named Job. Your story is inspirational. It shows young women that even though they are faced with adversity, they can still persevere. I am amazed at your strength and courage you showed when most people would have given up completely. The fact that you were able to continue on your path shows the strength that you have*"

~*Shawon Williams*-APOOO Book Club

"*I had to keep picking it up to see what was going to happen next.*"

~Michelle Larks-Author of *Keeping Misery Company*

"*I have so enjoyed reading your book. You are such an inspiration.*"

~Tinisha Nicole Johnson-Author of *Searchable Whereabouts*

For anyone, man, woman, or child, who is facing adversity, please read this book. Marie is a fine example that trouble don't last always!

`*Southern Girl Review*-Amazon.com

To Navette

A Girl Named Job

You are a friend & a gem all rolled up into one!

Love,
Marie Antionette

By Marie Antionette

Cauzing Elevation Publishing, LLC

PO Box 159

Trenton, NJ

A Girl Named Job

A Girl Named Job
By Marie Antionette
Revised Second Print
www.mzmarieantionette.com
www.myspace.com/mzmarieantionette

Cauzing' Elevation Publishing, LLC
PO Box 159
Trenton, NJ 08601
http://cauzingelevationpublishingllc.webs.com/index.htm

Edited By: Leila Jefferson

ISBN-13   978-0-9823633-0-0
ISBN-10   0-9823633-0-3

Library of Congress Cataloging-in Publication Data has been applied for.

Cover Design by Day'Quan Jabree'© Marie Antionette
Biblical Quotes from the King James & American English Version 2001translation.com

Printed in the United States
Published 2009

A Girl Named Job

CONTENT

Just so you know...

One is quick to recall their own good deeds, the deeds they've done for others and the hurt others have caused them. But how quick one forgets all the hurt and pain one has caused someone else... I have nothing go gain by spreading lies and untruths about anyone. For those who have been in my corner and have supported me, saying thank you will never be enough. For those who are fussed that I have written these memoirs. Well, if you think you're mad now, imagine how I felt when you were taking me through all of the unnecessary bull-shit.

WE CALL THOSE WHO ENDURED BLEST!

JAMES 5:11

IMAGINE LEARNING AS A CHILD YOU WERE GOING TO BE GIVEN UP FOR ADOPTION AGAINST YOUR MOTHER'S WILL. WHAT IF YOU LEARNED YOUR CONCEPTION WASN'T PLANNED, BUT INSTEAD, WAS THE RESULT OF AN EMPTY ONE NIGHT STAND. A REVELATION LIKE THAT COULD LEAVE A BITER TASTE IN ONE'S MOUTH...

THE ARRIVAL OF SOMETHING SWEET

My life began on March 29, 1970. As told to me by my Nana, my mother was a virgin when she conceived, (at least that's what she thought) and she and my father were never a couple. Just two teenagers who were diggin' one another and eventually, temptation and hormones took over. As the story goes, my mother's labor began while she was on the bathroom toilet of her parents' house. When Nana finally realized what was going on, she ran and called for an ambulance. However, because a bad winter's storm left the roads covered with snow, they waited over an hour without sight or sound of an EMS. (Nana said the snow was damn near ten feet deep.) Fearful that medical assistance wouldn't make it to us in time, Nana resorted to calling her beloved companion and family friend, Mr. James M. Reaves, to come to our aide. Once he arrived, he drove the three of us half way across town to St. Francis Medical Center, formerly called St. Francis Hospital. There, the three of them were met at the door and almost denied entry based on some of the most absurd reasons ever heard, the most outlandish being, my mom's delivery had already begun and they had no room for unscheduled admittances. Yeah right! They made it sound like we were an inconvenience. As if an emergency could be scheduled...

Maybe they were short staffed because of the storm and had received a lot of call outs. And maybe cows fly through the air, too! If you ask me, their reasons were nothing more then little *white lies* and their only basis for not wanting my mother to deliver at their facility was because she was non-catholic, black, and had minimal or no insurance. Regardless to their attempts to shun us away, I was born on Easter Sunday, March 29th 1970 at their facility. To my parents and half of America, this was a day to remember and celebrate the resurrection of

Christ. And because I was born on this day and constantly reminded of its significance, I grew up thinking my life would be just as hard as his. It's funny how traditions, stories, and beliefs can have such profound influence on a person's psych. Never have I read anywhere in the Bible where God, his disciples, or Christ said for us to celebrate an Easter, a resurrection, or a Christmas, and yet we did that and then some all the time in His *holy name.* (I only recall Christ saying remember the Passover.) Still, regardless of the date or worldly celebration behind the day, knowing certain facts about my birth allowed me to build up a unique admiration for my mother. If I thought my life was going to be rough, only God knew how hard she had it during her pregnancy. So, in addition to Christ and Easter, my born day was a wonderful occasion indeed. Just for different reasons.

Entering the world at 6 lbs and some odd ounces, the name bestowed unto me has a variety of meanings. My first name, *Marie,* comes from the English from of the word *Mary* or *Maria,* and is interchangeable with the Greek name *Mariam* or *Mapia.* The true definition is not known for certain, but several theories include; *Sea of Bitterness, Rebellious,* and *Wished for Child,* all which have proven to be truly descriptive of me. At the same time, the Egyptian's define it as *Beloved.* In conjunction, my middle name on the other hand, provides a much needed balance to its predecessor, for *Antionette* means *Graceful & Fortunate* and *Sensitive & Friendly.* I know this because I've done my research. How in the world did my Mama know I would grow into the very definition of both names combined, I don't know. And although I have acquired several nick-names like *Murf, Molly, Ree-Ree & Red,* my birth name is what describes the real me. My mother had no idea she was giving me a name that carried such prestige. She just knew she was naming her baby after a queen!

After my arrival, one would assume my mother would have had a three day recovery in the hospital, followed by a warm reception at home with family and friends. Yet, that was far from the case. In our situation, I was told that prior to my birth, arrangements were made for me to be put up for adoption since neither my mom nor Nana could afford to take care of me. Some preacher from North Jersey and his wife were to be my adopting parents, but in the end they never showed. Only

God knows how happy my mother was that they didn't. *What could have changed their minds? Maybe it was the snow, but if they thought the snow was bad what on earth did they think they were going to do with me? Good thing they never showed...*

As told to me by my mother, the adoption was all Nana's idea, not hers. My mom wanted to keep me but because she was only seventeen, didn't have much say in the matter. My mother was of average height and weight; about five feet five inches and one hundred and twenty pounds. Her mahogany skin tone always complimented her reddish brown hair that she routinely wore in a neatly blown out afro. Her visual made you think of those ole' 70's movies with the strong black female revolutionaries as the main characters. But sadly she lacked the character strength needed to stand up to my Nana. She had no choice but to adhere to her mother's orders, and after I was born, wasn't even allowed to see me. (I would have FLIPPED!) When my mom's friends heard the news she had her baby, they all ran to the hospital to see us, unaware of the situation at hand. Once mommy told them about the adoption they were outraged, but at the same time sympathetic. Together, they devised a plan to dress my mom in street clothes and pretend she was a visitor. This way, she could sneak pass the nurse's station and down to the nursery. Being as none of the nurses had really seen my mom, who would be the wiser? There was just one catch; nobody knew which baby was me.

Seeing everyone gathered at the window, an unsuspecting nurse pointed me out when asked which baby was the Cook baby. It only took my mom one look before she broke down and started to cry. No longer could she accept, go along with, or bear the thought of giving me away. Two days after my birth, a different nurse paid my mom a visit and asked if she was aware the adopting parents never showed. I wish I knew a way to describe my mother's joy at that time because from what she's told me, she was under the impression I had already been taken away. I guess *ecstatic* would be a good one, but regardless of her feelings, it didn't change Nana's mind. She still **did not** want the responsibility of another mouth to feed, and felt my mom was incapable of handling the responsibility herself. So instead of adoption, Nana shipped me off to Plainfield, NJ to live with her nieces and sister. (A decision I know for sure, she later ended up regretting.) To look at my Nana, you wouldn't expect her to be so stern. She was of fair complexion, had a coke bottle figure and wore her thick long hair, in a long curly wet set. She only stood about five feet-five inches tall and weighed about one hundred and fifty pounds. One was so often taken back by her beauty they didn't suspect she could be a rose with thorns.

I guess Nana's reasoning for sending me immediately was to prevent mommy from becoming attached. But considering I'd grown inside of her for the past nine months, it was way too late for that. Attachment wasn't the issue, it was detachment that was tearing my mother apart. (Maybe it was Nana who didn't want to become too attached to me, huh?) I believe to this day, that is why my mother and I are so distant from one another and have never established the typical mother-daughter relationship. We were never given the opportunity to bond, but instead were torn apart like velcro from a strap. Nana's nieces came down from North Jersey and took me back to Plainfield with them despite my mother's feelings, and to make matters worst, had the gall [*nerve*] to antagonize her by bringing me back and showing me off, but told my mom she wasn't allowed to hold me. *"If I can't hold my own daughter then why the fuck did you bring her down here!"*

After that, my mom began to act out horribly in order to hide her pain. She started getting high, staying out late, and sometimes not going home at all. Honestly, I don't see how anyone could have expected anything different. I mean, what did they think? Did they think she was just going to forget about me and go on to live a normal life? Did they think she was going to go back to school and act as if nothing ever happened? I can't even begin to imagine the emotional distress she endured after knowing how badly she wanted to keep me. It's amazing she didn't loose her mind! Eventually, Nana grew tired of my mom's crying and cutting a fool, she broke down and sent her to Plainfield where she and I were reunited. I believe I was about three months old at the time. This must have seemed like an eternity to my mom.

During this period of my life, I don't mention anything about my father or his feelings towards the situation. That's because when it comes to him, they're two very different stories and somewhere in-between lays the truth. As I recall from stories told to me later on down the line, Nana and mommies' account, is that my father denied me from the start and wanted nothing to do with me. They say his claim was my mom had gotten pregnant by one of his homies, [friends] not him. I know this had to have been a hard pill for both my mom and Nana to swallow, since it implied my mother was promiscuous instead of a virgin. My father, on the other hand, states he had no prior knowledge of my mom's pregnancy until after I was born, and therefore, couldn't have denied me. He also states he was in the Marines during her pregnancy and didn't return home until the summer of '71, a full year after I was born.

Luckily for me, I was given a photo of him which was taken during the summer of 1970, proving he was indeed in the military as he said, but it doesn't mean he didn't deny me. Nana never denied my father was away, but said *his no-good ass* only ran off to avoid dealing with me. So who's telling the truth and who's telling a lie? Don't know, don't care, none of it really matters to me anymore. (Key word, anymore) Raising a child can be a frightening experience, especially if you're not prepared and have to do it alone. If Nana, with all of her experience, didn't feel she and mommy combined could raise me, what in God's name did she think my dad was going to do? I believe Nana felt she was doing what was best and her actions were in the best interest of me and my mom. Yet, at the same time, maybe my dad thought he was doing what was best too! I believe all of them had their reasons for doing what they did, and if you ask me, all three of them were scared.

By the time the ordeal with my mom and her cousin's was over, she and I were permanent fixtures in each other's lives. Nana and Pop-Pop had completely fallen in love with me, and mommy had seemingly forgotten all about my dad. She even got married and gave birth to a second daughter who she named *Tasha*. I guess the status of being married gave her the security she felt she needed to raise her family properly, which in her eyes, was something she'd never been given credit for in the past. We all know how back in the days of old, it was frowned upon for a woman to have children out of wedlock. Yet, history has proven to us, everything that glitters ain't gold. Just because Mama was married didn't mean she was living the good life.

I have vague memories of living in W. Trenton on Oakland Street with my mom, sister, and her new husband. I can loosely recall the beatings she endured at his hand, and hearing her screams and cries for help. My most dreadful memory of life with him, is of me and my sister hiding behind the bathroom door while watching our mother fight for her life. So, even with a father in the home, our lives turned out to be a living hell. His abuse ultimately caused Nana to come rescue us, taking us back to live with her and Pop-Pop on Spring Street. Tasha, on the other hand, remained with her father since neither mommy nor Nana could withstand his continued threats and abuse.

ONE'S DEFINITION OF FAMILY IS ACCURATE ACCORDING TO THEIR REALITY AND THEIR REALITY ALONE...

NANA'S HOUSE

The way I see it, family's the foundation that sets the stage for one's life, and for the first eight years of my life my family consisted of only three people, Nana, mommy, and Pop-Pop! They were my only care-givers, they were the only ones I answered to, and they were my sole protectors and providers. Nana, although married to my grandfather, was head of the house-hold and the one who called all the shots. Pop-Pop, a disabled Vet, didn't do anything or have much to say aside from, *"give me a cigarette or fix me something to eat."* (That was until you piss him off.) My mom… Well, mommy pitched in wherever and whenever Nana grew tired, which wasn't very often.

I had a trio of extended family members too; Mr. James, Uncle Pete, and Mr. or Uncle Yap. All were very good friends of my grandmother and helped us out as often as possible, but only at Nana's approval or request. God forbid someone make a decision or take an action without her consent, it was like breaking all ten of the commandments at once. Out of the three, she and Yap were like sister and brother and he was the only one who could give her a run for her money. Sometimes the two of them would sit in her room at go back and forth with one another for hours, then pick the same discussion back up the next day and continue their debate. Yap wasn't afraid to tell Nana she was crazy and although the two of them fussed a lot, one could tell they had a great deal of love for one another as well. As for me, I was the only child in the house and the apple of everyone's eye, so it goes without saying that I was spoiled beyond belief!

Growing up I realized I could easily have anything I wanted by implementing the strategy of playing one parent against the other. I quickly learned how to manipulate Nana and mommy, and nine times out of ten ended up getting my way. If Nana said no I'd run and ask mommy, and if mommy said no I'd run and ask Nana. Being as Nana was *seemingly* an uncontrollable control freak, it was always easier to get a yes out of her after mommy had already said no. Therefore, I made a practice of always going to my mom first. It's funny how that played out because everyone looked at Nana as the tough one and mommy as being timid. Yet, regardless of their strengths or weaknesses, neither in my eyes could compare to the real head of the house, my Pop-Pop!

Pop-Pop, for lack of a better term, was *that dude* and would *curse* mommy and Nana out at the drop of a dime. Pop-Pop had the ability to set things off like a backyard barbeque and it would tickle the hell outta me to hear him going at it with either mommy or Nana, and sometimes both. After listening to the two of them rant and rave all day about what should be what shouldn't be and what ain't, to hear him break his silence and say anything was like a summer's breeze swooping through and rejuvenating our home. Nobody ever knew it, but every time he cursed at them I'd say to myself, *that's right Pop-Pop you tell 'em! What you gon' say about that mom/Nana? Hun? What you gon' say about that!*

As I recall, my mother always called her father *Cookie* instead of *Dad* or *Daddy* and I hated that shit with a passion. There were so many times when I wanted to leap up in her face and tell her to stop talking to him that way. I felt regardless of what he was or who he wasn't, he was still a provider, she still resided up under his roof, and he was still an immediate part of her life. *Not like my dad who didn't exist.*

I often wondered why Nana allowed her to get away with that shit, but at the same time, knew not to dare question her. Pop-Pop's disability limited his mobility tremendously. He needed assistance to get in and out of the bed, and standing up and sitting down. He hated to be left sitting in one spot too long and would raise Cain if you forgot about him. So, one day while sitting on his pot, [portable toilet] he must have started to feel a bit uncomfortable and began wiggling around a lot. When my mom noticed him, she yelled, *"Cookie, what the hell you doing!"* But, she said it with such a tone and with such contempt; it stopped me in my tracks. Pop-Pop, on the other hand, not giving two fucks responded, *"I'm trying to take a shit! What's wrong with you? Can't nobody take a shit 'round here!"* Then, my mom, who was use to the liberty of saying what ever the hell she wanted replied, *"You better sit down before I smack you!"*

9

WOAH! I'd never heard her get out of pocket like that before. She must have forgotten her father served and survived WWII and had piping hot West-Indian blood flowing through his veins. A thoroughbred to say the least... I could have sworn Nana was going to intervene in this one, but instead, stayed up in her room, which actually shocked both of us. Then, Pop-Pop again not giving two fucks about anything or anybody, (except me of course) rose up on his one good leg, held himself as steady as he could, and replied, *"I'll smack you the hell back, I'll break ya god damn neck!"*

Talk about comical... It was the funniest shit I'd ever heard! I almost pee'd on myself, overwhelmed with laughter. Imagine an amputee with only one leg, getting up and smacking the shit out of somebody. If accomplished, it would have given new meaning to the term *Stand-Up Comedian!* I couldn't help but wonder how the hell he was going to manage that one, but knew he could if pushed to do so. I guess Pop-Pop simply grew annoyed with my mom's disrespect towards him just as I did, and decided to *put his foot down!* (No pun intended) I also believe that's why Nana opted not to mediate because she knew her daughter was way out of line. As for my mom, she did what was best and walked off into the kitchen *quietly.* My Pop-Pop was the only *blood male relative* I knew as a child growing up, and I grew very dependent upon him. Before he took sick, he was a slim built man who stood at least six feet tall. He and my mother shared the same complexion, mahogany and his skin was smooth and unblemished. His voice was deep and slightly harsh due to his years of smoking Pal Mall non filter cigarettes. Looking into his eyes was like stepping into a library. He had so many stories to tell and he was the filler for the void that was rapidly growing inside of me.

****

Our living conditions were anything but traditional and our daily routine never changed. Nana worked five minutes away from our home, and home was a moderate, three bedroom house in the middle of the block. (Moderate for our location.) My daily walk to school (Junior #5) could have been a mere ten minutes, but because I had to cross by *Nana the crossing guard* every morning, (at the corner of Passaic & Willow) my ten minute stroll was converted into a twenty minute hike. Although, I must say, I am grateful Nana made me go the extra mile in order to ensure my safety. *"I can't set an example for others if my own don't mind me,"* is what she use to say. I tried my best to find a way around her, but that lady was a God fearing, law abiding woman who would have made me cross at that corner whether she was a guard or not. Oh well, crossing at the corner wasn't all that bad. At least I was able to hit the store before school and pick up my best friend. Plus, crossing at the corner wasn't half as bad as the clothes.

On top of being an employee for the great City of Trenton, Nana was also a very good seamstress who loved fashion. Nana loved to show off her talent, I just hated it when she chose to use me as her display model. Plaids and striped patterns from Sears, checkered and floral ones from Dunham's, Nana kept me looking like the black Marsha Brady! It was like those were the only patterns the woman knew how to buy. She stayed killing me softly with embarrassment 'cause she picked out shit she liked, to hell with what I wanted. I guess that was the best she could do considering she had to take care of four people on one income. (Oh, aside from the green check that came at the beginning of the month which nobody would explain). And although I fussed about her taste in fashion, she put all the love she had into creating my garments. It was just another way for her to show me how much she cared.

Learning how to play one against the other wasn't the only thing I learned by way of observation. Being as I saw Nana as the dominant one and envied the way everyone jumped at her command, I began to mimic her behavior, unaware I naturally possessed the same knack. My mom was the rebellious one and had a unique way of zoning everything and everyone out. I figured if I utilized that trait correctly, it too could work in my favor. Mommy use to lock herself in her room whenever Nana became overbearing and by doing so, she drove Nana crazy. And with the two of them going at all the time, as well as taking care of Pop-Pop 24/7, there wasn't much time left to do anything with me. Since Nana was the shot caller, I grew up looking at my mother as a bigger sister with authority more then my mom. After a while, I grew bored with my simple life and started acting out just to gain attention. I use to tag up my walls with markers and spray paint like they were the sides of a Bronx subway and allowed my visitors to do the same. Nana said she couldn't believe how a child, who was once sweet as pie, could cause so

11

much hell and destruction and if I could get a hold of the Devil, I'd probably destroy him too! I use to laugh when she said stuff like that and my rebuttal would always be, *"Nana, I act just like you!"*

"No you don't, she'd say. *Don't you put that lie on me! You don't act like me you act just like ya Father!"*

Nana hated to take the blame for anything, even if she was at fault. Though by being so defensive, she never realized how confused she made me with her statements. (A trait of hers I grew to despise and vowed never to repeat.) How the hell could I act like someone who didn't exist! For as long as I could remember, she always told me I had no daddy. If there was no daddy, where did the statement come from and how could I duplicate his actions?

****

Our lifestyle was modest. Nana had a car and back then, it was the shit. It was a cream colored, '71 Oldsmobile Cutlass with a black vinyl top. It resembled a racing car, for lack of a better description, and she only drove it when it was absolutely necessary. *"I don't want to put too many miles on it,"* she'd say. *It's the only car I got and I ain't about to muck it up!"* Nana killed me when she substituted her swears. Who did she think she was fooling? It all meant the same in the end.

There was one air-conditioner in the entire house, and of course, it had to be in her room. After a long and tiresome day of work, all she wanted to do was go in her room and relax. So in the summer if you wanted to escape the heat, you had no choice but to join her in her room. *"Sit yo' ass down and be quiet! Niggas draw heat and talking don't make it no better!"* Nana was one who liked the finer things in life, but didn't believe in having anything in excess unless it was to accommodate her. I guess that's why three out of the six TVs we owned were in her room and needless to say, she was the only one who had cable. However, I will admit she did allow me the privilege of watching Saturday morning cartoons each and every weekend till around 12:00 in the afternoon when *Soul Train* came on. (Nana loved her some Don Cornelius!)

With three TV's on at once, it's amazing she was able to keep up with everything, but she did. She could tell you every dumb move the *Mets* made, and she stayed cursing out *Mookie Washington.* She could answer every question from every game show; *The Price Is Right, Hollywood Squares,* and *Match Game 76.* Plus, she kept up with who was screwing who on every soap opera; *All My Children, The Young & The Restless, General Hospital,* and *The Bold & The Beautiful,* way before the plot was revealed. Funny, Nana always complained about not having money and we even stood in food lines for milk and cheese, yet, she made sure she had enough to pay for that cable and maintain her Tel-lie-visions.... Let me find out my Nana was just selfish...

My grandmother was one tough *cookie* there's no denying that. Her authority was like an *iron fist.* Just like Pop-Pop, she was a riot when she became angry, but at the same time, she was the most disciplined woman I knew. She didn't tolerate any nonsense and loathed filth and laziness as if it were an incurable disease. I guess that's why she stayed yelling at my mom about that nasty ass room of hers with clothes piled up from the floor to the ceiling. I guess that's also why mommy stayed in her room as much as she did with the door locked. It prevented Nana from saying anything about the site when ever she walked by. *Yet, when the door was open I always saw her writing... I wonder if she was writing about some of this shit right here...*

Nana's non-tolerance of sloth and filth was a trait I grew to admire and understand. Though for the life of me, I could never quite figure out the relationship between her and my grandfather and how she and Mr. James became *so close.* Nana was always preaching about right and wrong, and if you stepped out of line she was quick to put you back in check. The woman was a *Libra* and acted like the scales of justice were created by her and her alone. So how she managed to build such a strong relationship with a man outside of her marriage baffled the hell out of me. Nana and Pop-Pop did nothing but argue, and although she took very good care of him; cooking and cleaning like any wife would, all I ever saw them do was fuss.

I wish I could have witnessed a more loving relationship between the two considering how much I loved them both. (Still do) Though I'm sure it was there at one time or another, they managed to make two kids with each other. To the naked eye, anyone would have sworn she and Mr. James were the happily married couple and Pop-Pop was just an ill family member who resided in the house. To my knowledge, Pop-Pop never said a word about their situation and not once did he complain. That alone caused me to favor him over the women, and in my eyes, that made him *the head of the house,* regardless of who called the shots.

Pop-Pop and Nana had one son who they named after my grandfather, William J. Cook III aka Butch. Sadly, he was killed in Plainfield at the age of 19, one year after I was born, and Nana witnessed the accident. My uncle was working underneath his car when some friends came to visit. They were unaware he was under the car and one of them hit the vehicle, the car jack slipped, and my uncle died instantly! For a long time Nana and mommy blamed Pop-Pop for the incident and carried resentment in their hearts. They were mad because earlier in the week, Uncle Butch had asked Pop-Pop for some money to fix the car and he said no. Yet, we all know it wasn't Pop-Pop's fault and he would have given his son his last dime had he known such a fatal accident was going to occur. Pop-Pop would have traded his life for his son's and his death was something none of them ever got over. Maybe that's why Nana always said, I should have been a boy...

****

Proverbs 13:24, "Spare the rod, spoil the child," Nana took that verse to heart. Although I didn't get whooped [spanked] a lot, the sermons and preaching were just as bad. Thinking back, the only real whooping I can recall is when I was about ten or eleven and I'd just gotten my braces. This was after I wore an un-removable retainer for nearly two years in order to fix an overbite. The orthodontist advised me not to eat anything solid or hard for an about an hour or two because the glue needed to set on the brackets. But what did I do? No sooner than I walked into the house, I went straight to the refrigerator and got two pieces of chicken and an apple. At first everything was cool because I picked the chicken apart instead of biting down into it. Of course I couldn't do the same with the apple and that's where I fucked up!

Nana was in the hall removing old paint and wall paper from the walls when I approached. She had a paint spatula in her hand when she looked up and noticed I'd lost like nine of those new brackets. She was so mad she commenced to tearing me up right there on the spot with little compassion. That spatula of hers was cutting the daylights out of me. She struck me so many times with that damn thing my body went numb. Those licks were coming so damn fast and from every direction, I couldn't catch my breath to scream. I tried as hard as I could to block as much as I could, and by the time she was done with me I was extremely sore. Not only was I sore, but I looked a mess. There were red whelps all over my arms, back, and legs but that didn't phase Nana. All she saw was the additional $300.00 she was going to have to kick out due to my disobedience. Other than that, the only other whooping I can think of was the one I got the time I refused to wear my galoshes and my brand new Penny Loafers and socks got soaked from the rain. And again, Nana was hotter then a piece of coal and my bottom paid the price for her fury. After that, my discipline was dished out in the form of punishments and or threats, but in order to avoid all that, all I had to do was go to school, mind mommy and Nana, do my chores, and keep curfew. As if it could ever be that easy.

****

Our family was well known and both of my grandparents were known by either *Cookie, C.B* (C.B was just for my Nana) or plain ole' *Cook*. I use to think mommy and Nana were very fortunate to have so many friends and neighbors who'd frequently check in and lend a helping hand either around the house or with Pop-Pop. It was my assumption, back then, that they needed the extra *man-power* considering the man of the house was disabled. Yet, it was also obvious that most of *them sorry bastards* were only interested in my Mama. However, being they knew Nana was *no joke* and would have *a pure t' fit* if they came to occupy all of mommy's time without offering a hand, they extended their services, what ever they may have been. It was like a requirement of Nana's and a screening process that told her which *niggas* were worth while and which ones were worthless. In our situation, Nana didn't believe in entertaining company unless it was going to benefit everyone. She felt if people were ignorant enough to see our needs and still not offer any help, then it was best they kept it moving! But even with that strategy, it was still kinda difficult to keep all of the *riff-raff* away. *"Ain't none of dem niggas no good, they only lurking round, waiting to take advantage,"* was Nana's take on 'em all.

As hard as it was to accept Nana's truths, nine times out of ten she was right. Most of those worthless *suckas* weren't any good. Some of them actually managed to get close enough to us that they were

15

successful in carrying out their underhanded deeds. Just like Nana said, they only *lurked* around so they could case things out and learn our routine. Then, they'd rob us later when no one was around. Some would even return to the scene and pretend they had no knowledge of what had gone down. *As if the streets didn't talk.* My mom didn't have the same keen perception as Nana, and it sometimes took her longer to put two and two together. But Nana stayed on point, and at the slightest sign of trouble would cut you off in a heartbeat. She dared those *sap suckas* to return or else. Shit was deep back then, and I had to take it all in the best I could if I wanted to keep up. Clearly, situations like these were a contributing factor to me *knowing too much for my own good,* as Nana would say. How could I remain a child when I was in an adult world learning adult things...

Remember when I said Pop-Pop was the highlight of my life? Well, he was also the one I felt closest to back then, too. I've often wondered if he was aware of my feelings, but somehow I know he was. I was the only one in the house he didn't yell or curse at, and of course that made me feel exceptionally special. Nana and mommy use to be members of a high ranking bowling league, and one night a week they'd meet on Route 1 at Colonial Lanes in Lawrenceville. I had to have been about seven or eight at the time because I don't remember my youngest sister, Nette, being born yet. Anyway, they had their one night when they'd go bowling and on that night, I'd sit home and babysit my *Beloved Pop-Pop.* Since Nana felt I was rotten enough to destroy the Devil, the concern for my safety must have eluded her when she and mommy went out. (Even though she knew we'd been preyed upon in the past.)

Regardless of my grandmother's assumptions, there were several nights when I was afraid to sleep upstairs alone in my room. And on those nights, I'd go down stairs and jump in the bed with Pop-Pop. Despite his decreasing physical condition and strokes that rendered him unable to speak and incontinent, I still saw him as my protector. Nana use to say Pop-Pop was *as ornery as a bull in a china shop,* and if that were the case, nobody would mess with him and with him, I'd always be safe. (So I thought.) When lying in the bed with Pop-Pop, it was always damp... I don't know what I use to tell myself to get past the warm, wet sensation, but what ever it was it worked! *Nana use to swear Pop-Pop intentionally made a mess just so she would be forced to clean it up. But considering he was a man of pride, I think he was more embarrassed than anything to admit he needed our help.*

****

"Pissy!" That's what people use to say when they walked past our house and caught a whiff from within the house or from the porch because Pop-Pop couldn't make it to the facilities in time. They didn't know if indeed he could have made it to the bathroom, he would have. They didn't know his diminishing condition placed limits on him and they had no regards that the man they called pissy, a drunk, or a bum was someone I loved dearly. He wasn't pissy, he just couldn't help himself, and who were they to call him out of his name. My Pop-Pop was a man with a passion for preserving life, but between the war and the loss of his son, he just felt like giving up. So if drinking allowed him to forget about his troubles, then so be it! Who the fuck were they to judge?

In his day, my Pop-Pop was a bad mother--,shut yo' mouth! He was a Medical Engineer, a damn good chef, shot a mean game of pool, and after the war worked for the Pennsylvania Railroad until he was injured. He'd served both his country and his family, and had lived through his fair share of suffering. The last thing he deserved was to be called out of his name by a bunch of disrespectful ingrates who knew nothing about him.

I remember how enraged I'd become when ever I heard anyone speak foul of him, and it got to the point to where they said it without cause. They just knew he pee'd on himself and therefore, felt justified in making their comments. Even after Nana had cleaned the porch with Pine-Sol and bleach, people still walked pass and made ill remarks. I grew to hate that shit so much and I tried to confine myself inside to avoid the humiliation. The embarrassment of their remarks didn't bother me as much as not being able to do anything about it. I utilized the solitary confinement trick learned from my Mama in order to hide my anger, but that tactic grew old quick and only made my empathy for Pop-Pop that much greater. Instead of decreasing my anger it increased. And at my age, all I had was energy to burn, so what else could I do but go outside? However, just because I went out didn't mean I had to socialize.

Nine times out of ten, I chose to sit alone in the park or by myself on an abandoned porch.

To this day, I still I loathe the word *pissy,* but it doesn't bother me as much now as it did back then. I have countless, precious memories of my grandfather and they all tell a story of the man he was, not what others thought of him. Like the time he managed to walk me downtown to the *Five & Dime* in order to buy me a piano that played *Old McDonald.* He wasn't completely disabled at the time but still had difficulty walking. It took us nearly an hour to walk four blocks, but he did it just to put a smile on my face. Pop-Pop spent his last $5.00 on that piano, (Instead of spending it on a bottle of wine.) and when ever he heard me playing it he'd call me into his room so the two of us could sing along together. I also enjoy reminiscing over the days he sat and played checkers with me knowing he was the better player, but instead always let me win. My grandfather was a *jack of all trades* and I can think of a million ways to describe him, but pissy ain't one of 'em!

The extended members of my family weren't as intense as my immediate, but the memories are just as dear. Take my Godfather, Uncle Pete, for example, who was also that dude and too cool for words. Uncle Pete was just like Nana, law abiding and hard working, but unlike Nana, didn't have any children. I got to see Uncle Pete every other Saturday after his part time job and waited patiently for him to show. I did so because I knew once he arrived I was in for a treat. (Nana use to tell me her and Uncle Pete could have been a couple but Uncle Pete didn't want any kids. I guess he later grew to regret that decision considering how he took to my mom, me, and later on Nette.)

Uncle Pete use to take me (and my little sister once she arrived) to my favorite spot, which at the time was McDonalds. Without fail, I'd order a Quarter Pounder w/Cheese, small fry, and chocolate shake. (They didn't have happy meals back then.) And if we didn't go to McDonalds we went to Halo Farms for a 5lb box of cookies. I reminisce over my days with Uncle Pete like they were yesterday, just as I do with Pop-Pop. I'm very grateful to have been blessed with his love and kindness, as well as the role he played in my life. I loved the sound of his voice, the way he said our names, and how his mustache and goatee use to tickle me every time he gave me a kiss.

Unfortunately, I lost Uncle Pete when I was about nineteen to prostrate cancer. After his first surgery and hospital stay he seemed okay, but right before his second go round he told me he knew he wouldn't be returning home. He told all of us that. I didn't quite understand what he was trying say at the time and had no idea how real those words would turn out to be. Uncle Pete passed away in the hospital shortly after his second surgery. I didn't even get a chance to say good-bye. I guess in his own way he was trying to tell all of us good-bye, and after his death I grew increasingly close to Nana's friend Mr. James.

Mr. James... No one in the Cook family or anyone who knew the Cook family could ever forget Mr. James. He was the man everyone thought was my Nana's husband but wasn't. Instead, he was her beloved companion in life, her friend, her provider, and in my opinion, her everything! He was the kindness most generous man I knew and any and everything I could want or imagine I wanted, Mr. James saw to it that I got it. All I had to do was ask. He, just like Nana, Pop-Pop, and Uncle Pete, made sure I wanted for nothing. To Mr. James, I was the big baby. That's what he called me and that's what I remained until the day he passed away. If I had to pick a favorite memory of him, it would be the time I saw him sing with his Barbara Shop quartet and Sunday nights when he took Nana out for dinner. Because I knew this was their weekly routine, I'd raise all kinds of hell with Nana just so she'd let me tag along. I use to hate sitting at home eating my mom's cooking. All she ever fixed was hot dogs, boxed Kraft Mac-n-cheese, or beans and franks.

DAMN! I ate so much of that shit it was pathetic (although Nana with her fried okra and stewed tomatoes wasn't much better) and that's why I always looked forward to going out with Nana. Even on the nights she refused to let me go, Mr. James made sure she brought me back a doggie bag. The anticipation alone use to thrill me to no end, but as for my mom, it probably made her feel like shit. I wasn't aware of it at the time, but my actions made her feel like she was wasting her time cooking for nothing. Like, why even bother when I wasn't going to eat anyway. Mommy just didn't know how much I hated that mess and I didn't realize she was doing the best she could with what she had. *"I'll wait till Nana comes home,"* is what I use to tell her. I now see how those words were a slap in the face. She named me after a queen and I acted like a

19

brat. But, I did enjoy it when she popped *Jiffy Pop-Pop Corn*... It was always my favorite snack.

Looking back on my actions today, had I been my mother, I would have sent my ass to bed on an empty stomach. Then, maybe I would have grown to appreciate her efforts. Maybe she would have done so if she didn't feel she'd later have to answer to Nana. However, things have a funny way of balancing out, because just like mommy hated for Nana to bring me back a doggie bag or take me out to dinner, Nana hated it when Mr. James allowed me to tag along and order whatever I wanted. Including dessert, regardless if I finished my meal or not. In the end it made no difference who took the lead, whether it was Nana, Pop-Pop, Uncle Pete, or Mr. James, my loving and dysfunctional family always spoiled me rotten!

"DADDY'S LITTLE GIRL." THE PHRASE HAD NO SIGNIFICANCE TO ME WHATSOEVER AS A CHILD GROWING UP. THEN, ONCE I LEARNED ITS MEANING IT WAS TOO LATE FOR ME TO APPRECIATE IT. THE LITTLE GIRL IN ME WAS NO MORE BECAUSE EVERYONE, EXCEPT MY DADDY, WANTED TO PLAY DADDY TO ME...

WHERE'S MY DADDY

Nana's most infamous question day in and day out was; *"Why you got that girl round all dem niggas'?"* She'd ask my mom that every time she saw me around any of her male company. Any male company, she didn't care who it was. *"You know you ain't got no business entertaining them niggas 'round that girl!"* Entertaining? What did she mean by that? I thought the men who came to see mommy were her friends. What did she mean by entertain? Were they paying to come see her? These were my Mama's friends *so I thought* and I didn't see any harm in them coming over to visit. 1st Corinthians 13 verse 11 reads: *"When I was a baby, I used to talk like a baby, think like a baby, and reason like a baby."* Having said, it's clear to see why my thinking couldn't over-stand the wisdom of my wise ole' Nana. Shit, at the time I don't even think my mom fully understood what Nana was trying to express. I say that because no matter what Nana said, all mommy said was, *"Yeah, mommy, I know...."* Then she'd go on back to what Nana called, *entertaining*...

I grew up knowing most of my mom's friends by either name, face, or both. The first one I can recall was Mr. Payne, also known as JP. JP was a service man, he was in the military, and his visits were short and far in-between. Still, each and every time he was on leave he'd make 67 Spring Street one of his first and last stops. Every time JP came around he'd take mommy out, and I'd sometimes catch the two of them kissing when they thought no one was around. I use to think him and her were in-love and that the two of them would get married one day. Mommy seemed so happy when he was around. Not like when he was away... Then after a while his presence started to fade, and after a few years, he stopped coming around all together. So, I guess him and mommy weren't in love after all...

The next *joker,* as Nana would say, was a cat named Ernie. I don't remember his last name but I do remember his looks. He was *hot!* Each time that man entered our home I'd look up at my mom as if to say, *wow mommy he's cute!* He was tall and dark, but to call the man handsome would be an understatement. He looked like he was straight outta of Hollywood or the star of a Black Cinema film. If I had to compare him to anyone, it would be Wesley Snipes. Ernie was in the military just like JP. I don't know if mommy had a thing for cats in uniform just because, or if it had something to do with her father, but for the longest time, those were the only type of men I saw visiting. Then again, maybe military men were they only men available back then, I don't know. I remember one day asking him if he was in the Army too. That must have struck a nerve because he looked at me slyly and responded *"No little lady, I'm A Marine,"* in a certain, but non threatening tone. Then he looked over at my mom and smirked. (JP was in the Army. Maybe Ernie didn't know Mama and JP were friends too…)

That's basically the only memory I have of Ernie, other then just seeing him come and go like anybody else. And just like I thought her and JP were going to tie the knot, I thought her and Ernie were going to do the same. As a matta a fact, they even told me there were going to do so. Ernie's exact words to me were, *"Me and ya Mama' are gonna get married."* So once they said it, I believed it. But guess what? I don't have a step pop named Ernie or Ernest, or anything of the sort. JP and Ernie are the two I can recall early on with no reservations. Mommy seemed better when they were around and she spent all of her free time with them. I figured since Nana never cursed them out, they were good to go. Guess I was wrong…

When I think about it, I probably wanted my mom to get married more then she did. (Deep down, I wanted my mom and dad to get married and give me a little brother or sister, but from what I was told, my dad didn't exist?) I witnessed her sadness when she was alone as well as her joy when someone came to see her. Nana saw it too, and made sure we knew it by broadcasting, *"You sure do perk up when dem niggas come 'round, don't you!"* So, I started to think that maybe *dem niggas* were the only people who could make mommy happy. Maybe if she got married again, she'd be happy all the time! Plus, mommy needed to get married so the three of us could live in our own home and I could have a daddy, being Nana constantly reminded us of how much I needed one….

****

JP and Ernie were decent, but not everyone who came to visit was so noble. Like this bright-skinned nigga named Pete. No, not Uncle Pete, just Pete. Pete was nothing more then a smooth talking, corny ass, wanna be pimp who hung out at B.T.'S Lounge on N. Willow Street. Pete came around quite often and pretended to be big on my Mama. I say pretended because just like Nana's intuition, my third eye allowed me to see straight through his sorry ass. I could sense God warning me to be cautious of that man. His interest in my mom didn't seem to be as great as his interest in Mama's little girl. *Me!* Each time this bastard came to visit he'd beckon me to come and sit on his lap. Each time I did, it felt like a hammer was poking me in my rear and the back of my thigh. Pete use to bounce me up and down on his leg and my innocence warned me his actions weren't good. So every time I saw him walking towards our house I'd pray he'd just keep going. Sometimes he'd look and wave and sometimes he'd tell me to tell my Mama he'd be back., but instead of the message being for her, it felt like he was directing it towards me. His words and the sight of him caused me great fear, but I never displayed any sign that anything was wrong. I didn't think anyone would believe me.

Off guard, Pete would catch me outside and ask me to go and fetch my mom for him. Hesitant, yet afraid he'd tell Nana I was being disrespectful, I'd comply. But as soon as the deed was done I'd flee the scene. Having grown sure of his ability to intimidate me and at the same time conceal his actions from everyone, Pete got bold and began grabbing me by the arm pulling me back towards him. His cover-up was to tickle me playfully, forcing me to laugh. Then he'd let out a fraudulent sigh of, *phew that's enough,* and sit me on his lap in order to gain his arousal. Most of the time, I'd just sit with a blank look on my face trying ever so hard to ignore it. Then when that failed, I'd wiggle and squirm awkwardly hoping it would sway him into releasing me. (Never once realizing my movements only excited him that much more.) Neither method worked, but the most frightening part of all was it took place right out in plain sight, all while talking and smiling up in my Mama's face. .

Encountering *Pete the Perv* was never a thrill for me, even if it was for him. The last run-in I can commit to memory about his sorry ass was of him and mommy sitting outside talking. The two were sitting on opposite sides of the rail and when I approached, he grabbed me by my waist, pulling me to his lap as if I were his child! I tried to get my mom's attention by giving her a long, evil look as if to say, *aren't you gonna' say anything, don't you see I don't like this man?* But she never caught on and Pete made me feel dirty, like I was wrong. The longer I sat, the dirtier I felt, and the angrier I became. Finally, I jumped up and shot him a look that could kill, restlessly staring him in the eye with the burning desire to *spit* in his face. My mom then asked, *"What's wrong Ree'?"* Without saying a word, I just walked into the house, damn near knocking her off the porch as I swung open the door.

After that, Pete's visits declined considerably. Although we'd sometime cross one another's paths, he never attempted to grab or utter a single word to me again. This is how I know he knew he was wrong. And if he knew it and I knew it, why couldn't mommy see it? Maybe she just didn't have those motherly instincts Nana spoke of or maybe she didn't feel the need to have them since Nana was always pulling rank, I don't know. I just hate to think she was so wrapped up in *entertaining* that she ignored the obvious.

Years passed and I thought I'd forgotten about Pete's mischievousness, but every time the two of us would see each other in the streets, that same eerie feeling from before always managed to return. The difference was I was no longer a little girl, no longer could I be intimidated by him, and Pete could detect the change. Upon sight, he'd drop his head and avoid eye contact with me. This action gave me the feeling of ultimate power but I never felt the need to expose him or pull his card. He did that all by himself! Dropping his head and speaking in a low tone only confirmed his guilt and told the story of his shame. I was now just as sly as he once was, but with a stronger state of mind that was unmatched by his own. Two things I could tell, he didn't want to confront but instead tried to make peace. Anyone observing his behavior could tell he was suspect but all I wanted him to do was step out of line. *"Just please step out of line, just once,"* I'd say to myself, *"so I can light yo' sorry ass up."* And if I couldn't do it, there were plenty of *niggas* around me who would!

Next on the list was a guy named Jimmy, and he was a smooth one as well. He spoke like *Pretty Tony* from the movie *The MACK,* but with the humor of the one and only *Richard Pryor.* Jimmy, although one of mommy's friends, was more like the big brother or uncle I didn't have. No matter how long or short his visits, he always took the time to kick it to me about paying attention to my Mama and getting good grades. Jimmy seemed pretty cool and he also seemed to be one of Nana's favorite. Aside from Uncle Shelton and Mr. Yap, Jimmy was the only one allowed in the house when mommy and Nana weren't home.

The relationship between mommy and Jimmy could be compared to the home-boy and home-girl relationships of today. I never saw them as a romantic couple, but his presence outlasted many others. Personally, I never had a problem with Jimmy crossing the grain with me but he did blemish his record when he attempted to violate my mother. It was a chilly fall day and Nana wasn't home. Mommy was in the house when Jimmy stopped by and I was out on the porch, damn near bored into a comma. No longer able to ignore then numbness in my fingers and toes caused by the frigid weather, I decided to go back inside to thaw out. That's when I heard my mom, in no uncertain terms, repeatedly say, "*NO! NO! NO!*" Softening my steps in order to focus on where her voice was coming from, I realized the two of them were up in her room. This immediately raised a red flag because although Jimmy seemed to be one of Nana's favorites, nobody, and I do mean nobody, was ever allowed upstairs without her permission. Ever, ever, ever! But Nana wasn't home at the time so I guess her rules didn't apply.

As I crept further up the stairs, I could hear what sounded like the two of them wrestling and my mom was still saying no. I didn't know what to do. I thought I was being quiet but Jimmy came out and peeked over the banister. *"Marie, go back down stairs baby!"* my mom yelled from her room. I hesitated for a moment, just as I did every time she told me to do something, then I heard her begin to cry. I didn't realize it at the time, but I had just interrupted his plans and saved my mom from being raped! I slowly walked downstairs and back out onto the porch and waited for him to leave. Once he was out of sight, I ran back inside and walked up a few stairs, but stopped again because I could still hear my mother's weeps. This time they were louder then before. I still didn't know what to do or what to say and I didn't want her to be mad at me. So I did the only thing I could do, I sat down at the foot of the stairs and cried as well.

Jimmy didn't come around for a long time after that because just like Pete, he felt the guilt of his actions. Yet, when he did start to show his face again things seemed to be okay between him and my mom, so I guess she had forgiven him. But, just because she was able to forgive didn't mean I was able or willing to forget.

Slowly but surely, Nana's fear of my mother's entertaining was coming to the light. The repeat episodes of men coming and going, here one minute gone the next, had started to take its toll on me. But it would be years before those issues came to surface. I saw Paul, the muscular motorcyclist who was also in the military, Willie, the gentleman of all gentlemen, and Carl, the educated-intellect who, in Nana's eyes, was, *"all talk and no action."* These men who casually dated my mother in the long run turned out to be nothing more then *friends of the family*. But there was this one guy who changed the meaning of the word *friend* forever in my eyes, and his name was *J. Gillette*.

Mr. Gillette aka Gilly, was a very familiar face in our home and someone I grew to view as another extended member of the family. Gilly knew mommy and Nana by way of my Uncle Butch and after his passing, continued to come around and *show his respects* as they call it. Clearly, Gilly was attracted to my mom but it was also just as clear she didn't feel the same. Nonetheless, he hung around and his counterfeit display of concern for the family allowed his real motives and intentions to go undetected. Almost every day he'd come over and watch T.V, help out around the house, or check out the Sunday night oldies from 7-10 on "WDAS" with *DJ Harvey Holiday*. The two of them use to have me cracking up as I watched them *"cut a rug,"* doing the bump, the hustle or the robot, as if they were in a Soul Train dance line. Nothing about Gilly seemed to set off any alarms, and unlike her other friends, he kept his distance when it came to me. He was very tall and dark skinned, and had chiseled features that reminded me of the grim reaper. In passing he'd speak or pat me on the head, but other than that, I can't say much about the brotha except he was indeed a *wolf in sheep's clothing*.

Gilly knew everything about our family, therefore infringing our security wouldn't be a problem if that's what he wanted to do. The nigga was like *Santa Clause*. He knew when we were sleeping and when we were awake. He knew when Nana worked, where she worked, and what time she'd be home. He knew my grandfather was immobilized and the only man in the house. And, he knew what night Nana and mommy went out to bowl, which served as his plus point. Knowing that the two of them would be out of the house for at least four hours one night a week, gave him the advantage he needed to execute his plan. A plan nobody was aware of until after the damage was done.

As I recall the events of that one particular evening, everything seemed normal. Mommy and Nana were getting ready to go bowling and Pop-Pop and I were both ready for bed. The only thing unusual was I decided to stay upstairs in my room instead of going downstairs to be with my grandfather. Then, right before I drifted off to sleep, I heard a heavy knock at the door that startled the shit out of me. *Who the hell is that?*, I thought to myself. Everyone who knew us knew my parents weren't home. At first, I thought was it was mommy and Nana coming back to retrieve something they forgot. But after calling their names a few times and getting no response, I grew fearful. Slowly I walked downstairs, tightly holding my *Stretch Armstrong* action figure, thinking it would protect me. (Nana use to say I could knock a person out with that thing if I hit them the right way, so naturally he was the first thing I grabbed.)

I thought it could have also been Mr. James or Uncle Yap, but even they knew my parents weren't at home. Plus, they would have announced themselves as soon as they heard my voice or called ahead of time. Scared and frightened, I carefully pulled back the curtain and then breathed a sigh of relief. Although it wasn't Nana or mommy, it was a familiar face. It was Gilly. But what did he want? He, of all people, knew my parents were out, especially considering he'd just left no sooner then the two of them walked out the door. Why was he here?

"My mom n' them not home," I said, while holding back the curtain to the window. *"I forgot something in your grandpa's room. I just want to pick it up,"* he responded. Viewing Gilly as a family member was one thing, but I still knew not to allow anyone in the house when mommy and Nana were out. Not even him. Plus, something about Gilly didn't look right. He had this weird look in his eyes, more like a gleam to be descriptive. And, he kept trying to open the door even though he knew it was locked. *"Okay, I'll go check,"* I said, then walked away. Entering Pop-Pop's room, I did a quick review to see if I could find whatever it

was he left behind but I saw nothing. Everything in Pop-Pop's room belonged to him and nothing was out of place. I headed back to the door but by the time I got back, Gilly had wedged his foot in-between the door and the wall and was attempting to un-do the chain lock. (Nana swore up and down that little thing would increase our safety and eliminate intruders. Boy was she wrong. *Mental note: Chain locks only prevent children from busting into their parent's bedrooms…*)

Gilly busted though the door with the force of a bulldozer and all I could do was stand there and look at him, paralyzed by fright. The man who I once viewed as a member of the family turned out to be nothing more then another bad guy. My first thought was, *How in the world am I going to get him up out of here?* There wasn't a damn thing Pop-Pop could do in his condition and I didn't have the courage at the time to clunk him in the head with my heavy, gel filled action figure. What if he took it from me? I knew from the door, Gilly was telling me a lie because out of all the time's he'd been to our home, not once did he stop and say two words to Pop-Pop. So why would any of his belongings be in his room now? With each step he took, the fear inside me grew immensely. I just knew he was going to kill me and Pop-Pop and I was terrified I wouldn't be able to stop him. I tried pleading with him to just leave because Pop-Pop was asleep but he paid me no mind. He kept walking towards me and I continued backing up.

Gilly went into Pop-Pop's room and began tossing shit here and there. He pretended to be looking for something, but of course he didn't find shit because he hadn't left shit! I think there may have been a moment or two when I felt brave enough to hit him, but knew I didn't have the strength to knock him the fuck out. Gilly spent about ten minutes tearing the room apart before I yelled at him to stop! I didn't want him to wake Pop-Pop up but after all of the commotion, it was too late. Pop-Pop woke up to the sound of my voice and rolled over to find an intruder standing at the foot of his bed. My eyes were wide and filled with horror. Frustration was written all over Pop-Pop's face but the concern for my safety quickly filled his eyes. Pop-pop didn't know much about what went on in the crib, but he knew for sure Gilly wasn't supposed to be there. At least not at that hour. There was an awkward moment of silence as the three of us stared at one another, then our intruder exited the room and headed for the stairs.

Gilly grabbed me by the arm with a vice like grip and held me like a hostage. He ordered me to walk in front of him as we *tip toed* up the steps and he kept asking me, *"Is there anybody else here, is there anybody else in the house?"* If his intentions were to scare me, he'd accomplished his goal, and because I was in a panic of course I told him the truth. *"Hell no ain't nobody else here!"* (But there should have been.) By the time we reached the top of the stairs the pee I'd been holding was trickling down my legs and had soaked my pajamas. Now I was the pissy one…

With way too much force, Gilly pushed me towards my mother's room then asked once again, *"Is there anyone else here?"* I've always had a temper with an extremely sharp tongue and being scared didn't make things any better. So when this fool asked me again for like the fourth time was anyone else in the house I screamed to the top of my lungs, *"No, ain't nobody else here!"* (I really screamed because I wanted someone to hear me, not because I thought he couldn't.) Unappreciative of my little stunt, Gilly shook me with frustration and told me, *"If you're lying to me I'm a get you!"* (Gonna get me, nigga you got me!) So now I'm scared, pissy, and mad because homeboy is making threats and I don't have any defense. In addition, we both knew he wouldn't be talking so tough if my Nana was at home. Shit, he wouldn't even been there that late if Nana was at home!

Gilly entered my mom's room and reached into the top of her armoire where she kept all of her loose change and trinkets. There he found a bank I'd made for her in school out of a Pringle's potato chip can and a bird feeder made out of a plastic milk carton. Both of them were filled to the max with loose dollar bills, quarters, dimes, and nickels. It took an entire semester for me to complete both projects and almost six months for my mom to fill them up. Sadly, it took less then two minutes for his snake ass to clean her out, and at the same time, break my heart. At my age, a gift had more value to me then money, but I knew Gilly was wrong for taking both.

This man was off the hook. He'd broken into our house; *scared the shit out of me.* Tore up my grandfather's room; *scared the shit out of me,* and now he's stealing from my mom*; crushed the shit out of me.* I couldn't believe he was doing this to us after just sitting down at our table and breaking bread just hours earlier. It was time for his ass to go, but he didn't stop there. After finding my mom's stash he went for the jackpot. Nana's room!

Everyone who visited us knew Nana's room was the only spot in the house where you could find anything of worldly value. Nana was from the original old school as well as from the south. She didn't believe in entrusting all of her money to a bank, and therefore, kept a fortress hidden in her room. Nana kept our entire family savings buried in the bottom of her armoire, along with her best jewelry and important documents. In a million years, you'd never find anyone bold enough or stupid enough to enter into her room without her permission, and very few people knew about that cabinet. Gilly just happened to be one of the few. But why?

Gilly gripped the back of my neck and pushed me out into the hallway towards my Nana's locked door. Had I not been so scared, I would have broken down into tears. I was a stiff as a board and it felt like he was pushing me on a hand cart. Not one inch of me would bend, and all I could think about was Pop-Pop and what Gilly's dumb ass was going to do next. I don't think I've ever wanted to see my parents so bad. God, I wished they would have come home early or truly forgotten something and had to return. Gilly was a dumb ass, but he still had the upper hand. He stood me in front of Nana's door and said, *"There better not be anybody in there!"* At that moment, I managed to turn my head just enough to see him out the corner of my eye and thought to myself, *"Fool! In where... In there.... Dumb ass don't you see the pad lock on the door?"* (Yes sir, leave it to Nana to lock everything the hell up. Each time Nana left the house for long periods, she'd make sure to lock that damn door of hers. It wasn't just a security precaution it was paranoia. But in all her days on the earth I don't believe she ever thought anything like this could happen.)

I shook my head no, in response to his statement, but Gilly became nervous when he heard sounds from behind the door. He then realized it was a combination of Nana's television and her air-conditioner. Nana always left them on. *"Knock on the door,"* he said.

"Knock on the door?" Why, I thought, *"Ain't nobody in there!!!*

Gilly bust thorough Nana's door like the police executing a search and seize warrant. Somehow he managed to only damage the lock, but ironically, that was a good thing. Nana would have flipped had he broken down the door itself and left her with the responsible of replacing it. We would have never heard the end of it. I would have never heard the end of it! Once inside her room he told me to stand still as I watched him break into her armoire. Once that was accomplished the rest was history. It seemed like he knew exactly where to go. As I stood in disbelief, I looked across the room out of my Nana's window and noticed something I believe no one ever paid any attention to. Amazingly, if a person sat across the street on the abandoned porch, they could get a clear view of almost everything inside Nana's room. You could see her bed, her TVs, and that great big, double door cabinet, aka an armoire. Then I thought, *"Wow."* Gilly sits on that porch all the time, even when mommy and Nana aren't home. My thoughts were then disrupted by the sight of Gilly rambling through Nana's strong box. He helped himself to our savings and all our personal information. Gilly saw what he needed to see, took the box, and walked out the room. As for me, I just stood there watching, not knowing what to say or do.

Okay, no more confusion. It was now obvious we were being robbed and strangely it felt like I had assisted in doing so. Why was Gilly robbing us? I thought he was our friend. Now I had to process him as Gilly the neighborhood stick up man, which was kind of hard to do. Gilly must have noticed the wheels spinning in my head by the look on my face. He turned around in his tracks and told me to walk him to the top of the stairs. I would have resisted but that clutch of his was painful. Halfway down the hall, we stopped. Gilly noticed another perk. A fairly new, just cleaned, winter corduroy coat. It was one of Nana's favorites. He couldn't hold me, the strong box, and grab the coat at the same time, so he let me go and I made a bee-line for my room. After picking up the coat he proceeded to putting it on as if he'd worked and paid for it with his own money. He then continued on his way, and out of curiosity, I watched him descend down the stairs. He even said good-bye to me as he walked out the door. After he left, I stood there feeling guilty.

Once reality kicked in, I broke down crying like a wounded dog.

I wasn't crying because of what had happened, I was crying because I knew Nana was going *whoop my ass*! Surely she wasn't going to believe me, she never did! I knew she was going to put the blame on me. I was the only one in the house, and I didn't do anything to stop him. Damn, I could hear her now. *"Why didn't you go run and tell somebody you run ya mouth any other time? Why didn't you pick up the phone and call somebody, the police?"* My thoughts had me so shook I filled the house with weeps. It was hard for me to hear anything over the sound of my own tears. I thought the ordeal was over, I thought Gilly was gone...

I raised my head from my hands to wipe my face. Unaware of what I was about to see. He'd returned and I had no idea he was back inside the house. As he stood in front of me, I thought, *How long has he been here, is Pop-Pop okay?*

Nana use to tell me witches rode the backs of bad and evil people. Well maybe Gilly's witches liked me better then him because that's exactly how I felt. I couldn't scream, I couldn't move, I couldn't yell, I couldn't blink. I couldn't' do shit! All I could do was sit and stare as a paralyzing fear took over my entire body and mind. Then, he touched me and *whoa*, I blacked out. I was gone, I'd completely zoned out. I had no idea of his intentions and it felt like life had vacated my body. Gilly had his hands on an empty shell. He was talking to me but I couldn't hear him. His touch numbed me and I don't know how long he was in the room with me. I was just relieved as hell when he left. I started crying again...

All I wanted to do was run down stairs and hop in the bed with Pop-Pop but was too afraid to leave my room. So instead, I buried myself under the covers, forced myself to stop crying because I didn't want anyone to hear me, and rocked myself to sleep. I was terrified... (From that point on, I began to shy away from, and somewhat hate and despise, older men. I figured Gilly and Pete only got away with their bull because they were older, adults, and I was just a kid, a child. To this day, I still don't like older men, unless they remind me of my Pop-Pop.)

When I woke up the next morning, I prayed my memories from the night before were nothing more then scenes from a nightmare. Figments of my imagination... But when I looked out into the hall and saw Nana's coat missing, I knew all of it was real. Shaking like a leaf but

33

itching to tell the story, I ran past mommy's room into Nana's and said, *"I'm sorry, Nana!"* Nana was sitting on her bed doing a crossword puzzle, already expecting me to come and watch cartoons. Initially, I don't believe she even heard me because all she said was, *"Hey, Ree', what took you so long?"* So I got a little closer to her and said it again, *"Nana, I'm sorry!"*

"Sorry for what," she inquired? Then like a public auctioneer I began telling her the details of the past evening. *"First, I thought it was you and mommy and then....."* From the look on her face I could tell she didn't believe me, (Wow what a surprise...) then I told her to look in the bottom of her cabinet. Immediately she noticed the lock was busted. (I don't know how she overlooked the lock on her door being busted either, but then again, it was late when they got in.)

Nana was shocked and looked up at me like I was half crazy. *"Look, Nana, look,"* I said, while pointing to the bottom of her armoire where here strong box use to lay. Then, I told her about the things he took from mommy's room and about the coat he snatched from the banister. Nana then yelled for my mom who was already on her way and picked up the phone to call the police. *Mommy use to play possum at times just to avoid Nana's wrath...*

My parents were in shock and found it hard to believe my story. Then, they looked and saw all of their things missing and rationalized I couldn't have been making the story up. Our last name was *Cook* not *Abracadabra*! Mommy was really upset. She pulled me close and wrapped her arms around me. Nana was heated too, but I wasn't sure if it was because of me or because of the money. Everything else could be replaced, but she was pitching a bitch about my grandfather's pension papers from the Pennsylvania Railroad and the war. Nana dropped her head and let out a big sigh...

Mommy and I sat together and waited for the police while Nana made a few more calls. Talking about the robbery wasn't as bad as I thought it was going to be because mommy was the compassionate one. I mentioned nothing about him coming back a second time though. Compassionate or not, that was something I didn't want to talk about or relive. I could deal with it on my own and didn't want to add to mommy and Nana's worries.

When the police arrived, one officer talked to mommy and Nana and the other spoke to me. Nana did most of the talking on mommy's behalf, but mommy could tell I didn't to talk to the officer alone. I was afraid he was going to put me in hand-cuffs and take me away to jail. *"That's not going to happen,"* he said. Then he introduced himself and started asking me questions about the robbery. I guess he assumed the perpetrator was a stranger because he asked me things like what did he look like, how tall was he, bla, bla, bla. *"It was Uncle Gilly,"* I said. *"He's at our house all the time!"* After that the officer stopped writing and just looked at me. I returned his perplexed look with a dumb expression attached to it as if so say *what,* shrugging my shoulders...

Both officers wrote down our statements then started telling my mom and Nana how to go about filing a complaint to accommodate the charges. Then they strongly suggested I have a few sessions with a child psychiatrist, maybe even someone from the station or child services. Man, you should have seen the look on Nana's face when they said that. Filing a complaint was right down her alley, considering she was well known and highly respected by several members of the force. But talking to a shrink was out of the question. If the need arrived for me to be counseled, she felt she and mommy could do the job. Plus, Nana knew it would cause more harm than good if people found out we'd been robbed while she and mommy were out and me and Pop-Pop were home alone, utterly defenseless. She knew better than me how people would blame her for the incident, and by the end of the day, it was clear she was more upset over her money then she was over me.

To date, none of us have seen Gilly and his last known whereabouts were in Florida. We learned this by way of a package he mailed to us somewhere around my 12th born day. When the package arrived, all three of us were shocked and hesitant to open it. Nana broke the seal, viewed its contents, and the expression on her face switched to pure joy. Nana turned the manila envelope upside down, allowing its insides to fall freely to the kitchen table. Amongst the belongings was my original birth certificate, social security card, bank account papers I never knew existed, and a large sum of money. I guess after four years, his guilt finally got the best of him and urged him to right his wrongs the best he could. It was my birthday, but Nana was the one who received the gift. Seeing all that money put such a smile on their faces they had to share their thrill with Pop-Pop. As for me, I pretended to be happy because they were happy, and faked the excitement because they were excited. My true feelings, however, were of fear. The fear that Gilly would come back to finish what he had started.

After the initial excitement wore off, Nana calmed down and called the police. She told them about the envelope and the documents, but kept quiet about the money. (She wasn't stupid. She knew she'd have had to turn that cash in as evidence.) The police took the envelope, noticed the out of state postage, and said they'd have Florida issue a warrant for his arrest. Nothing else has been mentioned or done about the matter. It's been almost 30 years since I encountered that frightful night and although I've tried really hard, I haven't yet figured out a way to forget about it. I guess now I know why Nana didn't want mommy entertaining *dem niggas* around me.

****

After the robbery, mommy and Nana kept close watch on me but tried not to smother me too much. Basically, they just wanted to make sure I was okay and for the most part, I was. But it did bother me a little that I didn't have dad to protect me from something like that ever happening again. Out of all the men who'd come in and out of our lives, none of them were my dad and none of them were ever going to be. Nana and mommy continued to allow their selected male company over. But as for me, I didn't trust any of them. The only man I wanted to see or talk to was my dad, but Nana insisted he didn't exist. Knowing this was a lie, I one day asked my mom to call him up. I just assumed she knew how to get in touch with him. Then, off in the background, I heard mouth all mighty yell, *"Ya daddy ain't shit!"*

Okay, first I don't have a dad and now the nigga ain't shit. Knock it off! I'm not that innocent anymore. I know I have a father. What I don't know is what he looks like, where he lives, or why he doesn't come around to see me. Neither of them said a word but their looks to one another said, w*ell, answer the girl!* Then Nana walked away, leaving my mother holding the bag. Mommy then bent down to me and said in her quiet voice, *"You'll know your father when you see him. You look just like him..."* Wow, she finally broke her silence.

36

Months passed and I'd celebrated yet another born day. I was now nine and it had been a while since I said or questioned anything about my father. Then one day while sitting out on the porch, a man who I never saw before pulled up in a cream colored Volkswagen Buggy. You know the type of ride that looked like the cartoon character *Speed Buggy* .From the moment I laid eyes on him, I stared him down with curiosity. Usually the presence of a strange man would cause me to grow apprehensive, but dude didn't look the least bit threatening. It took me a few seconds to snap out of my daze, but once I did, I noticed something very recognizable about him. His smile... This stranger who I'd never laid eyes on before had the same smile as me. Then I thought about what mommy said, *"You'll know your father when you see him. You look just like him."* Her comment, combined with the butterflies in my belly and the thumping of my heart, forced me to blurt out words I never thought I'd say. *"You my Daddy!"* And I didn't say it like I was asking, I said it with utter certainty, like yeah, nigga, you my daddy!

After being caught off guard so many times, it felt good to be first on the draw for once. Without a doubt my declaration stunned him, his expression was of wonder, *"Who told you that"* he asked, but with confirmation in his eyes. *"My mom! She said I'd know who you were when I saw you because I look just like you!"* My heart was beating a mile a minute and I was nervous, but still very sure of myself. As I walked down off the porch, his smile increased. I reached out to him, put my arms around his waist, and said, *"Hi, Daddy!"* I don't think he was expecting such a warm reception, but shit, I never expected to meet him either. After years of being told he didn't exist and more years of being told he wasn't shit, to finally meet him was truly a dream come true. At that moment, I was the happiest little girl in the world!

To finally put a face to the title *dad* filled me with delight. I know my father saw the twinkle in my eyes as I looked up at him and I saw an even bigger one in his. I have my father's eyes that sparkle with question and brilliance. His sly smile, as if he were the cat that just ate the Canary, his golden tan complexion, gift of gab, and temper. He's not very tall but has a nice build, and carries himself with confidence and pride.

For a brief moment, it seemed as if no one else in the world existed but us two, and none of the things I thought I wanted to tell or ask were important anymore. My dad was from the streets just like Gilly and Pete, and eventually I knew he'd get wind of what had gone down. It wouldn't have surprised me if he already knew. I was happy all of the guess work was finally over. I was happy because even though Nana said he wasn't shit, he found it in his heart to come and see me regardless. But most of all, I was happy that my mom told the truth. I did look exactly like my father! (My dad's very cute…) Meeting him gave me the assurance there was someone out there just like me. Someone who understood me and who could relate to me, but most of all, protect me at all cost.

The two of us held a short conversation and hugged once more before he walked back over to his car. He told me he'd see me later. I smiled, then sat back down on the porch. When daddy's engine started up, the loud noise drew my mom's attention and she came to the door. *"Who was that, Ree'?"*

"That was my dad," I replied with a smile. *"Oh,"* was her only response then she walked off. (Again, what a surprise…) Nana, on the other, hand had to be the one to talk trash as usual, but that was to be expected. The way she downgraded everything was the main reason why I kept my feelings about my dad from her period. I didn't want to hear her mouth about how he was no good or how he was gonna disappoint me with his promises and lies. None of that ever made a difference to me anyway. *"Just because you don't like him, Nana, doesn't mean he won't love me. You just don't want to give us a chance!"*

I knew sooner or later the day would come when I would see for myself just how good or bad he truly was, but until then, I just wanted him in my life. It's kinda crazy now when I think about it 'cause I can't help but wonder if my mom had something to do with his visit. I knew she saw how much I wanted to meet him and I knew she knew what she and Nana was doing was wrong. Reflecting back on that day, I always think my mom was the one who encouraged his visit. Maybe she did make that phone call or maybe he came on his own, I don't know. I'm just glad the door to our relationship was finally opened and we finally got a chance to meet.

I learned a lot from those ordeals. I'd learned never to leave my kids unsupervised or alone for long periods of time. I'd always be cautious and careful about the company I chose to *entertain* and to pay extra close attention to my child's behavior, because their actions could be telling me something their mouths were afraid to say. I also promised myself I'd never prevent my children from having a relationship with their father without just cause...

THE DRAMA OF CONFLICT AND RIVALRY IS JUST AS NATURAL AS RAIN FALLING FROM THE SKY. THE KEY IS TO UNLOCK THE MYSTERY BEHIND THE CONFLICT AND FIND COMMON GROUND. RIVALRY HAS ITS PURPOSE IN LIFE JUST LIKE ANYTHING ELSE...

SIBLING RIVALRY

Being separated from my mom after birth was something my parents had to tell me. It wasn't something I could recall on my own, but being separated from my sister, Tasha, is something I can remember without assistance. For what ever reason, Tasha grew up viewing her grandmother as her mother and never had the opportunity to get to know our biological mother, *Marsha*. The circumstances surrounding our parting are just as confusing and conflicting as the stories I was told about my father. Yet, not a day went by that I didn't think about her and how much I wanted her back in our lives. I grew up knowing very little about my sister, except for the fact that we were indeed sisters. Nana had a few treasured pictures of the two of us and I use to look at them quite frequently. But growing up without her at times made me sad, especially when I grew tired of trying to *entertain* myself.

On several occasions, mommy and Nana drove me across town to see my sister. But far too many times, we were all turned away by her grandmother for reason's I simply could not understand. I use to wonder why mommy had to ask to see Tasha, being as she was her mother and all. But again, there were confusing and conflicting stories that a child my age simply could not comprehend. Nana saw how much our separation was tearing me apart, but she never caused a scene. We'd just drive back home quietly with me sitting in the back seat, pouting, on the verge of tears... No one could ever replace my sister, but there could be an equal.

****

Mommy and Nana were sitting in Nana's room on the bed one day when I walked in and noticed mommy's stomach was getting round and chubby. So I said to her, *"Dang, mom, you getting fat!"* Even though Nana was always first to have something to say, this was the second time I could remember her leaving my mom holding the bag. *"Well you midas well tell her 'cause it's too late to do anything about it now,"* she said.

41

Mommy looked at me and I looked back at her and asked, *"Too late to do what?"* Then, mommy said the words that would end my lonely days forever. *"I'm going to have a baby, Ree'!"*

"A baby, Mama?"

"Yes, Ree', a baby!" Wow, her news was so exciting! I had a million and one questions and I wanted them all answered at once. I can't remember our conversation word for word, but I do know it seemed like it took forever before that baby of ours arrived. Day after day, I drove my mom crazy by asking, *"Is the baby gonna come today, Mama'?"* And she drove me crazy by continuing to smoke them gosh darn *Kool Cigarettes! "Mommy, why you keep smoking? You know smoking not good for you! You gonna' hurt the baby if you keep smoking those cigarettes!"*

"Don't worry, Ree', I'm going to stop and nothing's gonna happen to the baby," she'd say. My mom tried her best to fool me into believing smoking wasn't going to harm her or my unborn sibling, but I knew better. Yet, despite my disliking to her nasty habit, she made me light her cigarettes off the stove when she was too lazy or tired to do so herself. Thus, she made me an unwilling contributor to putting their health at risk.

Mommy didn't stop smoking, but she did try her best to hide it from me. It didn't work though. I still saw the empty packs lying around the house and the smell was undeniable. The expectations of a little brother or sister gave me something to look forward to. Little did I know, my anticipation would later turn into feelings of competition, abandonment, and jealousy.

On the morning of July 12, 1978, I woke up and as usual, went straight into Nana's room. (I talk a lot of smack about my Nana but I love that lady like cooked food.) I paid no attention to my mom's empty room, but when I saw Nana's room was empty too, I made a bee-line downstairs to my Pop-Pop. To my surprise, Pop-Pop was already dressed and sitting outside on the porch. Usually, this meant Nana was done with her chores and was out running errands, but it was way too early and I hadn't even eaten breakfast yet.

I greeted my grandfather at the door while still rubbing the sleep out of my eyes. *"Hey, Pop-Pop, where's everybody at?"* Since this was actually prior to his second stroke, he was till able to respond clearly with no defects to his speech. *"Ya mom took ya mom to the hospital, she's having the baby!"* Excited by his news, I asked him, *"What chu' say, Pop-Pop,"* just because I wanted to hear him say it again. *"Ya mom went to the hospital, Marsha's having the baby!"* (Pop-Pop use to call both Nana and my mom my mom because it just made his life a lot easier...) Pop-Pop told me my mom had a baby girl and her name was *Annette*. I laughed at his pronunciation because that wasn't her name. Her name was *Altavese Lynnette*. But to make life easier, Pop-Pop just threw both names together and called her Annette. I knew what he was trying to say because mommy and I had sat down and chose her name together. We got *Altavese* from *Sammy Davis Jr.* wife and *Lynnette* was a spin of my middle name *Antionette.*

Aww man, I couldn't wait for my new baby to come home and play with me. I was going to do everything with her. *"Dang, Pop-Pop, when they say they coming home?"* Pop-Pop didn't know exactly when they'd be back, so in the meantime, I just sat down with him on the porch and waited.

Three days later when mommy and the baby came home, I couldn't' wait to hold her in my arms and see what she looked like. I'd never seen a new baby before and I was in total awe at how tiny and small she was. And Pale! *"Can I hold her, mommy, PLEASE!"* Nana told me to go sit my ass down and mommy told me to wait a minute. She said she'd bring the baby to me once she got situated. Mommy placed the baby in her crib and I stood there adoring her tiny little feet, hands, and her chubby, round cheeks. *"Can I pick her up, mommy?"*

"Go sit down Ree', I'll bring her to you!" I didn't like mommy's response. She sounded like she was mad at me. So as usual, I ran and told Nana. *"Nana, mommy won't let me hold the baby!"* Nana just looked at me and shook her head as if to say, *lord this chile'.* Nana told me to sit down again but she didn't sound frustrated like mommy. So, I parked my rear end in the chair next to Nana's bed and waited like mommy said. After a few minutes, she brought the baby in to me and I was so happy, I almost cried. Finally, after what seemed like an eternity, I was holding my new baby sister in my arms. It was an experience I'll never forget and it was at that moment I realized I wanted to be a mother

for certain. Nette now gave me someone to protect. The two of us were going to be best friends and no one would ever separate us. She would be the reason why I'd never have to find a way to entertain myself alone again. She was so precious…

****

Okay, what's going on? Mommy said she was having a baby so I would have someone to play with. Well, it's been over a month and I still don't get to play with the little girl. Ever since the two of them came home all they did was sleep. I didn't care if mommy slept because that's all she did anyway. But, I didn't expect the baby to sleep all the time, too! Every time I turned around the little heifer was either lying in her crib sleep, lying on the bed sleep, lying with my mom sleep, lying with Nana sleep, or they were patting her on her back trying to put her back to sleep. Damn, what was wrong with her? Why'd she have to sleep so much? My playmate plans were fading fast and all I could do was admire my new baby from crib-side.

Once again I was confused, frustrated, and didn't understand the circumstances surrounding the situation. This was not how I envisioned things. Watching from court side wasn't as exciting as being a part of the actual game, if you know what I mean. If she was always sleep, when would I get the chance to spend time with her? Then it hit me. Whenever Nette cried, either mommy or Nana would run and pick her up. So, I guess the same would apply for me. All I had to do was wait until she cried and be the first one on the scene to rescue her. Then, they would see how much I loved and cared for her and would let me hold and play with her a lot more. It was a great plan, but guess what? The heifer never cried when I needed her to. It did me no good for her to cry while I was asleep, in school, or doing chores. I needed her to cry when I was bored, playing all alone. Her timing was all wrong, so now what?

Smack, slap, smack, slap! That was the sound of my hand connecting with Nette's tiny little face, turning her as red as a strawberry, forcing her to cry since the only time I was allowed to chill with her was when she was awake and in her crib. I made sure I woke her up while she was still in the crib! When I look back on my actions now, it's hard for me to even forgive myself. I mean, she was so small. But God knows I didn't mean her any harm, I just wanted to play with her. After making her cry, I'd pretend to just be entering the room. Then I'd pick her up and begin to rock her saying, *"Look, mommy, I got her. Can I feed her now? Do you want me to change her diaper?"* Sometimes she'd say, *"Yeah, go ahead,"* and other times she'd be down right furious that she was woke too early from her scheduled nap. Nobody understood all I wanted was to play with her and I was going to do so by any means necessary. On the other hand, I didn't understand I could play with her all I wanted, but first I had to give her time to grow up. Damn, how long was that gonna take?

A year's time can go by in the blink of the eye and before I knew it, my little sis was turning one. Everyone was excited! Mommy was busy making plans for her first birthday, Nana was too, but I was wondering why she still couldn't walk yet. Nana always yelled at us to, *"Keep that girl off her feet,"* or she would become bowlegged and walk like she had rickets. I think Nana just liked to fuss because everyone could see the girl was already bowlegged! (She was born that way.) Plus, we didn't have to stand her up, she was doing that all on her own. She could stand, she just couldn't walk.

On Nette's first birthday the entire family was outside with our neighbor and friend *Chrissy J.,* (aka Aunt Chrissy R.I.P) and I was determined to make Nette walk. She'd already begun to take a few independent steps but her confidence needed reinforcing. That was my job! Mommy stood Nette in the middle of me and Aunt Chrissy as we stood on opposites sides of the porch and let her go. At first she just stood there bouncing up and down, smiling with those deep, pot hole dimples in her cheeks. (That girl has the deepest dimples I've ever seen!) She dropped down on her bottom a few times, but I kept picking her up coaching her until she finally got the hang of things. Once her confidence kicked in, there was no stopping her. I was so proud. This was the first time the two of us had accomplished something together. My baby sister was walking all because of her big sister, me! It was a long time coming, but now the two of us could finally play together. *Good thing they never found out I use to smack her in order to get her attention. Lord, Nana would have killed me if she knew that...*

Okay... I got my new playmate, she's finally able to walk, and mommy trusts me with her a lot more. I should be happy right? Wrong? I now had another dilemma on my hands. Attention… Ever since Nette arrived, all the attention was now on her. I never realized how much attention mommy and Nana really paid to me until it was gone. Not only were mommy and Nana always in awe over her, but all of our family, friends and neighbors were too. Now everything was about Nette. I mean, I still got fed, clothed, and yelled at, but other than that, it was like Marie who? It was so unfair. Why did things have to change? I mean, sure she was cute with those big brown eyes, head full of curly hair, and dimples so deep you could swim in, but why did I have to loose or share the attention?

Take my good friend Resa for example. Resa and I had been friends for years and were so close we called each other cousins. *You know everybody in the hood got a play-play cousin.* Everyday after school, if and when I was allowed to have company, Resa would come over to play with me, but without fail, ended up playing with Nette. Resa was very pretty, soft spoken and pleasant to be around. With her short brown hair and mocha complexion, she reminded me very much of my mother. It use to piss me off when Nette and her played together because Resa already had three sisters, why'd she have to come and steal mine? Nette wouldn't even let the girl get across the street good before she jumped up and ran straight into her arms. Naturally, I became jealous, but no one picked up on it. After a while, I did everything in my power to keep the two of them apart. If I took Nette outside, I made sure she sat on my lap and if I took her to the store, I made sure I held her hand. If I saw Resa walking towards us, I'd pick Nette up and hold her, but without fail, she'd fuss to go with Resa anyway. It use to hurt me so much that *my little sister* wanted to be with someone else, but it wasn't her fault. Nette looked at Resa the same way that she looked at me, as a big sister, and Resa was so nice to her. I couldn't blame Nette for liking or loving her the way she did. But I still didn't like it. It still hurt.

I had a lot to learn about being a big sister and by no means was I use to sharing the spotlight or my possessions with anyone. That was my number one mistake right there. I looked at Nette as a possession and not a human with feelings just like me. I was only willing to share her if the mood struck me or if she got on my nerves. I spent a lot of time resenting our new situation and the change in my attitude wasn't going to occur overnight.

I confess my feeling to Resa sometime in late 2007 and I told her how ashamed I was to admit such a thing. I'm glad she never knew about my jealousy and I'm also glad she was able to laugh about it years later. As for Nette, I confessed my actions to her as well, like how I use to slap her just so I could get to pick her up. I thought she would have been pissed to learn about it, but instead she just smiled and said, "Oh, Murthy"... *Murthy is her special nickname for me....*

****

Getting use to Nette was one thing, but I had to do the same with two more siblings who lived across town with my dad. Now for someone who was spoiled and not use to sharing, this wasn't just a confusing headache, it was way too much to absorb. I had two sisters by my mom but only got to see one, and now I've learned I have two sisters by my dad, who I've never even seen at all. It wouldn't have been so bad if they were babies like Nette, but no, they were just as big as me! Where did they come from and were they the reason my dad couldn't come see me? So many questions ran though my mind but the number one inquiry was; w*ho's gonna be the damn boss* cause *I'll be damned if I'm gonna let somebody I don't even know order me around!*

The idea of having siblings was beginning to wear me out, nevertheless, Toy *(my father's wife)* and my dad wanted all of us to know each other. The first time the three of us met, they piled us up in the car and took us to Veterans Park in Hamilton. I barely knew my dad and although his wife was very nice to me, I would have rather traded in my two new sisters for dolls or something. Those were my initial feelings, but eventually I saw the benefits in having playmates my own age and size. Plus, since they were my sisters, they'd be just like me and like all things I liked, right?

Veterans Park wasn't too far from home and had I known my way back, I would have left. To any idiot, it would have been clear as to why I may have been a bit shy or reserved, I was surrounded by four people I barely knew. But what was up with Kedya and Nikki? I tried to initiate play with them and they brushed me off like I had cooties or the clap! Maybe they viewed me as the outsider and didn't want me to infiltrate their alliance like I didn't want anyone to infiltrate me and

47

Nette, I don't know. What I do know is the rejection was not to be desired and I ended up playing alone until....

Keyda and Nikki played on one side of the playground and I played on the other. Keyda took after her mother in looks, complexion and build. Both were brown skinned with short brown hair, but Nikki like me, looked just like our father, and her hair, just as long as mine. Little by little, space between us began to decrease until we were close enough to hear one another talk. I thought this was our ice-breaker but on the contrary, it only led to conflict and then a fight! I don't even think our parents knew what was going on until it was almost over. There the three of us were huddled up like we were going over NFL plays, but instead, were actually banging it out like gang bangers. Whop, whop, swing, swing, bam! I think the idea was for them to jump me but as it turned out, we all ended up fighting each other. They were hitting each other just as much as they were attempting to hit me and to this day, I still don't know how the fight began or who started it. If I were a gambler, I'd be willing to be the house that it was Nikki because for whatever reason Nikki (the youngest at the time) told Keyda (the oldest) I was bad mouthing them. However, Nikki knew damn well I hadn't said one word about either one of them to anyone. How could I? It was my very first time meeting them and we were the only three in the park. Who in the hell was I bad mouthing them to, myself?

As soon as our dad saw us pounding one another into the dirt, he and Toy came a running. Daddy broke the three of us up and tossed us aside like we were last week's trash. Nobody said a word, not even me, and it was obvious that our play date was now over. Daddy looked at his girls, his face filled with disgust, then turned around and headed back to the car. Mommy (Toy) and the rest of us followed. I definitely wasn't expecting our first encounter to turn out like this, but Keyda and Nikki must have been forewarned to be on their best behavior or else. I say that because Nikki kept trying to cop a plea, but her cries fell upon deaf ears. To each of her appeals our father's response was, *"Shut up!"* I know it was mean to laugh but it was funny as hell. Nobody saw her rolling her eyes at me and nobody saw her giving me the finger. As if I was the problem? Once we got back to the car, daddy started preaching to us about keeping our hands to ourselves. That was funny too, considering three people had to squeeze into the back of that tiny little Volkswagen Buggy with no A.C. How could we not touch one another and we were all hot and fidgety?

Nobody said a word on the ride back home, not even my dad and Toy. I was cool with the silence because like Nana said, *niggas and talk create heat,* but Keyda and Nikki seemed real paranoid. I knew I had nothing to worry about because I hadn't done a damn thing wrong and wasn't about to let anyone blame shit on me either. Not even my sisters! But I was in for a rude awakening once we all got back to the crib.

As soon as we pulled up in front of the house, Nikki and Keyda started to wail like they were at their best friend's funeral. DAMN! Did I miss something? Why all of a sudden did they break down like that? Keyda was whimpering and shaking her head no, and Nikki was trembling so hard it looked like she was *Crunk* dancing. What the fuck happened? I must admit I was a bit lost, but I wouldn't be lost for long. As soon as our dad opened the front door he ordered all three of us to go upstairs. Then, he picked up the first thing in his sight, his Timberland work boot... As the three of us made our way to the stairs, Keyda and Nikki bowed their heads in what I thought was an admission of guilt or shame. I chose not to copy their actions, unashamed and totally unaware of what was coming next.

Keyda stepped only one foot onto the stairs and, *wham,* our dad swung that boot like he was batting for the NY Yanks! He caught Keyda right in the head, leaving her with a little nick on her left ear. Nikki was next and if you ask me, she got it the worst because her thrash was dead center, right in the top of her head. Although her flinch and moan was minor, the look on her face depicted she was in a lot of pain. In my mind I was thinking, *I know he's not about to hit me like that too,* but things do happen in three's. However, instead of hitting me with the boot still in hand, he threw it at me and caught me in the back. Once he'd let out his frustration, he left us with something to think about. ***"Ya'll family and family don't fight against each other, they fight with each other!"*** My dad and Toy went into their room and Keyda and Nikki went into their separate rooms and shut their doors. As for me, I sat dumbfounded and mad at the top of the stairs. This was some bullshit!

Scriptures say the tongue is mightier then the sword. My dad proved that statement to be true, but I don't think it was his intention to do so. Sure, I was a little sore from the tussle in the park and the boot to the back didn't make matters any better. But my discomfort didn't come from anything physical, it was all emotional. Until that day, nobody had ever spoken to me like that before. His words weren't so much harsh as they were effective and profound. Family... You don't' fight family! It had been a rough initiation but in less then a day, I'd become just as much a part of their family as I was a part of the family I'd grown up with. In a million years, I'd never trade in my Mama, Nana, Pop-Pop, or Nette, and nobody would ever come before them. We were unique to say the least. Yet, there was also something very unique about the way things operated within their union as well. In their home, nobody received special treatment, as opposed to where I was from, where I was the favored one. The lesson my dad was trying to teach us all was about unity, not just punishment for our actions. It's a given we're not always going to get along with each other but *by no means would we resort to tearing each other down.* That's not what family is about...

To this day, there have been plenty of times, and I do mean plenty, when I wanted to knock Nikki's head clean off her shoulders. I'm more then positive she has wanted to do the same to me as well. Hell, looking at the bigger picture, I'm sure we've all felt some kind of way about one another at one time or another and not all of those feelings were positive. Yet, I firmly believe the *NO FIGHTING* speech is what impelled us all to seek peaceful resolutions to our disputes, even if it meant not speaking to one another for a while. (I got pulled over once and used Nikki's name to get away. I avoided going to jail and paid the ticked immediately, but that didn't stop her wrath once the incident showed up on her abstract. She wouldn't even hear my explanation and was so mad at me I had to run to our dad for help. *"That's your sister, Marie,"* he said, *and you have to find a way to work that out with her on your own.* But, Daddy, I cried.... (Of course this was years later.)

In time, I learned how to balance out my love and fear of having siblings, and got better with sharing the attention. But as soon as I thought I was out of the woods, *Daddy Dearest* came along and told me him and Toy were having another baby! It was another girl, and they named her Gayle after her mother. Being as I was a little older, I wasn't as jealous over her as I was Nette. But wait, they weren't done yet. In a few more years they had a fourth baby. This time it was a boy, *Kenny Jr.!* Wow, I had a baby brother, what a relief. I was beginning to think I'd never get a brother. Now I have five siblings. All of us unique, but at the same time, very much alike. I was just hoping Kenny would turn out to be just as rough as me since Nana use to always say, *I should have been a boy!* (By the way, Toy is just a family nickname for my father's wife but I address her as mom because over the years, she's been nothing less…)

In the end, I felt it was okay my dad hadn't been there for me in my earlier years because he was busy on the other side of town giving me sisters, brothers and best friends for life. Ha, ha, and Nana had the nerve to say he wasn't shit…

Nikki and I still fight to this day, but instead of throwing punches, we fight with words. Ouch, they hurt worse, but I guess that's just how sisters do.

I kept breaking my neck trying to fit in, not realizing my potential to be distinctive and **STAND OUT!**

PRE TEEN SHIT

A nyone who knew me during my days as a youth can attest I was one of the prettiest and well mannered girls on my block. But regardless of that fact, Nana wouldn't allow my looks to go to my head and constantly reminded that true beauty came from within. "*Looks will get you but so far, Ree' and in due time, good looks fade. Respect, on the other, hand is a virtue.*" I guess she became worried that I'd become full of myself and day after day, stressed to me the importance for a young woman to carry herself with dignity. I was taught to be seen not heard, to speak with a soft tongue, be slow to anger, and to pick and choose my battles wisely. Well all I can say is, "*Nice try, Nana.*" I guess it's always easier to tell someone the lesson then to teach it by example. Nana tried her best to tell me what was right, but the very things she taught me against, were the very traits I seemed to pick up. She was loud and so am I. You can hear both of us a mile away when we speak, and if we're excited, you can damn near hear us around the corner. I never saw my Nana back down to a challenge, and I don't even entertain the thought! Her tongue was sharp as glass and mine is sharper then a double edge sword. The only thing I got right was the part about showing my elders respect. Aside from self respect, the other topic she preached round the clock was to show my elders the respect they deserved. "*They've been on this earth longer then you, Ree'. They know a bit more and you'll be lucky to become so wise.*" Nine times out of ten, she was talking about herself.

Nana was right, respect does outweigh vanity. Even though I botched the task of being *dainty,* I never disrespected any adults. I was far from an angel, but I was nothing like some of the youth we all see and hear growing up in our society today. Even my grandmother, who never agrees with me on anything, will back me on that one. Nana wasn't one to coddle, and she loved you with strict, old-fashioned Ellaville, GA love. Tough Love is what she liked to call it. Tough love! She kept me on a short leash and I was allowed very few privileges. If I went outside, the furthest I could go was the front porch. If I got off the porch, it was only to walk to the store. If I walked to the store, I had to tell them if I was going to the one on the corner or the one across the light. And God forbid someone wanted to walk with me, then that would take them an additional ten minutes to decide if they trusted the person or not. By then, whoever I was going to go with grew impatient and bounced, which was fine by them because now I didn't want to go. They knew what they were doing…

Nana knew the time would come when she'd have to give me a little space. She knew there was nothing she could do as a parent to stop my growth or curiosity, and she knew I needed some form of a social life. At first she'd say I could socialize in school, but my friends from school were the same kids from my neighborhood. Plus, in school we didn't have time to socialize as much, even during lunch and recess. Everyone from my block hung out in the same cluster, and that cluster had two hang out spots; Mr. Warren's porch and the park in the middle of the block. Nana didn't mind if I sat on our neighbor's porch, even though we all knew he hated us to do so, but she couldn't stand for me to go into that park because it prevented her from seeing what I was doing. None of the other kids had restrictions on their comings and goings like I did. I was the only odd ball.

Speaking of the other kids, I didn't have as many friends growing up as I would have liked. Not because I wasn't likable, but because Nana picked and chose most of my friends for me. She said she had he reasons and that the majority of the people I associated with were up to no good. *"They gon' get yo ass in hot water, you hear me. Just watch and see!"* I never wanted to believe her. It reminded me so much of what she used to say to my mom. Though, I guess it was her job to see the things I didn't.

Nana use to also tell me to stop being a fool for others and to stop letting everyone use me. At the time, her words seemed rather harsh but truth is truth, and Nana wasn't one to bite her tongue. Nana held me in very high regard and because of this, I went through a lot of drama with my peers. I kept breaking my neck to fit in, not realizing my potential to be distinctive and stand out. A lot of the girls who knew me were dreadfully jealous of me, and for no legitimate reason, because we all had our strengths. Nonetheless, there were those who resented me because I had long, healthy hair and Nana wouldn't allow anyone to play in it. Some hated me because I had semi-fair complexion and claimed I looked like a Puerto Rican. (I thought about explaining to them that I had grandparents with Dominican, White, West Indian, and Native American backgrounds, but I doubt if that would have made any difference. Besides, no matter how you broke it down, I was still black!) Others were envious for reasons unknown, and the rest disliked me simply because they were miserable inside their own skin, and I was a happy person who knew who to smile. It seemed like I couldn't win for loosing.

****

Out of everyone I ran across, Resa and Shell were the only two who Nana allowed me to chill with without putting up a fuss. Though every now and then she'd say I was being a fool for them too! Resa and Shell lived right down the street from us, which was a good thing, then later moved across the street, which was even better. Both of our families were long time residents of Spring Street and knew each other very well. But because Resa and Shell played in that park most of the time, Nana felt they were putting me up to no good. (I wonder if she ever thought it was me who put me up to no good.) *"I can't see what cha doing,"* she'd say. But Nana that's the point, I'd mumble to myself. Yet, regardless of who did what, the bottom line was, if I couldn't keep my *black ass* out of that park, I'd have to find contentment with just sitting on the porch! Nana made her instructions very clear, and it was often difficult to abide by her rules and at the same time maintain a friendship with others.

Paying heed to Nana meant being ridiculed by everyone else, and being laughed at by my peers was worse then having no one to chill with at all. I didn't realize it at the time, but Nana was well within her rights for being so protective of me. She knew most of the older teens and young adults who hung there conducted risky behavior and indulged in activities that she didn't want me to have any part of. Shit, I even got yelled at for doing simple shit like cheers and drills. *"Stop gyrating your body like that! If a man sees you moving like that, he gonna swear you know something!"* What the hell did she mean by that? How bad could Mississippi be? You remember, M.I. crooked letter, crooked letter, I,

55

crooked letter, crooked letter, I hump back, hump back I. Mississippi! It was one of the most popular drills back in the early 80's, but Nana dared me to do it. *"I don't give a damn what the rest of them do, Ree'! I don't want you doing it period!"*

Nana said my biggest problem growing up was trying too hard to do like others. She said I worried way too much about what somebody else was doing instead of paying attention to what she was trying to instill in me. Now that I was forbidden to do the drills and hang in the park, the girls didn't want to hang with me. The only fillers I had to avoid complete and utter loneliness was to hang out with the fellas; particularly Man and Larry.

Man was Resa and Shell's only brother and Larry was their younger cousin. Now girls will be girls and just like with my sisters, Resa, Shell, and I weren't always going to get along. When this occurred, Man and Larry always served as suitable substitutes, although Larry always seemed to make matters worse. Without fail, he'd try familiar manipulation tactics he thought would convince me he could get me back into his cousin's favor. I was never that naïve to fall for his game and because I refused to be his flunky, he ended up taunting me over the disagreements and causing more confusion. Larry always operated with an ill motive in mind, and because we were both born under the same zodiac sign, we constantly bumped heads. I guess he thought he was the only one who could be as slick as a can of oil. Nana was semi right, I did allow people to take advantage of me from time to time in order to have a friend, but I knew the difference between a friend and an opportunist.

Man, on the other hand, was *The Man*. His character was suave and meek and his intentions were never malicious or self motivated. He was the only one who never found reason to be mad at me and would sit and chill with me without prejudice. With him as an ally, I found it easier to *fit in* with his sisters. Resa was never a problem, but sometimes Shell, at times, could be unkind. In many ways, Man was the protector and big brother amongst my peers and we all looked up to him in one way or another. He was always sincere, he always had my back, and he never tried to abuse or take advantage of me like some of the other guys I chose to associate with. Needless to say, his actions made me feel loved and accepted. Although I had a little brother, he wasn't old enough to hang out with me and besides, he was still my *little brother*...

On several occasions, Man aka Claude, would see me sitting alone, trying to *entertain myself,* and out of simple, good heartedness would take the time to sit and play a few games of backgammon with me. Back then we called it *Acey~Deucey* or *Ace's Deuces.* There were even a few occasions when Nana was in a good mood and she allowed him to come in and help me set up one of my many race tracks or construction sets. (Yes, Nana really wanted me to be a boy and missed her son so much I often had to take his place.) Man's friendship was wholesome. He gave me a sense of security just like Pop-Pop, and at times, seemed like my only true friend in the world.

In time, Nana saw that restricting me from the park only made the temptation greater. She knew I'd defy her, regardless of the consequences, just as long as I got the satisfaction of doing the opposite of what she commanded. She eventually removed the park from her *do not enter* list and once that happened, a lot of my old disputes simply disappeared. But just like she suspected, new ones took their place.

Nana only saw the bad aspect of hanging in the park; spin the bottle, hide–n–go-get, smoking, and getting high. She paid very little attention to anything else. I guess it never dawned on her I liked civilized and constructive activities, like soccer, dodge ball, and baseball; even though she knew I loved baseball with a passion, just like she did.

****

From coast to coast, every hood and set are basically run the same. Certain individuals call the shots and others just join in and follow suit. Based on that I have to laugh, since today I am a leader amongst leaders. I was always excited and eager for others to include me in their plans, but I never got the chance to call any shots. That privilege was only given to a select few and they were Resa, Shell, Man, and Mike.

Mike was another *big brother* figure among all of us, but most of all he was Man's best friend. The two of them were like a pair of shoes, when you saw one you saw the other, and most people who knew them thought they were brothers. I guess in a sense we were all like family to each other, but unlike the family you share a roof with, things between us often became very competitive within our circle. This was something else Nana griped about because she saw the obvious. Resa, Shell, Man, and Mike were always the ones to coordinate a gathering for some type of sport activity. But no matter who played or who didn't, regardless if you won the toss of a coin or picked the magic number; in any game, the same individuals always served as team leaders or captains and they always picked their favorites and friends first. Resa, Man, and Mike seemed to keep their choices neutral but be that as it may, I still ended up sitting on the side lines more then I would have liked. Shell, on the other hand, only picked me when there was a need to even out the teams and even then, they often skipped me in rotation. On top of that, I was always given the worst positions, the worst pitches, and got hit more times than the ball itself. True, I wasn't the best player, but they didn't give me much room to learn either. This is why Nana used to say I was being stupid in order to have friends. That was until Generous came along.

Generous was another friend of ours, a bit older, who lived directly across the street from the park. Generous would often partake in the games we played and was quick to settle a dispute or attempt to mediate. He was a beacon of light and ensured the games were played in fairness. No one ever saw him indulge in any reckless activity and if he wasn't in the park with us or in the house, he was down at the church preparing for Sunday service. Clearly, his spiritual upbringing contributed to his moral integrity and I, for one, appreciated his unbiased take on things regardless of athletic ability.

Nana didn't like me hanging with anyone older then me, but Generous had my best interest at heart and surprisingly, she never fussed about him either. In many ways, he was a lot like Nana and use to become so frustrated with me when he saw how I let others treat me unfair. He encouraged me to demand to be treated equally and to stop sitting on the sideline feeling sorry for myself. *"If you don't stand up for yourself, girl, nobody else will!"* I wish he would have lived long enough to see that change take effect in me, but sadly, he was killed on New Years Eve prior to me turning twelve. Generous was loved by everyone who knew him and he was truly one of the most caring individuals I've ever known. He had the personality of a Prince and a heart that wouldn't stop giving. He wasn't a thug, but he wasn't going to let you walk all over him either. Everyone was sad when they heard the news of his bereavement, and although I don't remember all of the circumstances surrounding it, I do remember Nana saying God don't make no mistakes.

Nana was right, God never makes a mistake, and in the strangest way, a part of Generous still lives with me today, in a way that only God Almighty could have orchestrated.

The passing of Generous was a shocker to everyone because tragically, he was murdered; yet nothing hit me harder then the death of my dear friend Claude aka Man. Man's passing in '87 was overwhelming, and it was the first time I actually experienced physical pain while mourning. Man's passing not only affected his family, it tore a chunk out of our neighborhood and our community. I've often replayed that day in my head and the details are so vivid, it seems like it only just happened. It was a beautiful spring day and Man had promised he'd go with me to Motor Vehicles so I could take my driver's test. Ironically, his sisters were also waiting for him to accompany them to the movies. When he exited his house, he told his sisters he'd be back then walked across the street and jumped into the car with our neighbor Obe'. Before Obe' sped off, Man yelled out the window *"I love you!"* His sister and I found that to be a tad bit out of the ordinary, but never in a million years would we have guessed that would be the last time we heard his voice.

Resa and I sat on our separate porches waiting for her brother to return, but ten minutes after his departure they received a call. It was the police, there had been an accident and Man was seriously injured. Truth be told, he died on the scene, but out of compassion, the authorities waited until the family arrived at the hospital to break the news. It was one of the saddest days of my life and even looking back at old pictures of him can cause me to tear. Sadly, everyone knew how reckless of a driver Obe' was, and we all felt it was only a matter of time before he killed himself behind the wheel of a car. It's so surreal that he was the one to walk away from the crash without a scratch and Man was the one who lost his life.

Nana, mommy, and Pop-Pop never got over the death of Uncle Butch and no one who knew Generous or Man will forget about them either. True, *God don't make no mistakes,* but God isn't the cause nor the source of bad things to happen either...

****

Which came first, the chicken or the egg? According to scriptures it was the chicken, and speaking of scriptures, it's remarkable how certain events were foretold and predicted thousands of years ago and we have the privilege of seeing them unfold today. Hmm, I wonder if I would have lived back then would the predictions pertaining to my life been just as accurate? Would anyone have been able to predict I would experiment with PCP [Boat, Wet, Fresh] followed by the loss of my virginity at the early age of twelve?

EZK aka Mr. Keys, the younger brother of Generous, was someone I trusted and admired from a far. He was handsome beyond words with a swagga that just wouldn't quit. The two of us never had any romantic encounters, but I was just as attached to him as I was Man and Mike. Keys was the definition of a *ladies man* and had a true gift of gab. I often watched his wheeling's and dealings from a distance and being my senior, he must have detected my curiosity and my thirst to try things out first hand. Keys was our neighborhood dope man but he wasn't careless with his affairs. He had a gang of followers but kept his circle tight. Everyone respected him, no one ever crossed him, and he had more money then I'd ever seen before in my life. He was charming, had a great physique, and would knock a mother fucker out quicker then you could light a match. All of this and more held my attention, but for a pre-teen, he was way out of my league.

Regardless of Keys' choice of lifestyle or his means and methods of making money, he was far from a villain and never forced anyone to do anything they didn't want to do. Those who chose to be in his company did so of their own free will, and everyone who hung around him indulged in the same extra circular activity as he did. The new school learned their ways from the old school and just like today, back then you either had to *get down* or *don't come around*. Nothing personal, but birds of a feather do flock together! Fugitively speaking, I was a bird without a flock but I wouldn't be for long, and I was about to *get down* for all the wrong reasons.

Despite his ability to attract women like a moth to a fire, Keys did have a girl; her name was Peaches and during the course of their relationship, they had a son who they named Kyron aka little Keys. Now, Nana despised Keys activity, but she'd never deny me the joy of going to visit their son. I wasn't as close to Peaches as some of the other girls like Shell, but Nana knew my maternal nature ran deep. I couldn't resist babies, and in her eyes, sitting with Peaches and her son was better than sitting with anyone in that damn park. Before I knew it, I was a regular face down at the Parker residence, but I was so fascinated by the freedoms of the older crowd, my intentions to see the baby were often altered. The door to temptation was now wide open and it was only a matter of time before I'd take the plunge and start to entertain behavior unbecoming a young lady.

****

It was a warm summer's night and the younger crowd had just concluded an enjoyable game of baseball in the park. As the sun set and the street lights came on, we knew it was time for us to exit the grounds so Keys and his crew could take over. *Although even in broad day light, if they wanted the park to themselves, none of us would stand in their way.* As I sat on the abandoned porch diagonally across the street from my house, (The same porch Gilly sat on when spying on us.) I noticed one of my girlfriends chose to stay behind with Peaches and chill. I didn't pay much attention to what they were doing, but I did take note that Keys and his boys were all smoking joints. I don't know what made me want to test the waters, but out of nowhere, I decided I wanted to smoke one too. I'd never been up to the challenge in the past, but fuck it, if they could handle it, I could handle it, too.

I walked over to Keys like a small pup seeking a treat from their keeper. I never got the chance to part my lips to ask anything before he popped the question, "*You wanna try this?*" Eager to do so, I shook my head before answering. Keys passed me the small, tightly rolled joint, I took a few strong pulls, and in seconds, I was in another world. I'd never tried marijuana before, but I knew I wasn't supposed to be that damn high. It felt like I was standing on the outside of my body looking in, and the only thing I could think was, *Fool! Who told you to be so brazing?*

Wow, Nana was right, this shit will fuck you up! I'd witnessed plenty of people get high, but none of them looked like they felt like this. Every bit of reality seemed to escape me and the most I could hear were echoes. I tried to focus but nothing seemed to stay in place. Everyone was talking slurred and moving in slow motion. My head was spinning, I felt flush, and for some odd reason, I was taking huge steps in order to walk as if I was a giant. What the fuck was going on?

Keys drew my attention, *"Yo', Murf, you okay?"* Clearly, I was

61

off my deem, [off point] but because I wanted to hang with the big dogs so bad, I lied and said I was fine. Slowly I made my way to the front of the park and it seemed like that alone took about a half hour. The background sounds of babble and laughter seemed to vibrate my body. I looked down at my house and it looked like it was a mile away. Damn, what was wrong with me? I needed something to drink badly, but didn't feel I could make it down to the store. Luckily for me, Keys and his crew decided they wanted to go to the store too, and just simply tagged along.

At the most, the consequences for breaking curfew and coming in late would get me nothing more then a day or two inside the house. But walking into the house high, would have probably got me shipped off to a convent! I knew I was pushing my limits, but if I was going to face the music, I needed to do so in a better state of mind.

As we approached the corner I stared at the light, waiting for it to turn green. As soon as it did, I took off down the middle of Calhoun St., walking the double yellow lines, mimicking the sounds and actions of a train. I thought I was a Choo-Choo ya'll, and I was chugging along as if I had a car full of passengers with smoke coming out of my mouth. In other words, I was O.O.O. totally *out of order*!

I never knew weed could mess you up like this, my mom and aunts smoked weed all the time. They didn't think I knew what was in those manila twenty-sacks that use to be lying around the house, but I knew the difference between a cigarette and ciga-weed! I wasn't that stupid and just like with cigarettes, the smell of weed is undisputable. But why was I having such a bad reaction? It was like I couldn't control my actions. Cars were honking and beeping at me because I was disrupting traffic, and the lights and adrenaline rush made me so dizzy, I thought I'd black out.

Somehow, someone must have guided me out of the street onto the sidewalk, and that's when Keys handed me some white shit to drink. At first I refused because I didn't want to get any higher, but he forced me to drink it down. Within seconds I felt better and the concoction almost instantly crashed my high. Everyone was laughing at me except him, but once he saw I was good to go, he let the laughter out. Nervous but thankful and amazed at how much better I felt, I laughed along with everyone else. I didn't want anyone to know how scared I was and for the life of me, I didn't want to look like the true fool I really was. Keys and his crew then headed back down to the park and at the same time, escorted me to my house. As the lot of us walked and talked, Keys keep a close eye on me, and for some reason, that made me feel accepted. I was still wondering somewhat, how I managed to get so high after only a few tokes, but listening to their conversation helped me to put two and two together.

Keys could have just as easily left my ass at that corner to fend for myself. He could have allowed anyone to take advantage of me, and more so, could have had his way with me himself if he so desired. But that didn't happen, because like I said, he wasn't a villain. He may have played devil's advocate but I did what I did because I wanted to do it. Curiosity killed the cat but milk and mayonnaise brought me back! For anyone who has ever been under the influence of PCP or a similar narcotic, you know far too well what I mean. As it turned out, the joint I shared with Keys wasn't just filled with marijuana. It was a marijuana joint treated with PCP. PCP is a narcotic that was developed back in the 1950's. Its initial purpose was to be an intravenous anesthetic, however, was banned due to its mind altering effects which cause humans to hallucinate and sometimes obtain super human strength. It also caused users to act irrationally. *Hmm, you don't say...*

Clearly, I wasn't prepared to handle such a substance, but because I wanted to be down and craved the acceptance, I continued to indulge, thinking it would help build up my tolerance. However, continued use only contributed to longer highs that took just as long to come down. There were times when my sense of direction was totally out of whack and other times when I was rendered damn near immobile. I knew the effects of that shit could cause long term, even permanent damage, yet, I continued to smoke it until I was eighteen. The fact that I was putting my life in danger every time I smoked that shit didn't faze me, but the hallucinations were more frightening. I remember one night it got so bad, I thought I saw a solid statue turn its head, look at me, and start clapping its hands. That's when I knew I had to hang it up. After surviving that trip, I went home, threw away my stash, and told my mother to tell everyone who came looking for me I wasn't there. I needed time to detox and it worked. But twenty years later, looking up at that statue still freaks me out!

I guess you can call me one of the lucky ones compared to several of my peers who also fell victim to the fad, then graduated on to harder, more addicting substances. I thought PCP was as bad as it could get but I was terribly mistaken. After that, crack hit the hood and that's when shit really got messed up. The effects of that era are the closest I've ever seen to modern day genocide. Pushers eventually became users and users gave birth to a new breed of hardened hearts and spiritually dead youths. In a course of five years, it wiped out nearly three generations and sadly, we are still trying to reverse the effects of that man made destruction today. (I heard it was the CIA, but don't get me to telling stories...) True, I'd made the choice not to smoke *Wet* anymore, but that didn't mean I would be able to walk away from the game. Once you've had a taste of the forbidden, the allure is almost impossible to resist.

****

Anyone who sold anything back in the late 80's early 90's had an Up-Town [New York] connection, and little ass Trenton was one of the hottest spots on the E. Coast. The trafficking between the two states was like a non-stop relay race; and we built such a clientele, we had the dirty south coming up north to cop from us. Every dope boy I knew, including Keys, kept a substantial stash of what ever you needed. I remained close to them all and in turn, picked up on how to hustle and make profit in the game. Once they saw how easy it was for a *pretty young thang* like myself to get my shit off, they started fronting me bundles of their shit to knock off. Abu', another top dog back then, took notice of my dealings and offered me the opportunity to get down with him. Abu' was on the same level as Keys, just with a different cluster of customers. Abu' was also an Aries, but unlike my old pal Larry, the two of us made excellent business partners. My cut was 70/30, 60/40, and sometimes I didn't have to hand over anything at all, Abu' just loved to see me get my grind on. Nine times out of ten, he'd assure me my sales by sending all of his regulars to me and trust me, we never had to worry about stepping on anybody's toes because there was enough money out there for everyone and their Mama!

Shit was sweet, and even though I shouldn't have been exposed to the life, it felt good to be able to buy what ever I wanted, when ever I wanted. Nana knew something was going on but she couldn't put her finger on it. She never asked any questions though, and I guess that was because she wanted to spare herself the heartache and aggravation. As the years progressed, rumors began to circulate about me and Abu' as well as me and Keys. Yet, contrary to un-popular belief, all I did with either was learn the game, get money, and get high!

**********.

By now, everybody knew me as *Mrs. Cook's* granddaughter and was aware that most of our dealings had to remain on the hush and out of sight. Nana use to say, *"It's not what you do but how you do it,"* so with that in mind, I hid all of my activities from her except my admiration for little Keys.

Peaches and Keys' first born son was now a year old and Peaches had started to bring him outside more. By far, he was one of the handsomest babies I'd ever seen and not even Nana could argue with me on that. His dirty blond hair and big, brilliant smile caused me to fall head over heals for him, and because he was so beautiful, I volunteered my services to Peaches if ever she needed a sitter. Nana said I was too young to sit a baby, but said she didn't mind as long as Peaches or Keys supervised me. I argued I didn't need anybody to watch me and on top of that, Peaches and Keys knew I'd never cause little Keys any harm. Nana said she wasn't concerned about him as she was me, because she could tell he was a mischievous little Imp. In other words, he was a handful!

As usual, Nana was right, that little boy was a handful. By now, Keys was going on two and Peaches and I had become more familiar with one another. I use to go down and sit on her porch and wait for her to send the baby outside. I figured since he was always running up and down the street causing havoc, what more trouble could he get into by being with me. (That last statement will take on a whole different meaning later on in the book…)

Peaches now had another son, little Bryant, and she couldn't chase up and down the street after Kyron as much. I thought occupying his time would calm him down, but that little boy was crazy as hell, and stayed shocking the shit out of me. At two years old he had the mouth of a grown man and would curse a person out in a heartbeat. If I didn't know any better, I would have sworn he was related to my Pop-Pop because his tongue was sharp and his temper was lightning quick! He wouldn't hesitate to call you a *Bitch* if you aggravated him and although

I knew he was wrong, he kept me cracking up. (Maybe that's why Nana said I needed supervision while watching him?) Truly, he was too funny for words. I don't know what drew me to that little boy but I adored him from the top of his head and all that dirty blond hair, down to those tiny little feet that kept me chasing behind him. He was a rare little rascal, but at the same time, he was so innocent; and just like Nette, he was my baby...

The association between me, Keys, and Peaches set the stage for future events. But nobody, and I do mean nobody, could have seen what lay ahead for us as a result of an alliance made by a twelve year old little girl.

Nana's fears for me were unfolding right in front of her eyes and there was very little she could do to stop it. I hung out with a rough crowd but at the same time, learned the do's and don't of the streets. Each day of my life was an experience and each lesson was quick, somewhat confusing, and sometimes painful. I rushed my way through puberty and allowed myself very little time to prepare for the next phase; consensual, immature sex, take one! Action...

****

Sex, intercourse, having relations, whatever you want to call it; was introduced to me with such rawness, it's the one thing I truly wish I could do over. Age twelve was the magic number for me it seems. It marked a milestone in my life and a turning point. You know most girls start to *smell themselves* around that age as Nana would say, and of course yours truly wasn't any different. Nana could see the obvious changes in my body as well as my attitude. My breast were beginning fill out and I had begun wearing a big girl bra instead of those super hero *Underoos*. Nana hated them anyway because she said you could see my nipples, and you could. Plus, my hips were as thick as pizza dough from all of the pork and oatmeal she use to feed me, and boys became the topic of all of my conversations. In addition, I was now wearing my thick, long, dark hair out instead of in pony tails, my body was firm and

shapely, and my attitude was full of curiosity. The writing was written on the walls and she knew it was only a matter of time before I did something really dumb!

"Keep ya dress tail down and ya pants zipped up, Marie!" That was my daily reminder not to fool around, and when ever I walked out the door she'd yell, *"You better not get yo' ass in no trouble either!* Okay, Nana, okay I hear you, damn. Just like my Mama, I'd agree with her just so she would stop fussing. She knew I had to find out everything out the hard way. (No pun intended) *"A hard head makes a soft behind all the time, Marie."* I swear that woman had a saying for everything.

Nana was good for telling me what not to do, but she never warned me about the consequences if I decided not to follow her advice. Telling me, or any teenager, not to do something is just like placing a bottle in front of a toddler and telling them to leave it alone. It just ain't gonna happen! However, had Nana sat me down and talked to me about such things, *maybe* I wouldn't have been in such a rush to experiment. It just seemed like she was always trying to keep me from having any and all kinds of fun, therefore, my mind stayed set on rebellion. Having me check in every hour and reporting my whereabouts only minimized my exploring, it didn't put a stop to it. I still had to go to school and that meant six hours of freedom, six hours of boys, and six hours to plot, explore, ask questions, and set shit up. *Where there's a will there's a way...* That was one of her sayings too...

****

Girlfriends! Girlfriends are timeless treasures who you never quite forget, regardless of how good or bad your times were. They're the people you envy, cherish, fight for, fight with, and above all, tell secrets to. I had more girlfriends in school then I did at home, and our lunch period served as our time for social networking. Every Monday thru Friday, a group of us would occupy the corner of our favorite table and swap stories about who we thought was cute and who was our latest crush. A select few, however, were able to elaborate on more mature dialogue like; whose house they went over after-school and what took place. All of it aroused my curiosity, but for the most part, all I could do was sit and listen with nothing to contribute. Collectively, their declarations sounded like testimonies from a session with Dr. Ruth. They made having sex sound so simple and so exciting, I felt like I was missing out.

Despite raging hormones and a wild imagination, there were

still a few obstacles that kept me from taking things all the way. For starters, I didn't like any of the boys who liked me, and those I did find attractive were scared to death of my Nana. I didn't want to get into anything and not know what I was doing, so I sought advice from those I thought were experts, but they provided me with little or no help at all. *"How does it feel? Does it hurt?"* Nobody would say and nobody would tell me what I should and shouldn't do. Most found my curiosity amusing. That alone frustrated me, and my frustration led me to seek my own answers. The most I'd done with a boy was kissed him or allowed him to rub [grind] up against me. If we did that long enough my panties ended up all wet and creamy and I'd run in the house and change. None of the girls who claimed to know so much could explain that one, but the more it happened, the more I realized I was experiencing those grown woman urges and desires Nana use to talk about..

I don't know too many girls who will admit to having wet dreams or creamy jeans as a young woman, but it is what it is. Sure, I can sit back and laugh about it now but when my twat [vagina] became all tingly and my tootsie [vagina] started to roll, I thought something was wrong with me. The constant moisture in-between my legs had me embarrassed to confide in my parents and tell them what I was experiencing. I contribute that to Nana keeping me ignorant to the facts of life... She didn't even explain to me what a period was until I got one.

****

My best friend back in Junior High was a Hispanic girl named "Lissy." She was also very pleasant to be around, just like Resa. She had long dark brown hair, a slim build and thick yet shapely eyebrows that I knew my Nana would kill for. *(Nana complained her eyebrows were too light, and use to color them in with eyebrow pencil.)* Lissy was the friend I'd stop and pick up in the morning before hitting the store. She was brought up in a strict, Catholic home and that alone won Nana's approval because she never griped about me going to visit her. That was until she realized my interest was greater for one of Lissy's brothers than Lissy. Lissy had three drop dead gorgeous brothers and Nana could tell I had the hots for one of them because I couldn't keep their names out of my mouth. I tried denying her accusations, but eventually gave myself away by narrowing my conversation down to just one in particular. Not only that, but I'd use just about any excuse possible to get over to that girl's house. Even if it meant walking out in the freezing cold of winter, I had to be there.

The one I adored was named J.R. He had a slim, athletic build, smooth olive skin, dark hair, and chinky eyes. He kept me in awe and had me totally convinced crossing the line would be as easy as crossing the street! His subtle, sexy lingo kept me on edge and his touch warmed my innards like bread in an oven. Everyone could see I was head over heels for that boy, including his parents, who didn't hesitate to *cock block* the minute I knocked on the door. They were no fools and knew never to let me out of their sight or allow me in their home when Lissy wasn't there. Damn… I thought once I'd gotten past Nana's radar I'd be on easy street but seeing as his parents were also an obstacle, what was I to do? I couldn't take him to my house because that would have been a dead give-a-way, so besides his house, we didn't have anywhere else to go. I became so aggravated with the situation and at all our failed attempts, I just gave up. J.R, on the other hand, continued to push the issue but no matter how hard he tried, we just couldn't pull it off.

Sex sells, and people sell their sex stories regardless of truth, money, or who they may hurt in the process. It's just like prostitution, one of the oldest trades in the book. J.R was a popular dude and therefore, hung out with the popular crowd. The two of us never made it past first base but he created a reputation about me to others that *my cherry was ready.* I believe he did so in order to make himself look good, not to make me look bad, but in any event his bragging struck the attention of another young Latino male named Edgar. Edgar wasn't quite as popular as J.R, but hung out in the same crew just the same. J.R introduced me to Edgar one day after school while their entire crew was standing on the bridge, and from there our association with one another began. Edgar wasn't as smooth or charismatic as J.R, and he wasn't as tall, but he was cute and had a good sense of humor. I wasn't the least bit interested in having sex with him but didn't see any harm being his friend. I wasn't sure if I'd been handed off or what, but that's exactly what it felt like.

****

It was a Saturday afternoon. I'd completed all my chores and was free to go out. I told Nana I was going down the street to see some friends and she was okay with it, just as long as I wasn't headed towards that park. By now, Edgar and I had been kicking it to one another for a few months. He walked me home from school every day and before parting he'd always ask me for a kiss. I didn't consider him my boyfriend, but the potential was there. Although I still had a great interest in J.R, Edgar was good in the art of persuasion. Edgar lived on Hanover, just two blocks over. There was an alley six houses down from my house that took you from Spring through Passaic, and directly onto his street. I could have taken it but had I disappeared too quickly, Nana would have gotten curious. So to avoid that, I walked to the end of the street instead, then around the block, and Edgar was standing outside waiting for me just as planned.

Our *get-together* was a strange one and instead of Edgar inviting me inside his home, we stood outside in the cold making small talk and freezing our asses off. Okay, maybe he doesn't want to rush it I thought, then he started to ask me weird questions like the names of my past partners and when did I stop being a virgin? Huh? I had no idea how to respond and the only thing that came to mind was *experience*. I thought maybe Edgar was afraid to do the nasty because he thought I was inexperienced, so I made up two names and threw them at him just to save face. He then called me a *whore* but followed it up with a, *"Sike I'm just playing... I only asked because I wanted to make sure you weren't still a virgin. I couldn't do it if you were. I wanna hook up with you,"* he said, *"but I'd feel bad if I hurt you or took your virginity."* Huh? Is dude for real? After all the pressure he's applied? I knew right then and there I should have said good-bye, turned around, and headed home, but if I confessed the truth he'd call me a liar and I couldn't risk looking stupid. So I stayed, never realizing he was trying to be a gentleman.

Wow, I really needed someone to talk to and not just someone who was going to tell me what not to do. I needed to know the facts about boys, life, and what a young lady should and should not do in a situation like this. What I needed was a father...

The butterflies were fluttering so fast in my stomach I felt like I would throw up. Maybe it wasn't too late to turn around, but taking risk was a part of my nature. We stood outside a while longer and you could tell I was growing impatient. Edgar read the expression on my face, put his arm around my shoulder, and led me to the black top parking lot behind his house, formerly called *The Armstrong*. The Armstrong was formerly used as a parking lot/service center for city cabs, and after it was shut down the Papi's converted it into their playground/park. There was an old gutted out garage that sat remotely off to the right of the lot which the fellas used to escape the weather, and you could always catch someone out there shooting hoops or playing baseball. However today, it would be used for a different purpose. One that would leave me stained with embarrassed, ashamed, and full of regret.

For two consenting adults, a day of outdoor sexual activity may do wonders. It can open them up to one another, create new passion, rekindle old flames, or give them the rush of their lives. But for a twelve year old female virgin, it was a horrendous and frightful experience. Our bed was an old wooden door supported by two milk crates, the scene was dark, the climate was damp, and the temperature felt below zero! I didn't know what to expect from a first time, but I knew it shouldn't have gone down like this. I was also wondering why we were about to do it outside instead of in his house but I didn't want to look corny, so I didn't bother to ask. Edgar instructed me to lie down and then lower my pants. I shivered. I thought disrobement was something the man was supposed to do, but what did I know?

The weight of his body on top of me caused me to tense up from the coldness of the hard wood. (No pun indented) Then, without warning, he forced himself inside of me and I screamed like I'd been burned with a straightening comb! The sensation that flushed my body ran from the top of my spine to the tips of my toes and it was almost paralyzing. Tears flooded my eyes like a Tsunami and my agony bellowed in his ear. *"What the fuck,"* I thought to myself. He must have been thinking the same...

"Shh, Shh, Shh," he whispered as he tried to muffle my cries. The throbbing, the movement, the hurt, the intensity, was more then I could take. My cries echoed and filled the room, but Edgar didn't stop. He only slowed down long enough to gaze at me with a perplexed look. I forced myself to become a woman, way before my time, and before the deed was done, we had spectators viewing us in plain sight. Edgar tried to shoo them away but was more concerned with hushing me up. *"Hush, baby, hush,"* he said, it'll be over soon. His words were of no comfort,

and eventually I went numb from the pain. Why would a woman want to do this? What made this so fun and exciting? Anguish was my reward for wanting to be like others and mortification was my compensation for telling a lie. I'd crossed a threshold of no return and the only thing I proved was that risk and rebellion would land my ass in hot water all the time, just like Nana said. Once he was done I got up, I got dressed, and I said good-bye.

"Why you leaving?" he asked.

"I gotta go home! My Nana gonna' be looking for me soon." That was a lie too, but I had to say something. I made my way to the exit, then out of the cut appeared one of our mutual friends, *Izzy.* Izzy was of Islamic faith and hated to see a sista with anyone other then their own kind. Plus, I think he had a crush on me too, which didn't make matters any better. Izzy had been in the cut long enough to see my disgrace and when the two of us locked eyes, he just shook his head in disgust. The humiliation continued once I exited the garage because I was greeted by a squad of niggas, all gawking at me, eyeing me up and down and laughing amongst themselves. I walked away as quick as possible, but you could tell I was in pain. I never looked back, I never said a word, and I never returned to the scene.

It had begun to rain. That was a good, because I needed something to camouflage my tears. The streets were abandoned and that was good too, because I wouldn't have been able to withstand any more embarrassment. I took the long way home because I needed time to think, get myself together, and erase suspicion. Once I hit home I ran straight up stairs without saying a word to anyone, flopped down across me bed, and stared endlessly at my baby blue ceiling. Tears filled my eyes then flowed down the side of my face onto my pillow. I felt the urge to pee but my twat was throbbing like a sore thumb, my panties were sticking to me, and when I checked I was bleeding. Maybe a hot tub would make me feel better, so I ran a bath as hot as I could stand and submerged my body in it up to my neck. Within a few minutes, I was able to lay back and relax as the waters alleviated the soreness and washed away the evidence of my activities.

In our house, it was nothing strange for two of us to occupy the bathroom at the same time. There have been several occasions when one of us was in the tub and the other had to use the toilet or vice versa. I'd been soaking in the tub for nearly an hour and didn't think anything of it when Nana walked in. But instead of using the toilet, she just stood in front of the sink, with her hands gripping both sides. I tried to act innocent, but the look on my face illustrated anything but. I didn't want to make any sudden moves, so instead, I sunk down further into the tub until the water filled my ears and covered my chin. That's when Nana turned to me swiftly and said; *"Ya ass hurt now, don't it!"*

"What the fuck," I thought to myself. Does she have a crystal ball or something? How did she peep that out? My shock was almost indescribable and immediately I began shaking my head no while asking her, *"What chu talking 'bout?"*

"You know damn well what I'm talking 'bout, and when you get your ass out that tub bring ya ass on into my room!" Damn… My ass is hurting, my thoughts are scattered, and she wants to start. Truly, I was in no mood for her to be swinging on me or trying to hit me with anything, so in order to buy myself some time, I sat there until the water turned ice cold. Maybe she'll forget I thought?

When I got out of the tub I looked like a raisin. I dried off, got dressed, and was now ready to face the music. I walked into Nana's room thinking she was going to light into me but she didn't. Instead, she looked up at me, took a deep sigh, and told me to lie down. Hold up, I know she not bout to *whoop* me I thought, and I gave her a look like, huh? But whooping me was the furthest thing from her mind. Instead, she wanted to check me out to see if I was okay. Now, I don't know which is worst, getting your ass busted in shame while others watched, or having your grandmother play gynecologist and examine the damage. *"Damn, Nana, what you mean you wanna look? Look at what?"* Then she gave me a look of disappointment followed by the one that means *girl, you best to stop playing wit me!* I did as she instructed and just as with my mother some thirteen years ago, she saw the undisputable evidence of what she dreaded staring her in the face. I'd fucked up. I'd fucked up big time!

In my eyes things could have been worse, but in Nana's eyes the worst had already occurred. *"I bet yo' ass won't do it again, now will you?"* Unable to deny her accusation I shook my head no then replied the same, but Nana could only hope I was being truthful.

I healed from my experience, and therefore, thought I had experience. I also felt like I earned the right to boast about my initiation into womanhood to those I thought I needed to impress. I didn't tell them everything, just enough for them to know I'd finally taken things all the way. Some were appalled that I'd given myself to a *Rican,* some were amazed, and some admitted that their stories of having sex were only made up. However, the truth of the matter was nothing to be glorified and because of the truth, Edgar and I stopped speaking. This only proved the two of us shouldn't have committed the act in the first place, but because I wanted to be fast, I paid the price.

****

As with any saga in my life, each finale was grand. I say that because at the end of the school year, almost six months after my romp around with Edgar, me and my original puppy-love, J.R., finally hooked up. Out of nowhere, the flames between us had been reignited, however because I'd already had a taste of the forbidden and didn't like it, I was content with just having a crush on him and being his friend. The attraction was still there, but the urgency to take things to the next level had taken a back seat. Then, one afternoon after visiting Lissy, J.R told me to wait for him so he could walk me down to the door. In all my years of knowing him he'd never offered to do such, so right then and there I knew something was up.

As I slowly galloped down the stairs, J.R beckoned for me to slow down. I guess he wanted to be right on my heels. Once I reached the door he grabbed me by the hand, turned me around, and kissed me deep and slow. With such passion, it didn't take long for our bodies to respond to the rush and act on impulse. In no time, he had one leg out of my jeans and jacked up on the wall. He lowered his sweats and boxers down to his ankles, placed one hand over my mouth, and entered me with a single momentum. Within seconds, his thrusting caused me to release while tender, wet kisses on my neck caused heavy breathing and moans.

This time it didn't hurt so bad, it actually felt good. He erupted twice before it was all over and neither of us wanted to stop. His parents must have been sleep because we weren't at all quiet and had been going at it for at least a half hour. It had been a long time coming, but we finally pulled it off. He wasn't my first, but he erased the bad. It wasn't

74

the most appropriate setting, but it was better then an abandoned outdoor garage. Once we were done, J.R. walked me half way home and Nana never suspected a thing. Even if she did it didn't matter, because after my first encounter she put me on the pill. J.R and I never gained the opportunity to hook up again, but we thought and talked about it a lot. If anyone, he should have been the one to break me in, and I should have waited for him instead of jumping the gun. At least I was in-love with him, so I thought…

Image and reputation are nothing unless morals and integrity are the motivating factor behind them. Nana tried to instill that in me, but somewhere along the line, I lost the lesson. I wanted to build up a reputation and become popular. I wanted to be liked by everyone and I wanted to create an image. I was successful in doing so, but by doing so I created the wrong image and the wrong reputation. Nana and mommy did everything under the sun, everything they could think of to raise me right, teach me right, and protect me from the dangers of the world. But protecting me from the world wasn't the problem. It was protecting me from myself that was going to be the task of all tasks. And being that I was *Little Miss Know It All*, how would they ever stop me!

*BULLSHIT IS UNIVERSAL AND AVOIDING BULLSHIT
CAN SEEM ALMOST IMPOSSIBLE...*

HISPANIA'

Names, names, names; I got called more names then a blind umpire. I was corny, conceited, a Puerto Rican Lover, a wannabe, and a conceited, wannabe all rolled up into one. All of these names and not one of them described the real me. However, the mud slinging didn't bother me as much as the people who slung the mud, because half those bastards didn't even know me. They just fucked with me because they saw everyone else fucking with me, and since they couldn't beat the majority they decided to join them. (What a bunch of losers!)

Basically, it was just like Nana said. The majority of those who I called friends only associated with me because of what I could do for them, and once I stopped being their fool, their true colors shined bright. Being of a sensitive nature, this type of treatment was hard to accept, but it's not like I didn't have forewarning and therefore, should have been prepared. At this point in time Lissy was my only friend, and besides her, the only other person I hung out with on a regular was my boyfriend Ignacio, aka Iggy, aka Nacio. Iggy was way more then the ordinary boyfriend, he was also a good friend and a homeboy, kinda like Man. Iggy and I both went to Jr. 5 along with J.R and the others. Iggy was in the 9th grade and I was in the 7th. Everyday after school he'd meet me by my locker or out in front of the building and walk me home. Then, he'd stay there with me until I fell asleep. He did this seven days a week, for seven years straight, including holidays and weekends. At first Nana just though he was another crush, but after a while, she saw we were much more serious than that. We were like flies on shit, almost inseparable, and had been together so long, Nana started to claim him as her adopted son. (Good, now she can stop trying to turn me into a boy…)

Because of my relations with Hispanics and because I dated one for such a long time, very few of the black kids aside from Resa and Shell wanted anything to do with me. This is where the name, *Puerto*

77

Rican Lover and *wannabe* came into play. In guess because in school I sat with the Hispanics and during recess I played with the Hispanics, others though I was trying to be someone other then myself. However, it was just the opposite. I wasn't trying to be someone else, I just realized that with them I didn't have to play the fool or prove myself to be in their company. There was no need to seek acceptance and I didn't have to take unnecessary risk just to be down! The biggest challenge for me at that point in time was learning to become bi-lingual. Thanks to Ms. Felicia, Ignacio's mother, that task turned to be an effortless project. (While dating Ignacio, Ms. Felicia refused to speak to me in English, only Spanish. She taught me the difference between text book Spanish and the Spanish we all hear and speak out in the street...) Those who were talking shit, didn't even like themselves, so it's made no difference if they liked me or not.

To this day, I still don't see what all the fuss was about because Blacks and Hispanics have always had deep ties with one another, especially in the hood. Iggy wasn't ugly, dirty, disrespectful, disfigured, or dumb. He was just different! He was fluent in two languages and had a unique look about him that made you wonder was he a light skinned Negro or dark skinned Latino? Ignacio was straight hood, just not from our hood, and wasn't the least bit ashamed of his heritage. He had a stocky build but at an average height. He had a dazzling smile, dark hair with waves deep enough for gold fish, and a stride that surged with dignity. I respected that about him and that's what caused all the real wannabes to hate!

Iggy and I had to overcome a lot of obstacles during our courtship, from name calling to fights. But the one thing no one thought we'd be able to pull-off was gaining my Nana's trust. Nana was impressed by the way Iggy, (Nacio as she would call him,) carried himself, and therefore, had no reservations about him whatsoever. Plus, Nacio use to agree with her on almost every thing and that, of course, played in his favor. It took about two years, but she finally came around and began allowing me to go visit him at his house in Donnelley Holmes. For me, this was almost as exciting as going out of town because I wasn't accustomed to leaving my own hood, let alone venturing into the projects! Donnelley Homes aka *Divine Land* soon became my home away from home during the late 80's, and I got along with the folks up there better then the folks I grew up with. My mother, as well as other members of our family, couldn't believe Nana was being so lenient. Why was she allowing me, a rebellious teenager, to have so much freedom? Nana was no fool, she knew the likelihood for us to have sex increased with me being out of her sight, but just as with the situation with Peaches and Kyron, she felt anything and anyplace was better than hanging in that park. At that point in my life, having sex wasn't half as bad as smoking boat!

Nobody in Donnelley Homes viewed us as an odd, *inter-racial* couple. We were always viewed as *Murf & Igg*. (Nobody every pronounced the Y in Iggy's name.) It was only around my way that people divided us by race or ethnicity, but that was something we both learned to ignore. People could talk shit all day and night, Ignacio didn't care. Their hot air didn't prevent us from seeing each other and as long as nobody put their hands on us, he was straight! Funny, there was always somebody willing to sling slurs, but nobody ever wanted to throw a punch. Nobody ever crossed that line because everyone knew Iggy could box his ass off! Plus, his boys Sweet Pea and Cesar lived right around the corner, and they were nice with theirs, too! (Cesar later ended up crossing Iggy, but Iggy didn't learn of it until years later.) There was only one person dumb enough to try and test the waters, and because he allowed others to hype him up, he wound up getting his ass whooped!

K.D, a former boyfriend of about three weeks, ran off at the mouth one too many times for·Iggy to keep ignoring him. The two of them got into one night while Iggy and I were sitting on the porch, and K.D got the embarrassment of a lifetime. Iggy tried desperately to restrain from street fighting because he didn't want to lose his privileges as a boxer. But if needed, he had Nana as a witness to testify he'd been forced into defending himself. (He wasn't forced, but she would lie for him anyway. She was just as tired of their bullshit as he was.) I guess K.D assumed Iggy would be an easy task, being he was broader and heavier then Iggy was. But once it became clear K.D was no match for Iggy, several guys from the hood tried to jump in and save him. Nana dared them all to do so and swore she'd call the police on them if they did.

After that incident, Nana grew fearful the violence towards Iggy would only escalate, and with so much drama she didn't think the two of us would last. I argued her down that our love was strong enough to stand the test and that the two of us would be together forever! Iggy swore to Nana he'd always protect me, he'd always be her son, and that the two of us would never part. With such strong sentiments, Nana saw there was nothing she or anybody else could do to stand in our way. She knew love was the strongest and greatest gift in the world. It's a good thing she liked him so much, because if she hadn't, I would have surely ran away just to be with him.

****

Iggy loved my parents to death, and would have never intentionally done anything to disrespect them. However, by gaining Nana's trust we grew too comfortable and careless with our freedoms. We were never monitored, we were never questioned, and were allowed to remain at home, alone, while they went out. With liberties like that, the two of us carried on something terrible and never thought the day would come when we'd eventually get caught. Then, one day while the two of them were downstairs in the kitchen preparing dinner, Iggy and I were up in my room cooking up a little entree of our own. There was no door to my bedroom and in addition, you had to walk through my room to get to the bathroom. I believe my parents thought that would pose a deterrent to any naughty, but Iggy and I had gotten away with fooling around behind their backs so many times, the fact of not having a door didn't bother us at all.

The two of us never heard my mother as she crept up the stairs, and when she walked in on us lying but naked on the bed, I don't believe she believed her own eyes. She walked straight past us without saying a word and if anything, that scared us the most. By the time she exited, we were fully dressed but we didn't move from the bed. Instead, we just laid there like nothing had ever happened. Mommy went back downstairs with Nana, and we thought the two of them were going to kill Iggy and forbid me to ever see him again. A few minutes later, Nana bellowed for Iggy to come down stairs. Out of fear, I suggested we both just run out the door but Iggy said that would only make things worse. Iggy faced the music like a man and we lead them to believe we'd only committed the act once before. Surprisingly, Nana wasn't as upset as we thought she would have been, and she didn't fuss, yell, or raise her voice at either of us. Yes, she was disappointed we'd betrayed her trust, but she accepted her share of the blame for being so trusting in the first place.

Iggy and I were allowed to continue to see one another but refrained from fooling around at my house for a while. My mom assumed Iggy was my first, and she never knew anything about Edgar or J.R. Iggy, on the other hand, knew about my relations with both, because he was also a member of their posse and use to hear them speak about their dealings with me from time to time. Iggy said they did so in an attempt to piss him off but he never paid them any mind. On our first time together, Iggy asked me if I would consider him my first. He said regardless of what had gone down with Edgar and J.R, he loved me with all of his heart and they didn't, so what I did with them didn't count. He said sex is an act that should only be committed between people who love one another, not just for cool points. He made me promise I'd never give myself to anyone who didn't love me, regardless if the two of us last forever or not. I agreed to his promise, he kissed me, and the rest is history.

Ignacio was respectable, noble, and loyal. One has to accredit his mother, Ms. Felicia, for his admirable behavior, since like so many of us, he didn't have a father in his life either. Nacio and I learned a lot of lessons together, and he took his time teaching me just like a father. I could have been spared the lesson of learning back shots didn't mean doing it doggy style, but again... A hard head makes a soft ass, and this time I mean it literally!

****

Dealing with the petty shit in the hood wasn't any different than the bullshit the two of us hand to endure while in school. Jr. #5 was divided equally amongst Blacks and Puerto Ricans and for the most part, everyone got along. So why was there a day set aside at the end of the year for the two cultures to fight against each other, I don't know? During my 7th and 8th grade years, I managed to avoid the senseless chaos by either leaving school early or skipping school entirely. However, in the 9th grade, I wasn't so fortunate.

By now Iggy was already in Trenton High, but he always left

early in order to meet me at my school and escort me home. Iggy's cousin, Esmo, use to go to Jr. #5 too, he was infamous for his affiliation with the Kings, well known by everyone, and usually took lead of the Hispanics when the fights broke out. Esmo was tall and stocky with deep olive skin, thick, curly, dark brown hair and a mean attitude. Iggy never voluntarily chose to fight, but felt obligated to be on the scene for the sake of his boys and to ensure their protection. It was my hopes that everyone would realize there was no point to it all and walk away, but not everyone shared my views. There were even times when he and I would get into it over his loyalty, and I'd bitch because he was choosing his boys over me. *"This some ole' Slave Masta Bullshit, baby! We don't act like this, we don't hate each other like this! Why do we have to fight?"* As righteous as I may have sounded and as true as it may have been, it didn't change the fact that this ignorance still took place.

It was June of '85 and my last year in junior high. Several fights had already broken out in school long before the day was over and rumor had it, Iggy and I were two of the intended targets. Why, because we were a mixed couple and represented the very thing nobody understood, love and unity! The fact that certain individuals were so hell bent on seeing blood spill worried me. I knew my man was no punk, but I'd seen the damage done to others who decided to stand their ground and it wasn't pretty. Of course he had plenty of muscle on our side, Esmo, Domingo, Juan Jr., and countless others, but seeing people get stomped or struck with bats, bottles, and bricks, just wasn't my thing. By the time school let out several more fights had broken out, and the agitators were doing their job by egging people on. I knew Iggy felt the pressure to be with his crew, but I begged him to walk me home first and used sex as an incentive. I figured once I got him to myself, I could change his mind.

Ignacio and I walked towards the tracks, away from the mob of students and spectators, trying to remain unnoticed. We were successful in doing so but ran into another obstacle, his cousin *Chill Will*. Will and Iggy were close. Will was good people, but he was also a loose cannon. He took extreme risk, stayed in trouble with authority figures, and seemed to live only for the thrills. Will questioned Iggy, *"Yo', man, where you going?"* Iggy replied he was walking me home but was coming right back. Will didn't agree with his decision and said to him, *"Yo', man, come on, we got shit to do!"* I turned Iggy around and we proceeded to walk away, then Will pulled out a *rusty* old revolver and pointed it to my temple. He told me if I didn't let his man go, he was going to shoot me! I knew Will wouldn't really cause me any harm, but because he was so antsy, his actions were unpredictable. I looked over at Iggy, Iggy looked back at me then he told his cousin to, *"Put that shit away and stop fucking playing!"* Will stood there for a couple of seconds then he laughed and tucked his piece back into his pants, where it should have been. In my head I was hoping he would have shot his dick or something, just for being so stupid.

I held on to Iggy's hand, refusing to let him go, even after he made the choice to walk in the other direction. *"Go home, I'll be over in a few."*

"No" I screamed, *"I ain't going nowhere without you!"* Nana always said God watched over fools and babies, out of all of her catchy sayings, I prayed that one was the truest of all. Iggy saw that I was serious. He knew I'd never leave his side, and with that said, we both went along with Will to face what ever dangers lay ahead; like sheep straying away from their Sheppard. Up until this day, neither of us had any real beef with anyone throughout our three years at that school, at least nothing serious. This was about as serious as it could get, a racially motivated fight in which neither of us wanted to choose a side.

****

It's sad, but even with the presence of police, people still carried on like complete idiots. I guess that's because they knew the cops weren't likely to get involved unless an innocent by passer got injured. And when I say innocent, I mean a resident, a store owner, a teacher, or some other random adult who just happened to be walking by, never a student.

Regardless if a Latinos had any association with Esmo or not, they all viewed him as their Che' Guevara. But fret not, the same applied to the Negro's, the Nubians. We had our fearless leader as well, his name was Spencer, and he was our Marcus Garvey, our Minister Farrakhan, our Malcolm X, and just like Esmo, packed one hell of a punch! I don't think the two ever had any real beef with one another, but because each had half a school looking up to them, they buckled to their expectations. By the time the three of us reached the action, Esmo and Spencer were the main attraction, and people were lined up curb side, ready to see the two duel. Usually, the leaders of war sent the pawns and expendable ones into battle for them, but at Jr. #5, nobody was immune to combat; not Spencer, not Esmo, not even me.

Take this chick named Jayden Miller for example. Jayden was considerably bigger then me to put it nicely, always mad about something, and threatened any girl who smiled, spoke, or remotely looked at her so called boyfriend, Spencer. This made me public enemy # 1 in her eyes because Spencer saved me from drowning one day at the YWCA, and from then on, I was on her hit list. (Our gym was under construction and in order to take pool, we had to go around the corner to the Y.)

In school I tried my best to avoid Jayden, but after school was a total different story. Since most of us lived in or around the same neighborhood, we all took the same route home. Ironically, this was the same path the fights took place on, and even if you walked all the way around, you still met up with the crowd one way or another. With me determined not to leave my man's side, and Jayden acting as a magnet to Spencer, it's a no brainer the two of us were going to bump into one another.

Ignacio and I were merely spectators but as we watched Esmo and Spencer dance around in the street, Jayden eyed me down like a vulture plotting on its prey. I pretended not to notice her, but like a rodent in the desert, I knew I needed to either find a burrow or prepare for confrontation. The two of us never exchanged words, only dirty looks, but Jayden didn't need a justifiable reason to perform. The fact that I was presumably there with a gang of Latinos instead of on the side of *my own kind* was all the ammunition she needed. (As if Blacks and Hispanics weren't one in the same.)

As the crowd moved along, I tried getting Iggy's attention, but in a split second I took off down the street like a bolt of lightning! At first, nobody knew why, but they soon figured it out once they saw Jayden chasing after me. Iggy yelled for me to stop but I kept it moving. The thunderous sounds of footsteps running behind me made me push myself into fifth gear. I had a good head start on Jayden, so I wasn't worried about her catching up to me, but I wasn't about to let up or slow down either. I shot down Montgomery St. to Mill Hill, caught a second wind, ran through Mill Hill, up Broad, and then cut through the Pizza Parlor on the corner. (Currently it's Dunkin Donuts and it only has one entrance. Back in the day it had two, a side and a main.)

By the time I reached the commons I was able to blend in with the downtown scenery and take it down a notch. I was still moving a little faster than everyone else and constantly looking over my shoulder, but I was sure I was out of harms way. By the time I made it home, there was no sign of Jayden or the malicious crowd that followed behind her. I was safe for the moment, but tomorrow would be a new day.

Contrary to the selective memory of some, Jayden and I did end up fighting a few weeks later. Jayden was cool with a few of the girls form around my way and Shell just happened to be one of them. Every time Jayden came around I remained indoors just to avoid confrontation, but the more I tried to avoid her, the more she seemed to pursue. Thus, just like anyone else who had been chased for a period of time, I simply grew tired of it and decided to face my fears. Either she was gonna kick my ass or I was gonna kick hers, but I wasn't going to run and hide from her anymore!

I saw Jayden approaching as I stood outside and dipped into Shell's house to put some Vaseline on my face. Either Shell or her brother, (prior to his passing) gave me a pair of black Puma sneakers to put on as well. My heart was racing but I was ready. When I approached the front door, I heard Jayden outside talking tough about what she was going to do to me. She was always trying to impress, but all her talk did was fuel my adrenaline. (Never attack a person who's cornered. They'll do anything to escape!) I swung open the door, leaped off the porch onto her back, and tried to tear her face apart. I wasn't sure I was going to come out the victor, but nothing beats a failure but a try. I looked like a little monkey swinging from side to side as she tried to throw me off of her, but I was so afraid, there was no way I was about to let go. No one got their ass beat that day, but I did give a good exhibition of courage by standing up for myself and refusing to back down. It took three people to pull me up off of her and from that point on, she left me alone. No more Mr. Kutcher; no more *Punk'd*! When no one else has your back, you have to protect yourself *By Any Means Necessary...*

Jayden was expelled from school shortly after our confrontation, why I don't know. It would be nearly twenty five years before I saw or heard from her again. Sadly, our reunion wasn't a pleasant one and Jayden still had a lot of contempt for me, especially after she found out about my memoirs. Amazingly, she still wanted to fight me and even called me up with childish threats. I tried to appeal to the adult in her but apparently there wasn't one. In my opinion, she was still that same angry person she was when we were in the ninth grade and I refused to entertain her reasoning. Her anger after so many years only supports my recollection of our youth, and if nothing else, sheds light on her true character. Had I written Ms. Miller was my BFF, [Best Friend Forever] I doubt I would have gotten any static from her whatsoever. As for me, life is too precious to hold grudges and carrying a grudge requires way too much energy.

Jayden was the first in a series of *big girl* obstacles I'd have to overcome. Subsequently, others followed in her footsteps, but I'm no closer to understanding their reasons today then I was back then. There's a saying, *"God don't put no more on you then you can bear."* Although at the time I though the harassment would tear me down; all it really did was build me up, because I'm able to talk about it today.

****

In the late 80's, there were three girls who ran a constant ring of terror in my life, and I nicknamed them *Three Da Hard Way.* I figured the title suited them, considering each time our paths crossed, they'd give me a hard time. Tiny, Paula, and Lesha were the most horrible individuals I've ever had to encounter in my entire life at one time. The three of them rolled through the city like pack of hungry wolves, terrorizing young women from Donnelly to Miller Holmes. I'd never had any bad dealings with any of them whatsoever, and was baffled at how I became one of their number one targets. Not only did they pick on me without reason, but they jumped me on numerous occasions, sometimes in my own hood.

I knew Paula from school. She, Jayden, and Shell were all cool with one another, but our communication was never more then a simple hi and bye. Paula was slightly taller then me with a thick build and dark brown skin. When Shell and I started hanging tough, I'd sometimes walk with her when she walked Paula home down W. State Street after school.

At the time, Paula didn't seem to have any beef with me, and to my surprise, we actually got along. Needless to say, it came as a shock to me when she became a part of the assaulting trio, as if I'd done something to provoke her actions. As for Tiny, she didn't' even go to our school and the only time I saw her was in Donnelly Holmes when I'd go visit Iggy. Ig' would always tell me he thought she had a crush on him but cringed at the idea of her ever approaching him. Tiny may have been jealous of me because of Iggy, and if so, that would explain her actions. I don't have a clue as to what motivated Lesha to come after me, except the fact that she was Tiny and Paula's homegirl. I believe Tiny called the shots and the other two just followed her lead.

I had several run-ins with these three girls; but the most memorable and talked about altercation took place right down the street from my house, while I sat quietly at the corner of Spring and Calhoun. School was out for the summer and once the sun went down, the corner lit up. As I waited for others to come and join me, I sat on the porch of an empty apartment building directly across the street form Queen Esters. I'd just cashed my check and had copped a brand new pair of Patrick Ewing high top sneakers, (the blue and orange stripes off the white) when out of nowhere the three appeared. To them I must have looked like a sitting duck, and I could see bad intent fill their eyes. Tiny headed for me first and Paula followed suit. I got up to make a run for it but Lesha came up on my right side and blocked my path. I had nowhere to run and no time to react. One grabbed a handful of my hair pulling me down, and the other grabbed my feet and somewhat flipped me backwards. The combination of their tug of war caused me to hit my head on the cement step, and when I reached for my head, Lesha pulled me down again while Tiny removed my sneakers from my feet.

I guess the satisfaction of always outnumbering me wasn't enough for these young menaces, they had to humiliate me as well. No matter where you're from, getting jacked for your footwear or any other article of clothing is highly disrespectful. Plus, it wasn't like any of them could fit them either, they just took them because they had the upper hand. They knew I couldn't defend myself against all three of them without a weapon. And, had I made any attempt to do so, they probably would have cut my face. (That's just how some chicks rolled back then.) The three of them compared to me was like putting three pit-bulls against a defenseless kitten. My petite frame was no match against their height and body weight combined. So there I was, sprawled out on the porch, head throbbing, with no shoes on my feet. The chance of redeeming my pride or my property was far fetched since I knew they'd never allow me a fair chance. The best I could do was *take it on the chin* and hope they'd just leave me alone.

None of the females I knew would ever be brave enough to stand up to the three; but Clyde (aka Pupa,) Mike, and Solomon weren't intimidated by their tactics, plus they were males. Luckily for me, the three saw what had happened to me, felt it was wrong, and ran after my assailants to retrieve what was mine. I was grateful and flattered by their chivalry, but it did nothing to erase them embarrassment. As Mike handed me my sneakers, he asked me why the three of them kept harassing me, but at the time I couldn't give an answer. Though today, if asked the same, I'd know it was because they were blind to the negative energy that consumed them, and therefore had to release it the only way they knew how. Negatively!

Other quarrels between me and these three took place in other parts of town where I knew I'd be at a disadvantage. However, because I was in the company of others who were friends and family, I figured at least I'd have a fighting chance. Oops, wrong again.

In the summer of '85, shortly after the sneaker incident, a few girlfriends of mine asked me to get permission from my parents to attend a party at the South Trenton Boys Club. It was Trish, Starr, Betty, and Sherronda; girl's I'd grown up with and went to school with. Normally, I'd never go anyplace without Iggy right by my side, but I thought hanging out with the girls outside of school and home would be a lot of fun. My parents gave me permission to go, but of course had their reservations. I promised them I'd behave and had all intentions to stay on point. As the group of us traveled on our way, we were as thick as thieves. We smoked a few joints, more than likely there were treated with PCP, and we laughed like best friends at a slumber party. Yet, as soon as we entered the spot, I noticed they all left me standing alone and

I had no idea where they had gone. I peeked into the bathroom, hoping to find at least one of them, but the cloud of smoke was so thick, you could barely see your hand in front of your face.

Like a dummy, I walked into my doom and began calling out their names, waiting for a response. I stopped and stood in front of a sink, peeking under the stalls. When I stood up and turned around, I saw Paula over in the corner with Lesha by her side. Because of the smoke, there was a good chance they didn't see me, plus, they were smoking as well. I even thought without Tiny commanding them to attack, they'd even be nice and cut me a break. But no sooner then the thought entered my mind, Tiny exited the first stall and came rushing at me. Again, one grabbed a handful of my hair and all three of them shoved my face down into the sink. Not the clean sink that I was standing in front of, but the sink next to it all clogged up with dirty water. I tried holding myself up by bracing both hands on the side of the sink, but the pressure of all three of them combined with the punches made my efforts useless. The one who had my hair kept slamming my head into the sink and for the life of me I didn't know what I was going to do first, drown or pass out! I was just about to succumb to the hands of my attackers, when along came my relief. A girl named Ebony.

At the time, Ebony couldn't have been more then thirteen or fourteen, yet at the same time, she had plenty of heart. She was of average build and height, just like myself, Starr, Trish and Sherronda, and was the second person to come lunging out of the stalls. After her exit, she began fighting Tiny and her girls up off of me long enough for me to catch my breath and bounce. I felt kinda bad for abandoning her like that after she'd jumped in and saved me like that, but self preservation was my first priority. Prior to that evening, I'd never seen that girl before a day in my life, but made it my business to seek out her whereabouts and thank her for her courageousness later on. When I finally caught up with Ebony it was nearly two months later, out N. Trenton on Fountain Avenue where she lived. Surprisingly, she didn't remember much about the incident but that shouldn't have come as a shock since I suspected she had been smoking too. Being as those were the days when everybody was tripping off of that wet, I realize her actions didn't have to have anything to do with me, and may have purely been a reaction to her high. Be that as it may, she was still the only one in a bathroom full of girls who did anything to help me, and therefore, I felt she deserved my thanks.

Word of what happened at the Boys Club spreads just like word of what happened on Spring, and again, everybody who knew me questioned why. Of course I had no answer for them and was baffled by the whole thing, but not as baffled as when my girls told me they had been looking for me and was wondering why I'd left. Hurt and angry, they had influenced me to go then deserted me, I asked why did they leave me. I got every answer, but not the one I was looking for, and from then on I realized two very important things. First, it seemed to make no difference how cool I thought all of us were, it was obvious they were never going to have my back in a tight situation. Second, contrary to the concept of safety in numbers, I'd rather be alone than to risk abandonment. I also realized how sticking to my initial plan would have saved me from loosing focus. I had no intentions on getting that high that night. I only planned on smoking a few joints I'd rolled myself before leaving home, and shaking my ass all night long to the music.

Bad news travels fast and it didn't take long for word of what was going on between me and *The Goon Squad* to get back to my cousin LC. LC was about five years older then me; he was a body builder, well known, and feared in the streets, and him and Keys were like brothers. Keys nor L were pleased to hear about their terror on me and the first thing LC said to me was, *"Cousin, you gotta fuck one of them up! Even if they jump you,"* he said, *"you still gotta get the best of one of them. After that, I bet you they'll leave you alone!"* Easier said then done, I sighed, but at the same time he was right. I'd learned from battling Jayden that running would never solve the problem. (However, if I avoided running into them I wouldn't have to run.) But how could I get the best of one of them with the odds I was up against? Keys agreed with LC's advice, but said I could call on Peaches for help if I needed to. Peaches had about six sisters, all of them healthy in build, and when one of them fought, all of them fought. I took Keys advice into consideration, however, Tiny had already befriended Peaches, therefore, how much help would she be? Then, one night I saw Peaches and Tiny sitting on her porch as I walked by. Their snickering and taunts from Tiny confirmed my reservations, but I didn't bother to tell Keys because Tiny was my battle, not his.

There's a scripture that in part reads, "... *I make thine enemies thy footstool."* Nana didn't teach me that one but it's true. When a person's enemies rise up against them and appear to conquer, something always happens to put them back in their place, or under your feet as Nana would say. Tiny had several advantages over me, so when she tried to jack me again, I believe she thought she was going to get away with it. She probably would have too, had she not tried to take something from me that wasn't mine. I just so happened to be holding on to Keys radio while him and LC took a walk out north to *The New Park.* (That was the name of the park, The New Park.) Keys said they'd be right back; they had some business to take care of and the radio was going to slow them down. It didn't matter why because it was a big box, and I could see why he wanted to leave it behind. Everyone carried a radio back then, including me. It was the era when KRS-1, Public Enemy, Eric B & Rakim and LL Cool J's, *Can't Live Without My Radio* bumped through every speaker in the hood. There was only one catch, we both knew I'd have to remain down at the corner because if Peaches saw me with it, she'd surely have a fit!

(By now, Peaches and Keys were an on one minute, off the other type of couple. Peaches had mad [a lot] reservations about every female in Keys' life, including the ones who weren't screwing him, like me...)

The corner was crowded that afternoon. Everyone saw Keys leave me with his box but nobody spotted Tiny and her girls approaching the corner except me. By now, Keys and L were far, far away and damn near turning the corner onto Willow St. I was hoping Tiny and her dynamic duo would go down the other end of the block or hit the alley and cut down Passaic, but that didn't happen. They kept straight down the street, which meant trouble for me if they spotted me. At the time, Tiny was kicking it to one of my hommies named Chase and he just happened to be at the corner where I was standing. Damn! Here we go again...

I picked up the radio and started to walk off, then I stopped. I thought about what L said to me about fucking one of them up, and knew both him and Chase had spoke to Tiny about harassing me in the first place. I thought that would have made a difference, but again, I was wrong. The three approached me anyway and had the audacity to tell me to give them Keys' boom box, unaware it was his. Yeah right! Ya'll may have jacked me for my kicks and nearly drowned me in a sink full of dirty water, but I'll be dammed if you're gonna take something from me that doesn't even belong to me! Not today, not this time!

The three of them tried to surround me, but I wouldn't allow either of them to get behind me. I held tightly to the radio and Tiny asked me again, *"Let me see the radio!"* I've always been a smart ass, even when faced with danger, so I held it up and said, *"see."* Then, her and her goons started threatening me, saying how they were gonna fuck me up if I didn't give up the radio, blah, blah, blah. I looked over at Chase, who was leaning on the fire-hydrant, he looked over at Tiny, and all three reluctantly walked away. I breathed a momentary sigh of relief but no sooner then they were off my ass, along came Peaches. Now she's telling me to give up the radio but in my mind, if Keys wanted her to have it he would have left it with her in the first place. He walked right past their house on his way out North. It didn't matter to me if she was his girl or not, he left it in my care and I felt responsible for it until he came back to retrieve it.

Ironically, Peaches' actions played in my favor because now *The Three Bears* are aware that the property they tried to take belonged to Keys. It also made them aware of our friendship, therefore, they respectfully took a huge step back. They may have been big and bad, but they knew Keys didn't have a problem whopping their ass if his shit would have gotten messed up on their behalf, and there was nothing Peaches could have done to stop him.

As for me, I knew Peaches was trying to chump me off too, but I didn't want to get into it with her over her man's shit. I handed the radio over to Peaches and put an end to the animosity. Peaches got what she wanted and I walked off from the corner with my head hung low. By the time I reached my porch I saw Keys and L walking back from the park. When Keys saw Peaches with the radio he took it from her and returned it to me with a smile. He said I could hold on to it as long as I wanted to and not to give it to anyone but him or his mother. Nana was sitting out on the porch at the time and overheard what Keys said to me. She couldn't help but add her two cents by saying, *"That radio is going to be the start of some trouble if you ain't careful!"* I took the radio, shook my head, and went on about my business. I knew Nana was concerned, but really, I was already knee deep in a pile of shit to begin with!

Before the age of eighteen I learned, women often allow their emotions to override their intelligence when it comes down to their man, or so called man. It's never been a practice of mine to blame any female for my feelings, because the man you claim to be yours is more responsible for protecting your feelings than anyone. I believe if more women realized that, they'd save themselves a lot of unnecessary heart ache and pain.

By now, I decided it was time for a change. First, I weaned myself off the lovely, [Boat, PCP] then switched my circle of friends. Nana was proud of me for doing so, and even happier when she found out my new buddy was someone so close, we called each other sisters. My girl Roz, who Nana simply adored, became my new best friend. Nana liked Roz because she was pretty, polite, and didn't hang out in the streets like someone with no home training. Nana knew Roz's family and had not one complaint about any of them. Roz and I pulled some stunts together, but nothing so horrible that it would land either of us in jail or put our lives in danger. In Nana's eyes that was a plus!

Roz lived about ten minutes away from me on Pennington Avenue, and since my enemies made my block their new hang out, I made her home my new hang out. Roz had long, pretty hair just like me, her complexion was fair just like mine, and she had a slim frame. Nana use to always say she should have been a model but trust me, Roz was way too shy to be in front of a camera to that extent. (Nana was right, she could have been the world's next Top Model!) Because the two of us got along so well and both had the strictest of parents, we thought we'd hang together forever. That could have and would have happened, had it not been for the three obstacles that got in our way. Tiny, Paula, and Lesha!

It was a Saturday afternoon and I'd decided to go check Iggy out at his crib, instead of having him walk all the way around Spring to see me. Iggy hated for me to travel alone, but I had Roz with me and figured popping up on him would be a nice surprise. Roz knew all about the beef I had with Tiny, and we were both a little apprehensive about the walk, though I figured we'd be okay as long as we took Calhoun Street instead of the Blvd., (formerly called Princeton Avenue.) I figured since it was such a nice day, everyone would want to be seen and the Blvd. was a hot route. Calhoun, however, was much quieter, had a lot less traffic, and nobody hung out on that route ever. The two of us were fine just like I expected we'd be, but once we turned off the main road into the projects themselves, our luck ran out.

Roz and I were a block shy from Iggy's building, and I would have called and told him to come meet us but they didn't have a phone. As the two of us stood at the corner waiting to cross, the car that sped past us had Tiny, Paula, and Lesha inside. I knew the three of them spotted me, but considering neither of them were the driver, I seriously doubted they'd stop just to harass me. Wow, how many times can a sista be wrong about the same thing!

Before me or Roz could step foot off the curb or turn around and go the opposite way, the driver Isis, hit a u-turn in the middle of the street and headed back our way. My first instinct told me to run to Iggy's house, but I wasn't sure if Roz would be able to keep up and I didn't want to leave her behind. Roz could have been a model, but I should have been a track star, because when I do the dash, I do the dash!

By now, I was use to their childish antics and knew the only thing they wanted to do was fuck up my face. So on that note, I balled up in a fetal position and protected my face. Their circus act beat down lasted every bit of ten minutes and the whole time LC's words kept echoing in my head. *"Fuck one of them up, Ree, Fuck one of them up!"* I wanted to, I really did, but I knew I had no win. Everyone wants to be a gangsta, but it takes a certain type of character to know when to accept defeat. I'd managed to stay off their radar for quite some time but Trenton is but so big, and eventually, everyone runs into everyone.

My relief came when the driver yelled to them, *"Let's go!"* The three of them then jumped back into the vehicle and drove off like nothing ever happened. My hair was a little messed up, but besides that, I was good. Once they were out of sight, I looked around for Roz but she was gone. When I caught up with her later on, I was mad and asked why'd she leave me alone? She said she was sorry but she felt going to get help was the best she could do. The two of us became distant after that, but I still loved her like a sister.

You know life is funny. Out of all the surprise attacks and ass whooping the three dished my way, not once did they scar me up, not once did I ever hit the ground, not once did I run, and neither time were they successful in getting away with anything they took or tried taking from me. I don't know if it was prayers, my good karma, or both, but I always ended up being one of the lucky ones. A lot of girls from that era who wound up in street brawls weren't as lucky. Some got their face slashed from one side to the other with box cutters and others took such a beating, they couldn't come outside for weeks. A lot were left with permanent scars but all of us were left with the memories of the evils that were dished our way…

****

As I grew older and became an adult, flashbacks of what Tiny and her girls put me through would sometime replay in my mind. I knew eventually I'd run into all three of them, and when that time came, I knew I'd be ready. Surprisingly, once it did happen, my reaction wasn't at all what I thought it would be.

Fifteen years after the fact, I ran into Tiny in the oddest of places. Church! I was seated in my usual spot in the balcony, when I noticed she was sitting directly behind me with her family. At first glace, I wasn't sure if it was her or not, but a person's eyes never change. Their features may change as well as their physical appearance, but the eyes remain the same. That's how I knew it was her, she had the same look in her eyes as she did years earlier but with a slight difference. I didn't want to admit it, but there was a touch of humbleness in them now, and I could tell she had been through some changes. A knot formed in my stomach and I could feel myself cutting my eyes. Naturally, my first emotion was contempt, but considering we were in a house for worship, I swallowed my pride and simply said hello. As I sat in the pew just below her, I once again though about all of the horrible things she'd done to me and all I wanted to do was ask her why? Why did she terrorize me and what did I do to her to make her dislike me so much? Then I remembered this old saying, *"If it doesn't kill you it makes you stronger,"* and that's when everything fell into perspective. Regardless if it was her intention to do so or not, she'd definitely made me a stronger individual in an indirect way. She may have been *the baddest* back then, but on this day, I was definitely the bigger!

I guess I'll never know the answer to my question, but after that day, it no longer mattered. I was happy and satisfied with my life and I wished her the same.

As for Paula, I ran into her all the time at my favorite hair salon, Mikey's Shapes N' Styles. Seeing her always made me feel anxious, but never threatened, and that's because she was no longer threatening or a threat. I wasn't sure if she and Tiny were still friends, but I never saw them together anymore. Paula was always at the shop getting her hustle on, selling boosted goods, and I was always in there spending money on my hair. (Gotta stay fly, ya know.) Saying something to her about the shit that went down fifteen years ago would have been beneath me as a woman and very childish as a mother. Being as my son was always with me, I didn't want to risk putting him in harm's way or have him witness me in a verbal altercation by stirring up old shit. My intuition told me Paula remembered her past acts but wasn't proud of the role she'd played. Upon sight, she'd always say hi to me and never spoke to me with an ounce of sarcasm or ridicule. Paula was a mother now and had another one on the way. I guess her perspective on life had changed, and just like Tiny, I wished her well.

Lesha, on the other hand, was a different story. Seeing her off and on use to unnerve me so much, I tripped and fell right in front of her one day. (Talk about reliving embarrassing moments.) Nothing happened, but I know she also remembered the hell she caused me, and the look in her eyes said she wanted to cause more. Out of the three, she was the one I despised the most and I doubt if I'll ever see past her evil ways. Lesha wasn't from my part of town, but some of the people she hung out with were. One night while walking down Passaic Street, I ran into her near the alley. Vengeance filled my heart and I wanted nothing more then to do to her what she'd done to me so many times before. Getting the best of her wasn't going to be good enough, I wanted to humiliate her and treat her like a clown the same as she had done to me. In a nut-shell, I wanted to do something to her that more then likely would have landed my black ass in jail for a very long time! In her state of mind, I knew she wouldn't be able to defend herself, but in the end, where would that have left me? What would have happened to my son? It wasn't a matter of swallowing my pride, it was all about opportunity. Then again, it wasn't even about opportunity, it was about choice. I could have proved my point, but it would have been the wrong choice.

I haven't seen Tiny since that day in church and sadly, Paula has passed away. I still see Lesha on occasion, and yes, the hostility is still there. Sometimes we speak, most of the time we don't, and I can tell she still feels she can intimidate me. Most people change, some change for the better, but some don't change at all... (R.I.P. Paula Wilson)

****

That was pretty much it for the fist fights and beat downs, but I still had a few betrayals to overcome. Iggy and I were still a couple but as we grew older, we also grew apart. (Nana said that would happen, but it took a long time.) Iggy had now dropped out of high school and I was in my sophomore year. He spent almost all of his time around the corner at his boy Cesar's house and let him tell it, Cesar was his right hand man. Cesar's family knew me from growing up around the corner and me and Cesar's little brother, Sweet-Pea, were in the same class. It was nothing unusual for me to pop up over their house to see if Iggy was around, and neither Iggy nor Cesar's family ever complained about me doing so.

Cesar and Sweet-Pea had two sisters, Jackie and Evelyn. The two were always very nice to me and kept me occupied while the boys did their thing. With so much hospitality in the air, I didn't detect the subtle plot Cesar was about to unfold, and had no idea things would get so out of hand. Then, one weekend it all came to the light, or at least for me it did. I'd gone around to Cesar's to check for Iggy but Cesar saw it as his golden opportunity to let his feelings known. After greeting me at the door, he said Iggy and Sweet-Pea were upstairs on the third floor and I could go on up. He then went down into the basement and I proceeded on up the stairs. As I'm walking up the steps, I'm calling out Iggy's name but I don't get any response. Once I reached the attic and saw nobody was there, I turned around and Cesar was right behind me. He then closed the door behind him and refused to let me leave. Afraid to walk towards him, I began backing up, which ultimately forced me further into his tiny little room.

Cesar grabbed me and pushed me down to the bed. I screamed but not a soul was home to hear me. Even if they were, who would hear my cries way up from the attic? He pinned my arms down and forced my legs apart with his. He was extremely strong and compared to my frame, had a massive build. I tried clenching my legs together, but his strength overpowered mine. He started kissing me, but it was repulsing and I wouldn't keep still. Somehow, he got my right arm in a position where if I moved it felt like it would break and he raised my shirt with his free hand. After that, he worked his way down, forced himself inside of me, and had his way. I begged him to stop but in some perverted form, I think he thought our involvement was actually romantic. I cried until it was over and he kept his hand over my mouth the entire time. In the process, he kept trying to tell me how Iggy was no good for me as if it justified his actions one bit. I left feeling torn, literally, and I knew no one would believe me.

Iggy placed Cesar at a higher regard then his cousin, Esmo, and I knew telling him about the incident would tear us apart. I didn't want him to have to choose between his best friend and his girl, and even though Cesar was in the wrong, I somehow blamed myself. (We women always do that after we've been victimized.) To make matters worst, Cesar kept trying me, and my attitude towards him changed so much I know Iggy suspected something but couldn't put his finger on it. I've been violated more times sexually than I choose to remember, however, the men who've committed these acts will probably never realize sex is nothing without *Love* and without *Love* the act simply does not count! No means NO!

Behind every cloud lies a silver lining; an array of sunshine, laughter, and good times. Although I encountered some pretty rough times, I also enjoyed plenty of good ones, with good friends who I'll never forget. Tito aka Ice, his brother Jose', and Ruben aka Special K, and Rasheed were three of my hommie-brother-friends; and I was their *MC Lyte*, their *Peppa*, the princess of the bunch. The four of us were as close as booty hair, but Tito and I had a special friendship that superseded the rest. Our adventures together covered everything from a-z, but our highlight took place in one of the worlds most famous venues;

Madison Square Garden, in New York City! I couldn't have been more then fourteen at the time but the memory remains fresh. It was my very first time out of town, aside from trips I'd taken with my parents, and I was way too young to hang, but wasn't about to let age stop me from having fun!

What the four of us witnessed was truly history in the making. We attended the very first Hip-Hop concert held at that arena, and the show stoppers were the legendary Run DMC, LL Cool J, along with Whodini. We caught the local, NJ Transit to Penn Station but couldn't figure out how to get to the Garden itself. Lord knows it was an amusing revelation when we realized the Garden was right above our heads. We bought the cheapest tickets available, but as luck would have it, wound up standing in arm's reach of the stage, with Hurricane (an extended member of Run DMC from what I understand) pouring us tall tumblers of Old English the entire night. I was as drunk as a skunk but had the time of my life, and nothing to worry about because those three would protect me at all cost. You can bet the house on that.

Slipping up once the chains are off is understandable, but I took it to the extreme and lost focus completely! I threw away opportunities which sadly aren't even offered to the youth of today. I threw away the chance to enhance my education, I ignored positive electives like; home economics, sewing, cooking, and learning how to swim. I dismissed my ability to play the violin, the clarinet, and the flute; all because I wanted an adventurous life with no restrictions and where I made all the rules. I made a fool out of myself is what I did, and it saddens me to see a new generation doing the same. Only today, they're loosing their lives and aren't getting a second chance at life like I did. Some people become a product of their environment because they have no choice, and others by choice. I made the wrong choices...

DROP OUT

D amn, where should I begin? Where did I go wrong? I believe the trap was set long before I ever realized there was one, and therefore, I had no idea of what to be cautious of. As with anybody, high school marks a milestone in one's life. But, if you're not prepared for the change, the pressure, or the environment, all of the wonders will catch you off guard and bam, you'll fall off track! It seems like overnight I evolved from mischievous to Maverick. A phase my parents were sure would pass, but instead, became my lame excuse for giving up and quitting.

My parents could shelter me from a lot, but they couldn't shelter me from life. In my 9th grade year, I'd trespassed at Trenton High so much, the guards thought I was a student before I was even enrolled, and by the time I became a sophomore, everyone though I was a junior! When September of '85 came around, I just knew I was the shit. I didn't get lost like a lot of the other students and I knew who would let me slide, (Skip and Slim) and who to steer clear of. I had all of my bases covered, so I thought, however, my new found freedom proved to be nothing more then a recipe for disaster and failure.

In the beginning I took things slow. I went to all of my classes, completed all of my assignments with ease, and learned the personalities of all of my teachers. That routine lasted every bit of the first marking period because by the middle of the second, I grew bored, lost interest, and didn't see the purpose of it all. I viewed high school as a seven hour social institution instead of an institution for learning. Everything we reviewed seemed to be nothing more then a repeat of some lesson I'd already learned in junior high. I thought I was doing someone a favor by showing up to class every day and thought very little about the reward I could have received in the long run. A certificate of completion, better know as a high school diploma!

At first, I only cut the classes I loathed, and always had a good excuse when I returned from my absence. The periodic thrill of getting away with it eventually grew into a habit, because there were never any consequences that I could see for my actions. After that, I began cutting other classes that I felt were easy and eventually my attendance began to decrease so much, I stopped going to them altogether. Of course, this caused me to fail in certain subjects, but mind you, when I left junior high I was an honor roll student with straight A's and B's. By the beginning of third marking period, ditching class had become such a part of my daily routine, I'd reduced my sophomore schedule of eight classes, to a senior schedule of only two or three. It was easy to go to homeroom, first, and second period, but I hit third period lunch and j it was all she wrote. The fat lady sang and I was out the door.

Math, science, and social studies were my favorite subjects, but I cut them so much, I couldn't even make up for the loss at the end of the year or on exams. I had no excuse whatsoever for skipping 6th period, because by then all three lunches were done and over with. And as far as 7th and 8th period went, I doubt if the teachers even knew I was supposed to be in their class. They probably thought I transferred out or something. There were times when I wanted to go to class, but hiding out in the bathrooms, smoking behind the school, or roaming the halls was just as easy. I guess the rebel in me forgot to have a valid cause, and although I hated rules, direction, and restrictions, I desperately needed them. By the beginning of the fourth marking period, I was failing every class by grades, attendance, or both; but I kept up with the charade, just to save face with mommy and Nana.

When my parents began to question why I never had any books, the only thing I could do was lie then change the subject. I thought I was ready for the world but the pressures of making new friends and settling into a new environment was a bit much. I put a lot into being free and being my own boss, and in the process, I paid the price for my foolishness.

****

Wilbur Section aka *The Section,* is the east side of town but not to be confused with East Trenton. My dad lived in this area, and I told the school I lived with him instead of my mom because they allowed students to go home for lunch if you lived close by. By now, Iggy and I were almost history and my girl, Lissy, had moved and was attending McCorstin High School in Hamilton. Trenton High was a huge facility and the largest high school in Mercer County. It took up an entire four square blocks, (and then some) and everyone in the city of Trenton went there. For most, if you weren't a part of a clique or had an older sibling attending you didn't even count. The overpacked class rooms and congested halls could be compared to an average day at Penn Station. Finding the right slot to fit into was going to be tricky, just like living round the way. So when a few girls from the area decided to befriend me, it felt like I'd hit the jackpot!

Vette and Miko, also known as *Even T* and *Mika G*, were members of a dance group called *The Lovers*. The section based group was becoming well known throughout the city and use to compete all over town against a rival group called *The Dogs*. From time to time I use to see them practicing their routine on the football field or battling it out in one of the halls. I've always loved the creativity and seductiveness of dancing, so it goes without saying this group captured my attention.

Vette was tall with a thin build, light-skinned and wore her strawberry blonde hair cut short. Her choice of color matched her skin tone perfectly and so did her pink and red lipsticks. Nana would cringe if I even dreamed of painting these *soup coolers* as she called them red, but Vette's tone didn't scream vixen like mine, so she claimed.

As luck would have it, she and I had common ground with one another even before our acquaintance was made. Our mothers both worked for the Department of Labor and had been friends many years. This thread definitely served as a plus in building our friendship, since making new friends wasn't always my best attribute. I use to always see Vette and Miko in first period lunch, and Vette would always invite me to sit with them at their table. That was an additional plus in my eyes, since nine times out of ten, people sat in their own cliques and no outsiders were allowed to join. Then, Vette invited me to her house after school one day and the rest is history. We hit it off like a grand slam out of Yankee Stadium, and her mother, father, brothers, and cousins welcomed me with open arms. Miko, on the other hand, with her deep caramel skin, head full of thick healthy hair with cheek bones like Queen

Latifa and was stacked like a brick house, was a was a different story. She and Vette had been best friends for years and apparently Miko, viewed me as a third wheel. I guess she felt threatened by my presence and thought I was there to separate or cause confusion between the two, but those were never my intentions.

Miko put a lot of effort into making me feel as uncomfortable as possible. She'd pull silly stunts, like planting letters in our lockers that slandered Vette and tried putting the blame on me. Then when that didn't work, she'd wait until I cut school with her ex-boyfriend Mario and tried intimidating me for messing around with him. I could see if I'd known about their dealings before hand, but from what I'd learned, Miko was someone Mario tried very hard to avoid and forget. Plus, she had a new boyfriend at the time (Sims) and nobody could understand why she had it out so bad for me. I was never afraid of Miko and had no problems with her aside for the fact that she had a problem with me. The shit's funny to me today, but back then, she had me worried. Her hostility toward me never escalated to the point where we exchanged blows, but overall, that's what she was aiming for. Miko was a bit bigger than me and was sneaky as all hell. I was aware of every plot she planned against me, but she never gained the opportunity to see them through. (The Lover's wouldn't let it go down like that and I know that pissed her off as well.)

Although she was very annoying, I excused Miko's actions because I knew she was going through a difficult time. Soon after I met her, she suffered the tragic loss of her brother Eric, who was also her best friend. I had the honor of meeting him a few times and from what I could tell, the two of them were extremely close. I sympathized with Miko, because I understood what she was dealing with and knew the majority of her actions were just her way of dealing with the pain. That rational shit pisses me off sometimes, it seemed like I was always the one to give pardon, when God knows if the shoe was on the other foot, the empathy wouldn't be reciprocated. However, despite our disputes, nobody had fun like Even T, Miko G, Charlotte, and Murf-Ski. (Charlotte was one of Vette's cousins.)

Miko may have carried a chip on her shoulder, but as the saying goes, one monkey don't stop the show. *The Lovers* were a huge group; Tony, Shawn, (Spit) Tyrone, (Up-Town) Corey, (Virgin) and little Bernie, were a few of the original members and they showed me nothing but love from day one. The issue of creating alliances still outweighed everything else in my life and as always, I ended up biting off more than I could chew. Cutting class had become a thing of the past now that I had friends to chill with, and I'd graduated on to skipping school altogether. But in order to avoid being picked up by truancy officers, we had to have a place to chill. This is when my naïve thinking got me into a heap of trouble.

I'd gotten word from Vette after homeroom that we were all going to go over to Corey's house to smoke and chill for the day. Some of the crew was already there and others were on their way. Because we didn't want to raise any suspicions, we split up and left the building from different exits. Once we arrived, the smoke was already in the air, ah, just in time. I grabbed a seat on the couch next to Vette and the party was underway. It was supposed to be just an ordinary, laid back day away from teachers, security, and police, and all was well until someone decided to snatch my cigarettes.

Newport's were like gold, and although they were no more than three-fifty a pack, (and you didn't have to be twenty-one to purchase them) my pack wasn't a party pack. I can't remember who the culprit was, but I gave chase and followed him. He darted for the stairs on up to the third floor and once we reached the attic, the door slammed shut behind me. At first, I thought it was the wind but when I turned around I saw someone behind me locking the door. Then, I looked up and saw that I was in a room full of niggas. Initially I was startled, but since their faces were all familiar, the troubled feeling quickly went away. The room was filled with smoke and at least three or four dutches were circulating around the room. If nothing else, I thought I was being invited to a private smoke session but realized I was mistaken when a gang of them grabbed me and drug me over to the bed.

If this was someone's idea of a joke, it wasn't the least bit funny. I kicked, squirmed, screamed, and scratched, but my efforts were no match compared to a bunch of doped up, testosterone driven teenage boys. They pinned me down and succeeded in disrobing me, but had a hard time spreading my legs apart. Then, Corey aka Virgin Lover, our host, climbed on top of me and attempted to do the unthinkable. In my head I'm thinking, oh hell no! I'll be damned if I go through this again.

My eyes began to water and my heart was racing a mile a minute. I was embarrassed, but I kept putting up a fight. Corey had definitely crossed the line. Having a crush on someone is one thing but this was a violation! I continued to scream, wondering why Vette or no one else was coming to my aide, then I remembered the door to the attic was locked. Corey, although a tad bigger then I was in size wasn't that much stronger then I was when I was afraid. I managed to free one of my arms, then grabbed hold of Corey's right shoulder and bit him until my teeth met. When he pulled back I could see his white meat, and blood was oozing from him as if he'd been shot. Corey then started screaming like a bitch and at that same moment, my cousin Antoine busted through the door, ran upstairs, and started slamming everyone who stood in his way. Little Bernie was standing over in the corner of the room the entire time but never got involved. I think he was embarrassed by their actions but at the same time, didn't feel he could stop them. Once Antoine arrived, they were the only two who helped me, everyone else just backed off. I was naked in a room full of niggas, people who I thought were my friends. Bernie collected and handed me my clothes while Antoine kicked everyone else out. As for Corey, he stood off to the side nursing his wound, claiming the whole thing was just a prank. Again, not funny!

I guess snatching my cigarettes was just a way to lure me into an ambush. After getting dressed, Antoine escorted me downstairs and Cory kept apologizing, but I was beyond forgiving. Had he been successful with his so called prank, I wouldn't have been able to tell a soul, considering I had no business being there in the first place. Everyone else stayed behind but Vette, Charlotte, and Antoine, who walked me back to school where I met up with Tony, my current crush. Tony was also a member of our clique, but limited his dealings and wasn't always on the scene. While the two of us sat outside the C building across from the AM/PM, I told him about my ordeal. As usual, I fought to hold back my tears and thought he'd think ill of me but he didn't. He told me he was sorry for my experience and felt he was to blame. I questioned how, when he wasn't even there? He said he felt their actions could have been directed towards him, since him and the fellas had a long history of competing with one another for girls. He apologized again and said he wish there was something he could do to help. Little did he know, just by being a shoulder to lean on was help enough.

Oh and speaking of shoulders, Corey's healed up fine, but to this day that scar remains as a reminder of his foolishness.

My reign of rebellion continued to rise, but I now realized the term safety in numbers didn't always apply, especially if you were gullible and placed yourself in someone else's private surroundings or unlawful situations. Antoine, although he was my night in shining amour so to speak, was the influence behind one of the dumbest decisions I'd ever made in my life.

It was a weekday and I was on my way to school. It was routine of me to stop at the Bodega at the corner of Walnut and Hampton, and maybe smoke a doobie [joint] or two before class. I never liked to indulge alone, but surprisingly, none of my crew was around. I did however, run into someone I use to associate with, but she and I had recently fallen out. Her name was Tuti. She was a bit pushy and needy, but what cut our ties was her mouth and catty attitude. Tuti was a short, dark skinned, stocky build girl who had moved up to Trenton from the south and in her short stay, had began a courtship with one of my closest friends, Lonnie. Lonnie and I were raised like sister and brother but once he decided to cut her off, she blamed me for the breakup. I guess Tuti wasn't good with rejection and after he refused to take her back, she started kicking my back in and talking real reckless about me as if I were some type of punk. Boy I tell you, every time I got into a brawl with a chick it was always over a man!

Long story short, Tuti and I tossed it up that morning on the corner, and to be honest, we beat the shit out of each other. She tried to cut me but couldn't keep hold of her weapon, and in turn, I cracked her in the head a few times with the receiver of a pay phone and slammed her face into the booth until someone broke us up. We were both bleeding, had knots on our heads, and scratches on our faces. I never liked to fight, I never saw a purpose in it, but violence begets violence and I'd been a victim for far too long. Once the bout was over, I remained on the corner trying to calm down and that's when Antoine came walking up and asked me if I wanted to take a ride with him to New York.

Now, I don't care who you are or what hood or set you represent, if a nigga come up to you and asks if you want to take a ride to New

York, you need to understand you serve a purpose for taking that ride. An out of town trip to the city is usually something that has been planned and they're not asking you to tag along simply because they need the company. That's something I had to learn from hands on experience and trust me, experience is the best teacher! Antoine said he needed to leave right away and I started walking with him before even giving him an answer. Clearly, actions speak louder than words and a getaway like this is exactly what I needed. Plus, since we'd be away all day, I didn't have to worry about truancy or my father running up on me and sending me back to school or taking me down to the board. Cousin had a car waiting for us in front of his house. The driver was obviously a junkie and his side kick was obviously a runner. I trusted Antoine and felt I was in good hands, yet need I remind you, this was the beginning of the *crack era*!

The ride uptown was a smooth one and once we arrived, Antoine quickly took care of his business and returned to the car. We didn't even have to find parking. We just threw the hazards on and double parked in the street. Before leaving Harlem, Antoine stopped at a Bodega, picked up a few Phillies, and we were on our way. This wasn't my first time to New York, but it was definitely a trip like no other. Once we hit the highway Antoine cracked the blunt and began to roll. Of course he asked me if I wanted to smoke, but being as though I'd been down this road before, I asked, *"Smoke what?"* Antoine then replied, *"Cousin, you know I ain't gonna give you not shit that's gonna hurt you!"* Then he fired it up, took a few puffs, and passed it my way. Being his little comment made me feel bad, I didn't bother to question him any further. But keep in mind that history does often repeat itself.

As soon as my lips touched the blunt they started to tingle, then I took a few hits and knew for certain something wasn't right. The weed tasted funny, my lips felt numb, and then my face. My head felt like I was experiencing an adrenaline rush, almost explosive, and my body felt weak and woozy. I could smell a hint of weed but a stronger aroma overpowered it. I passed the blunt back to Antoine, heard him say a few muffled words, then I was out like a light. The next thing I knew, I was being awakened by the voice of a Hamilton police officer. Wow! Not only couldn't I believe I'd been sleep or passed out the entire ride home, but we'd been pulled over and for God knows what! It took me a minute to compose myself and through my grogginess, I could hear Antoine's voice telling me to wake up, wake up.

Once I realized what was going on, I began praying Hamilton's finest didn't feel the need to perform their duties to the fullest and search the car. If that would have happened, all of our asses would have been hauled off to jail! Bad enough I'd cut school and was in a rent-a-wreck with a non-licensed driver, we also had one hell of a bomb hidden somewhere in the vehicle. Not bomb as in boom, bomb as in enough crack to send our asses away until we were old and gray! Oh my God, what if it was planted on me? Shit, bad enough it was already in my system! I though for sure Antoine was someone I could trust, but like Nana always said, *"Trust no man!"* I knew now the blunt he'd rolled was laced with coke. I'd never smoked or sniffed cocaine before, but knew what type of effect it could have on someone from the many conversations I'd had with others who used it.

While waiting for the police to decide out fate, I did some thinking. Maybe going to school wasn't such a bad idea. Maybe this was God's way of telling me I needed to straighten up and fly right or things would only get worse. When I woke up that morning, I never thought I end up in a fight, take a ride to New York, or be deceived into doing drugs. The way I saw it, weed was harmless, but cocaine, well cocaine on the other hand is a powerful drug... Hamilton wrote us a ticket and said we were free to go. Antoine kept apologizing for not letting me know the blunt was laced, and I would have talked to him about it once we got home but there was no time. As soon as we got back around the way, Tuti was on the corner talking shit and waiting for me apparently. From the way she was going on, it sounded like she wanted a rematch. I don't know why, she already looked like a mummy!

After the adventure I'd just had; I would have stomped the shit out of that girl, left her lying in a pool of her own blood, and blamed it all on the toxins in my system. It had been over an hour since I hit that blunt but the after effect was worse than anything I'd ever gone through before. I swear, it felt like I could chew bricks! Maybe that's why all the crack babies of our time are so quick to fly off the handle and shoot one another up. I'm no expert on the matter, I'm just saying... Tuti followed me from the corner of Walnut and Hampton, all the way down to

Monmouth. A crowd had begun to follow her, I guess the fed into the wolf tickets she was selling, but I kept it moving and Antoine was right behind me. When she saw she couldn't gain my attention, she threw a bottle at me that barely missed my head. That's when a riot broke out. A few months later, I heard her grandmother packed her things and shipped her back down south…

****

Aside from my association with *The Lovers*, I had a couple of love interest of my own. I never made it to my senior year, but that didn't stop me from stealing the hearts of a few seniors. Biggs, aka Mr. Biggs, was my first official boyfriend while attending *The High*. Biggs was tall and light skinned with wavy hair and had an uncanny resemblance to the artist Run (Rev. Run) from Run DMC. Biggs, like most men of his type, had a bunch of groupies waiting to do whatever he asked at the drop of a dime, which in truth only turned him off. Briggs knew he was a good catch but hated it when girls threw themselves at him. I guess that's what attracted him to me, I was just the opposite. Briggs saw my rough, tomboyish outer shell as just that; a shell to protect the cute, intelligent, diamond in the rough. Plus, he loved the no-nonsense way I carried myself. He said it reminded him of his mother. That was a huge compliment, because his mom is a beautiful, strong, black woman.

Biggs and I began dating towards the end of the school year and remained with each other after school let out. Our relationship out of school was a hell of a lot better than it was while school was in session. I charge that to the fact that both of us were first class flirts who were very desirable and very cute. Popularity sometimes plays the con role when it comes to matters of the heart. I lot of chicks wanted a piece of me because of Briggs, but he wouldn't even entertain the thought. Instead, he'd flaunt me in front of their faces and shower me with hugs and kisses. Then, he'd look back at them and laugh, calling them, "*silly ass scaly wags*," and daring them to lay a hand on me. He spoiled the shit out of me and added a little lady to my character.

Biggs was hardheaded and rebellious just like me, and this contributed to our love to hate and hate to love you courtship. Our parents use to tell us we were dangerous for each other, and they were right because we pulled stunts that had them worried to death. For instance, take the time I stayed away from home for three days. Briggs and I staged an argument that both of our parents could hear over the phone. Then, we both stormed out of our houses under the pretenses of cooling off, but instead, met each other so I could in turn, spend the night with him. Briggs' mom worked nights and had no idea I was camping out at her home. During the day, Briggs would show his face and pretend he hadn't heard from me, while my parents kept calling his house, worried out of their minds. When the weekend came to an end and I returned home, I told my parents some story about me being stranded in Newark with no money. I even added the dramatics of being robbed. Nana fell for my tale, hook line and sinker, and it was my mom who surprisingly told me I was full of shit. I guess since Briggs hadn't called the entire weekend but did so as soon as I walked in the house, was a give away. And here we were thinking we were slick...

Prior to Briggs, I was attracted to the captain of our football team Deek. Deek appeared to be the total package; looks, well known, liked, and athletic. Yet, being as I was the new girl on the block, I had to wait in line just to gain his attention. I didn't like that!

As with any superstar of any high school, Deek dated the Valedictorian type. Her name was, ahh, I can't remember her name but it doesn't matter. She never gave me any trouble and from what I could see, was oblivious to who her man really was. Her girl, Tracey, on the other hand, was a pain in my ass. She kept her eye on Deek as if she wanted a piece of him herself. Tracey knew I had a lustful desire for Deek and told me his chick would see me if I didn't back off. I guess my actions were kinda obvious, but the hell if I cared. I was sweet sixteen and was use to getting my way. I would have grown bored with our game of cat and mouse had it not been for my girl, Bernadette, who was also interested in Deek's boy, Gumby. When Gumby and Bernadette hooked up, so did me and Deek, but I wasn't at all impressed with his performance. He may have been a *jock* but he left his game out on the field. I later on found out that the two of us were related by marriage. I wonder if he was aware of that fact, prior to....

It had been a long run, but as the saying goes; all good things must come to and end. No doubt I made my first year of high school tougher than it had to be, but when I started out, I had no idea my first year would end up being my last. Senior cut week was the week directly after finals. Since final grades were being recorded and absenteeism no longer held any weight, all of the seniors ditched school that week in preparation for graduation. None of *The Lovers* were seniors, but we participated in the event anyway.

There was a beautiful patch of land behind Hetzles Field out east Trenton. We nicknamed it *The Grass Field* because that's all there was. It was the perfect hide out and ultimate chill spot. Being as not many would be willing to go through the lengths we went through in order to get there, we were never had to worry about party crashers or the police. Sometimes we'd spend the entire day there smoking, drinking, and watching the trains go by. It was the one thing we did that didn't get me into any trouble, until...

There were only two routes to the field if you lived in Wilbur Section; East State Street and Greenwood Ave. Greenwood was the long route and nobody liked to take that way except me. I'd even break off from the rest of the group and go the opposite way, just to avoid running into or crossing paths with my dad. So, why'd I allow Vette to talk me into deviating from my normal routine I don't know, but I'll tell you this, it almost got the both of us killed! (Figuratively speaking.)

See, although we'd come up with a lie to cover our asses, I wasn't really planning on running into to him so early. Though in the event he was out and about, we were going to say we were walking back to Vette's house to pick up her books that she so conveniently left behind. It was a simple lie but not effective. I'd been so successful in ducking my father in the past, I didn't think he'd care now, considering it was the last week of school, but nope, wrong again.

I don't know who spotted who first, but you could see the terror in my eyes once I spotted him. Nearly two blocks away from his home and only three away from our safe haven, there he stood in his usual spot right outside of Willie's Lounge. My first reaction was to turn around and run, but it was too late. So, I slowed down my pace in order to collect my thoughts. I don't know why, but for some reason, the lie about the books wasn't coming to mind. As for the rest of the crew, everyone but Vette crossed the street. They knew what time it was and believe you me, none of them wanted to get into it with Big Country!

"Wassup, Murf?" Whenever he called me Murf, it was an indication he knew I was up to no good. Vette thought it was cute, but I

was all too familiar with his undertones. *"Dad, I'm walking with Vette..."* He wouldn't even allow me to finish. The look in his eye turned to stone, and without saying another word, I turned and did an about face. I tried to get as far away as quick as possible, because I knew things could get pretty bad had I attempted to talk my way out of it. Then I heard he say something to the effect of, "I better make it back to the school before he did..." Right then and there I knew what I had to do. There was absolutely no need in trying to beat him to the school and he was driving. Only a fool would attempt such a stunt. Yet, didn't the description fit me considering I was foolish enough to walk past his house?

I had a nice head start, but the school was still four blocks away. As I heard his car approach, I dipped off into E. State Street Park until the coast was clear. I knew once he arrived at the school he'd find out I'd been cutting a fool and wouldn't hesitate to do the same. So to avoid the embarrassment, I dipped into E. State park until I felt he was out of range then made a dash for the bridge. It was time for me to take my ass home and face the music. Either I was going to repeat the 10th grade or I was going to sign myself out of school and get a job. Over the summer I weighed my options and at the time, I thought I'd do better by getting a job than return to school. I felt I was capable of making it in the real world and feared if I returned to Trenton High, I'd fall back into the same pattern. I saw a degree from the school of hard knocks more important than a degree that could eventually earn me six figures. Nana always said I was too smart for my own good. Little did I know, most of life's lessons are repetitious because you need more than one chance to get them right.

Once my parents learned the truth, they were disappointed but didn't flip out like I thought they were going to. Plus, no one was more disappointed in me than me! I knew I could do better and should have. I just didn't know how to get back on track. I knew there was no way Nana was going to keep taking care of me after pulling a stunt like this. If I was grown enough to make decisions for myself, then by all means, I was grown enough to provide for myself, too. So provide for myself is exactly what I did!

THEY SAY IDOL HANDS TO THE DEVILS WORK. IF THAT'S TRUE, THEN THE DEVIL SURE DID HAVE HIS HANDS FULL WITH ME...

DISAPPOINTMENT

When you make your bed hard, don't complain about having to sleep in it! I say that because at first I enjoyed sleeping late and not having to get up at the crack of dawn, but it didn't take me long to grow tired of that routine. Since my mom now worked for the state, I'd ask her to help me find a job but nothing opened up immediately. I began purchasing the morning paper to look through the classifieds to see what positions were available and who would give me an interview. I may have been a high-school drop out, but I had secretarial skills that could be put to good use. I was a good typist and excellent communicator, and somebody had to have some use for me somewhere. I lucked up a few times and landed a few sweet office gigs that lasted for about two months each. The pay was fair and I received on the job training that could help me in future positions. But for several months I couldn't find anything, not to mention there weren't a lot of people willing to hire an eighteen or nineteen year old (depending on how old I told them I was) drop out with no GED. Being a responsible adult was harder than I thought it was going to be and there were plenty of days when I just said fuck it, and slummed around the house in self pity.

In time I knew my efforts would pay off but until then, I needed a way to earn cash. I didn't want to get wrapped up in the streets again because I'd surely lose focus on working. Just because I didn't go out didn't mean people didn't come and hang with me indoors. My parents saw how serious I was about maintaining my focus and therefore, cut me some slack and allowed me to have company as long as I kept it cute. Meaning, they didn't want any funny business going on, and that meant no sex, no selling or smoking dope as Nana would call it, and no running in and out. I agreed to their terms and in turn, Nana took the time to become familiar with all of my friends and even addressed them by their street names. If you didn't know any better you would have sworn she'd become soft but she didn't. She just saw the bigger picture; we'd be safer indoors than out. In the end, I believe that's all she was concerned with, our safety, and I'm glad my past acts of promiscuity didn't cause her to have reservations.

Although the names and faces of those who visited me never changed, some brought change into my life. The people who held me down in-between jobs were: Boss, C*Divine, S*G, Almighty, and Universe. Boss was a flashy brown skinned brotha with a hefty stocky build. C*D was short, with a medium build and flawless chocolate skin. S*G was fair and short due to his Italian blood line but had a head full of thick curly hair. Almighty was on the slender side, but shared the same smooth complexion as C*Divine and Universe was thin, quiet and caramel.

Our day together would begin around 10:00 a.m., and I could always count on S*G or C*Divine to be the ones to wake a sista up. The morning agenda was predictable, everybody wanted breakfast! Which meant the fellas brought the food and I prepared the meal. Cheese eggs, beef sausage, and toast was our common menu, and S was the only one who'd volunteer to help me clean up the mess afterwards. Then on occasion they'd splurge, and instead of having me cook, we'd all walk down to Willie Mitchell's where we ate steak, peas, fish, and grits. If we ate nothing else for another twelve hour period we were good because Mr. Mitchell knew how to hook some food up. Afterwards, we'd head back around the way where I'd put my hustle and talents to good use.

I wasn't a Chinaman, but I knew how to make a dollar out of fifteen cent! I had a forte for braiding hair, and The Gods of the Five Percent Nation all had a preference to wearing their hair in cornrows. (The Gods being; Universe, S*G, C*Divine & Almighty) This capacity I possessed not only kept a few bucks in my pocket, but amazed the shit out of my Nana. Everyday when she'd return home from work, she'd stop and stare at me in wonder. For the life of her she couldn't figure out how I could braid so well and how I could do so many heads in a day. Nana could give you a nice pig or ponytail, but she didn't know how to *"braid to the scalp"* as she would call it.

Nana had respect for my gift, and it kept her quiet about me not doing something constructive during the day. However, there was a catch, while I had somebody trapped doing their hair, Nana would lecture all of us about doing something with our lives and not becoming content with our present way of life. Nobody ever gave Nana any lip and I believe that was out of respect. But what stunned me was how soft she'd talk to them, considering she'd always been so stern with me. I guess most parents are harder on their own than they are others, but on the real, I believe she chose to be that way with them because they reminded her of her beloved son.

****

It was during this period of my life that I began to figure out who I was. I'd had a hard time finding myself up until now, but I guess with all of the pressures removed of trying to fit in, I had time to put things into perspective and sort things out. I began to study a lot and read; things I could have done in school but didn't find of interest. The fact that I spent so much time in the company of others who did do so encouraged me to do the same. It was refreshing to follow the lead of someone for a change and not end up regretting it. The literature I began examining is best known as *Lessons*. A lot of adults use to laugh and comment when they saw a group of us studying. They said we were being foolish and the stuff we were reading was foolishness as well. But of course, I wouldn't let it go down like that, and I'd ask, *"How can you be so sure it's foolishness when you won't have an open mind to read it for yourself? You can't deny the facts but you won't accept them either...?"*

I could elaborate more but the topic itself is so controversial, why not save it for another book. I will say this though, what I learned from reading those "Lessons" have helped me open my eyes to things our grandparents will forever be blinded to. Peace to the Gods and the Earths. We call them God, 'cause they were made in his image. They call us Earths because we reproduce just like the earth!

Since braiding hair no longer cut it, I got a job at Burger King on Olden Avenue out Ewing. I stayed there for quite some time, and would have remained there longer had I had reliable transportation. Oh yeah, Nana had a car, and both her and mommy knew how to drive, but once it was parked you could forget about it. Nana didn't care if you were stranded in AC or hanging off the side of a building, she wasn't going to move her car and she wasn't going to lose her spot. She'd always give me a ride to work but that's not when I needed her. The bus that traveled that route stopped running at 9:00 p.m., and my normal shift didn't end until 10:00 p.m. Plus, I worked overtime which meant I didn't leave until 12:00 a.m. I often hiked a long, dark, and scary walk home down Prospect and I couldn't believe she could be so unreasonable. She knew I needed her for that ride, but every time I asked she said no!

I don't know what it was about those old people, but they just had to have their cars parked directly in front of the house! Nana wasn't the only one, I had a few neighbors who were the same. Two doors down and it's a tragedy! Then, either they're up all night or have you up all night waiting for someone to move so they can pull up or move back. Amazing!

I was so hurt when I had to quit my job, and I blamed it all on my Nana. I felt if she would have been willing to pick me up or at least let my mom pick me up, I would have been able to stay. She wasn't even thinking about the money she was causing me to lose out on. Two hours of overtime was equal to my regular four hour shift. Combine that with my regular pay and it was like getting a check for eight hours each day. Not to mention the raise in my rate for being willing to take on the additional hours. So, in return for her unwillingness to assist me, I began stealing money out of her purse as a form of payback. I think more than anything I was hurt because she was being hypocritical. On one hand she was telling me to do something with my life and when I did, she refused to help me out.

Nana never caught me with my hand in the cookie jar, but she knew it was me. Once I obtained employment elsewhere and needed her to cash my check, she refunded herself whatever I'd taken before handing the rest over to me. I know my actions had to have hurt her but at the time, I felt I was justified. Damn I was wrong.... I was so wrong! I was so wrong! I was so wrong!

My spoiled lifestyle had become a problem. It wasn't that I didn't love having Nana and Mr. James at my beck and call to scoop *the big baby* up, and fix all of the wrongs I'd created for myself, it's just that it wasn't happening anymore. So what did I do when things stopped going my way? I had a temper tantrum for about two years. I hung out with the fellas and stayed on the go, which was a lot better than hanging with chicks because disputes were always resolved, peacefully! Though gradually, just like Nana suspected, most of them became involved in the drug game, and our group of six dwindled down to only two. Leaving me and S*G (Sun God) as the new dynamic duo.

I'm not sure if anyone picked up on it or not, but Neil aka S*G and myself, had a slight attraction for one another. Yet, I knew from past experiences not to mix friendship with sex. It's just a bad combination and it never works out. I liked Neil, but I loved our friendship even more. Neither of us had our heads screwed on right and screwing around would have complicated or ruined things all together. He never saw it that way though, but what man does?

In any event, the two of us became the best of friends and whenever you saw him you knew I wasn't far behind. Neil lived on Passaic Street, and his mom was as strict with him as Nana was with me. She didn't allow Neil to hang out all times of night and if he pushed the issue, Ms. Lucy wasn't afraid to set his ass straight! The both of us had an 11:00 p.m. curfew and one minute late could land us in a heap of hot water. We use to try that old trick of changing the time on our watch thinking that would allow us at least an extra twenty minutes or so, but our parents weren't beat! *"Ain't nothing new under the sun, Marie..."* Damn, I can hear Nana's words echoing in my head at this very moment...

As I recall the moments that made our friendship so strong, I'm reminded of when S*G invited me to listen to the new Farrakhan tape he'd just copped from uptown. He said the tape was so deep it would have been unfair for him to listen to it alone. *Now tell me that ain't game!* No doubt he felt the tape was worthy and that I'd enjoy every word, but boys will be boys, game recognizes game, and S*G was looking real familiar, if you catch my drift. I knew he had an ulterior motive on his agenda, but I accepted his invitation just the same. There was only one setback to our plans, we couldn't listen to his speech together without one of us breaking curfew. Either I was going to have to chill at his house, (which wasn't going to happen) or he was going to have to chill at mine. I didn't think that was going to happen either... So in order to resolve our dilemma, S*G asked me for my math, [phone number] and said he'd call me once he got in the house. He said he'd play the tape into one receiver, pick up the other extension in the next room, and the two of us could listen and talk to one another that way.

It sounded kinda crazy but it worked. For over two hours we sat in silence while listening to the controversial, yet very wise minister. At some point we both fell asleep and Ms. Lucy startled the shit out of me when she yelled for her son to get off the phone! When I looked at the time, it was 3:00 a.m., and Neil tried to play it cool, but I heard him telling his mom, *"Shh, calm down."* Then, she got on the phone and embarrassed me right along with him. *"Well who are you that my son is willing to fall asleep on the phone with you?"* My first thought was how did she know I was a girl? I was so afraid she was going to be mad once she found out it was me. As for Nana, had she known we'd been *holding up the line* so long, I know she would have flipped, too!

When S*G came over the next day, he was all smiles and giggles. He said, *"Earth wants to meet you!"* (Earth is another name for Mom, Mother, or Mama) Reason being, she felt I was a good influence on him since I could persuade him to meet curfew. However, I was so shook, I hid myself from her for months. I know she meant well, but that only made me more nervous. Considering Neil had the same influence over me as I had on him, I was afraid she'd see the attraction as well. Yet, regardless of the positive, there were times when the two of us should have been separated. I say that because playing devil's advocate is so much fun when you have a trusted party egging you on...

****

It was a hot summer's afternoon. Everyone was out and about; mommy and Nana were sitting out on the porch, and S*G and I had just walked up. Obe', the next-door neighbor and driver of the car my dear friend Man was killed in, had just walked out and asked if anyone wanted anything from the store. *"Oh yeah, could you bring me back a pack of cigarettes,"* my mom asked? Obe' took the money from my mom and proceeded down to the corner. Truth be told, I wasn't really feeling him every since the accident. I know every man has a conscience and has their own burdens to bear, but seeing him alive and well just didn't seem right. At lot of Man's friends, self included, felt Obe' had escaped justice and therefore, were waiting for some form of street justice to take place. Though out of respect for the deceased family, everyone played it cool. That was until he gave us ulterior reason to act up!

Obe' was about five feet-eight inches tall and weighed about one hundred and eighty pounds. He was dark skinned, with dark short cut hair, a slight southern accent and the story of his actions could be learned by reading his facial expression and his eyes. While the four of us sat on the porch, we noticed it was taking Obe' too long to return from the store. Nearly a half-hour had gone by and my suspicions told me something wasn't right. My mom, on the other hand, wanted to give him the benefit of the doubt so S*G and I walked down to the corner to see what was taking him so long.

Just as I suspected, when we reached the store, Obe' was nowhere to be found. I knew that motherfucker had run off with my mom's money; that faggot had been getting high every since the accident. I went ahead and brought my mom a pack of smokes then took them back to her. I told her Obe' wasn't at the store but she still wanted to have faith he'd return. I wasn't as optimistic as she was and took off again in search of him. When Neil and I returned two hours later, Obe' still hadn't come back with my mom's smokes or her twenty dollars. By now, we both felt we had good reason to fuck him up.

As I paced back and forth, pondering what stone I'd left unturned, Obe' appeared from out of the alley way. He approached us slow and wide eyed, which clearly indicated he was fucked up! He told us some lame ass story about getting jumped at the corner then robbed for the money before getting the cigarettes. As soon as he opened his mouth, I knew he was gonna lie, but at least I though he was going to try and make it believable. I guess his addiction, his guilt, or both had finally gotten the best of him since he'd decided to play the only family on the block that still showed him the slightest ounce of love. I was ready to fuck him up right then and there for taking from my mom, but my mom implored me to let it go! In my mom's eyes, it was only twenty dollars, but for me it was the principal. S*G walked me off down the street to cool of and Obe' went back inside his house. This was the last straw, first he's responsible for the death of a loved one and now he's stealing from my mom. Time for his ass to lose something too! Eye for an eye, tooth for a tooth!

S*G and I chilled until the sun went down and all the neighbors went indoors. I didn't know what I was going to do to Obe', I just knew I wanted to hurt him as much as he'd hurt me. He'd taken a son from one mother and money from another. So, it only seemed fair for his mother to take a loss as well. Obe' didn't have anything of worldly value, but his mother had just purchased a brand new Pontiac Fiero. As my anger festered inside of me, I knew my stupidity could land me in jail but I didn't care. S*G and I were excellent car thieves at the time and could hot wire a train if we had to. But taking off with her car wasn't what I had in mind, instead, I wanted to destroy it!

The best way to disable a car, in my mind, was to damage the engine. However, S*G said doing so would create too much noise and cause us to get caught. So instead, we settled on vandalizing it beyond recognition. We'd need a few things in order to pull it off, but S*G had no idea I had intentions on taking things so far. After gathering a few bottles, bricks, and sticks, I told S*G we needed to climb up onto my roof. *"What roof,"* he asked. The roof to my house I replied! How else would we be able to accomplish the task and remain undetected?

S*G thought I was out of my mind but I was dead serious. After collecting everything we needed for the attack, the two of us jumped the fence, climbed the tree, and pulled ourselves up to the roof. In my delirious state, my fear of heights escaped me but soon returned once I started looking over the edge. Everything we tossed down either bounced off or caused very minimal damage until we dropped the cinder block. Good thing most people had their air-conditioners on or we would have woken someone up. The sight of her smashed windshield and dented roof brought me temporary satisfaction, but once we lowered ourselves to the ground I wanted to take things further.

I was tickled by my destructive act and for the most part, Ms. Nelly's car looked like it had been in a bad accident, yet, it could still be repaired. S*G suggested we take it, burn it, then dump it but had we done so, I'd never get the satisfaction of seeing her face when she saw the wreck. So what did I do? I ran inside, got some laundry detergent, sugar and a Pepsi soda from the refrigerator, then dumped it in her tank. Then to add insult to injury, I picked up the shattered brick that lay in the street, and finished the car off. By then, I didn't care if people woke up and saw me or not. True, destroying Ms. Nelly's car wasn't going to solve anything. It wasn't going to bring Man back and Obe' still got away with my mom's twenty dollars. But knowing I did something instead of just taking it on the chin, at the time, made me feel a lot better.

The next morning I woke up to the sound of my Nana's voice. As usual, she was already outside performing her morning chores, and mommy was talking to Ms. Nelly. *"Who would do such a thing?"* I heard my mother ask with concern. I tried to remain quiet as I stood at the door but mommy noticed me and motioned for me to come out. As I approached their semi circle, I noticed them shaking their heads in disbelief. Since I already knew what to expect, I didn't think I could fake being surprised but I didn't have to. Viewing the damage in the light of day was totally different then what I saw the night before. I'd really messed that car up!

As the three of them continued to ponder who and why, I blurted out their unsuspecting answer. *"I did it, Nana! I did it!"* There was a brief moment of silence as their faces froze in shock and wonder, followed by my Nana asking, *"Ree, why?"* By now all of Ms. Nelly's attention was focused on me as she awaited my answer. *"Because of Obe','"* I shouted! Nana then dropped her head as if she couldn't believe her ears. Ms. Nelly then looked at my mom and my mom turned to me and asked, *"You did all this because Obe' ran off with my twenty dollars? Ree, Ms. Nelly gave that back to me."* "

No, mom, not just because of the twenty dollars, because Obe' took my cousin away from me and nothing happened to him! We lost somebody we love and he's walking around like nothing ever happened. He's a crack head, mom, why doesn't he have to suffer the way we do! How come he can get away with his shit and not have to pay!"

Finally, the anger had been released and it was clear to everyone why. Obe' and the entire situation had finally gotten the best of me. Either that, or I was the devil himself. There was another brief moment of silence followed by my Nana grabbing me by the hand and making me apologize to our neighbor. I did as she asked but it wasn't like I was being sincere. Nana always preached an eye for an eye, so why did I have to apologize? Little did I realize Ms. Nelly had no more control over her son's actions than mommy and Nana had over me.

Just moments after I gave my confession S*G came walking around the corner. I could see the look of paranoia on his face as he approached not knowing what to expect. S*G greeted everyone then the two of us hugged, at which time I whispered to him, *"Shh, don't worry, I took all of the blame."* I then walked off to the side with him, while Nana and mommy tried to negotiate some sort of payment arrangement with our neighbor. Ms. Nelly showed nothing but disgust each time she looked my way, but good thing for my parents she was an understanding person. Ms. Nelly didn't want any more problems to occur and she didn't want to send me to juvi jail. She knew Nana and mommy were good, honest, hardworking people who couldn't afford to pay for my mischief. So instead of going through the drama, she'd report the car had been vandalized, and let the insurance company write her a check for a new vehicle.

Now, would you believe after all that energy, I had the nerve to turn around and feel bad? What started out as rage had now dissolved into shame, and I was forced to look at my handy work until the tow truck came and hauled it away. It was then that I realized how wrong I was and to no one's benefit either, because nothing was gained in the end. As for Obe', every time I saw him he just looked worse and worse, which proved to me that he was paying for his actions even if he wasn't behind bars. A life as a junkie was no life in my eyes. I had taken Nana's words and had twisted them around just like a lot of people do when they are provoked by temptation and anger. Ms. Nelly never knew S*G had anything to do with the damage done to her car, but if she did, I know for sure she would have changed her mind about pressing charges.

****

Neil and I managed to remain trouble free until my 18th birthday, and that's because most of my time was now spent with my new boyfriend Pharaoh, my best friend Amber, and her cousin Kareem, who I just happened to have a huge crush on. Kareem use to warn me to *be good* because I could no longer be protected by my parents or juvenile law. It was a Friday evening and it just so happens I was on my way around the corner to visit Kareem, when Neil pulled up grinning like a Cheshire cat from ear to ear. *"You need a ride?"* he asked.

"Yeah, drop me off around the corner," I said.

Once inside the car, I immediately noticed a handkerchief tied around the neck of the steering wheel but I didn't trip. I wasn't going to be in the car that long, so why question the obvious? The total time the two of us had to be together was no more then two minutes tops. I was already half way down the street but we got stopped by the red light at the corner of Spring and Calhoun. I was then that S*G handed me a 12' inch screwdriver and said, *"Hold this for me."*

I looked down at the screwdriver, then at him like he was crazy. Then, he motioned for me to put it out of sight, so I hid it inside my jacket sleeve. While making our turn onto Calhoun, we heard someone yell, *"five-O,"* but we didn't see any signs of them. We hit the next inner-section and were about to make a right on to Passaic. There wasn't any *no turn on red* sign's posted but S*G still decided to wait until the light turned green. Once we made our turn, he pulled over on the left, jumped out, and told me to do the same. He'd given me no warning he was going to bail but because I didn't see any po-po, I thought I was straight. Wrong! As soon as I exited the vehicle, I noticed a black van with tinted windows parked across the street and my boyfriend Pharaoh was riding past.

With no proof I'd done anything wrong or out of the ordinary, I slowly started walking to Pharaoh's car but I was nervous as hell. Pharaoh' was about three inches taller then I was, and shared the same complexion. He wore his hair cut low, usually in a fade and walked with a unique and well paced gangsta toddle. His husky build only added to his appeal and his Asian like eyes combined with his butter soft skin and baby face kept me mesmerized. He was handsome as all hell with an uncanny resemblance to Shea Jackson, aka Ice Cube, but he was five cans short of a six pack and one had to always expect the unexpected when crossing his path. Nine times out of ten, he was creeping as well but if he suspected me of the same, he'd damn near kill me! In any event, I kept it moving towards him but stopped in my tracks when I heard a description of me over the police radio. *"Black female, wearing a green jacket with orange lettering, on foot headed west."* I was so scared when

I head that I almost pissed my pants. I tried making it to the car but was grabbed before I could do so. Pharaoh had no choice but to pull off or go to jail with me. Out of all the things I should have gotten in trouble for and should have gotten caught doing, why now would I get caught for something I didn't do?

Without any explanation, I was cuffed, read my rights, and thrown into the back of a paddy wagon. Pharaoh circled the block but could do nothing except watch them take me away. I'm not sure if he saw me in the car with S*G or not, but I'm more than sure he wanted to know what was my charge. Considering I had to be to work at the *Police Station* by 8:00 a.m., I know we were both wondering how the hell I was going to get up out of this one. What would I tell my boss? Would I even have a chance to explain?

After building up a good reputation with the temp agency I worked for, I was given a long term assignment to work at the Trenton Police Department, pending a civil service exam. I had eight months in and now this.

While in transport to the station, Pharaoh followed behind us in his car and kept signaling to me to jump. I knew he was only trying to make me laugh, but at the same time, I knew he was serious. Pharaoh loved to take risk and had a phenomenal gift of gab. So, I guess he had something in store to tell the police had they decided to pull over and stop him from driving so close. That boy didn't have license the first!

As the arresting officers escorted me into the back of the building, a few of the other officers were shocked to see me in custody. Like who would have imagined me, little Maria, in cuffs and pending a search? However, considering not one of them could perform a search and there was no female copy on duty at the time, I wasn't worried about that 12" inch, which was still concealed inside my sleeve. I was told to take a seat and they even removed the cuffs after one of the officers began talking to me about work. But all jokes and smiles came to and end after I was informed Carol was on her way in.

Carol was my boss and had the most seniority among all the clerical at the station. She was their primary back up when a female suspect needed to be searched, and I knew she wouldn't be happy to see it was me. Carol hadn't been told who she was being called in for but once our eyes met, her expression was of pure disappointment. As I stood paralyzed with fear, I watched the shoulders of the five foot- seven inch woman drop to her side, while the expression on her full, cappuccino complexion face, turned from wonder to disappointment. I knew I'd broken her heart, she thought so highly of me. I didn't know how I was to convince her I was innocent, knowing the hidden evidence would cause reasonable doubt.

Carol took custody of me from my holding cell and performed the duty she was called to do. She patted me down, she had me remove my jacket, shirt and pants, but that screwdriver remained out of sight. She even asked me to shake my belongings but thank God, she didn't make me go to the extreme. All she needed to do was show arresting officer she'd searched me as ordered and her job was done. After the search I was released on O.R and in an effort to spare me further trouble, one of the detectives offered to give me a ride home. By now, I guess Pharaoh found someone else to lay-up with because he was no where to be found. Damn! I was only in custody for about an hour but it really didn't matter, my plans for the night had been ruined anyway.

The next day at my arraignment, I appeared in front of a judge and was charged with receiving stolen property. *"What? Receiving! I didn't receive anything!"* Since I didn't seem to know S*G's real name, I took the charge alone. I stayed on S*G's ass for over two years to go down to the station and tell the truth, but that was just like talking to a brick wall. Surprisingly, I was able to keep my job, which meant somebody was looking out for me. Maybe it was Ms. Carol, maybe it was God, more than likely, a combination of the two. Neil and my friendship survived the ordeal, but not without going through a very long time out. Today, Ms. Lucy recognizes me as one of his closest and longest friends and I have to agree. The two of us have maintained a twenty year friendship despite our ups and downs. I was able to forgive him for letting me take that charge because I knew the car was stolen when I jumped in.

My life had undergone some pretty serious changes within the two years I was out of school. My mom now had a boyfriend and the two of them were bad for my image. He was too bossy, one hundred percent suspect, and had habits I didn't approve of. My mom was in love, and therefore, didn't see what I saw. But when she allowed him to move in I began searching for a way out. Pharaoh and I were starting to get serious with one another, but he wasn't always the answer, considering at times, he was often the problem. At times I ran home to escape Pharaoh, and other times I'd run to Pharaoh in order to escape home. I was somewhat needy and those needs couldn't always remain hidden. I had crutches to get me by, Universe and Kareem, but one can only run from their problems for so long.

...LOVE IS PATIENT AND KIND. LOVE ISN'T <u>ENVIOUS</u>, IT DOESN'T BRAG, IT ISN'T CONCEITED, 5 IT DOESN'T SCHEME, IT DOESN'T JUST WATCH OUT FOR ITSELF, IT DOESN'T STIR THINGS UP, IT DOESN'T HOLD A GRUDGE, 6 AND IT DOESN'T REJOICE OVER UNRIGHTEOUS THINGS. RATHER, IT REJOICES OVER THINGS THAT ARE TRUE. 7 IT COVERS EVERYTHING, BELIEVES EVERYTHING, HOPES EVERYTHING, AND ENDURES EVERYTHING. 8 LOVE NEVER FAILS...

SEARCHING

The year 1988 marked a pivotal turning point in my life where I knew things would never be the same. For starters, Nana moved out of our family home in the end of '87, and her absence in the home caused me to become depressed. I may have been her *big baby* but she was *my rock*! It never dawned on me I'd one day miss her yelling and screaming, or her calling us ungrateful, lazy ass niggas. She was still, by far, the most influential person to ever touch my life. Without her, I felt as if I were a foster child being tossed about from pillow to post. I usually loathed hearing her constant lectures and scolding, though I now realized they were all delivered with good intent. Dealing with the death of my Pop-Pop, who passed away in October of '86, was bad enough. But with her gone, our house would no longer be a home, and family as I knew it took on a total different meaning. In essence, there was no more family, it was just me!

I tried very hard not to display signs of resentment, but I knew my mom's new boyfriend had a lot to do with Nana's moving out. Nana didn't believe a man and a woman should live together unless they were married. She believed it imposed a bad impression on children and was highly disrespectful for the woman to accept such standards, as well as it being disrespectful to the Lord. Her absence meant our environment would lack not only balance, but character as well.

From the moment Eddied moved in, I could see things taking a drastic change for the worst. His obnoxious, militant ways put a damper on my lifestyle, and served as nothing more than thorns in my side. (Marsha and her military men… I'll never understand it…) Just the sight of his skinny ass, his greasy over activated Jheri curl and beady little eyes embedded into that smoky, ash-grey skin of his made me want to puke. I already had enough on my plate with Pharaoh and his controlling and manipulative ways and didn't need a pretend stepfather adding to those troubles. The world as I knew it had begun to fall apart and the conditions forced me to seek refuge. Hence, my life on Passaic Street began.

****

Passaic Street had always been my home away from home, without me having to give up familiar surroundings. It was where I found peace and laughter, and where my courtship with Kareem actually began. Kareem aka Kim Jones was someone I'd had a crush on every since I was a young school girl. Every time I saw him, I'd stare and say to myself, *chile, he's in a class all by himself.* However, I was far too shy to let my feelings be known, and instead, covered them up by hanging out with his cousin and my best friend, Amber. I recall days of standing on the corner speaking to him whenever he walked by. I noticed how he'd sized me up in one quick glance without noticeably staring or being rude. Then, one day he shocked me by telling me, *"Baby-Gurl, you're like a fine wine and should not be touched before your time."* I didn't have a clue as to what he was talking about but it sounded just as good as he looked. Kareem was Hershey dark chocolate dark. Combine that with his classy and fashionable wardrobe, footwear, stride that oozed with coolness, rugged mature looks and boyish charm, and you got yourself one fine piece of eye candy!

From that day forward, every time we saw one another he made it his business to remind me of my worth. His favorite analogy was to compare me to a vintage bottle of Don P. I remained in awe of his catchy metaphors and sayings, and eventually began enjoying his company; yet, by doing so caused a great deal of conflict, confusion, resentment, and even betrayal.

Kareem and Pharaoh were never friends, just business acquaintances. Reem [Short for Kareem] was aware that Pharaoh and I were dating, and I knew the price I'd have to pay if Pharaoh ever found out I was going to see him. Crossing Pharaoh wasn't something I'd intentionally planned, but his cocky and arrogant ways often pushed me to the breaking point. I was in love with Pharaoh, but found myself more compatibility with Kareem. I knew I'd never be able to hide the guilt of sleeping with someone else, but didn't think Pharaoh would find out, considering he slept with someone else all the time.

Kareem's timing in my life was impeccable. Just as he and I were befriending one another, Pharaoh, in turn, had to go away and do a small six month bid. This didn't necessarily mean I'd be free to do as I pleased, it just meant I'd be spending plenty of nights alone. The two of us did our best to maintain our relationship. We communicated with each other by letter, phone, and messenger. However, our separation did allow me the opportunity to appreciate someone who wasn't as sneaky and manipulative as he was.

My attraction to Kareem was more intellectual then sexual, but that's not to imply any lack thereof; I just adored his wisdom. Kareem was always polite, optimistic, and never failed to make me laugh. While Pharaoh was away, I spent a lot of time at his grandma Jean's house under his wing. Both Amber and grandma Jean were aware I had a crush on Kareem, and neither seemed to have a problem with it. The only thing that got on grandma Jean's nerves, was the way I use to try and hide my intentions. It was insulting to her for me to sneak in and out of her house as if she wasn't the wiser. I'd even hide out in Kareem's room all day in order to spend the night, as if she wasn't aware I was doing so. She knew I was a bit younger than Kareem, but not even that posed an issue. Kareem was grandma Jean's pride and joy, and anything that man wanted was okay with her.

Kareem was one of the better changes in my life, and he took the time to talk to me just like my Nana. He helped me make sense of, and put to rest, a hurtful and misunderstood past, and my attachment to him grew immensely. I loved the way he'd spend hours entertaining me, Amber, and her younger brother, Aimer. Sometimes the four of us would never leave the room, except to go to the bathroom, we were so engulfed. His impersonations, antics, and well learned Caribbean accent held us as a captive audience, and sitting around watching *Sun Splash* videos and listening to reggae artist like *Coca-T* and *Tiger Man* made you feel like you were a part of the live crowd.

Kareem was another who liked to dine at Willie's Restaurant and I believe it was him who put the rest of us up on it in the first place. Regularly he'd send me and Amber down town to pick up a take out order, and once we were done eating, we piled right back into that room to resume our fun. Being with him allowed me to escape the real world, where all of my problems and disappointments were. He could detect my

132

feelings for him were growing stronger, and regardless if we were an official or public couple or not, his feelings for me had grown as well. Allowing me to drive his car, a 1995 Peugeot, that he himself barely drove was the first sign. Amber said that was his way of letting me know he was *diggin'* me. But ironically, I dug a hole for myself by being so quick to jump behind the wheel, considering no sooner than I did so, Pharaoh busted me while home on a weekend furlough. I figured since he had a curfew, he'd be indoors at the time but he wasn't. Since it was Amber's idea for us to go out and joyride in the first place, I used her as my excuse and said we were going to the drug store to pick up her grandma's prescription. I doubt very seriously if Pharaoh brought into my story or not, but he let me go without making a scene.

****

When Pharaoh finally returned home from jail, I was under the impression he was being detained another sixty days. This wasn't something I heard third party on the street, that's the message he gave to my mother to relay to me. I figured if anyone was going to tell me the truth it would be him. But as it turned out, I was the main one he was trying to catch off guard! I had prior relations with Kareem but it wasn't a regular thing. I knew how I wanted to be when Pharaoh came home for good, and I maintained myself accordingly. Then to find out I'd been saving myself for a man who was still seeing someone else anyway got me down. I had been enduring the chaos of staying at home and dealing with my mother's new boyfriend, just to receive his calls. I'd cleaned up my act and wasn't spending as much time around the corner as I had been because I patiently awaited his return. And now he's not coming home....

I walked around to Kareem's. One thing led to another and I wound up spending the night. I don't know who was surprised the most, me or him, but considering I had just gotten caught walking out of another man's house at 10:00 a.m., I believe it was me who was taken off guard. I almost fainted when I saw that boy and his small entourage of followers. They parading him down the middle of the block as if he were some big time celebrity. My first thought was to run back in the house, but I'd already locked the door behind me. I was hoping it was just a bad joke, that it was someone who looked liked Pharaoh, maybe a twin brother I never knew about or something. This just couldn't be!

Pharaoh and I met in the middle of the street and the thought of being within his arm's reach paralyzed me with fear. Before he could say a word, my guilt broke through and I asked the obvious, *"I thought you weren't due home until…"*

The two of us kept our cool, well at least he did, and I explained my actions. In other words, I lied and said I was coming from visiting Amber. There were a few early morning spectators on the block, Boss and Uni were among them, and they stood off in the backdrop, shaking their heads. (Nobody could understand why I put up with Pharaoh's treatment, they all knew he had a problem with his hands.)

Pharaoh wasn't fooled. He knew I had been up to no good but wouldn't risk causing a scene. So, he put off his interrogation until the two of us were alone. This way, there would be no witnesses to his actions. Before the two of us parted, Kareem walked outside and chuckled when passing us in the street. Later that night when Pharaoh and I were alone, he grilled me over and over about why I was at Kareem's house so early, and over and over I gave him the same response. Without my confession, he'd only be guessing. I knew Kareem would never kiss and tell, so all Pharaoh had to go on was his own assumptions. But confession or not, he whooped the shit out of me that night…

Pharaoh was abusive from day one! The two of us hooked up while I was still smoking boat, and he was in the practice of powdering his nose. I wasn't aware of his activities at the time and didn't find out about it until years later. Though, it does explain why he locked me in the trunk of a rental car and drove me around trying to scare me into leaving my ex-boyfriend, Prince. Pharaoh used excessive control in which I thought was only a passing phase. However, once I realized my life was a Déjà Vu of what my mom had endured during her first marriage it was too late! I couldn't walk away…

The day Pharaoh saw me walking out of Kareem's door marked the beginning of the longest ass whopping of my life. From then on, each and every time he put his hands on me, he'd justify it by throwing that day up in my face. He even took me to this little hotel on the opposite side of Mastories' and whooped me so bad he damn near broke my nose.

Because Pharaoh and I didn't have any ties holding us together, he was a lot more forceful with me then he was his son's mother, Samantha. In the end, I guess he figured I'd eventually become so fearful of him he wouldn't have a problem keeping me in line. But I was just as rebellious as he was, so the two of us stayed bumping heads. (Pharaoh is a calculating, risk taking, meticulous, outspoken Aries too!)

Nightly, after checking in on his son, Pharaoh would pick me up from my house and drive us up Rt. 1 to the *Red Roof Inn,* where we'd spend the night. Because I hated to stay in the same house as my mother's boyfriend, it seemed ideal. But there were plenty of nights when I took that ride and sat on the passenger side contemplating, *"If I jump out and roll, I might survive."* What occurred with Pharaoh during the day, determined how well our night would go. If anyone pissed him off, if Samantha gave him grief, or shit just didn't go his way, I paid for it! There were times when he got so out of hand, I thought other guests or management was going to call the police. Lord knows I wish they would have…

Pharaoh damn near beat me into a coma some nights, but his overall, ultimate goal was for us to have sex. I took more slaps, punches, and black eyes from that man, than from all my street fights combined. Pharaoh had a need to feel empowered and he instilled so much fear in me, I was afraid to move, speak, leave, or tell anybody about what was going on. Not that people were blind, they just chose not to get involved. It was crazy how he wanted so much control over me, but at the same time, continued to deal with his son's mother. Of course he ran the typical game: *"I only deal with her because of my son,"* and I believed him because I needed his lie to be the truth. Then, just like any other woman, I grew tired of sharing him. He had me convinced nobody would want me besides him, and like a fool, I believed that too! He was a far cry from the young man who had once shown me shivery by retrieving my sneaks. He was a master of disguise, a beautiful book cover with a dark interior.

Pharaoh had me faded by more ways than one. Fear was his number one tool, but finances also played a huge part since I was no longer working at the police station. I had my hustle, but he played his part as well. Even when and if he wasn't around, he made sure someone in his crew took care of me; made sure I had food in my belly and paper in my pocket. When he wasn't beating the shit out of me, he treated me like a Queen! I'm not sure if it was his guilt or his true feelings, but the lifestyle he provided me with allowed me to live fabulous and carefree. I even took his son's mother shopping with his money while he was locked up. I knew once he found out he was going to have a fit, but I did it out of spite as a message to him for forcing me to keep up the charade.

****

Kareem and I dated each over a course of two years but eventually we fell apart. Having alternating relations with both men made me no better than Pharaoh for ignoring the possibilities of an STD. Had either of us would have contracted anything, we wouldn't know who in the world to blame. I grew increasingly weary of that possibility and knew something had to give. Though for the most part, I was just tired of all the running, lies, and sneaking around. I didn't have any kids yet, and I was too young to get burned out. In addition, Kareem had other playmates, and among them was his daughter's mother. But unlike Pharaoh, didn't feel the need to hide anyone me from her or her from me, and that in turn, brought out the cattiness in both of us.

It was Christmas Eve and Amber and I had just parked the Peugeot and were walking in the house. Before we could open the door, we saw 'Reem and his daughter's mother feuding in the middle of the front-room floor. Grandma Jean was in the middle of them trying to calm Kareem down but it didn't seem to be working. By the time it was all over, grandma Jean was screaming for the both of us to get out of her house! Since I'd already made plans to spend the holiday with him, I left very disappointed. A few minutes later Kareem drove around Spring Street, picked me up, and took me back to the crib, but it was obvious he was tired of the sneaking and the games as well.

I was mature for my age, yet still very immature, and my conduct spoke louder then anything. Kareem knew I'd return to Pharaoh regardless of how he treated me, and the best way for me to learn anything was with him out of the picture. In his eyes, it was straight lunacy for me to run to him for healing; then right back into the arms of my abuser after my wounds had been healed. Plus, it seemed pretty strange for Pharaoh to know so much about our dealings, if neither one of us was running our mouths. His knowledge of us two and the details he knew about, didn't settle to well with the God. I lost Kareem as a lover, but years later we wound up being the best of friends. I also lost my safe haven and was forced to return home.

****

Everyone is capable of change, but Eddie hadn't changed since the day my ex-boyfriend, Briggs, introduced us to each other a year prior. Briggs and Eddie had become co-workers after Briggs left school and Eddie was now Briggs' supervisor. Briggs use to tell me all about Eddie's lifestyle when we were together, and how Eddie was a loose cannon who loved to spend money. I warned Briggs to be cautious of someone so careless, but he wouldn't take heed and in the long run, ended up introducing the misfit to my mother. Nana didn't take to well to Eddie once she got to know him either. She said she couldn't stand a nigga who always had an *Oh poor me story,* and could tell he was no good.

Not only did Eddie always have some sob story to tell, he was also a hypocrite and extremely judgmental. When all of us lived on Spring Street, he us to condemn Prince and Pharaoh for how they earned their living, yet he was getting high every time someone turned their back. I guess it never dawned on him that Briggs would let the cat out of the bag but he did, considering how clear it had become that he was caught up as well. And even before Nana moved out, Eddie attempted to regulate shit as if he had some type of authority over me. I'll never forget the time Pharaoh gave me money to go to the grocery store then cook for the family. He knew how I loved to do little things like that for my parents, but Eddie even found a way to ruin that for me.

After finding a ride to the store (one of Pharaoh's cousins) then taking the time to prepare a meal for an entire family, it blew me away to later find out not a crumb had been saved for me! Before leaving the house I made the statement, I didn't care who ate what, just as long as they saved something for me. It wasn't too much to ask, but Eddie didn't think so. He took the liberty of finishing off everything that was leftover, including what Nana had set aside for me.

Normally when I'd been out and about all day, I'd just grab a quick bite at the corner store before taking it down. Though considering there should have been a home cooked meal waiting for me when I walked in the house, I didn't bother. Discovering my food was gone caused a huge argument and Eddie had the audacity to say, had I been in the house I wouldn't have missed out! Missed out! Nigga, if anyone should have missed out it should have been you! I couldn't believe this dusty dark brown, frail framed, Jheri Curl, be all you can be reject was standing in my face, in my home talking shit. To no surprise my mom quickly jumped to his defense, claiming he didn't know the set aside food was for me. As if that made matters any better…

I don't know what came over my mother, but she seemed to care more about his junkie ass then she did me. The two of us then began to argue and I backed myself up the stairs and into my room. By now, Nana had gotten involved and was trying to calm everyone down but my mom kept coming at me full force! I tried to leave the house but Eddie stood in the doorway blocking my path. I turned back around and headed for the bathroom just to get away from both of them, and my mom decided to follow behind me. She was determined to make me hear what she had to say, but sadly, she'd already lost me the minute she took his side. Tempers were flying and all I could concentrate on was my Nana's voice yelling, *"Marsha, leave her alone! Marsha, leave her…"*

Attempting to keep peace with my mom wasn't working. She kept waving her finger in my face, and I kept shouting for her to get out of my way. By now, all I wanted to do was lay down. My heart was pounding, my head was spinning, and then she pushed me… Why'd she do that? Never in a million years would I have though about lifting a hand to my mother, but in the blink of an eye, I'd kicked the shit out of her as if she was someone in the street. I didn't do it out of disrespect, it was just reflex.

My mom and I began to tussle and I could hear Nana crying in the background. Before it was all over, the top bunk had fallen down on top of both of us, and my mom had gotten hurt. Eddie was now willing to move out of my way, and Nana was pleading with me not to go.

As I walked down the stairs, I could hear Eddie yelling, *"Let her go!"* Nana couldn't stand to witness what had come of our family, and I couldn't stand taking back seat to someone like him. It hurt to leave that night because I wanted to make sure my mom was okay. I left, not because of our argument, but because I was ashamed of my actions towards my mom. Eddie was the cause, but that didn't ease my guilt. About two weeks later, Nana told us she was moving.

****

Home as I knew it had taken a change for the worse. Nana still came around to say hi, show her love, and check up on everybody, but Eddie bitched after each visit. Eventually, he convinced my mom to leave the house and Spring Street behind. He said they needed a fresh start, someplace bigger that didn't have so many old ties to it. I don't know how she didn't see through his bullshit, but they packed up their things and bounced. Nana tried to talk her against it, and had she known my mom was going to leave, she surly would have stayed. But mommy wouldn't listen and traded in thirty years of precious memories, for a two bit, two and a half bedroom resembling a hole in the wall out in E. Trenton.

Eddie kept bragging about the deal he got, but when I saw the spot I couldn't believe my eyes. The comparison between our old home and our new house was like night and day, or sugar and shit! Eddie was from one of the roughest parts of Camden, and in Camden a house like that may have been a step up. But the way I saw it, we'd left a mansion and a decent neighborhood for something way less desirable. Wall Street was a tiny, one-way street, a long ways from Spring, Passaic, and Willow where Nana lived. It was dreary looking with a lot of drug activity and several abandoned buildings. To be honest, it looked just like a street in Camden!

I didn't embrace the move one bit, especially not in the dead of winter! Mommy knew Eddie and I didn't get along, and now I was being forced to live under his roof and abide by his insane rules. I tried to make the best of things for her sake, but I still felt like an outcast. Then once the two of them got married, (and no I did not hold my peace) he moved in his three, never before seen daughters and it was all she wrote.

Eddie had three daughters; Kathy, Darla, and Yvonne, and with five girls under one roof, someone had to know it was going to get congested. I believe it was Eddie's intentions to push me out permanently in the first place. I literally had no privacy and my possessions and money were beginning to disappear; yet nobody seemed to know how. Mommy asked me to give our new situation a chance, but taking on three new sisters at once was just too much for me to deal with at the time. Mommy wanted a family and Eddie provided her with just that, plus independence away from Nana. I was of age now and free to do as I pleased. My mom didn't force me out the door, but she didn't make it easier for me to remain. Pharaoh had no place for me to go because he was still trying to pacify Samantha, and Nana couldn't take me in because she lived in a building for seniors. So, I used my mom's spot to change clothes and wash, but my home for the time being was the streets.

I wish I could have gotten along with my mom's husband. I believe it would have brought us closer. Instead, because of him we only ended up drifting further apart. Eddie had a need to enforce, and he did so whenever and where ever he saw fit. He even made my mom lock me out of the house because I missed his new curfew by a few seconds. I looked up to the window where I saw my mother standing and looking down at me. Then, I saw Eddie walk up to her side and close the curtain. It was so cold outside. The snow was mixed with freezing rain and I had no place to go. By now we were living on Southard Street and we had good neighbors, but I was too embarrassed to knock on their door. Instead, I walked around the corner, cut through the school yard, climbed over the fence into the yard, and slept inside an old stove that had been set out on the porch for trash.

The way I saw it; Eddie had humiliated me, embarrassed me, and had successfully turned my mother against me. There was nothing left for him to do. In the morning, my little sister woke up and saw me lying down on the back porch. She called for my mom and Eddie walked down and opened up the door.

The changes Eddie took our family through were ridiculous. When Nana got wind of what happened, she extended her sympathy to me but could do nothing about it. She knew why my mom let him take the lead, she knew why she felt the need to have a husband. It had been her who instilled that moral or thought in her mind. But she had no idea he would cause such confusion in the process. As for our next door neighbor, Aunt Desa, she felt the same as Nana. She couldn't stand Eddie no further than she could throw him, and told me before I spend another night out in the cold, I better knock on her door and let pride go. I tried to find a way around it, but ended up taking her up on her offer more then once. Her daughter, Stacy, and I were real close, but Pharaoh didn't like me over there. He thought her cousin Ryan had a crush on me, and my reason for spending so much time with her was because of him. Pharaoh was right on one count, Ryan did have a crush on me but the feeling wasn't mutual. He was cool but my purpose for being there wasn't him.

****

Running from pillow to post wasn't any easier then living with my mom and Eddie, but Uni and Boss helped make my bumpy road a bit easier. Although I tried to maintain a low profile and keep to myself, the two still picked up on how late and frequent I was hanging out. This lead them to believe I was either hustling or using, and neither was the case until Boss put a package in my hand and said, *"Do you!"* He said it didn't make sense for me to be out hugging the block with empty pockets, waiting on some nigga to do for me when I could obtain the means to do things for myself. What he said sounded good, and clocking my own dollars made a lot of sense. I got down with Boss, formed a business alliance with two associates, Geech and Mook, and the three of us spent nearly every night burning down the block. It wasn't the lifestyle I set out to achieve, but a sista had to do what a sista had to do, and selling dope was something I knew how to do well.

Working for Boss was cool but I got tired of turning all that money over to him. Off 5gms I had to turn in $150, which only left me with about $50 in my pocket. Then one day my girls stepped to me with a proposition that could help us all. We were going to stop working for Boss and go independent. Shit, since we were the one's taking all the risk, why not be in total control? That was all I needed to hear, and from then on, all that I grinded up was mine. When Boss finally came to me for his dough, I told him I used it to put oil in our house. Without reprisal he let me slide, and from then on I was my own Boss! (I really did use most of that money to put oil in my mom's house, but the rest of it was used to re-up on my own.)

Pharaoh didn't like the idea of me hustling, and if he caught me there was no telling how he'd react. So to cover my ass, I employed others to bring me sales and keep look out for him and the police. Uni allowed me to use his home as a fall out shelter, but eventually things heated up between us after spending so many nights. Uni knew Pharaoh's M.O., and he hated to see me with bruises all over my caramel skin. I use to try covering them up, but when you have to see and one eye is black, there isn't much covering up you can do.

Pharaoh use to do the dumbest shit. There was this one time when he kidnapped me and locked me away for days at his father's house. (RIP Johnny Cake) The room he held me captive in had nearly ten locks on the outside of the door and a lock on the phone so no one could call out. The fool even had the nerve to cut my hair, then turn around later that night and try to make love to me. If I said no, there would be a price to pay and considering I wasn't going anywhere, I didn't see the need to make my stay unpleasant. In the morning, he'd leave and go about his day, making periodic stops through out the day to bring me food and drink as if I were is prisoner. What disturbed me the most weren't his actions, I knew he was crazy but his mother, Ms. Carol, knew what was going on, she even sat with me one afternoon. But to my knowledge, never said a word to Pharaoh about how wrong he was for holding me against my will... (RIP Ms. Carol)

****

Pharaoh and I went from one extreme to the next. I guess that how young love goes in the hood when the men are angry and the females are lost; both trying to find their way. I went from selling for Boss, to being my own boss. I went from spending nights at Uni's house to hanging out all night with Sissy, Scribby, Sam, and Starsky. Sometimes Pharaoh and I fought, sometimes were like two peas in a pod. Sometimes he was my night in shining amour, sometimes he was a savage. Sometimes I was an angel and sometimes I was, well...

Sissy was a good ally because she wasn't catty and always had my back. She was straight up, held no punches, and was about one thing; her money! She would have been a gem to have around when I was going through my changes with Jayden, Tiny, and the rest. But at least she was there when Betty and I had our bout. Had it not been for her, I know I would have gotten jumped, but Sissy wasn't about to let it go down like that. She made sure everybody knew the two of us were going to shoot a fair one, and once it was over, it was over! As for Uni, every cat in my life had an ulterior motive when dealing with me, but I guess it goes along with the territory.

In my eyes, Pharaoh's jealousy couldn't be justified. He was living a double life and manipulating the emotions of two women at once. Yet, that didn't stop him from acting a fool or humiliating me out in public. In addition to his actions, he'd drag our mutual friends into the middle of our mess, causing a bigger mess in the process. He'd have Pook, Freedom, and Sam cover for him and he one day made Foo' chase me down so he could beat me up. On this occasion, Pharaoh took me to the back of Shiloh Baptist Church and hit me so hard, my head hit the car and I fell out. I had nine earrings in my right ear and one of them got embedded in my ear due to his punch. The Nefertiti black onyx and gold earrings I was wearing wound up cutting the side of my neck, leaving me with a visible scar as a reminder of his treatment for over two years. There was never a dull day between the two of us and if there was, we made up for it down the line.

****

With very little stability in my life, it was hard to sit down and figure out my next move. Occasionally I'd go back home and chill with my mom and sisters, but as soon as Eddie started up I was out. In all honestly, I felt like a motherless child. I had not a pot to piss in, nor window to throw it out of. Then out of nowhere, Pharaoh told me he'd secured a spot in Donnelly Holmes, and he and I could crash there until I figured something out. (Not that he needed a place to crash, Samantha only lived around the corner on the Blvd.) Due to our rocky past, I was hesitant to give him even more control, but he promised he'd never put his hands on me again, and of course, I believed him and agreed to chill. If nothing else, it provided me with temporary relief to an on going battle that had been wearing me down. Surprisingly, the two of us actually started to get along better and acted more like a couple instead of opponents in a boxing match. It was definitely a pleasant change for the better, life was grand…

Since Donnelly Holmes was such familiar territory for me, there wasn't much need to go back around Spring, except to see Shantell and Moe'. I was very happy with Pharaoh and he seemed to be happy with me as well. However, misery loves company and Samantha wasn't willing to just let us be. I'd never disrespected Samantha and had no problem with that fact that she had a son with Pharaoh. I actually

143

admired him more because he was a father and took such good care of his baby. So when she came marching up to our apartment one Sunday morning, demanding to see him and screaming for me to get out, you know I wasn't the least bit pleased.

Samantha was equal in height to Pharaoh with a deep brown skin. She wore her short dark hair, neatly gelled into a pony tail, and although she wasn't very flashy, certain characteristics about her stood out. I never quite understood what he saw in her, but maybe looks wasn't the attraction. Pharaoh tried calming Samantha down and at the same time, tried to convince me he wasn't messing with her anymore. However, if that were the case, she would not have been so emotional and upset to find me there. He locked her in the bathroom and me in the bedroom, while he attempted to negotiate himself out of yet another mess. It wasn't until she left that I discovered the reason behind her hysteria. She was pregnant again, and there was no doubt in my mind it was his baby!

I thought all of our drama had been put to rest, but apparently that wasn't the case. Pharaoh had ongoing issues with Samantha and I had unresolved issues with Kareem. Because every change that occurred in my life happened so quickly, I never had the chance to tie up loose ends. I had clothes at Pharaoh's spot, clothes and personal belongings at my mom's crib, and several items remained at Kareem's. In turn, I still had one of Kareem's leather jackets and just happened to be wearing it the day he ran up on me at the corner store on the Blvd., (682) across from where Samantha was staying.

Kareem had never been disrespectful, arrogant, or insulting to me, but on this day he was all of the above. I didn't even see him enter the store, but as soon as he saw me he demanded I give him back his jacket. I had no problem doing so, and it wasn't like I was going to keep it. (Okay, I was going to keep it but it wasn't like he was gonna miss it. The man had so many clothes he could start his own clothing line!) But the way he asked for it was rather embarrassing and it gave others the impression I'd stolen it or had it without his consent. I thought he'd give me the opportunity to return it to him later, but instead, he was cruel and wanted it right then and there. That wouldn't have been a problem had I been wearing a hoodie or something underneath, but I wasn't. All I had on was one of Pharaoh's t-shirts and that wasn't going to be enough to keep me warm out in the freezing cold. At this point, Kareem had nothing but contempt for me, and swore up and down I'd been playing him by telling Pharaoh about our dealings. I don't know why he would assume such a thing considering it only put me in harm's way, and I was just as baffled as he was as to how he knew so much about our past dealings.

Kareem took his jacket, rolled his eyes, and walked out. Spectators looked on and laughed, and I walked out a few minutes looking a fool. Once I returned to the crib, I had to confess to Pharaoh that the jacket I'd been wearing belonged to Kareem, however, I was only wearing it because all of my winter wear was still on Passaic at his grandmother's. Pharaoh wasn't as fussed as I though he would be but he did order me to go retrieve all of my belongings at once. Considering Amber and I were still good friends, gaining access to my things wouldn't be a problem.

****

As if matters of the heart weren't enough for me to deal with, I also had to worry about street credibility on top of it. I'll be the first to admit I've put myself self in harm's way more than once, but I'd never drag anyone else into my shit. So, how did this guy named Mike end up threatening me because he though I stole some of his people's shit is beyond me. Yes, I allowed myself to be a mule on more than one occasion and for different people. Yes, I transported coke, crack, marijuana, and at times, guns across state line and was paid well for doing so. I'm not proud or bragging about my actions, but even when conducting unlawful activity, I've always been honest and upfront. A person's credibility depends on their integrity and respect. Damage one and you might as well leave town…

As I was told by my accuser, several ounces of crack cocaine were missing from a package I'd delivered. After the discovery I consented to a search which I hoped would prove my innocence. Yet, even after I came up clean it still didn't clear my name, and because I couldn't get rid of that type of weight without raising a red flag, people assumed I'd given it to Pharaoh to add to his wealth. Their assumptions were wrong and in all honesty I know it was *the connect* who threw grease in the game. He knew I'd be returning home alone and he knew

145

I'd serve as the perfect fall guy, or girl, in this case. Pharaoh told me not to worry, but he wasn't the one receiving the threats. It was no fun looking over my shoulder or peeking around corners in order to stay safe, but as the saying goes, *shit happens!*

****

Four years passed and despite the infidelity and birth of a second son, Pharaoh and I remained together. Like a gypsie, I moved from Donnelly Holmes back to Southard; from Southard to Stuyvesant. I landed a decent job on S. Olden Avenue at Central Motors, brought a car, and lost them both a year later. Materialism and monetary items were of no interest to me anymore, and it would take a lot more then a permanent address to fill my void. I was ready to give up my NY state of mind and concentrate on the things that mattered most in life. Things like family and the unconditional love of it generates. I missed home cooked meals and hearing voices in the house other than mine. Pharaoh didn't mind constantly relocating and had a honeycomb hide out in every section of town. He said he did so because of his lifestyle but I knew better. And besides, no matter what happened, he could always go back home to his mother which was something I could never do. Ironically, after all was said and done, I ended up right back on Spring Street across the street from where I grew up. For the next two years, 76 Spring Street became my new home sweet home, complete with family, good food, and all the comforts I'd missed so much.

While back on Spring, Pharaoh was right around the corner at his mom's on W. Hanover. (At least that was his official address.) It would have been sweet of him to allow me to stay with him and not inconvenience family, but that didn't happen. (Minni and Aunty never looked at me as in inconvenience anyway.) True, I spent plenty of nights with him there, sometimes weekends, but having me there on a full time basis would have prevented Samantha and the kids from coming over and that would have been a problem. Again, I never had a problem with Samantha and respected her position as the mother of his children, I just didn't appreciate all of the lies he told in the process, while trying to maintain me, her, and others. Though, regardless of how thin he spread himself, he still took care of my needs, wants, and desires.

With no way to hide what was really going on, my cousin Shantell proved to be a great source of relief. The two of us were extremely close and she'd speak up for me when I was too embarrassed or depressed to do so for myself. Had it not been for her, I probably would have ended up back out on the streets. Shantell was very young and still growing into her looks but depicted the picture of pure innocence. After loosing my job at Central and being evicted from my apartment on Stuyvesant, she was the one who asked Aunty if I could stay with them for the night. When Pharaoh dropped me off, I had all of my things stuffed into two hefty garbage bags. When Aunty saw my belongings sitting in the hallway, she took it upon herself to take them upstairs into Moe and Shantell's room, and the rest is history.

Stability had been restored and so was my sanity. Aunty was my new, positive mentor, and although she was very young at heart, she was very well grounded and set in her ways. She reminded me of my mother with her dark skin and short dark hair. But she wasn't as quiet as my mom, instead, she was quite loud like me. Minni was my enforcer and disciplinarian just like Nana. She was of medium height but due to living the good life of home cooked soul food meals was pleasantly round. Nevertheless, she was full of wisdom and advice and quick with her hands too. David (Shantell's little brother) and Dayquece' (Moe's baby boy) were the youngins in the house, and grandma, who was fragile yet sassy was eighty-nine at the time and the eldest in the home. The bond which formed between all of us was unbreakable, fun, and sincere. Even Debbie, Moe's mom, played her part in some of the most pivotal stages of my life, and her brother, Tye', was the ultimate prankster.

With nothing but time on our hands, the three of us lived like college roommates on break. We played spades all night with Minnie, Angi, Debbie, and Judy (RIP), then stayed up till dawn watching black cinema on cable. We sat on the porch guzzling 40oz while trying to prevent the scent of the weed from hitting Aunty's room. On Thursdays we hit West Indies and Fridays we'd sit up in Klotz. We did our chores, we ran our errands, and then we'd shower and get pretty so we could strut up the Blvd., with all eyes on us. Silly Rabb, Swing, K-Hog, and Whip were our homies out North and the entire *"808"* was our family around the way; Great, Paz, Black, Mucho, Science, Fedo, and Loge. We cracked jokes with Biggie June, Tommy, Ace, Solomon, and Sun Born;

we exchanged lessons with O*G, and got the best hook ups at Meechies, via Chino my Godbrother, aka Ralph.

My life was full of fun and adventure and Pharaoh saw that as a threat. I guess he feared I'd cut up now that I had a bit more freedom, but shit, I did that anyway. He was never faithful to me and me being unfaithful to him is what pissed him off the most. I loved him and I was in love with him, but I was tired of being his fool. I was tired of sitting up waiting for him, knowing damn well he wasn't going to show. Then having to justify it and make excuses to the people who loved and cared about me the most.

Amusement wasn't the only thing the three of shared collectively. There were also some very fundamental, inspirational, and spiritual moments that helped mold us into better individuals. We joined a community choir (Tony Booker and Praise Power) and toured throughout Pennsylvania, New York, New Jersey, Maryland, and Delaware. We met Tony through our aunt Grace when they were both singing in Rapture and Revelations. Tony became our friend, trained our voices and kept our hair looking fierce. While in this lifestyle we sang our hearts out and learned things about ourselves and others that aided in our growth. Then, just as the seasons change, so did our daily lives. Shantell, who was now a very attractive grown woman with a fiery disposition, went off to college at Fairley Dickerson University. Moe who had the looks and build of a modern day Mary Wilson moved in with her son's father and I moved out after landing a job with the State on the strength of my mom's connections. (The fact of my mother getting me that job, whipped away years of bad feelings and regret.) I was sad growth caused us to go our separate ways, but nothing in the world could ever keep us apart.

After I became permanent, I moved into a quaint little neighborhood in the historic area of Trenton, and Pharaoh and I spent nearly every night together. This was my fresh start and I wanted nothing more than to transform my house into a home. Who knew my dreams of doing so would turn into nightmares of a dormant and secluded hell. A hell so beautifully disguised, no one could hear my cries, see my scars, feel my fears, or wipe away my tears.

As if Pharaoh's cheating, lying, and hot temper weren't enough to deal with, I also had some heavy shit of my own to take into consideration. The one thing Pharaoh used to justify his behavior with Samantha was the one thing I couldn't do for him. Give him a child. It was a hard pillow to swallow, considering how much I loved children and wanted to start a family of my own. However, I'd been told over and over the possibility of my having children was almost next to zero. Therefore, I fed into the notion that I wasn't woman enough for him and, therefore, accepted his behavior due to my infertility.

I never gave up wanting a son, but out attempts to get pregnant continued to fail. Both he and the doctors tried to convince me it just wasn't meant to be, but I was never willing to accept such a fate. The thought of going childless was too much to bear, and the desire for motherhood wouldn't allow me to become bitter or selfish. I brought gifts for Pharaoh's two sons when holidays rolled around, and became Godmother to two very special little boys, Quece and Teo aka baby Kevin. People who knew me always asked why I didn't have any kids of my own, and on the other hand, I kept hearing rumors about my man fathering children all cross town. Pharaoh denied every account but if I pressed the issue, his guilty temper caused him to lash out and hush me up. A lot of outsiders looked at us, looked at me, and thought I was the happiest girl in the world. My inability to feel complete allowed me to let go of my self worth and ignore the obvious. Kareem was right. No matter what Pharaoh did, I was going to be with him regardless. He was my first love and I wanted to be with him until death.

****

Although material items and gifts weren't what I needed, Pharaoh made it awfully difficult to pass them up. He believed money could buy him anything, even forgiveness, and on a lot of occasions I proved his theory to be true. Whenever things got really out of hand, he'd do something unnecessary, like buy me the biggest herringbone necklace he could find or a new car to pacify me. But no good deed goes unpunished as they say, and just as sure as he brought cars for me, I also had to let him register his cars in my name. Years later, the decision to be so generous ended up costing my license.

With all my heart I believed Pharaoh and I wanted us to love one another for the rest of our lives, I just don't think we knew how. Any man who claims to love you in one breath, then turns around and slams you into a wall and gives you a concussion in the next, isn't worthy of such loyalty or love. His charm and charisma had a way of making me forget about the anxieties in our relationship. But his rage often had me scared for my life. He saw nothing wrong with our dealings and dared anyone to tell him any different. He would disappear for a week, bounce to Maryland and not even call, then turn around and drive me all the way to Florida and reconcile all differences. He'd wine and dine me until I could stand no more and sex me endlessly until we both passed out. He was a true ladies man and his gift blinded me and caused me to surrender to him completely. I lived a life filled with lies and deception and I did it for so long, it almost seemed normal. Nobody could understand how I could stay with him and not complain, and at times, I didn't understand it either.

Part II

MY EVERYTHING

After undergoing years of testing, going to specialists, and seeing different gynecologists, I finally knew the answer to my infertility issues. I had Endometriosis and PCOS, more commonly known as Poly-Cystic Ovarian Syndrome. These two conditions altered a woman's normal menstrual and ovulation cycle, often causing multiple miscarriages, ovarian cyst, tubal pregnancies, and countless failed attempts to conceive. Now why in the world would I of all people have to have this stupid abnormality? And why couldn't somebody fix it! All around me were women having babies who didn't take care of them. Crack heads were having kids born to their addictions. Teenage mothers were getting pregnant just to hold on to a man and gain financial security, and I had to have this stupid condition. All of my sisters had children *(except Nette, she was still too young)* and all of my friends had babies, too. I felt so odd being the only one without. As if I didn't deserve to be among them or had this huge blinking banner overtop of my head that read *Barren.* Sometimes the knowledge of my condition caused my thoughts to become so hopeless. While watching them with their children I'd think to myself, *"This may never be you. And no matter how much you smother someone else's child, you may never know what it truly feels like to be a mother."* The bond between a mother and her child would forever elude me.

Regardless of how dysfunctional the relationship, Pharaoh and I were in agreement on having a child. Therefore, no matter what was told to me, I persisted without cease to become pregnant. I began a series of treatments, which consisted of hormone replacement pills and steroids to regulate my cycle. However, once I stopped the treatment, my period stopped again as well. I was even told that because I tried so hard, I lessened my chances by lowering Pharaoh's sperm count. I confidently assured my physicians there was absolutely nothing wrong with

Pharaoh's sperm. But they continued to urge me to bring him in for consultation. He refused just as I knew he would, and because we wouldn't do things their way, they stopped my treatment all together.

Pharaoh was down on us having a kid, but he knew he wasn't the problem. He wasn't willing to self serve himself just for them to come back and tell us something we all already knew. I pleaded with my doctors to concentrate on just me, but they said they wouldn't take things further without testing him as well. So now I'm pissed, but just because they refused to expand my options, didn't mean other options didn't exist. I nearly lost my mind trying to find a cure for my ailment, and when all else failed, I went to the wisest person I knew for counsel. My Nana!

Nana was extremely candid, and if she knew anything she couldn't wait to tell you. If nobody else could help me, I knew she could shed light on my situation and point me in the right direction. Initially, I didn't know how to explain to her that I wanted a child out of wedlock, especially by a man who in her terms wasn't worth *"a buffalo nickel!"* Though, I'd hoped she'd appeal to my maternal side and understand why this meant so much to me. She did, and after our talk she told me the only doctor still living who could and would help me in getting pregnant was a man by the name of Dr. Gindhardt. Dr. Gindhardt was a fertility specialist and use to be her gynecologist when she first moved to Trenton. *"A lot of folk don't like him,"* she said. *"They call him a butcher! But if you want to get fixed he's the man you need to go and see."*

I took Nana's advice, called the good doctor, and tried making an appointment. But wouldn't you know it, he didn't accept my insurance. If I wanted to see him it would have to be out of network and the cost was $45.00 per visit. In addition, I'd have to pay out of pocket for prescriptions, testing, and all other treatment. I told Pharaoh my dilemma of how my insurance was useless, and he agreed to pay all the expenses. I was so happy I think my heart skipped a beat. I ran straight to the phone, and immediately scheduled my first appointment. A consultation of course…

Nana said Dr. Gindhardt was old *"fuddy- duddy"* with a peculiar sense of humor and she wasn't lying. While taking down crucial information he was sure to slip in a joke or two just to make me feel at ease. He said it would be a few weeks before he could obtain my medical records so until then, I just had to sit tight. My next appointment with the Dr. didn't take place until the flowing year in January of '92. By then, he'd obtained my files from Mercer Regional OBG and the results from the laparoscopy performed by Dr. Sheppard in '87. Those two months of waiting felt like an eternity, but it was worth it. His diagnosis was the same as all the others but he offered me a solution that others didn't. Surgery! He said surgery would increase my chances of becoming pregnant by 80%. Though, after adding in the cost of the anesthesia and hospital stay, the procedure itself would run me close to $5000.00! There was no way in the world I could foot such a bill, but before I allowed despair to set in the doctor gave me even more good news. *"You won't have to pay the whole thing up front, Marie. The hospital only requires a minimum of 10% down, the rest can be billed to you."*

I couldn't believe my ears. After years of testing and disappointments, my dreams were finally going to come true! With no hesitation, I asked Dr. Gindhardt to schedule my surgery as soon as possible. I didn't even wait to speak to Pharaoh or any of my family because my mind was firmly made up. It wasn't until I got home later that evening that I told Pharaoh my good news, and at first, he wasn't so sure I should go through with it. He didn't trust modern medicine and the idea of surgery freaked him out. He thought I was making an emotional decision; okay duh, becoming a mother is an emotional experience! I told him despite the risk, I was willing to take the chance, because a life without children, in my eyes, wasn't much of a life at all.

Pharaoh was truly a blessing to me during this time, and provided the 10% down payment needed to have the procedure done. Prior to my scheduled surgery date, the two of us took some time off from our normal routines and did some horseback riding at a quiet ranch somewhere out in PA. The time off was truly therapeutic, but once we returned, the drama began all over again.

My surgery was scheduled for the end of February, which gave me a few weeks to prepare. Yet, instead of concentrating on the operation I had to deal with gossip circulating about Pharaoh and my old ally Amber! Yes Amber! As rumor had it, the two of them had been seeing one another and Amber had begun to claim him as her own. Excuse me! Now I knew Pharaoh was a dog, but only snakes can get that low! Then I though about it and realized there may have been some truth to the buzz. The two had become mighty close over the years. Too close if you ask me. Though, I thought it was on the strength of me, her brother Ameer', and their cousin Pook. Never in my wildest dreams did I think he was actually attracted to the girl. If anything, I felt he looked at her as a little sister. Then I did a play back in my mind of some scenes and situations and a lump formed in my throat. *"That son of a bitch! How could he?"*

How could he fuck my girl? How could she fuck my man? I let this bitch drive my car, wear my clothes, spend the night at my crib, I treated this bitch like family. I broke bread with her, treated her like a sister, and had her back whenever trouble came her way. I thought her little goody-goody ass was my friend but as it turned out, she was just using me in order to get close to him. Now it made sense as to how Pharaoh found out so much about Kareem and me. It was through her! She was the leak and she was the only one close enough to the situation to know so many details. Since way back, he had been manipulating her and picking her little brain, and her dumb ass was stupid enough to let him do so. This is why the two of us drifted apart after Kareem and I stopped seeing one another. I thought she felt some kind of way because me and her cousin had broken up but that wasn't the case at all. She didn't care about me or him one way or the other. She didn't care about the friendship or our privacy. All she cared about was getting her claws into Pharaoh. The heifer had been *dick-matized*!

How could I have been so blind and naïve? Amber was Kareem and Pook's first cousin, and Pook was like a brother to me and Pharaoh. Based on that alone, she should have known not to cross that line but above that, she was supposed to have been my friend, I trusted her! Pharaoh, on the other hand, should have known I was going to find out about the two of them sooner or later but as usual, his ego blinded him into believing he had everything under control. How could they stoop so low? No wonder Kareem was so callous towards me. He must have thought I knew!

155

This was definitely one for the books. No, I was no angel but regardless of who I crept with, I never fucked any one in Pharaoh's camp, any of his boys or any of his family. Even if they wanted to do me and could care less about him, I still gave him that respect and never crossed the line. No wonder he was so enthused about taking me to that ranch. That fucker knew he had screwed me over big time. I questioned Pharaoh about his dealings with Amber and he confessed that she liked him but the attraction wasn't mutual. He said he kept trying to tell Amber nothing would ever come of the two of them, but he wasn't able to convince me that he'd never slept with her. I knew Amber all too well to fall for that one and I knew Pharaoh even better. I had a choice to make. Allow their dealings with one another to ruin my chances of happiness, or go ahead and proceed with the surgery as planned. I kept thinking to myself what in the world did he see in her, but at the same time I thought the same about Samantha. I will admit, the thought of him being with her turned my stomach, but at least I hoped he was smart enough and considerate enough to strap up!

****

On the morning of my surgery I arrived at Helene Fuld Hospital accompanied by my mother, grandmother, and Pharaoh. My soon to be *baby's daddy* stopped at the billing desk prior to my check in and paid the $500 down payment as promised. The three of us were then directed to my room, where we were met by the floor nurse, and the nurse who was going to prep me for the procedure. By 7:00 a.m., I was being rolled down to the operating room and when I last noticed the time it was 7:20. The anesthesia then started my drip and before it took affect the good doctor said to me, *"Okay, Marie, this procedure will only be good for about one year so once you heal, get busy making your baby."* Damn, there goes that peculiar sense of humor again, but this time with a touch of pressure. A year wasn't a whole lot of time considering all the trouble I'd had in the past. I hoped that would be enough time, were my thoughts as I drifted off into a deep sleep.

After the surgery, I woke up in my own private room in undescribable pain. A nurse was checking my scar, and I was moaning for someone to come and help me. Then my doctor walked in and said the surgery went well. I tried to feel my cut, which went from one side of my stomach to the other, but it was covered up with gauze and bandage. Dr.

156

Gindhardt then wrote me a prescription and instructed me to begin taking it after my next cycle, which hopefully would be in March. He gave me a six month supply plus one refill of a fertility drug, *Clomid,* and my dosage was three pills a day each month for ten days. He said the pill would assist me in conception, but to beware that most people who used it wound up having twins, triplets, and even quads!

Twins would be nice I thought to myself while trying to stay attentive. Though I knew darn well I didn't want to have any more than two at a time. Dr. Gindhardt then bid me farewell and went on his way. Our dealings with one another were now complete. From here on out, I would go back to seeing my regular gynecologist and the only time I'd have to see him again is if complications were to occur due to the surgery. Once he left, my Nana and mom came into see me and Nana said I looked like pig that had been gutted open. I guess she was trying to be funny, but at that moment, the last thing I wanted to do was laugh. Every move I made hurt, even movement from my toes and fingers hurt my belly. I sure as hell hoped this worked because I was in too much pain for it not to.

It took two months for me to heal, a month for me to walk upwards, and by the time I returned to work I was still quite sore. Due to my limited mobility my baby sister, Gayle, moved in with me and she was truly a God send. Had it not been for her, I would have surly injured myself trying to do more than I was capable of. Pharaoh wasn't much good at caring for me while I was on bed rest, but he did make sure I had every necessity and plenty of money as usual. Dr. Gindhardt had his craft down to a science and I am pleased to say it only took six months after my surgery for me to become pregnant. I hadn't missed my cycle, but because I was on medication, I was on the schedule to come in and have blood work done each month. Over the past six months I'd had my hopes lifted time and time again by false readings and high HCG levels, and when the results came back negative, I became pretty depressed.

In October of '92, I went in for my appointment, had my blood drawn, then as usual, waited until after 3:00 p.m. to call for the results. When I arrived home around 3:30, Pharaoh was in the house mixing on his turn-tables so in order to have some quiet and privacy, I took the phone with me into the bathroom while I made my call. The receptionist put me on hold after I gave my name and when she returned to the line she said *"Ms. Cook, your results are positive."* I almost dropped the phone when I heard her comment and then I began to whisper to her as if it were all a big secret. *"Are you sure?"* I asked, still very much in shock, but at the same time very excited. *"You are, Marie, DOB 3-29-70 correct?"* *"Yes,"* I replied in an enthusiastic voice. *"Then yes, Ms. Cook, I'm sure, your results are positive, you are pregnant."*

****

There is no word in the English language that can describe what I felt at that very moment. Excited and speechless would be an understatement. Without saying a word, Pharaoh could see happy written all over my face, but he didn't bother to ask what it was about. Instead, he waited for me to say something to him which I didn't. I chose to hold on to my good news and share it first with the person I loved the most. My Nana! Then after telling her, I called my good friend Laurie, who up until a month ago, was also experiencing a hard time conceiving. Laurie was a white girl but she had a mouth, ass, and the attitude of a sista. She damn near burst my ear drum screaming through the phone in response to my news. The two of us shared each other's desire for motherhood and were excited beyond control that we both had little *Buns N the Oven.* Once I was off the phone with Laurie, I made a bee-line to my mother's to share the news with her and my little sister, but tears of joy overpowered my announcement. My mom was beyond thrilled to know she was finally going to be a *Nana,* and my little sister was jumping for joy because she was now going to be a *Ti-Ti* [Aunt].

One may wonder why Pharaoh wasn't the first I chose to tell considering he was the father and right there when I got the news, but the answer to that is quite simple. This would be his third child, and frankly, I didn't feel he would be as excited as I was. I wanted to first share my news with those I knew would share in my passion before having to confront him and deal with his reaction. So after running all around town I finally went back home and told him the news. The shocked look in his face said it all, but after a few minutes and a brief moment of silence, he gave me a big hug and expressed his happiness. In all honestly, that was all I wanted, and was so thankful he hadn't grown to regret our mutual decision. I truly believed our child was created out of love and that alone was Pharaoh's greatest contribution to our relationship. From that point on, I would be ever grateful to him for the seed of life he planted inside of me. *My Everything...*

****

My first prenatal appointment was on October 16, 1992. I remember it well because it marked the 6th anniversary of my grandfather's passing. Because back then I was so superstitious, I felt the date held significant value concerning my pregnancy, that my child's birth would be blessed and that the sex would be a boy. I didn't have a lot of morning sickness, but in the afternoon and evening, that baby gave me hell. On top of that, my sense of smell was heightened more then I could stand, and I despised the stench of cooked meat and my sister's perfumes. My siblings, Yvonne, Darla, Kathy, and Nette were sympathetic to my condition, so instead of fighting with me, they just ran and hid every time I came around to avoid hearing me say, *"Ilk that shit stinks!"*

Because I'd had such a difficult time conceiving, my doctor regarded me *as high risk* and took extra precautions throughout my entire term. He was concerned with the 80lbs I'd gained by my ninth month and figured I had gestational diabetes. He advised me to slow down with the starches and sugars, and to try and drink more water, and if possible, eat less meat. I tried to follow his advice but was under the impression that the baby ate just as much as I did and I didn't want to let him go hungry... You can call it foolish or greedy, but I ate everything in sight!

While carrying my child I did everything I thought a mother should do to ensure the relationship between the two of us started off on the right foot. I sang to him, read books to him, talked to him, and placed head phones on my belly so he could hear the sweet sounds of music. Nana warned me to be cautious of my actions during my pregnancy because everything I did and endured affected the baby. She wasn't so much concerned with my behavior, but was very concerned with Pharaoh's and how he acted towards me. She knew how disturbed I was when in my 4th month, I saw Samantha in town looking as if she too was with child! Of course I questioned Pharaoh about my sighting, but as usual, he denied the claim, and because I wasn't ready to have my perfect world shattered, I ignored my very own eyes. I tried extra hard to ignore all of the bullshit between the two of us purely for the baby's sake and was extremely cautious about how I carried myself. I worked extra hard to maintain the ideal image of one who was in a loving relationship because my desire to have a family was the only thing that mattered. *I guess that's what the book of Genesis meant at verse 3:16; Conception, sorrow, and desire... A subject that has many interpretations and often misunderstood...*

My efforts to nurture my child were relentless and I was inquisitive over every test, every ultra sound, and kept a journal of his movements and his sleeping patterns alike. Normally, one would only get one ultra sound which was to help determine how far you were. Though in my situation, I had one at twelve weeks, one in my fifth month and another in my eighth because they though I was carrying twins. When it came down to the advice of others, I was extremely critical about their input and only took heed to the wisdom of my doctor and Nana. I even managed to piss people off concerning my shower because there were certain items I wanted to get on my own without the contribution of others. Some charged my pickiness to my condition but that had nothing to do with it. This was my first child, my first shower, and I was going to be the boss of my own show. Yet, despite my lack of diplomacy, my shower turned out to be the ultimate experience and I received all of the major things a new mother and child would need. I damn near had two of everything, including the items I forbid people to get. The generosity of those who pampered me during my nine months made me realized how loved and respected I really was. My best friend, Esha, who was one of the prettiest girls I knew, with skin so flawless, simple lip-gloss would cause her to stand out in a crowded room, was the coordinator of my shower and managed to have my mother and Nana attend which was a very pleasant surprise.

The clock was now beginning to wind down and I only had eight more weeks to go before my reason for living would arrive. Throughout my experience I use to always tell my doctor I knew the exact day I conceived. Yet, gidgets and gadgets made him doubt my calculations and he said that pinpointing the exact date was nearly impossible unless you were a virgin. (Yeah, just like they said having a kid would be impossible, too!) My first ultra sound gave me a due date of May 28th and my second gave me one for the 19th. I was cool with the 19th since that was Malcolm X's born day, but my calculations said the 22nd, which was a day after my mother's born day. The 22nd was the date I was looking forward to delivering on, but on May 19th at 10:00 a.m. I woke up in what I though was a puddle of my own urine. This came as an absolute shock to me considering I never had a weak bladder or any little accidents during the middle of the night. I had dreams that I was using the bathroom, but always managed to wake up before anything trickled out. However on this occasion, my entire bed was soaked and so were my pajamas. I also noticed that the flow was constant and didn't stop, which scared me. So as usual, I picked up the phone to call Nana while making my way to the bathroom.

When Nana answered the phone, I told her I was scared; I was in the bathroom and I couldn't stop peeing! I was hysterical and frightened being I was home alone, and my first thought was that there was something wrong with the baby. My night before had been a restless one, with me tossing and turning the entire night. I was groggy and cranky, and not as refreshed as I normally would have been. I was damn near in tears while seeking my grandmother's wisdom, however, she was as calm and cool as a cucumber. I could hear her chuckle in between my blabbering, but finally she managed to stop long enough to tell me my water had broken and I needed to get to the hospital! This had to have been a *Déjà-vu* for her as well, since twenty three years ago she went through a similar experience with my mother as she was about to give birth to me. *"But what if the baby comes before I get to the hospital?"* Again, she tried to contain her laughter but I was so comical, all she could do was laugh.

I thought the fact of my water breaking on its own was a good thing. Over the past month, doctors had made three different attempts to induce my labor but all three times they failed. On May 13th I had two clamps inserted into my cervix with the hopes they would encourage dilation. After two days of discomfort and pain, they removed them for fearing I'd catch an infection. Then, on the 16th and 17th, they administered a gel to me that they claimed would definitely work after being inserted into the cervix three times a day, three hours apart, but that failed too.

161

With a wide leg walk, I wobbled back to my room, called my beloved, and told him, "*it's time!*" Just like Nana, he was able to keep his composure while assuring me he'd be out front to pick me up within five minutes. My bags were packed and my papers were in order, but I didn't want to leave me house in such a mess. I also didn't want to go to the hospital without cleaning myself up but didn't think I had time to do either or. So, I wrapped a towel around my bottom and stood out on the porch. I would have sat but it would have been hell trying to get back up. I felt a bit *crampy*, as if I was about to have my period, very anxious, and uncertain of the unknown. My patience grew thin as the five minutes turned into fifteen, and just as I was about to call Pharaoh for the second time, his brother Sunny pulled up, honking the horn, yelling let's go! I was reluctant to get into the truck. This was not a job for a brother, this was the responsibility of my man. I didn't need a ride to the grocery store or around the corner to be dropped off, I was about to have his child. How come he wasn't there to escort me and where the fuck was he at anyway?

My anxiety had now reached its peek, but at the same time I needed to get to the hospital. Sunny was a sweetheart and he could tell I was feeling some kind of way, rejected even. So out of compassion, he rubbed my belly as the tears fell from my eyes and told me Pharaoh would make it to the hospital as soon as he could. I knew he was doing his best to comfort me while at the same time trying to cover for his brothers neglect, but his efforts were in vain, and nothing he said or did made me feel any better.

Once we arrived at the hospital, as feared, Pharaoh was no where to be found. The only familiar face I saw was Ms. Jessie, Amber's mother, as I entered the room to be monitored and prepped. She and Amber were in the close-in directly across from me, and I could hear Amber's moans and groans of discomfort. Oh did I forget to mention, my home girl Amber was pregnant too, and from what I'd been told, my brother, Wayne, was the father. Made not a damn bit of difference to me though because she and I had stopped speaking a long time ago. I found out about her pregnancy when we ran into each other one day going into the hospital. I was there for some tests and she was walking out with her mother and younger sibling. Her family cheerfully spoke to me but Amber acted as if my presence offended her. I thought she looked cute with that little belly sticking out in front of her, especially compared to my big ass huffin' and puffin' in the hot heat. Then, she rolled her eyes at me and I was like damn! What was that all about? How ironic was it for the two of us to wind up in the same hospital, at the same time was too much of a coincidence.

From what I could gather, it sounded as if Amber was going into labor herself. Her mom kept coaching her to calm down and breathe, and it kinda made me wonder was she going to be alright. My concern for her and her child grew, but for the life of me I couldn't figure out why. Then, a nurse came in and hooked me up to an IV, strapped a monitor to my stomach, and said she'd be back.

As I lay in the bed, my cramps became stronger and the monitor was going crazy every four to five minutes. I tried to zone out and not go into a panic, and I tried calling Pharaoh but he wasn't picking up his phone. Then out of nowhere, Amber began talking aloud saying, *"I'm going to have my baby before she does!"* I could hear her mom telling her to hush and be quiet, but that shit didn't bother me. *"Okay, you're going to have your baby first, fine, knock ya self out,"* were my sentiments. You nor your baby, have shit to do with me and mine, so what's your point? Then, the nurse returned with my family and Pharaoh and they all escorted me up to my room. It was now 12:00 p.m., and the most I felt were cramps. I figured the labor pains would kick in sooner or later and estimated the whole thing to be over by 5:00 p.m. If not by 5:00 p.m., then surely by 8:00 p.m. that evening.

Three hours later I was still sitting feeling nothing more than some damn cramps! Staff feared if I kept leaking I'd have what they call *a dry birth;* so as prevention, they started me on a Pit/IV to help induce my labor. Two hours later, everyone except Pharaoh had to leave. The medicine had begun to take its effect and initially I refused any pain medication. Though by 12:00 a.m., I'd had all that I could take and was threatening the nurses to give me something for the pain or else!

What was taking so long? I'd begun to panic. The nurse assured me everything was okay and that long labors were very common. But it had been over twelve hours since my water broke and my baby wasn't anywhere close to being born. Pharaoh stayed with me through the night but snored more than anything. By the next morning I was drained and had experienced pain I only believe was depicted in horror movies! My family was worried and Pharaoh couldn't sit still. My mom tried talking to me but all I could do was curse. Nana sat in the corner praying harder than I'd ever witnessed her praying before. I believe she was crying harder than I was, which really freaked me out. Her actions let me know something wasn't right. On day three of my ordeal, a resident doctor came in and asked me what were my wishes in the event me or the baby needed blood. That right here just freaked me out, but my dad took the stand and told him we didn't do transfusions. (He's Jehovah's Witness and as for me, I just don't believe in taking someone else's blood or organs unless it's coming from a family member. What if they had something wrong with them that wasn't detected? Now I'd have it. I know they were only being pro-active, but no thanks!)

Before my dad left, he left me with these words. *"My Grandson better be here when I get back, Murf..."* That was his way of showing his concern and well wishes at the same time.

Nurses kept coming in to check my vitals and I kept screaming for them to *"get it out!"* Those pains were hitting me like a demolition crew, without any breaks or comfort in-between. Pharaoh returned to be with me day after day, but by the end of day three even he feared the worst. My family stayed by my side until visiting hours were over, and besides them, my only other visitors were Ms. Jessie and her youngest son. I though it weird for them to go out of their way to check up on me, but as it turned out, Amber's room was right next to mine to the left. Amber had given birth to her daughter on May 21st a little before midnight, so I guess she got her wish. She had her baby before I had mine. By 12:00 p.m. that evening, I was in so much pain my body went numb. The flowers on the wall now looked like weeds and the numbers on the clock had begun to disappear. I was delirious...

Wednesday had turned into Thursday and Thursday had rolled over into Friday. Friday had now faded away and I felt I had faded away with it. It was now Saturday the 22nd and I knew for sure I couldn't endure another day. A Hispanic custodian came in to clean my room and was thrown back when he saw me butt naked and sprawled across the floor. *"Mami, Mami, get up,"* but I didn't bother. I was afraid, weak, tired, and didn't care how I looked or who saw me. I'd been walked up and down the halls, placed in a whirlpool, and my baby still wouldn't budge. Labor wasn't my issue, it was dilation. They baby couldn't come out if I didn't dilate, therefore, there was nothing left for anyone to do except call my doctor.

When Dr. Kaji arrived it was nearly 2:00 p.m. in the afternoon and he was mortified to see I was still with child. Immediately he asked how long I'd been in labor, and after viewing my chart and seeing I was admitted on Wednesday, he told the nurse to prep me for an emergency c-section. My birthing canal was now dry and after four days of labor, I wouldn't have the strength to push even if I'd made ten centimeters.

On our way to the operating room, Dr. Kaji tried explaining to me what the procedure would be like, and that I wouldn't have to go through it alone because my *husband* could be in the room with me. Pharaoh was far from a husband, but I believe all doctors used that term out of simple respect. However, by the time I was ready for surgery our plans had changed. Blood test showed something abnormal with my blood. Under normal circumstances a doctor would put off surgery until things got better, but in my case we didn't have that much time. They needed that baby out! So instead of the usual method, Dr. Kaji opted to put me to sleep. Although this was a lot more dangerous than giving me an epidural or a spinal, it would assure the baby's birth and elevate the stress to his system.

Without delay, I had at least three people frantically working on me administering anesthesia, and Pharaoh had to leave the room and wait outside with the rest of my family. A tube was then inserted in my throat to prevent me from choking since I had recently eaten, and the next thing I knew I was counting backwards, 10, 9, 8… Seven was the last number I remember.

****

In recovery, blood was the first sight I saw and it must have shocked me so much that I went back out. A nurse came over to change my garments, then announced that I had just given birth to a healthy and very handsome 8lb 12 oz baby boy! Her words were like sweet music to my ears, so much that I didn't even recognize the pain I was in. After 86 hours and 23 minutes of long, hard labor and anguish and agony, my blessing had finally arrived. I was exhausted with a slight fever and chills, yet all I wanted to know was *"Where's my son! Let me see my son, please bring him to me!"*

Off in the background, I could hear people talking about my long labor and the experiments used to induce it. I couldn't make out everything they were saying, but I was later told by the head obstetrician that one of the physicians in charge of me would be investigated and questioned about his procedures. (He was later relieved of his duties.)

After I was changed, on orderly began to take me to my private room but we were held up in the up in the corridor by my family and Pharaoh, all who were anxiously waiting to see me to make sure I was alright. It was a joyful moment as they couldn't' stop bragging to me about how beautiful my baby was, and Pharaoh had a smile on his face as wide as a four lane highway! For him, that was quite unusual.

I was kinda fussed that they got to see my baby before I did and Nana and her crazy ass couldn't stop talking about how big his balls were. Nana! (My baby was born with milk in his testicles. It was nothing for us to be concerned about, just a strange site to see.)

Regardless of the excitement, the pain was more than I could ignore. Now that I was settled in my room, I wondered why it was taking them so long to bring my baby to me. Then, before I could say a word, in walked the nurse with the most beautiful sight I'd ever laid eyes on. My son Quan! His name wasn't Quan at the time, and he actually remained nameless until the day we left the hospital. Not that I didn't have a few names picked out already, but I'd been silly enough in the past to give them all to Pharaoh to name his other children. *(Dave' Tyqueese and Davon) So* we settled on calling our little soldier *Baby* or *Dough Boy* until we agreed on Day'Quan Jabree.

As I sat there gazing at him in awe, I was amazed at how tiny he was, yet it felt like I was holding the entire world in the palm of my hands, and in a sense, I was. This new life that I'd been blessed with had now become my entire world in a matter of seconds and because of him, my life would change for the better. Then, suddenly without warning, paranoia kicked in and because of his fair complexion, I questioned if he was really mine. I hadn't seen him when he was born, and prior to him I'd never seen a new born baby period. Why was he so white and so pale, and why was his hair so straight? I can't describe the feeling but my emotions abruptly caused me to blurt out, *"This ain't my baby, this a white baby!"*

As crazy as it may sound, for a minute, I actually though someone had switched babies on me. Everyone in the room stopped talking and looked at me as if I was crazy and Nana and her crazy ass just burst out laughing. *"Marie,"* she said, *"what makes you say that?"* On that note, Pharaoh exited the room and the nurse responded, *"Ms. Cook, this is your baby."* But why is he so white? *"It takes a while for newborns to get their color, Ms. Cook, but rest assured the child you're holding is the one you gave birth to."* Are you sure, I asked. *"Yes, Ms. Cook, I'm sure, and besides, you're the only African American mother on the floor."*

Quan must have sensed my anxiety or maybe it was just my big mouth that woke him up, but before I had the chance to speak another word, he opened up those beautiful eyes of his and that right there removed all doubt. Now that I could see all of his features, I felt ashamed that I'd even questioned in the first place. *"Oh My God, this is my baby."* I then drew him close to my chest and kissed him gently. Wow, I was truly amazed! God sure does answer prayers. That boy was an exact duplicate of his daddy (who had now returned to the room) with a smile that could melt arctic ice, just like his Mama. I'd gotten what I'd wished for, now the question was, could I handle it?

Pharaoh was the only one allowed to stay in the room with me and the baby after visiting hours. The rest of my visitors had to leave at 8:00 p.m. With daddy on my right and baby laying down with me on my left, I felt complete. Every few hours a nurse came in to check on me and the baby, then get on me for sleeping with him in the bed. *"You can accidentally roll over and smother him, Ms. Cook!"* I heard this a few times during the beginning of my stay, but once they saw I was going to sleep with him anyway, they decided to leave the two of us alone. I understood their concern, but there was no way I was going to roll over or accidentally do anything to harm my pride n' joy.

On and off throughout our stay, I was congratulated by many visitors and callers. Amber and her family dropped by my room frequently and Pharaoh stuck his head in to see her and her newborn as well. Had this been the old me, I would have had a fit knowing he was being so friendly with this broad. Though after the experience I'd just had, I was more then willing to let the past, stay in the past.

Our first night with our son was carefree and pleasant. But on the second night, his dad and I noticed something strange about him. His eyes were green (and I don't mean hazel either) and his skin was an odd looking yellow. This was noticeable the first night but neither one of us said anything about it. When the nurse returned, we brought it to his attention. *"This is also common in newborns he said, but to put you at ease, we'll order some blood work to rule out certain illnesses."*

Being this was a brand new experience for me, it hurt me to my heart to see someone stick my baby as he screamed aloud. I tried to hold back my emotions but hearing him yell and straining his tiny little lungs was too much. When I could take no more I leaped from my bed, causing pain in my abdomen, reached for the technician's arm, and told him to stop! Pharaoh blocked my attempt to stop him, but by then the blood had been drawn. The technician apologized for causing my baby to be uncomfortable, but was completely gentle with him nonetheless. I picked my son up and held him close in order to quiet him down. After that, I guess Pharaoh had taken all that he could stand, so once the two of us were back in bed, he left and went home. An hour later a Dr. came in and told me my son's blood work tested positive for Jaundice. He then said he'd have to be placed in a special care unit immediately and monitored 24/7! I was too through…

I am the first one to tell someone not to let their emotions override their intelligence, yet, I do it all the time. After all that I'd gone through, for anyone to tell me the care my son needed would be more than I could give was un-comprehendible.*" What the hell was Jaundice?"* As the doctor explained my child condition to me and what needed to be done, a nurse was rolling him down the hall. *"Jaundice is normal, but his levels are so high, we need to get them down before he can go home."*

"So what are you saying, doc? That my baby can't come home with me?" Again, I was too through…

For ten days I sat by my son's side while he lay in an incubator, baking under an infrared light. I changed his diapers, I changed his monitors, and held his tiny little hand through the hole provided, praying for him to get better. The thought of being separated from my son for any length of time made me think about my mom and how she must have felt being separated from me. After a few days, I was even allowed to take him out and hold him, but no longer than an hour. Aside from that, the only other time he was allowed from under the light was for feedings. At only four days old, my son and I had been through ordeals that would bond us forever. Normally, an hour or a feeding would have little meaning to me, but under the circumstances, an hour was like a little piece of heaven. Daily I looked forward to hear the news that my son was well enough to come home, but in-spite of his progress, it was never good enough.

Knowing how stressed I'd become, both my family and Pharaoh tried persuading me to just come home and let the doctors do their job. They said visiting the baby might be less stressful than staying at the hospital with him waiting for things to get better. I told all of them, *"If I leave this hospital without my son, it would be over my dead body! If my son doesn't come home, then neither do I!"* What type of good did anyone think I'd be at home, knowing all I could think about was my child? I use to get so pissed at the suggestion, I'd tell everyone to leave! I already had fears that they'd soon come to me and tell me I'd have to leave without him, so why were they compounding things?

On or about the 5th or 6th day of our stay, one of the nurses who had been assigned to take care of my son had a talk with me. At first she told me Jaundice was nothing to be alarmed by and that once his levels were down they'd surely release him. I told her I didn't care what happened, I wasn't going home without my son and I meant it! Taking notice to my depression and my sincerity, she took the liberty of explaining to me that my insurance would only pay for me to stay six days after the baby's birth. After that, if nothing was wrong with me, I'd have to go home, but the baby would remain because of his treatment. This was all I needed to hear and no sooner than she said that, I started to cry. For a short moment she sat there with me in silence but later shared another piece of information with me, and what she said afterwards actually cheered me up.

Although there was nothing really wrong with me. My stay could be extended if my blood-work showed I had an infection. So in order to fool the doctors all I had to do was have a fever when it was

169

time to check my vitals. A fever would give them reason to believe there was an infection and an infection was justification to keep me one more day. *"So how do I fake a fever,"* I asked? Vital are checked on schedule she said. So as soon as you know someone is coming down to check yours, just drink something hot like coffee or tea, and this will give you a high reading. I wasn't sure if her advice would work or not but I was willing to do anything in order to stay close to my child. Her tip, however, did pay off and due to the deception, Day'Quan and I spent his first ten days in the world, together in the hospital. But wouldn't you know it, later on a monkey wrench was thrown my way, one that would threaten my security and send me back into a frenzy...

Although Day'Quan's condition was improving, doctors said if he didn't show significant signs by his next reading, they were going to move him to a different unit. In this unit, nobody, not even the mother, could stay past the normal visiting hours of 8:00p.m., and nobody could spend the night. I was so distraught I rushed to my room and called my grandmother. I cried to her and told her what the doctors had told me and how I didn't want to leave my son. She prayed for me and the baby, but told me to remember that God knows best. Nana knew the faith of a mustard seed could move a mountain but at the time, my faith wasn't as strong. By his next reading, Day'Quan's bilirubin level dropped four points, but needed to drop four more before they could let him leave. They would release him if it reached ten, and the last time they checked it was at fourteen. Still kind of high...

Because of his progress, Day'Quan was now able to sit with me in our room when it was time for his feedings and such. I was so afraid that this would be my last time holding him before they shipped me out I didn't know what to do. After feeding my baby, I held him close to my bosom and the two of us drifted off to sleep. Well, he was sleep and I was laying there resting, trying not to worry. The light from the window was shining so bright, it illuminated his face. As I looked down at him I saw him smiling as if the angles were talking to him, (remember how the elders use to tell us the angels talked to the babies) and before I could compose my prayer, I looked up and saw a vision of my grandfather smiling back in return. Call me crazy, call it divination, or hocus pocus, but I saw an image of him just as clear as you see the words on this page. I wasn't sure if I was having a spiritual encounter or what, but it was definitely real. The energy in the room was different than before, as if someone had opened a window or something. My fears seemed to no longer exist and time seemed to stand still. It was an awesome feeling and I can't even say for sure how long it lasted. Once the image faded back into the bright sunlight, I looked down at my child and his smile was still there.

For the past seven years I'd missed my grandfather so much, I wasn't able to accept his death or let him go. More than a little I'd visit his grave site, sit down on his tombstone, cry, and ask why he left me before I had the chance to say good-bye. I use to beat myself up for not making it to the hospital in time and I couldn't forgive myself for the days I'd missed going to see him. Immediately, I picked up the phone and called Nana, who wasn't at all surprised to hear from me since I'd been calling her nearly every two hours every since the baby was born. *"Nana, guess what just happened?"* I went on to explain my experience to her and as always, she tried to provide me with a logical explanation. *"Well, Ree,"* I loved it when she called me Ree'. *"Maybe God allowed your grandfather to show himself to you when you needed him the most. Maybe that was his way of assuring you that Pop-Pop was okay and that Day'Quan was going to be okay, too!"* Being he was the first male child born on our side of the family besides my uncle, her theory made perfect sense. Then, right before the two of us hung up, the doctor returned to my room. *"Ms. Cook,"* he said in an elated voice. *"Your son's test results show his bilirubin level has only dropped 3 points,* (my heart dropped as he examined my baby boy, checking his eyes and tongue) *but we feel his progress will continue and therefore we're releasing the both of you from the hospital today!"*

I don't know what I did to deserve such blessings, but in a week's time my cup was truly running over. I was so excited my child and I could go home together I felt like I would faint! Nana was still on the line when the doctor told me the news and yelled out, *"Thank you Lord!"* I then hung up the line and immediately began packing our things. While sitting on the bed waiting for my ride, a nurse came in with papers for me to sign for the baby's birth certificate. I had gotten so overwhelmed with his condition, I forgot we never officially gave him a name. I called Pharaoh and asked him what did he think about naming our son Day'Quan Jabree'? (I was totally unaware Pharaoh also had a brother who's first name was Jabree' also.) Pharaoh agreed, although he wasn't there to sign the certificate. I was fine with that because had he been there, he may have wanted to give him his last name which would have caused a problem. Nana felt since Pharaoh and I weren't married, my son should carry my last name, which technically was the only way to keep my keep my grandfather's name alive for future generations. For my first born to bear his great granddad's last name was an honor and a privilege. *Thank you, Pop-Pop, Thank you so much!*

****

Motherhood was all that I'd expected and then some. My tiny one bed room apartment had everything we both needed. We had a crib and a bassinette for our son, but the three of us usually slept together because I was too spoiled to let him sleep alone. I needed to feel him next to me while he slept and I wanted to be able to respond to any of his needs in a moment's notice. For a short while, he suffered with colic which caused him to cry a lot. However, that was easily cured, believe it or not, by taking him out for a ride in the car or turning on the blow dryer until he fell asleep. True story!

My brother, Chino, (My Godbrother) became Quans' Godfather and my cousin, Shantell, became his Godmother. Although the two of them didn't have any kids of their own, I couldn't think of anyone I trusted more to take care of my son in the event something happened to me. The prefix on his name *Day* which comes from *David* has a translation which means "*Beloved,*" (Hmm, so does Marie) and the root *Quan* has a translation meaning, "*Warrior of God and Protector of the Children.*" Every since his birth, I have been amazed by his strength, courage, random acts of kindness, and utter understanding for the feelings of others. My son is now fifteen years old, and the time has gone by so fast. Because of the excess emotional baggage I've unknowingly carried over the years, I will admit I've at times allowed my feelings towards his father dictate our relationship, but I thank God those bad memories have been replaced with pleasant ones for both of us. In some of my darkest moments, my son has proven to be the one true friend who has never turned his back on me and if I could give back to him all that he has given to me, it still wouldn't be enough. He is without a doubt *My Everything!*

MY SON

You are my son
My only son
And I love you oh so much
Nothing can calm or comfort me more
Then your soft and gentle touch
When all the others come and go
You stick around to let me know
You care even when they don't
You are my son without a doubt
You lift my spirits when I'm down and out
And as you grow I know you will be
Not only my son but a friend to me

Dedicated to My Son Day'Quan Jabree' Craig Cook'

I would try to say something nice, inspirational, or catchy but fuck that! Keep your friends close and your enemies even closer, and never expect anything except the unexpected!

THE BULLSHIT

The conception of a life is sacred, and if the chemistry is right, creating one can be just as special. But don't be fooled, a baby won't wash away all of your problems or fix everything that has been wrong. It may bring the two of you closer, but then again in life, there are no guarantees.

May 22, 1993 by far was the happiest day of my life. Though thirteen days later I was hit with a revelation so devastating, it literally knocked me to my knees. On June 4th, two weeks after my son was born, I took him into town to have pictures taken. As luck would have it, as soon as we approached the strip, I was greeted by Ms. Jessie, Amber, and her newborn daughter, who were also in town to have baby pictures taken. I'd seen quite a bit of Ms. Jessie and Amber during my stay at the hospital, but this was my first time seeing Amber's daughter. Funny, I never though about it while I was there, but even Pharaoh had seen the little girl and here I was right in the next room and I hadn't?

Nevertheless, since I'd decided to let bygones be bygones, I greeted both of them with a friendly hello then asked could I see little Amber. (Although I'd heard the baby was my brother's, I didn't push nor ask who the father was.) Ms. Jessie jumped at the opportunity to hand me her granddaughter but the look on Amber's face didn't concur. In fact, she acted as if she didn't want me to see her at all. Then, with the two of them in my arms, I rocked them and complimented Amber on her baby's cuteness! *"What time was she born"* I asked? You know my mother's birthday is the 21st too, I said. *"Right before midnight,"* she replied, *"they're only a few hours apart."*

I continued to rock them and admire their good looks. Both of them had fair skin (as most newborns do) and beautiful hair. A few moments later, a friend of Ms. Jessie's approached, hugged the two of them and congratulated Ms. Jessie on being a grandmother. She then she looked at me holding the two kids and asked *"Amber, did you have twins?"* I guess since this woman didn't know me, she assumed both kids were Amber's. Instantaneously, Amber's face turned pale as her mother turned to the woman and replied. *"No, but they may as well be twins because they're brother and sister!"*

The proud smile I was displaying slowly began to dissolve as Ms. Jessie's words slowly sunk in. Did she just say they were brother and sister I asked myself? Then, I looked up at Amber but she turned away. Ms. Jessie looked at me, then went on to tell the woman that Amber and I were good friends, and our children were fathered by the same man. As if it was something to brag about! While taking in every vile word that came out of her mouth, my body went numb, my heart sunk into the pit of my stomach, and I fell to my knees, damn near dropping both babies. I don't know if they were aware I wasn't aware of this accusation or if they were intentionally trying to make me sick. Though what ever the case, they surely knocked me off my feet. I couldn't even bear to look at Amber, and when she tried to speak, her words fell on death ears. I wouldn't make a scene though. I had way too much pride.

After that I was done, I handed Ms. Jessie back her baby without taking another look at her and went on into the photo shop. Amber and her mom remained outside and I tried with all my might to hold back my tears. Now I knew why Pharaoh had seen the baby before me and why he'd been in and out of her room so much. He was probably there at the hospital with her when I got there. That's why she was talking so much trash when we were in the room together, and probably why he couldn't manage to come pick me up. But why would she put it out there that the baby was Wayne's? I was lost, confused, hurt, and feeling betrayed was an understatement. I was fussed, I was fucked up, and more then anything, I wanted to fuck someone up! I was so far off in a zone I didn't even hear the owner telling me to take a seat. By the time our session was done, my rage had grown but I continued to hold back my tears.

While our photos were being processed, the manager kept complimenting me on how beautiful my daughter was. *"He's a boy,"* I said, which only caused them to smile and compliment him even more. Then, I crossed paths with Amber and her family one last time as I was on my way out the door. They could see I was on the verge of tears, but that didn't stop them from stopping me and telling me how happy they were for me and that the baby looked just like his daddy. Oh I was so sick!

I couldn't get inside the house fast enough. I was itching to look that boy in the face and dare him to tell me another lie, but it seemed as if I'd just missed him. I laid my son down on the bed beside me, picked up the phone, and frantically dialed his number. He answered, but the sound of his voice made my heart stop. I avoided the immediate blow by asking him why didn't he stay, then went on to ask when would he be back.

"What's on your mind, girly," he asked, detecting a storm on the rise. At that point I said fuck it, ain't no need to beat around the bush. *"Pharaoh, I just saw Amber in town and she said her daughter is your daughter too!"* My voice was cracking as I struggled to form the words and Pharaoh just laughed. *"Murf,"* he said, *"you actually believe that bullshit? Girly, don't let that bullshit get you upset, that girl lying and she know it. I'm a talk to her about it, I don't even know why she approached you on no bullshit like that, for real."* He then went on to give me more detail as to how he was sure the baby wasn't his but that was neither here nor there. I'd reached my limit. Pharaoh never concerned himself with the consequences of his actions or who he hurt in the process. He had countless tools of manipulation, all which where highly effective. But, he fucked up when he failed to realize, *"Hell has no fury like a woman scorned."*

Pharaoh had done a lot of twisted shit to me in the past, but this was the straw that broke the camel's back! After all I'd gone through to have a child, his child no less, the thought of him fathering a child with Amber had me willing to commit a homicide. I couldn't believe she'd spent all that time in the hospital right next to me and I wasn't the wiser. As far as I was concerned, the two of them could have each other if it was all like that. The only person who mattered to me anymore was my son! Samantha was a nobody to me, a mere cushion for him to fall back on when all else failed. But I was his rock, and he'd fucked me over for a pebble. Once I'd completely healed and returned back to work. I did all I could to stay out of his way. Straight from work, I'd go pick the baby up from the sitter then go straight to my mom's house or around Spring to chill with Shantell and Moe. At night, I'd take my slow time going home and found myself spending more time at Klotz than usual. One night *(Thanks to Mr. Griffin)* I drank thirteen double shots of Courvoisier in a foolish attempt to wash away my thoughts. I believe I could have died that night had I not been forced to vomit a few times in an effort to sober up. Everybody knew about Amber's baby and everybody knew Pharaoh and I were still dealing with one another. This alone made me look like public dumb ass number one!

****

Pharaoh could have all the friends and associates in the world, but let me have just one and he had a fit. The guilt from his actions caused his paranoia to grow out of control and this lead to him ruining an alliance I'd created with someone I looked at like a sister. Mr. Hampton aka B*C had been a friend of mine every since my early childhood. Not only were we friends, we looked at one another as family and grew up looking at his biological father, Shelton as Uncle Shelton!

From what I'd learned from Nana and mommy, Uncle Shelton and Uncle Butch were as thick as thieves prior to his passing and Nana loved Shelton like a son. Teo', B*C's first born had been a part of my life every since he was born, and my love and concern for him was genuine, never accompanied by an ulterior motive. Deja was B*C's girl and Teo's mother. Deja trusted me. She trusted me as a friend and she trusted me with her son's life. I was her son's Godmother and my love and concern for him was genuine. But when rumors began to circulate about me and her man, of course she questioned me, wanting to know if Teo' was just a ploy to get closer to the man she loved. All I could to was deny any and all accusations pertaining to the negativity, but of course this put a strain on our relationship and hindered me from seeing Teo' all together.

Incidents like this made me reflect back to Nana's words on vanity and respect. Being pretty and well liked can be a gift and a curse. Deja, although just a pretty as me, had nothing to worry about when it came down to me and her man. I had enough on my hands with Pharaoh bugging out and reacting irrational. I didn't need her man with his quick temper and vain attitude adding to my troubles.

Pharaoh viewed everybody as a threat and for some unknown reason, B*C was at the top of the list. He accused me of sleeping with

178

B*C and claimed the only reason why I took to his son was because of him. That fool had lost his damn mind and I guess because him and Amber had been snakes in the grass, I had to be one, too. I couldn't defend myself against a lie, and if I couldn't get him to believe me, what more could I expect from Deja? I knew eventually the truth would come to the light, but until then, I had to literally roll with the punches.

Pharaoh's intuition led him in the right direction but had him barking up the wrong tree. My relations with other men didn't start until after I found out about Amber's baby. However, since I'd never been caught, I didn't see any reason to confess. My first affair was with my shawty, Baby Boy. I called him that because he was the oldest of two siblings, but his Mama treated him like her baby boy! He was the first individual I can say I actually cheated on Pharaoh with aside from Kareem, but it wasn't like I jumped at the opportunity to do so. It took a lot of persuasion on his behalf before I'd even give him my number, but once he broke the ice, I allowed him to lead the way.

BB [Baby Boy] was fly, [sharp] yet humble, and treated me with respect. He had chocolate skin, good curly hair, amazing chinky eyes and kissed like he invented the word. He never wanted to argue, he never wanted to fight; all he wanted to do was spoil me rotten and wrestle underneath the sheets. Throughout our time together we created some nice memories. We spent a Christmas together at his family's house in NY and took risk romping around in the back seat of his ride in the parking lot of his job. Everyday, regardless of our counterparts, we attempted to see each other and if that wasn't possible, we made sure we spoke to one another on the phone. Cutting him loose was difficult because of the feelings I'd developed, though I knew if Pharaoh found out he'd act a fool. Deep down inside I knew BB didn't deserve to be pulled into my mess and in essence, I sacrificed a good friendship for the one I felt obligated to be with. Shantell and Moe thought I was crazy for dismissing him the way I did. They didn't care for Pharaoh and hated the way he treated me, but at the same time, respected my decision to be with the father of my child.

After Amber, Pharaoh was never able to win my submission as easily as before, and others disregarded his self proclaimed authority as well. Tuck, another unethical delight on my romance menu, was someone I'd started dealing after I let Baby Boy go. Tuck had a deep chocolate complexion and what I like to call slits for eyes. He was lean and tall compared to me, and also felt Pharaoh was all steak and no sizzle. Our dealings took place out in plain sight, just like Pharaoh's dealings with Amber and Samantha, and he may have noticed us had he not been so busy trying to cover up his own dirt. Tuck and I had great sex together but just like Pharaoh, he had a dark side that I warned him to keep under control if he wanted the two of us to last. Over time, Tuck grew uneasy with our situation and claimed he wanted me all to himself. I couldn't blame him for not wanting to share, but at the same time he knew leaving Pharaoh wasn't an option.

Eventually, Tuck's selfishness caused him to act out of character and the two of us got into a fight right in the front of Shiloh Baptist Church. Apparently Tuck became jealous when he saw me at the bar *(Klotz)* socializing with friends, and when I refused to lend him some money, he decided to raise his hand at me. Wrong move dude, check mate, game over! After that night, he never gained the opportunity to apologize for his actions and I wasn't beat to hear any half ass explanations. I already had one hot-head on my hands, I didn't need two.

Although the flings with BB and Tuck were short lived, the two helped see me through some highly emotional times. Neither one could understand how Pharaoh could be so sadistic and uncaring towards a woman he claimed to love, and neither understood how the abused could stand to stay with the abuser. I guess I was a classic case of Stockholm Syndrome, but thank God my mom and little sister moved in over top of us or he would taken things too far and left me for dead.

Besides fear, our son was the number one reason for me staying with Pharaoh and keeping quiet. I didn't want to raise my child alone and regardless of how fucked up his father was, I felt he had the right to get to know him, I felt we had the right to become a family! However, all of that changed once Pharaoh was fingered as the gunman who shot another well known from our neighborhood, Mr. Griffin. Over the years, Pharaoh knew he could count on me for wisdom and advice that would get him out of almost any situation. He himself was no dummy, and one of the most clever men I've ever known. Though, no matter how smart either of us were, nothing short of a miracle could fix the mess he'd now gotten himself into, not even his gift of gab or pockets filled with cash.

I knew Pharaoh's temper would eventually land him in a heap of trouble, and because I still loved him, I allowed him to talk me into to testifying on his behalf when it came time for his trial. I told the courts Pharaoh couldn't have shot Mr. Griffin, because on the night in question he was at home with me and the baby. I knew my testimony wouldn't mean shit but Pharaoh swore up and down it was his get out of jail free ticket. The boy was smart, but at times, he was so smart he was dumb! Forcing me to vouch for him did his case more harm than good, and even his public defender knew I was telling a lie. The prosecutor in the case used me as a weapon against him, with hopes that my scorned emotions would place him behind bars.

Pharaoh wound up losing his case and even blamed me for the outcome of the guilty verdict. The judge gave him a date to come back for sentencing but until then, I was the sponge that had to absorb all of his frustration. Take for instance, the night he called me around onto Camden Street and smacked me around until my face and mouth were bloody. All because he couldn't have what he wanted when he wanted it. The countdown to his sentencing made life unbearable and because he felt he was loosing control over everything and everyone he placed ownership on, it pushed him over the edge. He may have been smart, but he was far from wise. He was quick to accuse but refused to listen to reason. He was constantly looking for something to be wrong instead of acknowledging what was good. There was so much going on behind the scenes that I didn't know about, so much that he wasn't willing to disclose. It was literally like sleeping with the enemy.

I don't know how he did it, but Pharaoh managed to get his sentencing date pushed back at least three times. Nearly a year after his trial he still remained a free man. By now, Amber and I had run into one another so much I couldn't stand the sight of her or her daughter. She use to send messages to me by way of my parents when ever she saw them in church, but I didn't want to hear anything she had to say. Then, one day I saw her standing at the corner with her youngest sibling and I approached her and asked *"What's the deal? If that's Pharaoh's baby, why not go get a DNA test to prove it."*

"I plan on doing so," she replied, *"but just like he denies my daughter to you, he denies your son to me as well, but I know he's telling a lie."*

Hun, I thought to myself. Wasn't that mighty kind of her to share that tidbit of info with me, as if it made her look any better. She even went on to tell me that he was blaming the baby on B*C! Oh, I see now. First I was screwing him and now he's the father of my child. Just like at first he was only screwing Amber, my closest friend, and now she's the mother of his child. I just laughed, because again, the way I saw it, both of them were crazy. Amber then went on to say that the only thing she wanted was for our children to know another and not be strangers. I thought it was mighty noble of her to say, but at the same time, I didn't see that happening. Until she could prove to me that her daughter was my son's sister, neither of us were going anywhere near her. I said that to her as I walked away and got back into my car, but I don't think she appreciated my tone.

Months passed and strangely, Pharaoh's actions reversed. Now he was coming in the house early, always eager to make love, and allowed me freedom like never before. I guess the thought of having to turn in somewhat changed his ways. He even had a going away party at the garage and sported me on his arm as if I was his prize winning trophy! His doing so not only shocked the hell out of me, but out of several others in attendance to bid him farewell. I should have known the sudden change was too good to be true. If it walks like a duck and sounds like a duck; you can bet your last dollar it ain't no mouse!

****

It was a Monday afternoon and I'd just gotten off work and was on my way around to the shop to see my man. He wasn't there at the moment, but his brother John said he had been looking for me; why he didn't know. It came as no surprise that he'd be anxious to see me considering he hadn't come home the night before and that was a definite no-no! I guess he was feeling some kind of way because I'd gone skating in Glassboro the night before, but when the two of us discussed it, he didn't show any signs of disapproval. He actually said it was okay… He knew who I'd be going with and he knew Solomon was my peeps and had been going skating for years. If he had any concerns he should have voiced them or maybe his silence was just to throw me off. Maybe he wanted me out of the way so he could creep around and play.

I drove around the area a few times, went up Donnelly Holmes and picked our son up from the sitter, and by the time I returned both of us were pulling up in front of the shop. Immediately I detected something was wrong by the troublesome glare in his eyes, and had I not known any better I would have sworn he was high. (Pharaoh got goofy off of one Budweiser so puffing trees was definitely out of the question. Besides, he hated drugs of any sort, even Ganja, which comes straight from the earth!)

That look, that all too familiar look, was one I'd seen far too many times in the past to forget. I'd seen that glare in Gilly's eyes and the one in Pharaoh's wasn't any different. A look like that only meant one thing. Somebody was about to get they ass beat, and ten to one said it was going to be me! As always, my first instinct was to put the pedal to the medal and speed off. I wanted to go anywhere but home, but knew it would only be worse once he finally caught me. Reason and logic had never saved me in the past, but faithfully I prayed that this time things would be different. When I pulled off Pharaoh wasn't even in his car and I don't know how he did it, but somehow, he managed to make it to the house before me and the baby. Once I got inside, he instructed me to send the baby upstairs to my mom. Again, the urge hit me to run but sadly, I was too afraid...

Reluctant yet cooperative, I complied with his request. I felt if I was going to have to go through it, our son didn't need to be in the middle of it. Then, no sooner as I shut the door and walked into the bathroom, he followed behind me and started in with his interrogation.

"Who'd you go skating with last night? What time did you get home?" The drill was all too familiar as well and because I was use to it, I gave him the explanation I though he was looking for, yet, he wasn't satisfied. Repeatedly I gave him the same answers, but over and over he told me I was leaving something out. We were at it so long, I started to wonder was I leaving something out? *"What am I not telling you?"* I asked.

"I don't know, you tell me," he shouted!

Because I knew no answer would satisfy him, I walked out of the bathroom into our room and sat down on the bed. Pharaoh, in turn, walked into the front room and began smashing everything in sight, including the pictures of Teo' and Quan. He tore all of the pictures down and then pointed to Quan and told me to take a good look at what I saw. *"Take a good look at what,"* I asked, and that's when he pounced on me like Tom pouncing on Jerry.

Arguments and fights were nothing new between Pharaoh and me, but we'd never gotten into it like this before. It was if he were striking me with all of his strength and I just knew for sure he was going to leave me laying there unconscious. I was so afraid, I was scared to scream, and wondered if my mom heard us but prayed that she didn't. She was the last person I wanted to know what was going on considering her past with her ex. She could do more good by just keeping an eye on my son.

It seemed like the two of us were going at it for hours and by the time he was done, he'd literally beat me beyond recognition. That boy punched, smacked, choked, and dragged me across the floor because he swore I'd gone skating with B*C instead of Solomon. He also claimed that the photos of Teo' and Quan proved Quan looked nothing like him and exactly like B*C. (So I guess Amber was telling the truth...) By the time he was finished with me, there was a high pitch ringing in my head, a patch of my hair was gone, I was dizzy, and could barely see straight. He then jumped in his car and sped off, but not before I was able to grab one of his guns and give chase behind him. Out of all the times I needed a father, this was the one that topped them all...

With not a stitch of license, insurance, or registration, I swerved throughout the city with an unregistered firearm. I was more then sure had been used in a crime at one point in time. Yet, despite the facts or consequences, I stayed on his heels. I knew catching up to him would be nearly impossible due to red-light and pedestrians crossing my path, so instead of trying to follow him, I went to various spots where I though he might go.

Ernie's house was my first stop because Pharaoh and his cousin, Hass, were real tight. I thought maybe Ernie could call Hass for me and find out where Pharaoh had gone or was headed. Ernie was a good friend and knew all about Pharaoh's ways and temper. But after seeing the damage he'd done to me, his only words were, *"Murfy, GO TO THE HOSPITAL!"*

I knew Ernie had nothing but concern about my well being, but I also knew he didn't want to be involved. So instead of using him as the middle man I respectfully left his house, but I didn't go to the hospital. Instead, I made a b-line to Hass' crib, but I didn't have any luck with him either. My fury with Pharaoh had reached such a high, I wasn't just looking for him, I was looking for him or anyone who looked remotely like his ass. I felt the only way I'd be able to put an end to his torment was to kill him dead! Even if I had to die in the process that was fine by me, but after tonight, he'd never put his hands on me again!

I drove around for hours twitching that little ass .22 in my hand. Taking the bullets out and putting them back in. I stayed out until midnight but was so disoriented, I eventually had to call it quits. At this time, all I really wanted to do was hold my son in my arms and fall asleep. As soon as I got home and sat down in the chair, my mom brought the baby down to me and the two of us passed out. I was so tired I didn't realize I was still holding the gun. Then somewhere around 2:00 a.m., Pharaoh crept in, put the baby in the bed, and took the gun from my hand. I only saw the back of him as he was closing the door, but I made no attempt to make matters worse. I didn't know what was going to happen next or how things were going to play out. What I did know was there was absolutely no respect or trust left in our relationship, and from that point on things would never be the same. By now, aside from my son, Mary J. Blige *My Life* cd was the only thing I had to get me through the emotions. If people could look into my life and saw what was really going on, they would be surprised that I was still holding on.

The next morning, I woke up and prepared myself for work. I wasn't sure what I was going to say to everybody when they asked what happened to my face but, *"Mind your business"* is what came to mind. Pharaoh use to force me to hide his handy-work from the eyes of the public but I never had any shame. I wanted others to see what he had done to me because I wanted someone to do the same to him. At work, Ernie was the first one to see me and his one word said it all. *"DAMYUMM! You look worst now then you did last night."* Like that's what I needed to hear. He then went on to tell me that he knew Pharaoh had been looking for me but had no idea this is what he had in mind. All I could do was stand there and look at him with a blank expression because even the slightest of warnings would have been better than remaining silent…

****

Old habits die hard and breaking and abusive cycle is just as hard as trying to quit smoking or gambling. Pharaoh was use to abusing me as well as others, and I believe it had a chain reaction on those he chose to deal with. I say that because one day while crossing the street, Amber came flying down the road and tried her best to hit me. I mean, she actually swerved in my direction as I was trying to get out of her path. In return, I caught up with her at the light and returned the favor by trying to beat her senseless with streamline Mac Tools flashlight I kept in the back of the car for protection. Silly I know…

By March of 1995, Pharaoh was still a free man, the two of us were still seeing one another, still sleeping with one another, and still denying the truth. He was on now on short time and would soon have to turn in. Again, he's had a sudden change in character and every moment we spent together was a pleasant one to remember. Funny, it took me nearly eight years to figure out why he acted the way he did, and once I found out the truth, the clock had run out of time. My heart was heavy because there was no time for us to heal, no time for us to forgive, and not time to start a new. The poker faces had to remain in tact but our hearts, on the other hand, were falling apart. Pharaoh had to start his sentence on March 30th, the day after my 25th born day. How he managed to pull that one off will forever remain a mystery but I'm glad we were given the chance to spend our birthdays together. (Pharaoh's birthday is the 22nd.)

Our grand finale with one another was all that and then some, and as usual, he spared no expense to show me a good time. It was the first time I can actually say he did something with me from the heart, with no ulterior motive involved. He even went through the trouble of paying my baby sister to watch our son while we spent the night out. He put a lot of effort into making sure my 25th was a night to remember.

At our hotel we enjoyed a long, sit down shower, and I'd never seen a shower that you could sit down in before. Our next step was a hot, bubbly Jacuzzi where we sipped on champagne and aged cognac. It was a rare occasion for us to sit back laughing and giggling, but we did so while reminiscing over the good and the bad. He even went as far as to pick up some good old, earth grown *Ghanja,* and puffed a stogie with me which was the ultimate shocker.

Before giving myself to him one last time, my stomach filled with butterflies due to our intoxicating chemistry. Our bodies were one another's playground, and we stayed in sync with each other like the waves of an ocean. By the time we fell asleep, the sun was coming up, and I was saddened to know our run had come to and end. Pharaoh's last night of freedom *(my birthday)* turned out to be one of the happiest days of my life, and even though we knew things were about to change drastically, at least for once we treated each other like King and Queen.

The reality of what was about to be hit hard upon our return to the house. Pharaoh took one last look around, checked some items in his safe, kissed me, and then walked out the door. He didn't even want to say goodbye to his son. I guess he wanted to spare me the emotions. Once he was gone, I sat down and pondered all of my thoughts. Some good, some not so good, and then I experienced a sigh of relief. After that I cried. I didn't know what to expect, but I knew I'd have to deal with it. It was going to be tough to make ends meet without his help, but worst than that, I had to explain all of this to his son. Quan loved his father and after two years, being without him would come as a shock. How would I explain going to visit him behind plexiglass and why he couldn't come home anymore?

****

Just as when Pharaoh went away before, he made sure his family and associates dropped off a few dollars to me for whatever I needed. Things weren't as tough as I thought they were going to be, partly because I was able to borrow from my pensions. At first our visits were every Saturday, 10:00 a.m., and we were never late because the county jail was only two minutes away from our house. But once Samantha and I ran into each other as I knew we would, he changed them to Sundays, same time. After thirty-days he was transferred up north to Annandale, where I drove two hours each way, every Saturday, just to see his face. Upon his request, I'd stop at KFC and take food up there to him and other inmates, and on occasion, I even went through the trouble of cooking something myself. I arranged meetings between our friends in order to smuggle contraband into the facilities, accepted all of his collect calls, and made sure money stayed on his books. I did all any woman could do for a man locked down and three months into his bid, the fucker cut me loose.

I guess the fact of him being on the inside and me on the out was more than he could stand. Besides his own paranoid thoughts and assumptions, he also had to deal with the rumors, haters, and dick riders coming at him from all directions, feeding him just what he feared most. On the morning of my last visit, he called me at about 7:00 a.m., claiming he'd been trying to contact me for over an hour, but the phone just kept on ringing. Right away I knew something was wrong because his lie didn't make any sense. For one, he was in a correctional facility, therefore, an operator had to patch his calls in every time, and second, there was no way anyone would let a line ring as long as he was claiming he'd rung mine. In addition, I slept with the cordless under my pillow, how could I not hear it ringing?

Once he couldn't win that battle he switched to telling me what he wanted me to wear. Okay, maybe I'm trippin'. Maybe my man just misses me and doesn't know how to say it. So I went ahead with my visit as planned and before arriving stopped off to pick up a bucket of KFC for his boy. A guard escorted Day'Quan and me to an empty bench as usual and moments later, Pharaoh walked out with regret written all over his face.

"What's wrong?"

"Nothing, I just want to ask you a question," he said. I passed the baby to him and he pushed him away. This was another bad sign that something was wrong, but I hadn't put it all together. He passed the chicken off to his boy then asked, *"Who have you been fucking?"* At first I just looked at him like a lost dog or Scooby Doo. *"Who have I been fucking,"* I said while shaking my head. *"Is that what you just asked me?"*

"Who have you been fucking?" he abruptly asked again. *"Pharaoh I know you ain't call me all the way up here, just to start no shit!"*

The look of worry intensified on his face as the two of us sat staring at each other in silence. I wasn't sure if he was going to leap over the table at me or ask another ignorant question. Even our son could tell something was about to go down because the look on his face matched that of his father's. Pharaoh then looked up at me and said; *"If you not gonna tell me who you fucking, then I don't want you to come back!"* With pain flowing into my heart with each passed second, I sat and thought about his words. He was the one doing a bid, yet he was putting demands on me. After all he'd done to me, I still stayed by his side. I may have done my thing but he always came first. Yet, even though I maintained the same low profile as before, he wanted to threaten me with an ultimatum. I just wasn't feeling his demand and didn't deserve his disrespectful tone or behavior. *"If breaking up with me was on your agenda, Pharaoh, then you could have saved me the time, money, and gas by doing it over the phone!"* (As previously stated, the poker faces had to remain in tact.)

I was a hot as a red-pepper, but didn't break or back down. *"Okay, I'm gonna ask you one last time,"* he said, *"who you fucking?"* You see, maybe if there was someone I was seeing on a regular his question would have been relevant or justified, but there wasn't. I could see in Pharaoh's eyes that this was something he didn't really want to do. Nonetheless, because I chose to remain silent, he got up, walked away, and never looked back.

I couldn't believe it. After all we'd been through he was able to just get up and walk away like our eight years meant nothing. This wasn't the change I was looking for, but I have to admit, I knew it was coming. I tried holding my composure as I walked with my son to our car, but before I could open the door, I slumped over and broke down. A part of me was crying because it was finally over and the other was in tears because the end was so counterfeit. I'd allowed this man to ruin my credit as well as my license. I put cars in my name for him and didn't complain when I didn't get to drive. Even when he tried to play me with that B*C shit, he didn't want to call it quits. So how come all of a sudden did he want to let me go? I had no understanding to what had just occurred and was in no condition to drive home alone.

About one mile down the road, a State Trooper pulled me over because he saw me driving in distress. In other words, he saw me crying, a rare that could effect my driving. He asked if I were okay and of course

I said yes, but he could see I was upset. He allowed me to gather my thoughts after checking my credentials then allowed me to go on my way. But not before standing with me for about a half hour, as I cried my eyes out about loosing my counter part. He even let Quan sit in his patrol car, but of course he held on to the keys. *"This Pharaoh is a stupid man,"* he told me, *"and any man would be proud to have you as his lady."* His words were somewhat comforting and deep down inside, I knew they were true.

I arrived home safely two hours later. I drove the scenic route because I was in no hurry. Once in the house, I lay down across the bed and cried myself to sleep. How could he do this to me? How could he be so cold and callous? I was there for him during his trial. I lied on the stand while Samantha lay in a hospital bed giving birth to their fourth child. Yes, the fucker even had the nerve to have another one after our son was born. He not only screwed my best friend, but my best friend's sister too. (Oh, he didn't think I knew about that one.) And aside from walking away from me, he was walking away and shutting out his son, a son that we agreed to have. Never before had I hurt so bad, this even topped loosing a dear friend in death.

For days, I waited patiently for Pharaoh to call but my hopes for reconciliation were in vain. Occasionally, his brother John and sister Chippy (RIP) would come by to visit us, but I figured that was only at his request. Other than that, it was like the two of us didn't even know each other and our relationship never took place. He'd made his decision clear and it was nothing left for me to do but move on. A few months later, I got word that he removed my name from the visitor's list because Samantha placed an ultimatum on his head, *"either me or her!"* Any fool knew it was cheaper to keep her, and being as though they had four kids between them, the choice was a no brainer.

On occasion I wondered what it would have been like if Pharaoh and I never hooked up and I would have stayed with my previous boyfriend, Prince. Prince wasn't nearly as difficult to deal with as Pharaoh, and his only downfall was he was a follower and not a leader. What a huge turn off. I can't stand to see weakness in a man, at least not in one I'm dating. Pharaoh had me convinced he was the better man, so I left Prince in the pursuit of a better life. Oh well... And for the record, Amber's daughter did turn out to be Pharaoh's daughter as well. DNA proved that as soon as he went away. No need to cry over spilled milk though. What's done is done. But regardless of the circumstances, I was a mother and had a duty to make sure my son knew all of his siblings, regardless of my personal feelings. It's amazing we lasted as long as we did, but I will say not all of our time together was bad. Some of it was incredible and considering I wasn't his only one, I don't know how he did it, but I'm sure he had some help. Tiger Balm, Ginseng Root, or maybe both...

LOVE DOESN'T DISCRIMINATE AND THE HONEYMOON IS ALWAYS SWEETER THAN THE LONG HAUL. SOMETIMES TAKING THE TIME TO WEIGH YOUR OPTIONS IS YOUR BEST OPTION, AND EVEN THEN, YOU'RE NOT GUARANTEED TO GET GREENER PASTURES...

NEW DUDE

MY new found freedom was bitter sweet. The peace and serenity that had eluded my life was long overdue. Yet, I still yearned for companionship. I needed time to heal, but nothing heals a wounded heart better than love. I still had a lot of issues to work out. For starters, I had to quit flinching at someone's slightest move and I had to learn how to trust again. The stakes were now a lot higher because the one I chose didn't just have to be good to me, he had to be good enough to be around my son. I also had to get my business in order. I had to restore my driver's license, pay off my surcharges, and try to re-establish my credit. While dealing with Pharaoh, I use to sometimes give him half of my check just so he could, "get back on" as he would say. But by doing so I neglected to pay my own bills. Then, of course he'd never repay me the full amount at once, thus the cycle began.

In more ways than one, the summer of '95 was one of the' hottest summers ever! It was entertaining to see the way niggas switched their game up towards me now that Pharaoh was away. People who never said two words to me all of a sudden wanted to holla, others came from out of the wood work. But there was one individual who kept his game the same regardless of his presence, and that was Solomon.

Besides Chino', Solomon was the only other male in my circle aside from my son. The history between us dated back till when we were kids going to Junior #5, he was B*C's youngest brother and the cutest one out of the bunch. (They also have a middle brother who we all call Ace.) Solomon had rich mocha skin, a nice medium build and dark curly hair. When standing in the right light, you could see his natural reddish tones, similar to my mothers and he too had slits for eyes and resembled the hip hop artist Keith Murray. My past with Solomon and his brothers is lengthy, but he and I were always the closest. Although we knew we weren't blood, we all looked at each other as family or cousins. Then one day while hanging out at the corner store, all that cousin shit changed.

I was inside the store jaw wrestling with Chino when one of Pharaoh's boys walked in, his cousin Mike actually. Mike asked me how Pharaoh was doing and the only thing I could say was, *"I don't know, we're not together anymore."* This came as a shock to Chino and Solomon because I hadn't been so forthcoming about our relationship until now. The only people who knew about it from my end were Shantell, Nette, and Moe, but Mike knew how he was doing, and he knew Pharaoh had broken up with me. I think he just wanted to see where my heart was at.

Chino's reaction was like, *"what,"* and Solomon began smiling from ear to ear. Mike then turned around, smiled at me, and walked out the door. My intentions were to follow behind him but I stopped in my tracks. There was something about Solomon that held my attention, and I could read in his eyes he wanted me to stay. I'd never looked at him in that light before, but I liked what I saw. I liked the energy he projected. He asked me to confirm what he thought he heard me say and I repeated it again with no reserve. For the next twenty minutes the two of us stood in the corner, laughing and giggling about I don't know what.

Solomon was familiar with the ups and downs of my relationship with Pharaoh. He'd witnessed his handy work after seeing him slap me around a few times on Hermitage. Solomon constantly warned me to leave that cat alone, and I even ran to him the last time Pharaoh beat me up. The news of our break up was a shock to him as well as a relief. After a while, our conversation moved from inside the store to outside next to the fire-hydrant. The dialogue had changed from casual to comfortable, and plans were put into play to hook up with each other later on at the bar. I wasn't sure about what he had in mind, but my thoughts were straight in the gutter. Passers by, who saw us engaged in our chat, were yelling out to us like fourth graders on a school bus. Saying shit like, *"Oh, y'all know y'all wrong,"* and, *Oh, I'm telling!"* We laughed about that too, because they were acting as if they caught him with his pants down and my dress tail up!

Even though the two of us were simply talking, we were out on the corner at 10:00 a.m., looking as if we'd been struck by cupid's arrow. By 11:00 a.m., we parted ways, and I walked off feeling real sexy. Little did I know, that little conversation of ours would spark a flame resulting in us sharing an intimate relationship with one another for the next six years...

Prior to that day, Solomon and I spent a lot of time with each other swapping video tapes and kicking it about our favorite movies. We were both huge fans of comedy, cartoons, and the martial arts. We frequently hooked up with each other to catch a flick at the cinema and loved to watch Russell Simmons' *Def Comedy Jam*. There was nothing unusual for him to fall asleep on the couch at my house while Quan and I slept in the bed, and because I was so comfortable around him, he sometimes caught more than an eye full. Like the night he came over to pick up a few movies but ran in to Pharaoh's brother at the door. I knew to expect Solomon, but had no idea John was coming over too. When I went to the door I had nothing on but my t-shirt and panties. After seeing the look on John's face, I knew what he assumed but it wasn't like that at the time. Dude was just over there to pick up some tapes, and maybe puff some trees.

After that incident, the likelihood of us hooking up was a no brainer. The chemistry between the two of us was as thick as pea soup, but neither one of us were brave enough to acknowledge that fact. The secret crush we had on one another was now an obvious attraction, as we thought of more and more ways to see each other. The move that let the cat out of the bag, however, was when I started letting him use my car. I use to wok part time at Olan Mills on Whitehorse-Mercerville road, three nights a week with Shantell and Moe, and I use to have Solomon drop us off, then pick up back up. To return my kindness, Solomon agreed to babysit Quan for me so I wouldn't have to pay someone else. That right there is what caught everyone's attention because everyone knew how protective I was over my son.

Word about the two of us began to spread quicker than a strippers legs, and we felt the desire growing between us but were able to maintain our cools. I even suffered a falling out with Moe over our dealings because of a short fling the two of them shared as teens. In part, I understood her disapproval but I was hoping she would be happy for me just the same. I didn't want to sever a relationship over a man, but I was past the point of caring about what others thought of me or worrying if my actions pleased them. Solomon made me feel protected and loved, just like when we were teenagers, selling boat and robbing *cousin LC* because he refused to pay us. (It fucked his head up to see the both of us rocking brand new custom made New York Yankees starter jackets with M & M embroidered on the front in small cursive letters and our nick names embroidered on the back in huge century gothic font, with matching white Lee jeans and white on white Air Forces.) He even once saved me from being attached by cousin LC one night after he got way too high! Being with Solomon kept a smile on my face and flutters in my heart. There was no way I was giving that up!

Solomon and I were now almost inseparable but no lines had been crossed yet. He and I use to see each other at Klotz a lot but were never really in there together. By this time Shantell had gone back to school and Moe was pursuing her singing career. My only road dog out side of Solomon and Chino was my home girl Don. A lot of people thought with Pharaoh out of the picture, I'd be out in the clubs and bars shaking my ass like I'd lost my mine, but being a mother kept me grounded, and besides, I was never that chick in the first place. However, I did like to step out and get my drink on and this is where Minnie came into play.

Being as Minnie was nothing less than a grandmother to me, Quan grew extremely close to her, Aunty, and Debbie, while I was out socializing. On the nights when I wanted to go up-top, Minnie was my only relief. As for Don and I, we were like socialites on the scene and rarely had to come out of pocket for any drinks. On any given night we knew we could count on at least five of our boys to keep our glasses full, and knew we were in good company from the entrance to the exit. People looked forward to our attendance, including the owners and bartenders, and we looked forward to always having a good time.

****

They say that brown cognac is like liquid courage. I find all metaphors and analogies to have some reasonable truth, but I've never actually tested any of them out. That was until the night I lured Solomon to me from across the bar and he was unwilling to resist. From the moment he stepped on the scene, our eyes locked on each other and it was like tunnel vision. There weren't any extra stools for him at the bar so I scooted over on mine and offered to share my seat. He accepted and then ordered us both a drink. The two of us couldn't even exchange words because we were too busy blushing. Don, who was sitting to the left of me, didn't understand the sudden change in my actions but she wouldn't be left in the dark much longer. She saw Sol' (short for Solomon) sharing the stool with me on my right, but she also saw Tuck standing off over in the cut. Up until that night, Tuck and I had been seeing each other on and off but after that evening, we would be no more. This is why I never dignified Pharaoh's accusations about B*C or anyone else's about Solomon because Tuck was the one I had been fucking. He and I had been getting it in for the longest but Pharaoh was so stuck on B*C he couldn't see the forest for the trees.

After consuming what seemed like half the bar, the two of us were practically in each others laps. Slowly he began to stroke the inner part of my thigh while I sat there and purred like a kitten. Our actions hadn't been premeditated, but I love the feel of his touch as it warmed my insides and rushed my blood. I'd long anticipated this moment but wasn't sure how to respond. I was nervous and he'd caught me off point. I zoned out thinking of what could happen next, but was snapped back to reality by the sound of his seductive, raspy voice, *"You like that, don't you!"*

Hell yeah, I thought to myself while responding with a smile. Then, he gestured for us to go outside. By now, I've forgotten all about Don, but she'd understand. I can recall times when she dipped out on me too. I did, however, manage to shoot her a signal before walking out the side door. With the parking lot damn near empty, the two of us walked to my car. Then, Solomon grabbed my keys and allowed me the leisure of riding shotgun. He'd taken control of the entire evening so no need to stop him now. Inside the car, he picked back up where he'd left off, touching all the right spots, warming all of them right, and I just sat back and enjoyed the attention. As we exited the lot, he put on some smooth R&B which complimented our moods and opened the sun roof to alleviate the steamed windows.

After exiting the parking lot, we drove down Prospect with plans to stop at the pool hall, but once we arrived, he popped the question. *"So, do you wanna go to the pool hall or do you wanna chill with me?"* What... Pool? Solomon already knew the answer to that question, that's why he didn't hesitate to turn around. He hit a quick u-turn in the middle of the road and put the pedal to the metal as we headed back into town. To my house!

Usually my first time with someone causes me to become nervous, silly, and even shy, but this time around I was good to go. Solomon was far from a stranger to me, which made it a lot easier for me to maintain control. As we sat and pretended to watch *Def Comedy Jam*, I enticed him, licking the nuts out of the butter pecan ice cream from my spoon. He, on the other hand, maintained the light strokes up and down my thighs, occasionally gripping my ass and pulling me close.

Oops, there goes his hand, up under my shirt, OH MY! Ooh there goes his lips, against my tit's OH MY... Oh my was putting it lightly, it was more like OH MY GOD! Within a matter of minutes we were about to change the way we viewed and felt about each other indefinitely. There's a song by the Whispers that goes *"It just gets better with time,"* and that's no understatement. Until that night I thought I had the best of the best, but as I was finding out, passion came in all different shapes and sizes. We went from the couch to the floor, but never made it to the bed. As the sweat dripped from our bodies, a wet spot formed on the rug. Our rhythmic movements were encouraged by moans of pleasure and had it not been for my gold fronts, I would have bit a whole in my lip. Unlike other lovers, Solomon was able to bring out the fetishes I'd been too shy to share with others and complimented my natural freakish nature. Pulling my hair, slapping my rear, however he wanted it, I didn't care! The precise strokes of his shaft caused my sugarwalls to release like Niagara Falls. I would love to divulge more but that would turn this into an erotica!

About an hour later, exhausted and short winded, I made my way to the bed and crashed. Solomon stayed in the living rolling a Dutch and my plans were to smoke with him but I fell asleep. When I woke up the next morning and didn't find him lying in the bed next to me and I feared the worst. I felt used. However, to my surprise, he was only a few feet away, still sitting in the living room, smoking on that same stogie. His raspy cough drew my attention and when we looked at one another we immediately began to blush. Then, simultaneously, he reached for his boxers as I pulled the sheet up to hide my nakedness. Without saying much to each other we began to laugh and giggle like children on a playground. His eyes asked the question, *"Was it good,"* and mine responded with an affirmative, *"Yes!"* The activities of only a few hours ago left a burning question in my mind. *"Where do we go from here?"*

I had a good feeling about the two of us and it didn't feel as if our friendship had been compromised. Before dropping him off, I thought to myself how I should have let him move in with me when he asked a few months ago, but I didn't see it as a wise decision at the time. I still didn't view it as a wise decision, but my *kitty kat* had a mind of its own. Now here I am dropping him off to someone else's home but I thought to myself, it can't be that serious if he was able to spend the entire night out with me! (Misconception #1) Before parting the two of us swore to one another we wouldn't tell a soul about our night of passion, not even our closest friends or siblings. But just as we were making our pinky promise, one of our mutual friends Eddy Ed, happened to catch us riding down Willow Street first thing in the morning and gave us a look as if to say, *"Oh, y'all busted!"* We both acknowledge seeing him and threw up the peace sign in return, but we also knew our cover had now been blown. As for me, the promise we made lasted every bit of five minutes, just long enough for me to get my black ass back home and on the phone with Don.

"Girl, guess who spent the night with me," was the first thing to fly out of my mouth. Then, for the next sixty seconds I sat quietly while she ran off the names of individuals who she knew would repulse me and leave a bad image in my mind. Don had a good sense of humor, which is what made her so much fun and why she was the first one I chose to call. Then after the two of us could no longer stand the suspense, I gave in and told her who the lucky man was. But wouldn't you know the heifer wasn't the least bit surprised. *"Oh I knew y'all were up to something, y'all two kissing cousins now!"* The two of us then shared a laugh and I filled her in on all of the juicy details. Ironically, just as I was sitting on the phone spilling my guts to her, Eddy Ed was running his mouth to the block and Solomon was running his off to his brother Ace. Oh well, so much for keeping it on the hush.

Later that day when I went around the way to chill, I ran into the usual crowd of guys standing out front of the store. My boy Coop was among them and he grabbed me and gave me a friendly hug as usual. It was then that I caught Ace out the corner of my eye giving me a look that said *"Aight, Molly, watch it!"* (Molly was another one of my many nicknames like Murf and Ree.) Ace's reaction to Coop's affections is how I knew Solomon had spilled the beans. Not that I was bothered, and to be honest, I was quite flattered. Even as friends, my dudes were never

the type to claim anyone quickly or kiss and tell. So for Ace to know about me and Solomon really got me to thinking. After pulling away from Coop's embrace, I walked up to Ace and greeted him with a smile. Being as Ace was as silly as his brother, he grinned at me and giggled, which was his way of returning the love. After that, I faded off into the dark, jumped back into my car, and drove away. Solomon and I wouldn't hook up again until a week later but not because I didn't want to see him sooner. However, my monthly visit from Mother Nature put all action on hold.

****

Prior to our engaging, Solomon had no problem dropping by the house unannounced or at the spur of the moment. However, after our escapade, he wasn't sure if the surprised visits would still be acceptable. Because of this doubt, he resorted to other methods of contacting me. Being as there weren't many people who even knew where I lived, he asked Moe for my number, and for and for a whole week we spoke to each other daily just as all new lovers do. I thought his shyness would have prevented him from asking about our evening together but to my surprise, he didn't hesitate to ask when he could see me again. I was wooed by his interest because in my eyes, Solomon had always been a good dude. However, he mistakenly assumed I was trying to brush him off when I told him it couldn't be right away. I later put all his worries to rest once I invited him back over, at which time we realized our dealings with one another could far exceed casual or platonic sex.

After that second night, the two of us were like Jada and Mariah (By Your Side,) and the only time you didn't see us together was when I was at work. Yet even then, we still spent my lunch hour together which often turned into a two hour break. (Wasn't nothing Lazy-Boy chair and we sure didn't use it for lounging.) After lunch, I'd reluctantly return to work for about an hour or so, but by 4:00 p.m., we were right back in each other's faces. If you didn't see us on the block, you saw us cruising around town together, and when you didn't see either of us you knew what it was…

I was having the time of my life but I had one major fear. Rejection! I wasn't ready to be rejected and I damn sure didn't mean to fall for dude the way I did, but there was a rare sentiment between me and him, something we both acknowledged and didn't take for granted. Solomon riding shotgun to Philly with his boys had now been replaced with me riding shot gun to Philly with him. The same applied when going to New York or the skating ring in Franklinville. Oh, and speaking of the skating ring, I wondered what was going through Pharaoh's mind now that he knew me and Solomon were an item and not B*C. I knew word of us had reached him by now because cats in jail get the down-low quicker then cats out on the street. I bet he never suspected Solomon was man enough to pick up where he left off, but surely he knew I wasn't the type to screw one brother then move on to the next.

I guess it was natural for me to wonder what Pharaoh was thinking now that word of me and Solomon had hit the streets, but I wasn't alone. Solomon had a few questions about him too. I say this because he once asked me what I would do if Pharaoh came home and wanted me back and was I dealing with him just to piss Pharaoh off. He laughed after asking me, but I could tell there was a real concern to know the answer. I'm a firm believer that actions speak louder than words and in time, Solomon grew to realize that my sole purpose for having him in my life was because I'd fallen in love with him, not because I wanted to make someone jealous.

Solomon was someone I could admire because of his integrity instead fear because of iniquities. If such a thing really existed, I'd go out on a limb and say he and I were the perfect couple. However, love is blinding like the sun and allowing love to blind you can cause serious heartbreak if you're not cautious. It will also cause you to see only what you want to see, thus enabling you to create your prefect world. This type of behavior is cool if you live in a world drawn with a No. 2 pencil and an eraser on top. You could then just simply erase whatever or whoever got in your way and replace it with whatever suited your fancy. I didn't live in that world, however, and neither did he. Over a consecutive nine month period, the two of us spent every day, night, week, and weekend together with no problems. Pharaoh's people continued to drop by on occasion and so did Solomon's daughter's mother, but there was never any beef and everyone respected our dealings. (His daughter's mother use to always tell me I was stupid for dealing with him and the way she saw it, I could do much better, but I failed to understand how my stupidity, as she called it, affected her or anyone else.)

I had not one complaint about him and he had none about me that I was aware of, but that didn't mean our path to bliss was clear. Officially, Solomon still had a roommate and apparently he hadn't been so honest with her about our dealings.

Solomon was a good dude but he was a dude, nonetheless. The girl he had been dealing with prior to me was seemingly the sweet, quiet type who didn't bother anybody. You know, the type you can't trust! Well, long story short, her and Solomon were still seeing each other and she had become suspicious of his actions. Ya think? So now this cat's conscience starts to mess with him and he can't see himself breaking her heart. So where did that leave me? Smack dab in the middle of yet another love triangle with two options. Leave now and cut my looses which were zero at the time, or deal with it and don't complain. Considering I'd just gotten out of a dead end relationship that should have been a no-brainer but... The desire to be unconditionally loved was still leading me astray.

To make matters worst ole girl and I knew one another but she wasn't my girl, and I only contented with her presence to keep Solomon out of hot water. On occasion, the two of us would pick her up from work then drop her off just to get her out of the way, but the majority of our dealings took place once I began taking courses at the college and she just happened to wind up in one of my classes. The closeness was too much for comfort considering while the two of us were in class, he had my car. The funny part is she knew it, but never questioned me about it. At times I wish she would have, then I would have had a reason to say something but nothing was ever mentioned. I've always been able to use any situation to my advantage, but I wasn't going to go after blood and besides, I didn't view girlfriend as a threat in the first place.

Solomon and I were a cute pair and provided each other with perks we didn't receive in previous relationships. I can't tell you his roommate's story but I can tell you mine. With no complaints from either one of us, I was beginning to believe the stories others told me about the outside chick reaping all the benefits, while the one at home put up with all of the bullshit. In a nutshell, we made each other happy; nothing was broke and nothing needed fixing…

****

Besides personal companionship, Solomon and I created a family environment for each other's children, which was a high, mutual priority. Solomon loved Quan like a father and even disciplined him if necessary. Outside of his Godfather Chino and God-brother Teo', Solomon was the only man to have any direct contact with my child. At the same rate, I smothered his daughters with the same love and affection they'd receive from their natural mother and more. My relationship with his kids was totally different than the situation with Pharaoh and his other children because I rarely had any contact with them at all. Over the course of time, the two of them grew to love me just as they loved their own mother and I loved them as if I'd given them life. Quan looked up to Solomon and grew to love his daughters like sisters. There were very few occasions when I had to experience typical *Baby Mama Drama*, but it was to be expected when parties fail to communicate. I was in love with Solomon but I was no fool. I knew he played his part in the madness, but in any event, our kids always came first.

Years passed and despite the fact that we didn't live under the same roof, we were still very comfortable with one another. Maybe, a little too comfortable… As time progressed, my motherly duties caused me to fall back from Solomon's side in order to do more things with my son. He was five years old now, going to school and a lot more observant. The block was no longer a suitable hang out for the two of us and Solomon agreed. Yet, because I was no longer glued to his hip, others took that as a sign that the two of us were no longer together. True, the amount of time we spent together had decreased but the quality of our time spent grew. Just like Pharaoh, he made sure the two of us wanted to nothing and if we did, he was only a phone call away. Daily he'd remind me of how much he cared about me and whispered sweet nothing's in my ear like, *"What would I do without you…"* Once he even

203

said he was considering joining the Navy, and if he did, he was going to take me and Quan along with him. How sweet!

Solomon had always been conservative about his private affairs, and I'd never had any run in with anyone behind him. So when I started hearing stories about the various chickenheads swarming around him like bees to honey, I paid them no mind. I knew I was in good standings with my Bugga' and he'd done nothing to make me feel otherwise. My little sister even put a bug in my ear about the same thing and I still threw caution to the wind. After her, it was her best friend, and then my sister Moe, but I rebuked all of their claims. I thought Moe was basing her opinions on hearsay and I questioned why Nette's girl, Monica, would have any interest in my affairs period. *"Because I think you're too nice for him,"* is what she told me. But even then, I refused to take heed.

Solomon was a natural born flirt, and had been that was all his life. I knew he had that characteristic about him when the two of us hooked up and I wasn't about to pressure him to change. Besides, I had several admires of my own, and a few of them spent quite a bit of time chilling with me and my son out on the front stoop. I wasn't screwing any of them, so why did he have to be screwing any of the ones that hung around him?

I had no insecurities, and if people were going to run back and tell me things, then let them be good. Nobody questioned or said a word when Pharaoh was giving me black eyes, having baby after baby, and causing me hearing loss. But now that they see I'm happy with someone, everybody wants to be Action mother fucking News!

I knew my little sister would never do or say anything to intentionally hurt me, so maybe her stories were based on the accounts of others, too. With nothing influencing me but pure curiosity, I asked Solomon about the rumors and he disgustingly denied the accusation, therefore I happily let it go. Then, one afternoon while playing hooky from work, all of that security was washed down the drain after receiving a one single visit. Four years ago, I'd made an unwise decision by assuming Solomon's relationship with ole girl across town was something to disregard. I wasn't really sure if my caller was Solomon's karma or mine, but I will tell you this, his words shattered my world!

Kyron, aka Baby K, was one individual in particular who I managed to remain close with throughout the years and now he was all grown up, very sexy and went by a different name, "Droop." Standing about five feet-eight inches tall, his honey brown skin and alluring smile was a sight to behold. He and I were almost as close as me and Solomon, but instead of calling each other cousins we called each other sister and brother. For years I knew Droop had a crush on me but due to his age, I always kept him at bay. He was, however, very mature acting for his age and had been that way since a young pup running up and down Spring Street. In several situations, Droop proved his love and loyalty to me and without hesitation, I did the same. Aside from immediately family Chino and Solomon, Droop was the only other person I'd let watch my son and I trusted him beyond all doubt. On Fridays when the girls and I went out to the Indies, he'd watch Day'Quan for me and treat him like a little brother.

Droop wasn't conservative like Solomon, he was knee deep in the streets and didn't care who knew. He was strictly underground never flashy but loved to take risk. He was my eyes and ears on the streets and kept me up on the latest facts and buzz. So when he came over that day and told me the same exact thing Nette, Monica, and Moe tried to tell me, I knew he wasn't telling me a lie...

Droop had nothing to gain by lying to me, and just like Monica, couldn't stand to see me being played. Had the news been about the chick he was rooming with it wouldn't have hit me so hard, but to add an outsider weighted real heavy. (Mental Note: If a man will cheat with you, he'll cheat on you!)

I should have known something was wrong just by his visit alone. Droop never came by to see me that early in the day and his demeanor was never that serious. His eyes couldn't hide his concern and when he burst out and said, *"Molly, you know I'd never do anything to hurt you,"* I thought he'd done something bad to Solomon.

"Okay, Droop, I know you love me but how do you know your info is correct?" As if he'd ever been wrong in the past. *"I questioned Solomon about this shit before and he said it wasn't true."* But Droop knew beyond a doubt that Solomon had been lying to me because Dee-Dee, the girl he'd been rumored to be messing around with, was his cousin and he'd seen the proof. *"She's pregnant by him, Molly!"* I believe my heart stopped....

Now this was a new twist. I'd heard that Solomon and Dee-Dee were fucking with each other but I ain't heard shit about her being pregnant. But this was a lot for Droop to drop on me and I know his heart weighted heavy by doing so. Thus, in order to save face and any uncomfortableness, I said; *"Oh yeah I heard about that too, but if she is pregnant, he definitely ain't the father!"*

I knew Droop was telling the truth, but I couldn't deal with it right then. I couldn't let him see the hurt this revelation brought to me and I couldn't let him see me weak over yet another man. *"Well as long as you cool, Molly, that's all I'm worried about,"* and he dropped the subject. Then as usual, we cracked a few jokes, smoked on a bone, and he was on his way. He kissed me on my cheek as he made his exit and that was that.

The door shut, I turned the lock, and dropped down to my knees. I cried like a baby because due to Solomon, I thought my days of heartache and pain were finally over. What the fuck possessed him to go out and fuck up a good thing? With all of the drama he claimed to be going through with his roommate, it baffled me how he could be so stupid to bring bullshit into our circle. Didn't he know I'd find out sooner or later, or are all men truly stupid? How discrete did he think he was being when he was sleeping around on me right in plain sight? Fifty percent of our outdoor time was spent standing on that corner or inside the store with Chino and Meech. Shit, the two of us practically worked there. So how could he be so careless as to fuck with a broad from around that set? What, did he just not care about my feelings? Was all that talk about loving me and, *"What would I do without you?"* just talk? With each question a blade pierced my heart. Solomon had a lot of explaining to do, and if it killed me he was going to tell me the truth.

As I sat on the floor fighting with my tears, I thought about when Droop and I really became close. It was a few years back while he was in the youth house. In the letters he wrote me, he confessed his feelings and how he'd always been afraid to let them be known. He also talked about how he felt I was the only one who understood him, didn't judge him, or shoot him down. Back then, his ways and actions were cute because I knew he'd grow out of them. Taking that into consideration it made perfect sense why I was the first person he called when ever he got in trouble, stole a car, or ran away from home. He knew I'd always save him if I could, and because of my affiliation with his family, he knew I'd always try to make a bad situation look good for his sake. Now here he was all grown up, and he was trying to save me. How ironic... Maybe he was my good karma...

As I dried the tears on my now swollen face, I became angry at myself. For four years, I did all I could do to please him and keep him content. Not to mention the countless nights I sat up bagging pounds of his weed, or the fact that I allowed him to store it at my crib, putting me and my son at risk. I was down for him all the way across the board and this is the thanks I get? He goes out and fucks with an around da' way hoodrat, who's a dummy on top of it! Cheating one me was one thing, but he just added insult to injury by messing around wit her young, skinny, frail ass! At least he could have stepped it up and fucked with a broad who could offer him more than me. Oh fuck that! I got my ass up off that floor and got my shit together. I sat up in the window, rolled myself a stogie, and zoned out to *Project Window* by *Naps*. As the marijuana eased my mind, I asked myself, *"Are you really that in love with him to let this shit slide?"* What about Droop? Was I just going to pretend his visit never happened? Just knowing how the two of us got down, then to think about him with someone else, and a baby!

My heart was racing a mile a minute and I couldn't stop rubbing my hands together. The entire situation put me in the mind of the night I was on the hunt for Pharaoh, combined with finding out about Amber's baby. I had so many internal bruises it was hard to maintain any faith. The closer I got to that corner, the more anxious I became. I knew I needed him to tell me the truth, but at the same time, I wasn't sure I could handle it. Seeing him from a distance somehow put my heart at ease because at least that meant he wasn't with her. Then he spotted me and began to smile, but there was no way I could reciprocate the same, I was damn near in tears. I spotted Dee-Dee across the street and watched how she eyed Solomon as he walked towards me and my anger escalated. CONFRIMATION!

"Wassup, Molly," he said as he walked up and hugged me.

"Wassup, Bugga'," I replied with tears rolling down my face. (Bugga' was my pet name for him.)

"What's wrong, Molly, what happened?" I tried to contain myself but I couldn't, I had to let it go. *"Bugga', what the FUCK is this shit I hear about you and this young girl, who's running around claiming she's having your baby?"* The look on his face changed instantly and his chinky eyes got four times bigger. *"What chu' talking 'bout, Molly?"* Of course that was a sign of denial and then he dropped his head, which was the ultimate sign of guilt. He then took a deep sigh and said, *"Don't worry about that, Molly, I'm a take care of that!"* That was his confession!

Sensing things could quickly get out of hand, Solomon wrapped his arms around me and tried to walk the other way but I wasn't budging. *"What chu' mean don't worry about it! What chu' mean you gonna take care of it! Does that mean she's lying, Bugga' and making the whole thing up! How could she go around saying she's pregnant by you if you not fucking her?"* Then I pushed him and screamed, *"ARE YOU FUCKING HER, BUGGA' HUH, ARE YOU FUCKING HER!"* His silence and hesitation to respond turned my heart to stone. *"I'm sorry, Molly, I'm a take care of it. I didn't want you to find out about this BS in the first place."* I was so outdone I couldn't respond. I just stood there shaking my head thinking to myself, you sorry? You sorry and you didn't want me to find out. Wow… With nothing else said, he grabbed me by the arm and walked me to his car. Before getting in I looked across the street for the girl who'd crushed my dreams but she was gone. *"Stop crying, Molly"* was all he could seem to say. But if it wasn't for him and his stupidity, I wouldn't be crying at all, so I blacked out on him again. *"HOW COULD YOU DO THIS TO ME? Here I am thinking the two of you are just friends now the bitch about to have your baby!"* I swung at him but he blocked the blow. *"Stop saying that!"* he yelled. *"I told you I'm a take care of it!"*

Apparently, Solomon felt because, *"He was gonna' take care of it,"* I had no reason to be mad. Nevermind the fact he'd betrayed my trust by screwing someone else. I should just be happy he was going to take care of it and everything would be alright. Bullshit! *"If I can't trust you, Bugga' how are we going to make it? Did it ever cross your mind that one day I may want to have your child? Did you think about us and our potential future while you were fucking her, knocking her up?"* He cut his eyes at me and tried to respond, but each time he parted his lips I lashed out at him again. . Then he tried reaching for me but I pulled away. The thought of him touching me again made me want to spit in his face. I felt bad for myself, but even worst for Dee-Dee and her baby because he was talking like they were expendable.

Getting rid of the baby had to be his idea not hers, yet, I was selfishly pleased to hear those were his plans. After about a half hour of hearing him repeat, *"I'm sorry,"* over and over, I'd had enough. I got out the car, went into the house, locked the door, turned off the phone, and withdrew myself from everything. I was trying to block the pain Solomon had inflicted on me without cause, and at the same time, keep old wounds from re-opening. Why was this shit happening to me?

I needed desperately to lash out at someone but no one was around. Thank God my son was down the street at a neighbor's house when all of that shit went down. Quan loved Solomon with all his heart and would not have understood why his mommy was so upset with his surrogate daddy. For the remainder of the afternoon, all I could do was cry, and my face and chest hurt so much, I had to fall asleep. But as soon as I resumed consciousness and woke up, the pain returned and I began crying all over again.

I couldn't release my anger the way I wanted but emotions still caused me to act stupid. I couldn't see past the pain and, therefore, went into the closet, took out all of his things, and dumped them in the toilet! If I was gonna walk around feeling shitty then he was gonna smell the same way! I even though about hiding his stash but a lot of good that would have done considering I only had two rooms. By the time I got through throwing a fit, it was damn near 6:00 p.m. and not once did I bother to go check up on my child. For all I knew, he could have been half way across town and I wouldn't have been the wiser. My emotions had me all messed up but the reality of the matter was clear. Karma had come around to bite me in the ass at a time when I least expected it. Sure, it was all good when he and I were rolling tough together, dissing the chick he lived with, and disregarding her feelings, but now that the shoe was on the other foot, it didn't feel so good...

****

Later that evening, Solomon called me and asked me how I was doing? He made it sound like I'd had major surgery. I was hesitant to answer the phone but my heart won the battle. Again, he apologized and told me how sorry he was, then said he'd see me later. I said Okay because that's all I could say, but I wasn't up for a visit. We hung up and I went back to sleep.

So now what? Well, just like many of the other brokenhearted, we kissed and made up. Being as I was so in love with him, I was willing to forgive and forget as long as he was willing to straighten up and fly right. Time after time I'd forgiven Pharaoh for the same and greater, so why not Solomon? Who, unlike his predecessor, wasn't putting his hands on me or forcing me to remain under his thumb. The two of us managed to make it past that dilemma, but our relationship was never the same. Insecurities that were never there before seemed to always be present, and instead of remaining close to home, I found myself making frequent trips around the corner. To save face, I always made up a good reason for my pop-up, but truthfully, my only reason was to check up on him. I then realized by attempting to babysit a grown man wasn't going to solve anything nor could it stop it from occurring again if that's what he wanted. He knew what he had with me, and if he wanted to throw it all away for good, then nothing I did was going to stop him. I learned that lesson from Pharaoh.

****

While going through our relationship changes, I lived at 510 W. State Street. I should have known living there would only bring drama, because in my opinion, W. Trenton was nothing but drama. Munchy, Reese, Science, Tamar, B-Swian, Dre' Born X, his brother Pop, Cedric (RIP) Dough Boy, and Shamad, had taken the places of 808 and Spring Street, and Solomon couldn't stand my popularity among my new friends.

I will admit my first time meeting them wasn't all that pleasant. I was tired, I was just getting home from work with Day'Quan, it was hot as hell outside, and they were crowding up my steps. I wasn't sure if they would turn out to be friend or foe and I damn sure didn't need any nuisance with niggas selling drugs on my porch. It later became clear that they were just an ordinary bunch of decent, hardworking guys, who at the end of the day, just wanted to kick back like everyone else. For a short while I did fuss and fight with them about their presence, but decided it was much easier to share than to make enemies. The fact that all of us enjoyed the same social activities was just a plus!

It didn't take long for us to form an alliance and Dre' was someone I knew through my cousin Shantell and I knew Shamad through my girl Don. The rest I got to know just by being me, but now that I was become friendly Solomon instructed me to, *"tell them niggas' not to be crowding the porch!"* Either that or he wanted me to stay in the house. Hmm, you know that karma thing works both ways…

Not only was Solomon's request a bit extreme it was also unfounded. How could he have such reservations? If he didn't like the company I was keeping then he should have been my company. How could he expect me and Quan to sit up in that hot ass efficiency all day and night just to please his ego? Everyone I associated with was familiar with Solomon, either through the streets or through me, and none of them tried to cause us any problems. Whenever we were out on the porch and he approached, they greeted him accordingly and even asked and offered him to stay. This is how real they were towards him, yet he still acted as if they were the enemy. Munchy, Science, and Reese always offered him a beer and whoever had something to smoke always offered him first dibs. They did this all on the strength of me and how I felt about his nigga, and because they wanted to prevent any ill feelings. Real niggas do real things, but Solomon felt they were just trying to butter him up in order to move in on his territory.

Well, as it turned out, Solomon's instincts were right. There was one individual who had his sights set on me, but he wasn't one who smiled up in his face or tried to befriend him. He was very stayed to himself but was observant of everything around him. He saw how Solomon spent the majority of his time hanging out on the block, in the faces of others, and socializing at the bar; when he should have been spending quality time with me, keeping niggas like him off my trail. I saw it too, and felt helpless to do anything about it until he stepped in and filled the void. He was as sweet as pie and spoiled me to no end. But to deceive the man I loved put my spirit in turmoil. Hence, I chose to end the affair in order for us to remain friends. He wasn't my man, but he'll always be my X. I knew Solomon suspected something but he never said a word.

After a year of the same ole same ole, I started weeding out cats who didn't know how to go home. Science was no problem because he lived right across the street, but as for the others, they were drawing too much attention and had to go. I was still crazy cool with everyone but my home is my home. Munch and Reese, however, became my best friends, my confidants, and somewhat my protectors. I say that because I shared several insecurities with them about my relationship with Solomon that I feared anyone else to know. In addition, they kept me safe from Pharaoh's wrath once he started coming home on weekend furloughs. Something Solomon should have been doing but was too busy. Pharaoh must have gotten wind of Solomon's neglect and began harassing me the moment he was set free. I use to dread his visits because he used our son as his excuse to come by when really he knew it was all about me. He called frequently but we were never able to hold a civilized conversation, and on days when he'd come and pick Quan up, Reese would sit out on the porch with me until he dropped him back off at 11:00 or 12:00 in the morning! It was embarrassing for others to notice how unconcerned Solomon seemed to be when it came down to Pharaoh, and even more embarrassing for me to pretend everything was okay.

Conquering obstacles seemed to be my number one challenge while dating Bugga'. Let him tell it, there was no issue concerning Dee-Dee, although I still heard rumors about the two of them. Let me tell it, there was no affair with X and the drama with Pharaoh had subsided. He even stopped rolling his eyes at me when ever he caught me sitting out on the porch because the crowd had decreased measurably. But when it came down to my next door neighbor Carl, I had an uphill battle!

Carl aka Kenny had his sights set on me and he didn't give a damn who knew it. Just like everyone else, he saw how I spent most of my time at home alone and he felt he was the perfect individual to occupy my free time. Carl had a girlfriend, who he happened to live with. In my book this meant he was off limits. But Carl saw things differently and neither his girl, nor Solomon could slow down his pursuit. Solomon couldn't point the finger at X, but he was well aware of Kenny's intentions. Nearly every day Kenny would call for me to come out side and smoke some Haze with him and he didn't care if Solomon was around or if his chick complained. Even when he was out and about making runs, he made it his business to come by the crib periodically just to let me know he'd be back and would leave his Piff stash with me as his insurance. The two of us never became physical, but just because we weren't physical doesn't mean we weren't intimate.

I knew Kenny would be the reason for me getting my ass in hot water but that didn't stop me from finding him attractive. I knew he was a loose cannon, way too young, and I couldn't stand his partner, aka his ratchet! But none of that stopped me from finding him attractive either. I even tried reasoning with myself, telling myself I only hung out with him because he made himself so available but I knew it was more to it. Truth be told, I loved the attention and more so, I deserved it. Solomon would never admit it, but I could detect his jealousy towards the young boy, but as previously stated, had he been there occupying my time, he wouldn't have had to worry.

Without warning, Kenny had become a part of my daily and nightly routine. Then one evening, all of that came to a head when he called me out to talk after hours and Solomon unexpectedly crept up on us. I didn't even see the car until it was parked, and by the time I looked up, Solomon was already on the porch. Getting caught in an unexplainable situation is never a good thing, but had he been a few seconds longer, he would have caught his girl kissing another man, or *swapping spit* as Nana would say.

To make matters worst, Solomon had his kids and their mom in the car with him. I would have fussed at him about her but he didn't give me a chance to complain. He was too busy cursing me out about that, *"Mother fucking young boy all up in my face!"*

"You gon' make me slap the shit out of him, you watch," were the heated words that echoed in the hall as he brushed past me up to my apartment. Kenny then walked away because he didn't want to make matters worse, and of course, I followed behind my dude. I tried my best to clean things up but there really wasn't much I could say. He went straight into the closet, grabbed the sneakers I'd brought for the girls, and bounced. *"Keep ya ass in the house,"* he said, then slammed the door behind him.

About an hour after Solomon left, Kenny began to beckon me from his front room window that happened to face my bedroom window. I couldn't' believe it. After all that he still wasn't giving up. Now tell me what neglected woman could resist that. Not me I tell you, that's for sure. I knew the risk I was taking, but I got up out the bed and sat in the window with him, laughing and joking until the sun came up. Solomon never called, never came back, he didn't even do a drive by. I guess he wanted to save face with his roommate and this is exactly why Kenny felt so confident. He knew all he had to do was play it cool and wait for the opportunity to present itself. I knew it too, and that's why I decided to cool things down.

The relationship between Solomon and me had hit a curb at 40 mph and I wasn't sure what lay ahead for us around the bend. The motions remained the same but his attitude had changed. Now he was always on the move, cranky, and short tempered. I knew it wasn't me, but when a woman loves a man and forgets to love herself, she'll take on his mess in a heart beat, allowing his shit to bring her down just to please his ego. I knew I was with Solomon for the right reasons but his attitude was too much to ignore. Still, I dealt with it and hid it the best I could for the kids' sake.

****

Throughout each ordeal, Munch and Reese were still my dogs and use to crack up at the close call stories I'd share with them. They use to tell me *"That young boy gonna get you in trouble one day,"* but I wouldn't listen. To be honest, I wanted us to get into trouble. At least it would break the monotony of things. Sometimes the catch is just as good as the chase. They chuckled… I guess it was easy to be friends with Munch and Reese because they didn't judge me or think foul of me because I was being a woman. They knew Solomon had been cutting up and, therefore, felt I had the right to do the same. They even thought Kenny would be the one to break the two of us apart but I knew that would never happen because Droop wasn't having it…

Ever since Droop dropped the bomb on me about Solomon and Dee-Dee, I'd noticed a change in his actions towards me. He'd become a lot more protective, and made his visits to check up on me more frequent. He knew Bugga' and I kept that fire, and used it as his reason to come through when ever his cover was blown. Solomon was either oblivious to his intentions or again, just didn't care. He and Droop were cool and Solomon always addressed him as *little cousin* because he grew up with his father just like I did. Yet, despite any and all intentions,

Droop never spoke another word against Solomon, although I'm quite sure he could have. Then again, there was really no need to kick his back in because in his eyes he didn't pose a threat. Droop played his part, Solomon played his, but in a game full of players, someone's bound to get played in the end...

THEY SAY IF A PERSON TRY'S THE SAME THING TWICE YET EXPECTS DIFFERENT RESULT IS INSANITY...

DECEPTION

Towards the end of our fifth year together, Solomon said he wanted us to buy a house. Since he had no way to prove his earnings, of course it would be in my name, but it was still going to be our house. At the time, he was staying on Spring Street in a little three room spot not too far from the store, and split his time up between my house, his Earth's crib, his brother's or his uncle Bob out on Hamilton. (So he claimed) He said he bounced around so much because he wasn't living with his roommate anymore, and my efficiency was just too small. He used this logic to convince me he was serious about making moves with me. *"Some of my stuff is still there, but I don't be there,"* is what he would say.

I fell for the *Willie Bo-Bo* [game] and immediately got on my mission to find us a new home. Things were sweet again, so I thought, but that sweetness was soured by yet another dilemma. This time it was my health. First came the nausea, then the sluggishness, followed by a number of other ailments I never experienced before that worsened by the day. Immediately I thought I was pregnant, but reasoning dismissed that theory. I was on the pill! (Plus, according to doctors, my chances of hitting the lottery were better than my chances of getting knocked up.) Then, I thought it could have been a yeast or bacterial infection so I went to the drug store and copped some Vagasil. However, when that didn't work, I grew worried. This sickness was fucking me up and when I finally mentioned it to Solomon, his reaction didn't make things any better.

"I feel sick, Bugga', I don't feel right." Instantly he started acting all weird and nervous, and I looked at him like whoa, what's up with that? Instead of asking me am I alright, he was acting like he just got caught with his hand in the cookie jar again. I tried getting info from my brother Chino since the two of them were so close, but he didn't

know anymore than me, but did say he'd noticed he'd been acting a bit strange as well. Finally I broke down and made an appointment with my doctor, and that's when Solomon said, *"Molly, we gotta talk."* Hmmm, now that's a Cancer for you. I'd been with this cat for five years and if it's one thing I knew for sure, he hated to get deep. It was like he was allergic to heavy conversation and would break out in hives from the mere thought of doing so. Butterflies, began to flutter in my stomach, accompanied by the strong urge to vomit. This was a sign that what he wanted to talk about wouldn't be good. It was also a sign that things may turn out worse for me than anyone else. He went on to confirm my theory by adding, *"Oh, I ain't fucking with "Thing" no more, I'm a start staying here with you, alright."* Well now, ain't I the lucky one!

I guess I was supposed to be impressed by his deceleration, but considering the amount of time it took for him to step his game up, instead I was insulted. I'd been on the scene for too long for him to try to pacify me like that. Something was definitely wrong and Solomon was definitely holding back. Not only was he holding back, but he was switching shit up as he went along. He'd already told me he's stopped seeing that girl who he chose to call "Thing" when he moved around on Spring Street. Then, two days later he came to see me around 4:00 p.m. in a rental packed with all of his things and said he wanted to take me out to dinner. Five years! I'd been with this cat for five years and not once had we been out to "dinner - dinner." We'd grab a bite to eat from Taco Bell or the Pizza shop, but we'd never gone out to enjoy a sit down meal. Who the hell did he think he was fooling?

Solomon had no idea I'd already gone to the doctor to find out what was ailing me. He had no idea I already knew what he wanted our little talk to be about. My doctor and I had a long history together, so when I called him and told him about my symptoms, he made time to see me that very same day. After doing a few simple tests, he dropped the bomb of all bombs on me by telling me I'd contracted an STD. The medical term for it is Gonorrhea, but its better know as "Burned."

While my doctor sat and wrote me out a prescription, I sat in his office speechless. I hadn't been with anyone else in over a year, maybe longer, and regardless of that I always used protection and got a check up in the end just as a precaution. I'd never been sick a day in my life! With all certainty, I knew Solomon had given this to me, but I wasn't sure if he was going to be man enough to admit it. Therefore, I didn't say anything to him when I found out. I got my shot, took my medication, and waited for his guilt to eat him up.

At the end of the week, Quan, Solomon, and me, went to dinner at Red Lobster. I ordered my entree and a kid's meal for my youth, and we sat and ate all the Cheddar Bay Biscuits and salad we could. Solomon, on the other hand, picked over his meal and barely spoke a word. *"Is ya food okay, Bugga'?"*

"Yeah, it's alright," he replied. Funny, three days ago this nigga had so much he wanted to talk about and say, now he's sitting quiet as a roach with the lights turned on. I put on a good front, but I was just as nervous as he was. No longer able to stand the suspense, I broke the silence and asked; *"What's up, Bugga', what did you want to talk to me about?"* Immediately you felt the eeriness of a bad vibe swoop down over our table. Solomon dropped his head as if her were ashamed and let his fork fall into his picked over plate. He refrained from making eye contact with me as he mumbled, *"Molly, why you wanna ruin my appetite?"* Then, he leaned back in his seat in order to deal with the pressure.

As I waited patiently for his response, I said hello to a few familiar faces seated a few tables away. The look on their faces also confirmed they could feel the vibe, but I wasn't there to cause a scene and was cordial just the same. I returned my attention to Solomon and asked, *"what's wrong,"* with all the concern I could conjure up. *"Thing burned me,"* he said in such a low tone, I could barely hear him. *"What?"* I asked? He then took a deep sigh, looked around the room, and said it again. *"I think "Thing" burned me."*

Finally, I was able to breathe a sigh or relief as I took another bit off my fork. I then leaned across the table and whispered, *"I know, 'cause you burned me..."* His eyes got big as his face turned to stone. He was speechless, but remained calm as I repositioned myself in my seat, continuing to enjoy my meal. *"So you knew?"*

"No, I didn't know. I didn't know until I was embarrassed by my doctor who I respect like a father after my exam! Do you know what it felt like for me as he scolded me about having unprotected sex with a man whose not monogamous? He called you a fool and said I'd be one

too if I didn't leave you alone..." He then had the audacity to wrinkle his face up as if he'd given me bad advice.

"*I'm sorry, Molly, Word is Bond I'm Sorry. I though I'd gotten rid of that shit before me and you...*" Solomon became silent again as he glanced over at Quan who was now coloring on his menu. "*I'm just glad you told me the truth, Bugga'.*"

"*I'm sorry, Molly, I'm sorry,*" was all he could say.

I know I should have been pissed, but I wasn't. Solomon found out he was infected and got treatment immediately. His only slip up was when he failed to remember he couldn't drink while taking it. He thought he was in the clear, but obviously he wasn't. In the meantime, the two of us engaged and the rest is history.

I didn't fault Solomon for what had happened, because I realized he didn't pass it on to me intentionally. The two of us had been abstinent for a few weeks and it was obvious he was taking precaution not to infect me. The time apart caused me to become suspicious, but never in a million years would I have suspected this. .

I allowed that wound to heal just like the rest and before long, was back to house hunting as planned. I was sure Solomon wasn't seeing his former roommate anymore because let him tell it, she was the one who burned him in the first place. Yet, my intuition warned me that something still wasn't right. My nights were becoming restless and my dreams were becoming vividly strange and weird. I knew my premonitions and visions always had some significance to them one way or the other, but this was outright odd. A red-boned bitch with long wavy hair had been the cause of my sleepless nights, and it was so bizarre because I didn't recognize her face. Though without fail, night after night, I saw this same chick in my dreams and didn't have a clue why. It was beginning to wonder if maybe this person posed some type of threat or danger to me and/or my son. Then, maybe I was just fatigued from doing and thinking so much.

Spending all day at work, then driving around all night in search of the perfect home did take quite a toll on me. There were times when Quan and I wouldn't get in until after 8:00 p.m.; sometimes Solomon would come in with us, sometimes he wouldn't show at all. Then, I took notice that I only dreamed that dream when he wasn't there...

Every since our little dinner date, Solomon had been spending more nights out than in. When I questioned why, he said his uncle had secured him a spot out in Lawrence, but only so he could have a formal address. Not a damn bit of what he said made any sense to me, and if that were the case, why have me out searching for a house? Also, why keep this new apartment such a secret? I'd lived in that tiny ass efficiency for three years and he always found it accommodating in the past. I knew there was so much more to the story than what he was letting on, but I didn't have any proof.

One Friday evening in particular, I had a dream so vivid, it almost felt as if that girl was in the room with me. The next morning I woke up scared and afraid, and later on walked around Spring to clear my head and see my Bugga'. As the two of us stood outside talking, Solomon's admirer, Dee-Dee, stared me in my mouth so hard, she could have counted my fillings. I ignored her as usual because she was as significant to me as a grain of sand. Then a car pulled up and low and behold, it was her, the girl from my dreams. At first I just stood there in amazement thinking, this has to be a joke. Where did she come from, who was she, and why did I know her? The same energy I got from my dreams was the same energy I felt when she pulled up. Her presence made me nervous, angry, and curious. Then came the kicker; she spoke to Solomon and he dropped his head but spoke back just the same. Startled would be an understatement to describe the look on my face. I quickly turned my attention to him and asked, *"Who is that, Bugga?"*

Duplicating the same low tone he had at the restaurant he looked at me and said. *"That's Ivy, Molly."*

"Oh, well is Ivy a friend of yours?" I asked.

"Yeah she a friend," he responded, but the way he said it didn't sit to well with me. On top of that, a crowd had formed on Dee-Dee's porch with all eyes on us as if something were about to jump off. Without saying a word to him, I took heed to my gut and walked over to her double parked car. In the background I could hear Solomon mumbling, *"She just a friend, Molly, she just a friend."*

"Hi, I'm Marie, who are you?" She hesitated for a second, shot her eyes over to Solomon, then said, *"I'm Ivy."*

221

"Hi Ivy, did you come around here to pick Solomon up?" I guess she wasn't expecting that one and neither was he. She then looked over at him and asked, *"Should I come back?"* *"Yeah come back,"* he said. She then drove off in a hurry.

"Okay Bugga' you know what! I'm tired of this shit! First it was this bitch across the street," I said pointing at Dee-Dee. *"Then it was ya dick!"*

"Come on, Molly, why you so loud?" Solomon hated it when I got loud and he hated to be embarrassed. *"Now this! Well you know what, Bugga'? Fuck You! Fuck You! Fuck You! Fuck You!"* I began walking away and he tried stopping me but it was useless. I had taken all I could take and if I didn't leave right then, at that very moment, I know in my heart I would have done something I would have regretted for the rest of my life. My dreams and instincts never lead me astray. I knew he was fucking that girl. I knew he was still fucking Dee-Dee's dumb ass too. But why was I still fucking with him? Clearly he didn't give two fucks about me. I was giving him 110%, and all he could do was make me look like a fool. I couldn't accept it anymore. My anger was raging. I couldn't look at him anymore. I had to get away. I had to flee.

Moments after I left Solomon standing on Spring Street, my son and I were home and I was packing our shit! I only had one duffle bag but it wasn't big enough for everything. I was also in need of money and didn't have a dime to my name. So we went to my Nana's house and I talked her into fronting me my check. I promised her I'd sign my check over to her once I got paid and I'd even make arrangements with my job to mail the check directly to her. Since I was still using her address for everything, she knew the check was guaranteed to reach her no matter what. She gave me the money, five-hundred dollars, but I didn't tell her anything about my plans. I also asked her for a suitcase. She tried not to pry, but couldn't help but to worry. I'd never come to her for that much money before and for Christ Sake, what did I need a suitcase for?

She could see I was upset, but I assured her me and the baby would be okay. Before we left, she grabbed Day'Quan, kissed him, and told him to take care of his mommy. It was too hard to stand at the door with the two of them as she said goodbye, so I stood on the elevator and held the button until my son got on with me. As the doors to the elevator shut close, I could hear my Nana yelling to me, *"Ree, I love you, baby!"*

"I love you too, Nana!" I replied in a cracked voice while fighting back my tears.

My son and I returned home and I continued to pack our things. Day'Quan has always been a very observant child, but he never once asked where we were going or why we were leaving home. He too could sense something was wrong and from experience, knew just to let me be. I called Greyhound to see out how much two round trip tickets would cost. Then, I called the train station to see when the next local was pulling out. We then jumped in a cab and headed for the station. We arrived in Newark around 3:00 in the afternoon and our bus was pulling out at 4:25. Once on board, I held my son close and cried like a baby. I knew running away never solved anything, but I didn't know what else to do. I was afraid of my own emotions. Afraid of what I would do. None of my family in Trenton knew I was leaving. I didn't say a word to anyone, not even my sister. None of my family in Detroit knew I was coming either. I only had one number to call and that was my grandma Estelle's work number. Our eighteen hour ride from Newark, NJ to the Motor City was going to be a long one. I was hoping I could think of something to say to my family, which would explain my unannounced visit without telling them the truth. But then again, they always told me if I ever wanted to come, just come. I'm glad they extended the offer. I really had no place else to go.

Day'Quan and I arrived at the Detroit bus station at around 4:00 a.m. I believe our trip took longer than expected, considering we had a two hour overlay in Toledo, Ohio. That eighteen hours must have been actual driving time. I knew my grandma wouldn't be to work until 8:00 a.m. In the meantime, my son and I bunked on the floor of the station, on top of the lockers, and when possible, on the chairs. We weren't the only commuters using the station as our Quality Inn, and it felt really weird to be so far away from home surrounded by strangers. I prayed to God the two of us would be okay.

I called my grandma as soon as I thought she was at work. I told her I was in town with the baby and she told me she would be there to pick us up immediately. The station was now full with workers, travelers, maintenance, and the homeless. I kept Quan close by my side as he laughed and talked with all of the Mid-Westerners and their funny accents. He was having a good time already and had no idea mommy was in distress. Funny, I'd already begun to forget about why I'd run away. Something about the Detroit atmosphere made me feel free. Now, I'd never seen my grandma before and wondered if the two of us would be able to recognize each other based on family resemblance. All I knew is that she had blonde hair and she knew I had blond hair and gold teeth. I kept my attention focused on the door to be sure I didn't miss her and once I saw her, it was like looking into a mirror.

Once she smiled at us, I smiled back and my heart felt at ease. She looked at me then looked at my son and said, *"You're a Henderson, just like ya Daddy!"* Then she hugged me tight. Wow, it took me damn near twenty to get that hug and it sure did feel good. *"Hi, Grandma,'"* I said. *"I'm so happy to see you!"* Grandma hugged me with one arm and pulled Day'Quan close to her with the other. She placed a call to her son, my uncle Vance, to tell him she was with us and we were on our way to her house. Then, we piled in her little Ford Escort and hit the highway headed to the W. Side of Detroit. West Grand Boulevard!

Grandma lived in a high rise apartment complex on W. Grand Boulevard, right down the street from the historical Motown Recording Studio/Museum. It took us a little over ten minutes to arrive, but once we were there she proudly escorted us up to her flat and told us to make ourselves at home. Grandma was excited to see us both but couldn't keep her hands off Quan to save her life. Every five minutes she was hugging him and squeezing him tight. She said he reminded her of her son, my dad, and the both of them reminded her of my dad's dad, Chester. My grandpa's genes were strong and you could see the resemblance from one generation to the next. Seeing her distant relatives sure did put a smile on her face but that smile didn't mean I was pulling the wool over her eyes. Grandma was wise just like my Nana and could tell I was troubled. *"What's wrong, Chile',"* she asked. *"What some man done did to you that got you runnin'?"*

Were all grandmas so intuitive I wondered? Why couldn't I just be up there for a visit? Why did I have to be running?

"I'm Okay grandma, I just needed a break and I wanted to come see you, that's all." She knew that was a lie, but we could talk about that later, Grandma had to get back to work. *"I'll be back in a few hours. I'll stop by the store on my way home so I can cook for y'all later."* She

sounded so excited. *"Y'all keep this door locked. "Ya' Aun-t Cookie is on her way over here to sit wit cha'. Feel free to what ever I have, but keep an eye on ya Aun-t. You know she's my troubled chile."* She laughed as she shut the door. Quan and I then went into the bedroom to unpack then take a shower. The ride had me exhausted but I was too amped to sleep. I walked into the bathroom to adjust the water temperature for my son and the phone rang. At first I was going to ignore it but it kept ringing. I didn't want to be forward but I was family. It wouldn't do any harm to pick up and tell the caller grandma was at work and to call back later. My reasoning took a few seconds but by then, even Quan wanted to answer it. *"Hello..."* There was a short silence and then I said it again. *"Hello."*

    "What the hell wrong with you, Murf?"

    "Oh my God...Daddy?"

    The voice on the other end of the phone was indisputable. I had no idea how my dad knew I was in Detroit and at that moment, I didn't even care. Everything was starting to freak me out; the dreams, my grandma's intuition, and now this. I didn't let it stress me but it damn sure had me thinking. *"Whut's up, Dad. Ain't nothing wrong with me, I'm cool. You know I'm just like you. I just get up and go like the wind."* I had to say something to make my actions sound good. But I doubt if he was fooled either. (Getting a call from my dad was beyond ironic, it was out right freaky! I stopped by his house the day I was leaving but changed my mind about knocking on the door. I figured he wouldn't' want to be bothered with my silly matters...)

****

    Detroit is a beautiful city, the hoods are famous and downtown is huge! I saw Tiger stadium, the Lions football field, the Detroit Science Center, the Fox comedy hall, the Renaissance, and of course Hitsville Motown USA. I ate the best food, visited relatives on both the West and East Side, saw the Ambassador Bridge from Bell Island, and me and my Aunt Cookie smoked almost a half pound! Long story short, I had a ball, Quan was having a good time and the two of us were at peace. Then, in the middle of my second week, I began to feel homesick. I missed my own hood, missed my sister, Nana, and like it or not, I missed that damn Solomon too...

I had the Bugga' Blues, and although it felt great to get away, I had unfinished business to take care of back home. Now that I could think straight, I was ready to return and face the music. I never confirmed nor denied my grandma's theory that I was running. I didn't want to get her all worked up over something I knew I could handle on my own. Besides, it felt good to meet and see the rest of my family for the very first time and I planned on making Detroit a routine vacation spot.

Quan and I returned home on a Monday evening. I was sure I was going to enter my home and find it in the worst condition ever but to my surprise everything was in tact. On top of that, there were clear signs that Solomon had been staying there while I was away. Now ain't that something? While I'm here he acts as if he can't chill but as soon as I leave he wants to stick close? Niggas.

Quan and I weren't home a good half hour before I saw the lock on the door turn turning. My heart was pounding because I wasn't ready to see him yet and as soon as the door opened I had a fit. *"What the fuck you doing with my key"* I asked. It was a shock to see Solomon's boy, Shawn, open the door and not him. But because Shawn knew me and knew me well, he didn't hesitate to place my key on the microwave and back out the door. *"What the fuck,"* I though. I know this Nigga ain't been letting other cats use my crib. I know he's not that stupid. Seconds later, Solomon came busting in like he was five-o. I stood in the kitchen staring at him while he picked Quan up, swung him around, and hugged him like it was his first birthday. Then, he looked at me the same way a disappointed parent looks at their child. His presence alone made me feel weak, but I refused to break. He approached me. I turned away. He hugged me. I pushed him away.

We sat and talked for a while. Quan was exhausted and fell asleep in the room with the T.V on. Solomon and I never left the kitchen. He sweet-talked me and told me he missed me, as he sucked on my ear and kissed the nape of my neck. I felt my knees buckle because I missed him too. He began undressing me. I couldn't resist. I didn't want to. He denied having any relations with Ivy. He said their only business was business. He said she was helping him get the information he needed to buy a restaurant. At the moment, my heart chose to believe him. Then we began to make love. I shed two tears. One for the joy I was feeling and one for the pain. I knew I was only repeating a cycle but it felt too good to stop. The next day he took me to the car dealer and got us a Lexus. It was registered to me but he put up the cash. He said he had been planning on getting me a car before I ran off to Detroit. Funny, for once, we were on the same page because those were my exact plans for me and Quan once I returned. I didn't know if he was telling me the truth or not, but I knew the two of us would never manage with only one car. The Lexus wasn't a bad deal, but the Chevy Lumina I bought later on was even sweeter. I didn't mind having two cars in my name. At least I only had to worry about one payment.

****

On the flip side, Droop had gotten word that I was M.I.A. Upon my return he couldn't wait to get at me to see what was up. I knew after being away for so long, he'd be willing to tell me anything I wanted to know about Solomon and Dee-Dee. But what he didn't know is that I'd gotten myself in deeper with Solomon by signing for that car. Hopefully I wished, since he wanted to put the car in my name, he was looking to be in it for the long haul. Droop was predictable, and just as I suspected, he continued to warn me to watch Solomon because he was sneaky. Well now, isn't that the pot calling the kettle black!

Again, I knew Droop was being truthful, but by this point what could I do? Solomon was never around, always busy, and had a car in my name. I was always alone, always lonely, and had a car of my own. Droop always needed a ride and I always needed a shoulder to cry on…

Solomon kept trying to assure me his affiliation with other females was purely business related. However, I found it very hard to believe due to the change in his attitude when ever I popped up on the scene. He was always trying to rush me off or send me down to the house so we could talk there. We'd argue about me never going to this "apartment out Lawrence," and why I never drove the car; and he used it against me claiming I was too argumentative. Then, one day while securing things in the closet, I found a Valentines Day card to him from Dee-Dee and it was reeking with cheap perfume. The inside of the car was signed, "Love Dee-Dee." Her proclamation made me sick!

While storming around Spring, the hurt in the pit of my chest kept crying why? Why go through all of the trouble to hold on to me, if all he was going to do is hurt me? Why take me through the same shit I went through with the last man? Why not be better?

Solomon admitted Dee-Dee gave him the car, but said he had no control over it. He also claimed he left it on the porch, and she was the one who put it in the bottom of his bag before he walked off.

"Well if she did it, you encouraged her actions!" Solomon dropped his head, then disgustedly walked out the door. I stood on the store steps for a minute then spotted Dee-Dee walking across the street. She noticed me, then made an about face. I knew she was on her way to see Solomon, but seeing me foiled her plan. Turning around did nothing more then just piss me off. I jumped in my car and drove slowly beside her. She refused to look my way but I couldn't let it go. I had to say something. I had to let her know how I felt…

"You better fall back, or I'm a make you fall!" She showed her heart, said something slick back to me and that was all the ammunition I needed. I got out of the car and commenced to whooping her ass. *"If you want to play hard ball, bitch, then I'm gonna teach you how to play!"* I belittled myself because I wanted to prove a point, but didn't know who I was proving the point to. Beating her up wasn't going to change anything. But it sure did make me feel better for the moment!

The drama didn't end there either. A few months later I caught Ivy driving the Lexus, and to make it even worse, she had the girls in the car with her! I don't know what hurt the most. Seeing another chick pushing a car that was technically mine, or seeing another chick with the kids I've taken care of and loved like my own.

"Was this nigga stupid or what?" I called him but he didn't answer his phone, so I followed the car over into a PA laundromat. I called Solomon again, still no answer. I sat in the parking lot for a minute just to gather my thoughts, and when I walked inside, his youngest daughter Bear spotted me, and her eyes got as bit as melons. Then, his oldest looked up and stood stiff in her spot. I didn't say a word to either of them, but Bear ran over and hugged me around my waist. Ivy then looked up and was startled to see me standing there. For the sake of the children, I didn't want to make a scene. So I asked her if we could step outside and talk. She had no idea why, but agreed just the same.

"Look, at this point, I really don't care what you and Solomon do. You can have him for all I care but the car you're driving is mine!

It's registered in my name and so is the title. I'm not even going to trip about it this time, because I know this is all his doing. But I promise you, if I catch you behind the wheel of this car again, there will be a price to pay!"

Ivy wasn't disrespectful or arrogant like I thought she would have been, and I couldn't believe my ears as I listened to her side of the story. She told me she thought the car belonged to an older lady named "Marie" who lived on N. Willow in a senior building. I could tell she wasn't the brightest bulb in the pack, but regardless of her smarts, my beef wasn't with her, it was with him. I left Ivy and the girls at the laundromat to do their thing and found Solomon around the way, at the store, behind the counter with Chino and Meech. He could see the angry look on my face but had no idea of what had gone down. Ivy must have been trying to call him when I arrived because he kept pressing the ignore button on his phone. As I stood there with tears in my eyes, my brother Chino gave him a look of disgust. Chino was Solomon's friend, but he hated to see his sister hurt.

Without saying a word, I yanked Solomon's chain from my neck, threw it at him, and told him we were through! As I walked out, I yelled for him to take that mother fucking car out of my name or I was going to call the police and report it stolen. I jumped into my car with my son, drove home, and for the hundredth time, cried myself to sleep.

Solomon wasn't just unfaithful, he was a whore! He was sleeping with me, Dee-Dee, and now this bitch. Ilk! Droop was right, Solomon was sneaky but his sneakiness had now converted over to out right disrespectfulness. A few days went by and Solomon came down to see me, hoping to patch things up. He even had the nerve to give me an extra set of keys to the car as if that meant something. I threw the keys back at him and told him I wanted the car out of my name. He fussed, about doing so, claiming I was the only one he could trust. Ha, now ain't that a laugh. Trust? If you asked me he didn't know the meaning of the word. Solomon swore up and down nothing like that would ever happen again, and that he'd explain everything to me later. Later never came and neither did the explanation. Less than a month after our talk, I caught Ivy behind the wheel of the car again, and this time I wasn't so nice.

It's funny how it all went down because until I woke up with the munchies, I was in the bed sleep. I only went out so I could hit 7-11 and pick me up a beef hot-dog. On my way home, I decided to get off the highway and cut through the hood. It was late and the block was dry. I wasn't expecting to find Solomon or anyone else out and about at that hour, but one should always expect the unexpected.

Initially when I spotted the car, I though he was in it talking to someone on the sidewalk. Then as I approached, I saw he was the one on the sidewalk and she was behind the wheel. At fist he didn't see me and that's probably because I turned my lights off. But as soon as he did, he motioned for her to drive off but she was so busy fussing at him, she didn't pay him any attention. When I pulled up along side of her, I didn't even bother to acknowledge his presence. I just rolled down my window and upon eye contact said to her, "Now what did I tell you!"

Ivy looked at me but didn't utter a word. Solomon tried to say something to one of us but never budged from the porch. He saw me reach into my back seat for the bat, and that's when Ivy put her foot to the floor and sped off. I started to chase after her but did them both one better. Instead of getting myself into trouble, I threw the car in reverse, backed down the street to the corner, and used the pay phone to call the police. (I left my cell home since I didn't plan on being out that long)

I reported the car stolen just as I said I would and as I waited for the police, fussed to no end. *"Molly, why you,"* bla, bla, bla, I didn't want to hear it. I gave him an ultimatum and he chose to ignore me. He made his bed, now he had to lay in it!

I gave my report to the police and once they were gone, I jumped back into my car and took off. I didn't know if I was looking for him, her, or both but I knew I was going to find somebody. My Godson Dre' tagged along with me for the ride, but honestly his ass should have been in the bed sleep too. The two of us didn't have to go far because I ran into Solomon at the corner of Montgomery and Perry, waiting for the light. When our eyes locked on each other, his facial expression froze. Dre' froze too because he could tell it was about to be on. My light was green and I made a sharp left pulling up along side of him. The two of us were now blocking all traffic as I signaled for him to roll the window down. He laughed and me and said he didn't feel like it, then he rolled his eyes. His lack of concern for my feelings had hit an all time high and with the Lox *"Wile' Out"* playing loudly in my ears, I decided to take their advice and do just that. I think it was Swizz who set me off when he said, *"If you find your man cheating, come on, Boo, Fuck that, Wile' Out!"*

Solomon was still waiting for his light to turn green and didn't see me grab the bat as I exited my car. I told my Godson to pull my car out of the street and by the time Solomon looked up, I was busting the windows out his car! Solomon was in shock as he sat behind the wheel, unable to back up or go forward. The satisfaction of seeing the look on didn't alleviate the pain in my heart, but it was a start! It would have been better for the both of us if he would have just left me alone and taken the car out of my name, than play with my emotions and use me. I could take a lot, but everyone has their breaking point.

As glass shattered all over the place, it ripped cuts in my arms, hands, and even my neck. Solomon couldn't believe his eyes and by the time he got out of the car, I was working on the sun-roof. As I raised the bat in the air, Solomon wrapped his hand around my neck, but that didn't stop me from striking the car. I was in a zone...

Solomon and I never had any closure to our problems, we just let them fade away. I guess that was best considering he was never going to be straight up and honest with me. It's sad how we allowed ourselves to get to that point, because we started out as such a happy pair, as many couples do. The dust settled on our dispute and weeks later he came and informed me that he and Ivy were no longer friends. How noble of him to inform me after the damage was done. Had he been so caring in the first place, it would have saved the both of us a lot of heartache and pain.

SOMETIMES YOU GOTTA' MOVE AWAY TO MAKE A WAY...

ON THE COME UP

I n February of 2000, I made up my mind to move out of the hood, across town to the Chambersburg "Burg" section of Trenton, aka Little Italy. My decision to do so couldn't have come at a better time either because the community I'd grown to love was slowly falling apart. Spring and Passaic had begun to look like the lower east side of Harlem, and the projects were completely off the hook. As luck would have it, I wasn't even scheduled to look at the place I secured. I just happened to be riding down the street and spotted a "For Rent" sign in the window of a huge, second floor apartment. I pulled over to write down the number, and the gentleman parked in front of me in a green Nissan Maxima got out and asked me did I want to take a look inside. He said he'd been waiting for someone else to come do a walk through, but since she hadn't shown up yet he'd be glad to show it to me.

Before entering, I knew this would be my new home. Upon opening the door I was stunned at how shiny and bright the hardwood steps were that lead to the apartment. Once inside, I remained in awe at how roomy and immaculate the place was. Talk about lucking up! The entire flat had brand new hardwood floors, a huge eat-in kitchen, and the lighting was perfect. The room that would be my son's was the size of two medium bedrooms, had three large windows, and two walk in closets with enough storage for all of his toys and belongings. The master bedroom was located on the second floor and it was the apartment's best feature. It was the size of efficiency or a small club, with plush carpet so deep, you left foot imprints in it when you walked. Even though it was going to run me an additional $275.00, there was no way I was going to pass up such a sweet deal. In the end it would be worth it. My son was definitely worth it and, therefore, I was going to make it happen.

Quan and I moved in immediately and within a few months, were use to our new environment and enjoying ourselves. The only thing that concerned me at this point was the lack of children in the area for him to play with. Aside from the little boy next door, who was two years younger then him, there weren't any other kids in the neighborhood for him to play with. Columbus Park was down the street from us, but it was too far for him to walk there alone. So for the most part, after summer camp he was either in the house with me watching TV or around the corner at Peaches' house doing the same with her youngest daughter. It's funny how that played out too because I had no idea Peaches had moved from N. Trenton or lived so close. Seemed like no matter where I went, Droop and his family were always somewhere close by.

Things finally seemed to be looking up for me and my son it was about time. I was in a beautiful new spacious place. My son and I no longer had to share the same room or bed. And for the first time in my life, I had a car that nobody helped me get and I was current with my payments and insurance. Things were so good for us that I went out and got a second job at Super G to make sure I didn't fuck up or fall behind. When September rolled around, I enrolled Quan in Harrison Elementary, which was the best school in the area aside from Washington. I could have put him in Washington but it was a further walk. So Harrison was our choice until he became older and more responsible.

As for my relationship with Solomon, he and I were still an item and my move to *The Burg* decrease the stress between us two measurably. We were back to making love to each other again on a regular and the closeness between us felt good. My son was now able to see a glow on my face and his reciprocated the same, and that also warmed my heart. For what it's worth, Solomon now had the time to sit back and evaluate our situation and felt my moving out of the hood was the best thing yet. *The Good Life Bug* had finally gotten the best of him and due to his kid's mother experiencing some hard times, we all agreed that it would be a good idea if the girls stayed with me. This way, they too could go to a better school and live in a better environment. The two of them were already calling me mom and Quan always has a father figure. We had nothing to lose if we stayed on track, and the kids were all excited to her the news and were eager to move in.

Solomon had broken a lot of promises to me. So many I'd lost count. But to shrug his responsibilities with the kids was an all time low. I thought things were going well for all of us, but no sooner then the girls moved in, he was back on his shit and the stress had returned. Only this time, it was tenfold because I had two additional mouths to feed with nothing more being brought to the table. He knew I loved the girls but I could only do so much. Eventually, I had to go out and get yet another part time job just to make ends meet. This time it was a sit down receptionist gig at Lawrence Lincoln Mercury on Rt. 1. I thought Solomon would have been glad to hear I was back on my grind since he was still hounding me about getting a house. But as soon as I told him where I'd be working, he got spooked!

Having gone through the drama far too many times, I knew not to let my intuition be known. Instead, I sought answers from my brother Chino, but not even he had a clue to Solomon's strange, paranoid, and unusual behavior. Chino was never one to chose sides, and deep down wanted things to work out for Solomon and me. However, he couldn't ignore the fact that I was a magnet for drama, and that I didn't have to go looking for trouble because it was sure to find me! *"You got a good heart, Sis', it's fucked up but bad shit always happens to good people."*

Chino hit the nail right on the head. About two months after I started working at Lawrence Lincoln Mercury, my dreams of Ivy returned. I knew not to ignore them but I was afraid at what they'd reveal. What's done in the dark always comes to the light is what Nana always said. On that note, I saw a flicker of light one afternoon while on lunch break from my full time job. I was low on funds and needed to go pick up my check. On the way back to town, I jumped in the wrong lane and was forced to go straight down Franklin Corner Road instead of making my left. It was no big deal. I'd just turn around and head back the other way. When I did, I could have sworn I saw Solomon pulling into an apartment complex off to the right. I slowed down once I reached the entrance to get a closer look but the car was no where in sight. After realizing how paranoid I was acting, I laughed it off and said to myself, *"Damn, Molly, it's not like he has the only Lexus like that in the world. Stop trippin..."*

Paranoia can have its pros and cons, but in my case, it's always worked in my favor. Ordinarily, I'd be pleased for my man to pop up on me and see what time I was getting off, but in this case, I knew there was more to it. During the day he was elusive, but at night he wanted to check in. Something didn't add up. Then one evening I had that God awful reoccurring dream about Ivy again, only this time I could vividly recalled a phone number. I dialed it, and low and behold, the voice on the other end was a woman. It was Ivy!

Love is beautiful when it's reciprocated the same as it's dished out. But when you're in love and the one you're in love with doesn't love you the same, it can make you physically sick! My legs began to shake, my heart began to race, and my heart began to crumble. Now it all made sense! Now I knew why I kept dreaming about her when he wasn't there, and I was 100% sure it was Solomon I saw pulling into that complex out Lawrence.

I jumped into my car and sped straight up Rt. 1. I pulled into the same complex I saw Solomon pull into, and once I reached the first lot, I saw all the proof any love sick woman needed. The Lexus was parked in lot number 201 and up in the balcony was Ivy with her back turned to the glass. I didn't want to believe my eyes but I couldn't deny them either. I wanted to remove the tags from the car but didn't have any tools to do so, plus, I was afraid someone would see me and call the police. I'd set out for answers and now that I'd found them, I couldn't deal. Solomon had been dealing with that girl every since I went to Detroit. He was using me to take care of his children, while all along he was building another home somewhere else. Word on the street had it that he owed her father a large sum of money. I guess that's why he felt obligated to let her hold the car. As I sat there putting the pieces to the puzzle together, I wanted to throw a brick through the window but didn't have the will power to get out. I just continued to sit with the engine running, wondering what lie or excuse he would come up with this time to make this all go away. Moreso, I was thinking what could I do to make it all go away? I don't believe he was aware of how bad he was hurting me. I think he was too wrapped up in the game to even notice…

"BLACK MAN"

Black Man, Black Man,
When will you understand?
In order for me to be a **WOMAN**
You have to be a man.

Black Man, Black Man,
When will you see?
A single woman, wit a child,
That's not a family.

I bear a heavy load.
I stand strong when I'm alone.
So am I asking too much when I ask,
For my Black Man to come home?

Home the foundation of families.
Home the start of New Life.
I don't need diamonds & documents
To prove that I'm your wife!

Black Man, Black Man, what did I do?
To make you promise me things, you knew
You wouldn't stick around to see through?
Black Man, Black Man, what happened to **TRUST?**.
Now look at that word, what happened to tr**ust**?

Black Man, Black Man, the disappointment & disrespect.
Even though I will forgive, I'll never quite forget.
You were **DEEP** with ya' shit **Black Man**!

Black Man, Black Man, I'm definitely not a hater
But karma comes round, a lot sooner then later.
Black Man, Black Man, you ain't getting any younger

and every time you hit that block you look a little dumber.

Black Man, Black Man, I've done all that I could do.
To open your eyes,
To touch ya' heart
To try to get through to you.

Black Man, Black Man I'm neither bitter nor mad.
I've shed a thousand tears, but you're the one who's truly sad.
My sweet Beautiful Black Man......

Once again the joke was on me, and as usual, I was the last to know. I even heard that the two of them had run off and gotten married in Aruba. If so, it would explain his week long trip to Cali to make a pick up. Solomon was no different then Pharaoh, except he wasn't running around having kids by everyone he laid with. Solomon knew I was so in love with him, that I'd forgive him for just about anything. But being in love and being able to take care of three young children was something all together different.

By now, there was no more me and Solomon and the only thing that held us together was the car. Unexplainably, Dee-Dee moved in with his mom, yet he claimed to have no influence over her taking her in. Bla bla, bla, nigga! If Dee-Dee was good enough to live with his Mama rent free while I struggled and worked three jobs to make ends meet, then she was damn sure good enough to take care of his kids too! She longed to take my place and walk in my shoes, so now, here was her chance to do so. Turning my back on the girls was the last thing I wanted to do. I hesitated for days, trying to think of a solution that would save us all, but there wasn't any. In the best interest of everyone, I felt I had no other choice but to pack the girls things up and send them back to their grandma. His oldest daughter was mad at me but the youngest was really hurt.

"You said you'd love us forever," she cried as I told her it was time to go. *"I will love you forever, baby, but this is more then I can handle."* I didn't want to lie to her, but I didn't know how to make things better either. I was worried about their school and if he was going to be man enough to make sure they got there every day. I was going to

volunteer to pick them up in the morning but that would only keep the cycle of things going. Dee-Dee was there with them now. Let her see to it that they get where they need to be. I was through…

Solomon called my actions mean-hearted and selfish. He said I was taking my anger out on the girls when they had nothing to do with anything. It amazed me how he could be so conscience when it suited him. All he ever though about was himself! He didn't think about how the situation was emotionally damaging to me, the girls, and Quan. Poor Quan, he really loved Solomon too, and he had become so attached to the girls. How could he expect me to take care of those babies when he was out doing God knows what with God knows who. Even their mother understood my reasoning.

I couldn't believe it. Within less than a year of my move, all of my plans, hopes, and sacrifices had been destroyed. Foolishly, I continued to have sex with Solomon but in time, that faded away as well. I don't know how it happened, but as Solomon was falling back, Droop was coming on stronger then ever. Eventually, he became my full-time lover and I'd become no better than what I despised. I was fighting a endless battle between spirit and flesh, and I was losing the fight. Hopefully, I wouldn't lose the war.

I was still in love with Solomon but being with Droop helped ease the pain. He kept a smile on my face, and I was able to focus more on being happy instead of how to undo the past. He and I were so into each other, we didn't stop to think about anyone else. I didn't think about Solomon and he didn't think about his girl. Okay, here we go again…

****

Droop and I never considered ourselves a couple, but our dealings weren't as secretive as I thought they were. Nobody ever said anything to us about it, but not everybody was fooled by our brother sister act. I don't know why I always dealt with a man who had baggage, then expected things to change later on down the line. But in this case, I wasn't looking for change or a permanent relationship, I was cool with the two of us just having fun. Droop's chick was a good girl. She was pretty, smart, and didn't run in the streets. I didn't know his reasons for stepping out on her with me the way he did and I didn't care. Call it selfish, scorned, or what have you, bottom line is we were getting away with our shit and dared anyone to try and stop us!

You know, when the shoe's on the other foot you can always point the finger. But when you find yourself in those same shoes you're often too close to the forest to see the damn trees! I'm not making excuses, I'm just saying... In our little down-low situation, nobody was supposed to get hurt. All of his people, including his mom, rolled with the punches and supported our front of being brother and sister. All of my people did the same too, but there were a few who actually fell for our charade. Droop's girl, Blaque', was one of the few who took our alliance as platonic. On top of that, she wound up befriending me, on the strength of him.

At first it was cool and it started out with her just calling me on his behalf to see if I could come pick him up. That was the play-off. Then we started chilllin' with each other, smoking with each other at my crib, and hanging out. That then escalated to me meeting her mother, sister and brothers; as well as her grandmother, cousins, and father. Before you knew it, the two of us were hanging out with each other and he wasn't even around. In addition to that, we took little trips together to the beach, participated in family outings, broke bread with each other, and slept in each other's bed.

As twisted as it may sound, although I was screwing her man, I did grow to love Blaque' as a friend. I know it sounds fucked up, but there was a method to my madness. I played devil's advocate and double roles in order to protect her feelings, not break her heart. But when she started confiding in me about the problems she and he were having, it made me feel like shit! I felt like shit, but we didn't stop doing each other. This, by far, had to be one of the *"triflin'"* periods of my life. Fucking over Solomon didn't bother me as bad as fucking over Blaque'. She was so pretty with her model shape body, flawless mocha skin and eyes that never needed liner or mascara. If nobody else, she was the innocent one in all of this and didn't' deserve to be treated so unfair.

With a heavy heart, I tried reasoning with Droop about falling back but he wasn't having it. *"Molly, we been messing around for years... If we switch up now, people gonna start to get suspicious."* His logic made sense but our actions still weighed heavy on my heart. Especially, when Blaque' started confided in me about the trouble she was experiencing with him. There were so many times when I wanted to just drop a bomb on her and confess our actions, but at the same time, I knew the truth would be devastating. I, of all people, knew how crushed she'd be to learn we'd been doing her dirty right in her face. Sometimes, literally, right in her face! The similarities between me and Droop were parallel to those with Amber and Pharaoh. The only difference was I'd been messing with Droop long before Blaque' stepped on the scene, however, she wasn't aware of it.

In my alone time, I thought to myself how in the world could she not suspected anything, considering a woman's intuition always warns her to guard her heart. Blaque' was far from naïve, but it's a known fact that some women only see what they want to see. In the midst of my dilemma, the best I could do to ease my mind was retell Blaque' my story about Pharaoh and Amber. I'd tell her the story and compare Pharaoh to Droop with the hopes she'd compare me to Amber. This way I figured she'd catch my drift, but she never put the pieces of the puzzle together. I guess since she knew how in love I was with Solomon, she didn't think I could step out on him. Still, each and every time I had a chance to reflect on my past my conscience warned me to do one or two things, either A, confess to the girl about what was really going on *(Yeah right that wasn't going to happen)* or B, quit screwing Droop.

My intentions were never to come between the Blaque' and Droop, and I damn sure didn't mean to get as close to her as I did. In my eyes, he was just my young dude and regardless of my actions, my heart was still with Solomon. I could never see myself with Droop in the long run because of the huge age difference between us. But his age had nothing to do with his dick, and didn't prevent the two of us from catching feelings.

Being the oldest in the situation, I felt responsible for everything. I felt responsible for protecting Blaque', I felt responsible for protecting Droop, and I felt responsible if either one of them would have gotten hurt. My paranoia caused me to look at everyone under a microscope, including Droop, and trusting anyone was out of the question. As for Solomon, he didn't seem to have any suspicions, but that could have also been a front. Maybe he never said anything to me because in turn, he didn't want me questioning him. Then one day out of the blue, my boy

Munchy asked me were me and Droop really sister and brother. *"Yeah,"* I told him, with a tad bit of wonder in my response. Munch then laughed at me and said; *"Murf, that boy don't look at you like he your brother. That nigga look at you like he in love!"*

I tried to deny our involvement but it was almost impossible. Droop's aunts and cousins were always saying shit that put the two of us on the spot, and his father who lived way Up-State New York confessed he knew about our dealings, even before he went away! So, with all of this coming to the light how could Blaque' and Solomon still be in the dark? It didn't add up. Maybe Blaque' was just staying close with me so she could keep an eye on him. Maybe Solomon was staying close so he could keep the car? Maybe some of the puzzle pieces were still missing. Maybe I was just losing my mind…

As time progressed, believe it or not, my concern for Blaque's feelings grew greater than concern for my own. Every time I looked at her I was reminded of the hurt I endured when I found out about the affair Pharaoh had with Amber. However, the two of them were only exposed because Amber was dumb enough to get pregnant. Droop and I didn't have to worry about that because of my infertility. So unless someone literally caught the two of us in the act, we really had noting to worry about. This is what I told myself in order to sleep at night. But Nana's warning still echoed in my heart and head. *"Ree, Baby, what's done in the dark, will always come to the light."*

Maybe Nana just wasn't slick enough to get away with her shit like we were. That was something else I told myself in order to sleep. However, contrary to what I chose to believe, our cockiness and over confidence caused us to become careless and sloppy. He and I carried on as if we had license to do so. We were addicted to one another, and everyone knows addictions aren't good…

****

Sometime towards the end of July, shortly after another fun day at the beach, Droop caught a charge that landed his ass in jail. This put a definite damper on our *entertaining,* but just as with Pharaoh, I viewed his incarceration as a blessing in disguise. Something had to slow the two of us down. However, unlike Pharaoh, Droop wasn't looking to call it quits and was determined to keep in contact with me. With that said, he called me every morning on my job at 10:00 a.m. sharp, and we stayed on the phone until noon. If I was away from my desk, my girl Missy would take the call for me and talk to him until I returned. I knew accepting collect calls were against policy, but I had game to run down on them if they caught or questioned me. Besides, I wasn't the only one who did it and wouldn't be the last either.

Once my lunch rolled around, the two of us would hang up and he'd give me ten minutes to get across town to his mother's where our conversation would resume. This is when shit should have become real obvious to all those who claimed to be in the dark. I say that because Droop knew his chick would be there waiting on that same call, but would tell her to give the phone to me once I arrived. The man was relentless but I can't lie, I looked forward to those calls, because even from behind bars, Droop made me feel more loved than Solomon.

Blaque', on the other hand, showed signs of jealousy concerning the phone calls and even had the nerve to talk bossy to me one day like I was some type of sucka. She was really starting to show her colors now that he was away, and her actions confirmed my suspicions that she wasn't as sweet and naïve as others thought. Either that, or Peaches was throwing grease in the game by pretending she too didn't know what was going on. Blaque' had no idea that as soon as she was out of sight, Peaches was calling me on the three way so I could talk to her son! Ha, Ha, the things a mother will do for her child…

****

They say absence makes the heart grow fonder. Droop was only away for a minute but it was long enough for me and my twat to miss him. I didn't want to admit it, but I was in love with my best friend! With all that was going on and going wrong in my life, Droop was my security blanket. I never had to search for him, I never had to wonder, and when ever I needed or wanted him, he'd drop whatever it was he was doing just to be by my side. Amazingly, although Solomon and I still had our connections, I felt more obligated to Droop than him. It's also amazing that the entire time he was away, Solomon and I only had sex once. The date was August 28th, 2000, two weeks prior to Droop's release and ironically, it was out last time.

Due to a little help from yours truly, Droop was released on bail. However, it wasn't because he had the money; it was because I put my good name behind his, and signed his release papers. I had no intentions on signing any dotted line for no nigga ever again, but when Peaches came to me one evening at my part-time and asked for my help, I couldn't say no. As it turns out, both her and Blaque' tried to do so together, but didn't possess the right credentials. From the look on her face I could tell I was the last person she wanted to come to, but at the same time, I was the only person she could count on. She knew I'd do anything for Droop and she knew she'd only have to ask once. I know obtaining my help must have left a bad taste in Blaque's mouth. I mean really, what woman feels comfortable knowing another woman has to rescue her man...

As long as I wasn't at risk, I didn't see a problem with helping Droop out. Blaque' quickly told me not to worry because Droop had the dough, and if he didn't she did. Peaches concurred, adding she'd make sure the payments were made on time, and from there, the deal was sealed. Droop was released on the 6th of September, but the two of us didn't bump heads until the 10th. Although I'd signed for his release, I went out of my way to avoid running into him. I didn't really want to cut him off, but I didn't want to continue on with the lies. I utilized all the strength and willpower I possessed to refrain from slipping up, but felt childish for going out of my way to do so.

The 10th was a Sunday, Quan was at my mom's and I was on my way home from church. As usual, like after any service, I needed to cop a dutch for later on. I should have and would have taken the scenic route, but instead, opted to go up the Blvd. The streets were deserted; they always were on a Sunday morning and I just knew Droop was still home in the bed. Even if he was out and about at that hour, I didn't think he'd be posted up outside anywhere after just getting out of the pokey. But old habits die hard or either he was just hard headed, because as soon as I came around the bend I saw him standing right in front of 682.

Upon spotting him, I immediately slowed down due to disbelief. I wanted to keep driving and just toot my horn, but he got out in the middle of the street and flagged me down. I pulled over on Ingram, turned off the car, straightened out my dress, and got out of the car. I had my money in my hand and proceeded to walk in the store, but stopped to hug him in the process. His demeanor was so sincere, I could barely keep a straight face. His grip around my waist was a strong as a bear but at the same time, as gentle as a lamb. When I walked out the store, he walked to the car with me and after noticing the cigar in my hand, asked me if I wanted to smoke. Aww man, all I could do was laugh. To him my response was *"Yeah,"* but in my head I was saying, *"Yeah right, smoke my ass."*

Seven weeks! Droop and I had been apart from one another seven weeks, so it didn't take a rocket scientist to figure out what was going to happen once we got to my crib. The drive home was short and there was absolutely no traffic on the roads. Once we reached the crib, we locked the doors and propped chairs up against them as usual, then took it on up to the second floor. My heart was racing but not because I was nervous. I could feel my body getting heated just at the sight of him, and Droop's soft and clammy touch didn't make matters any better. I thought about Solomon and what would happen if he decided to drop by. What would he do once he couldn't get in and how the hell was Droop going to get out...

I stood up against the window and Droop sat down on the bed and removed his boots. He had on a pair of black Timberlands. You know *Boys N The Hood* wear Tim's all year long. I cracked the dutch and he broke up the weed. We rolled up and smoked, then rolled around under the covers until about 1:00 p.m. It was hot as hell in my room and we were without A.C. I wasn't in the habit of getting completely undressed while making love to him because we never knew when we'd have to jump up quickly and get dressed. But in all that heat, getting naked was unavoidable. Droop knew I was shy and use to anticipate my giggles each and every time he exposed my breast from my bra. That was the best part about being with him, no matter what the situation, he was always able to make me laugh.

Droop's strength was his honesty, and not only was he able to capture my heart, he was also able to keep it. He never lied to me and allowed me to have my way even if I was wrong. He continued to posses a childish charm, which despite everything else, showed his good intent outweighed his bad. As a teen I could never understand my admiration for that boy and as an adult I was just as puzzled. After our session, the two of us smoked again as I took him back to the Blvd, but by now, the streets were flooded. As I drove off, I heard one of his boys yell to him his chick had been looking for him, and to tell him she'd be back. I tooted my horn as a sign of saying good-bye, and he signaled to me he'd call me later. If adoring him was wrong, I didn't want to be right!

****

Shit was all fucked up and it would take a miracle to fix the mess we'd all gotten ourselves into. Amazingly, despite all of the cheating, disrespect, and tangled web of deceit, Solomon and I still found it very hard to walk away from one another. In October of that year, I started to feel sick again and immediately suspected him of being the source, contributing it to the last time we shared ourselves with one another. True, Droop and I had been together since then, but he was fresh out and didn't have time to catch anything, or at least I hoped not. No, I couldn't suspect him, he didn't have any strikes against him. It had to be Solomon!

Fearful of what my doctor would say if he found out I allowed the same man to sting me twice, I went to Planned Parenthood and got tested for a STD. The results were negative and I was happy I wasn't that type of sick again, but something was still wrong. While unaware of what was ailing me, I'd cut Droop off in order to protect him, and he repaid my consideration by busting off a few shots at my car while I sat in it. I knew he wasn't trying to hit me, but I was pissed because bullets do ricochet! I explained to him why I didn't want to mess around and he wasn't happy, just relieved it wasn't because of Solomon or anyone new. I laughed at his jealousy which he called concern, then gave in to desire as usual.

I don't know what makes sex so good between an older woman and a younger man, but what ever it is someone needs to patent it! For a man to let lose his moans of pleasure and state his claim, *"This is my pussy,"* will send a sista into a seizure of climaxes. Our lust for one another drove one another past the point of no return and our rebellious nature forbid us to see past the moment. The only thing that distracted me from him was the worry over what was wrong with me? I kept feeling sick and sluggish, just like before, and on that note accepted the fact that I needed to see my doctor. My cycle had been irregular lately so possibly I needed some hormone replacements to get it back on track. My last period was in the middle of August, right before Solomon and I had our last interlude, but it wasn't as heavy as usual. The results of my visit were shocking, and just like I expected, Solomon was the cause. Only this time I left with something a lot heavier to think about then a STD. They say lightning never strikes in the same spot twice, but I'd be one to argue that theory. Lightning had struck me twice, and with something I thought was totally inconceivable. For the second time in my life I was with child. For the second time in my life, I was pregnant!

****

Pregnant! Pregnant! Pregnant! Now how the hell could that be and they said it was impossible? I was sure my doctor was mistaken and I argued with him until he kicked me out of his office. He gave me paperwork to go get a blood work done to determine how far along I was, and to call him as soon as I was done. Pregnant! Just putting that word and me in the same sentence seemed universally impossible, nevertheless, the thought of having another child filled me with joy. I said it would take a miracle to fix the mess we'd all gotten ourselves into. Maybe my pregnancy was the answer?

On several occasions I tried telling Solomon I was going to have a baby, but I could never get up the nerve. I wanted to wait until the time was right, but that timing never arrived. Ironically, he was spending more time with me at the crib than ever before, and truthfully, I thought he'd notice the chance in my appearance and behavior. I was eating up everything in sight and every time he called me I was asking him to bring me something to eat. He use to joke and say, *"That's fat people shit, Molly,"* but I thought he was just waiting for me to tell him what he already knew. I'd even throw little hints at him like, *"Bugga' you gon' buy me some sweat-suits cause pretty soon I'm not gonna be able to fit these jeans,"* or, *"Can you go and get me some comfortable shoes because when my feet swell it's gonna be a mess trying to put these on."* Truthfully, I was just waiting for doctor Murthy to give me the results of the blood test. This way when I did sit down and tell him, I could tell him how far I was too.

It took two weeks before Dr. Murthy gave me a call, and by then doubt had returned. I thought the procrastination indicated he was mistaken when we did the urine test, because I'd been messing with Solomon for five years and not had I been knocked up, so why now?

The answer to the "Why," would continue to elude me, but I did get an answer to the when and how far. On November 13th, (Solomon's youngest daughter's birthday) I found out I was between 12-14 weeks pregnant or 3-4 months. Doctor Murthy apologized for taking so long, but due to my condition, wanted to be absolutely sure before he called and gave me the news. Initially, the possibility that it may be Droop's baby, crossed my mind a million times but now I knew that just couldn't be. Droop didn't come home until a September and if it were his, I wouldn't be that far.

"Marie, I want you to come into my office," he said, then switched me to the receptions to make an appointment. Dr. Murthy wanted me to have an ultrasound to further confirm how far I was. I was so excited I took Quan along with me, and the two of us leered in amazement at the little ball of life that was moving and growing inside of my body. It was too early to determine the sex, but neither one of us were concerned with that. Our lives were being changed at that very moment, and for the better I might add. It's a moment we'll never forget and one that instantly brought us closer.

****

It was hard to contain my emotions and I had so many calls to make. My mom, my sister, and of course Solomon, but the first person I needed to speak with was Droop. I don't know why, but I felt obligated to sit down with him face to face and tell him the news, before he started to see signs of it or heard about it from someone else. As a matter of fact, I owed him that much. I knew he would have a fit, but that didn't mean we wouldn't still be fly as always. We just couldn't fuck anymore! Essentially, Droop was a good dude and had a good head on his shoulders. I knew he wouldn't expect or try to force me into dealing with him knowing I was carrying another man's child. We were grimy but we weren't dirty!

I called Droop as soon as I got home, but instead of being upset, he was pretty cool. I told him the baby was Solomon's, and that he had nothing to worry about, assuming that if it were his, he'd want to hide the fact considering he lived with his chick. *"How you know,"* he asked? *"How do I know what?"*

"How you know the baby is his?"

"Cause I'm three to four months," I replied, annoyed that he'd question me in the first place. *"You sure"* he asked again? *"Yes Droop, I'm fifteen weeks! That means I'm four months. You ain't been home that long!"*

Droop acted like he knew something I didn't and I couldn't believe he was questioning me the way he was. He knew I'd never lie to him. Then he asked me to come pick him and Po' up so we could smoke some Haze. *"What? Smoke some Haze. Boy, didn't you just hear me tell you I'm pregnant!"*

I was so frustrated by his lack of regard for my baby's health I just hung up on him. I couldn't believe he asked me to go smoke, as if they baby wouldn't be smoking right along with me. This had to be the end. We had no business messing with each other in the first place. We'd had our fun, but the joy ride was now over. I had business to take care of and it was time for me to get back on track. Right after my conversation with Droop, Solomon walked in the house. I wanted to tell him about the baby, but he seemed pre-occupied. So I asked him what was wrong, and he replied he'd be bringing all of his stuff over later on. All I could think to myself was, Wow! Look at how shit just falls into place. It seemed surreal for him to say so, but I didn't bother to question him. I just went along with the flow, he chilled for a while then bounced.

****

At four months I was already busting out of my clothes, and I still hadn't told Solomon the news yet. It was a Thursday when he said he was going to move in, but by the following Monday there was still no sign of him or his belongings. I wasn't surprised. I was way use to his unfulfilled promises by now, but I still needed to let him know what was going on. We spoke quietly on the phone the following Thursday, at which time he said he was on his way to his mom's house to check up on the girls. He was funny like that. He had to make sure he told me his purpose for being there was for the girls and not Dee-Dee. As if I believed a word he said. I knew my chances of seeing him later on that night would be slim, so I took the initiative to meet him at his mother's after work.

When Solomon saw me pull up, he walked over to the car and jumped in. Before he could say a word, I politely interrupted him and told him I had something to say. He could tell something was weighing heavy on my mind, and in his normal, laid back disposition asked; *"What's wrong, Molly."*

"I'm pregnant, Bugga'!"

"You pregnant! By who?"

"By who, by you!" I couldn't believe he let that shit fall out of his mouth. *"How, Molly, and we ain't been together for a minute?"*

"I'm three and a half months, Bugga', that's how..." The car then filled with silence. I dropped my head then look at him from the side. He was speechless and his face displayed he was displeased. *"So you waited until, it was too late before you told me!"* Again, I couldn't believe he let that dumb shit fall out of his mouth. Who did he think I was, Dee-Dee? I know he didn't think I waited this long to tell him just to avoid getting an abortion, because an abortion never entered my mind! *"Fool, is you crazy? I just found out, Bugga'! I tried to tell you earlier but I wasn't sure and honestly, I thought you already knew."* By now I'm crying but he's still sitting silent. *"I'll talk to you later, Molly."* He looked at me with contempt and got out of the car, slamming the door behind him. The fact that he thought I was so desperate to be with him that I would try and trap him was more hurtful than anything. He knew, or should have known by now, that I was too real for games like that. Solomon got out of the car and went into his mom's, and I pulled off crying. This could not be happening...

Planned! Entrapment! Was this nigga high? I wasn't on any fertility pills, didn't calculate having sex on any specific date, and I didn't calculate my ovulation. It just happened! And he thought I was trying to trap him!

In any event, the worst of it was now over, or at least that's what I assumed. Things didn't go the way I had hoped, but the outcome was out of my control. A life with me was not on his agenda and I was cool with that. He could have been more considerate of my feelings but that's another story. At this point, all I was concerned about was Quan and the baby. I didn't even care about the car. He could keep it, sell it, or shove it up his ass as far as I was concerned. The whole thing hurt like hell but I knew I would be alright. God had blessed me to have another child and I wasn't going to let him steal that joy from me. The way I saw it, I was still on top of my game. I had my job, my car, my home and most of all, my beloved first born to see me through. So what I was going to be a single mother all over again. I'd done it before and managed just fine and there was no doubt in my mind that I could do it again.

The funniest thing happened that evening too. After crying my eyes out and up-chucking everything I tried to hold down on my stomach, I turned on the radio just in time to catch the "You Ain't Shit" segment on a popular Philly station. The hosts were asking listeners to call in and put their significant others on blast, exposing why they weren't shit! Usually, I turned when a station played anything but music. I hated to endure the sponsor's announcements, commercials, and those God awful shout-outs, with people shouting out everybody they knew within a five mile radius. But on this evening, the drama caught my attention. I heard people saying all kinds of stupid shit and I was like damn, I wonder if I call in…. Nah, I mean, don't get me wrong, it's not like I'd never called a station before trying to win some tickets to a concert, but I ain't get through then so why would I get through now. I need to stop thinking, cause as sure as I thought the phone would just ring and ring then eventually hang up, one of the host answered and asked me to tell the world why my other half wasn't shit!

I entertained them both, by screaming on Solomon, and how he was trying to play me out. But only a few people knew I called him Bugga, and I doubt if they were listening. Then about a half hour later, Chino called me cracking up. He hadn't heard me on the radio, but Solomon did and he had Dee-Dee in the car with him! Ha, Ha…. I wish I could have seen the look on their faces.

****

No matter how weak I had become over Solomon, the fact of becoming a mother all over again gave me strength and faith beyond belief. That too was a blessing from God and something no one could take away. The only thing I really had to concentrate on was putting some ends aside for when the baby arrived. I had no intentions on going to him or asking him for anything. Good thing I had a little hustle that kept me with a constant cash flow. I'd need that money over the next couple of years.

WATCH ALL, TRUST NONE!

BETRAYED

The state of New Jersey has a slogan, "Driving is a Privilege". I believe it's printed somewhere on your license or posted up at Motor Vehicles Agencies, and who ever came up with it wasn't telling a lie. Driving is a privilege in New Jersey and an expensive one too! Car insurance can run you just as much as your car note, so needless to say, that spelled trouble for mother fuckers in the hood who wanted to stay legal. Coming from where I'm from, you're lucky if you can pay your rent on time without having to kick out a late fee. Nine out of ten people in the hood couldn't afford car insurance but you needed proof of it in order to register you car, pass inspection, and put the car on the road. This is where my hustle came into play because I made obtaining insurance affordable.

As luck would have it, Quan's father left some blank insurance cards with me when he went away to do his bid. He got them off one of his customers who use to work at an insurance company. At first I though they were useless, until he showed me how to fill them out, and once we saw how much we could make selling them, it was all she wrote. I had about thirty or forty, and by the time I ran out of those, I found a way to scan the last one and produce as many as I wanted off that master copy. Technically, it was a blue collar crime, with white collar status. And just like those who committed white collar and every other crime of its nature, I kept a low profile and only dealt with a certain type. I had several clients, but to throw them off I pretended I was only the middle man. Directly, I dealt with about ten people, but those ten brought me about ten clients each. I sold the cards in-between $50.00-$80.00 a pop, (I gave family a discount) and sold anywhere from 5 to 20 cards a month, so you do the math. I was straight.

The cards were good to get you registered, pass inspection, or even show proof of insurance if you got pulled over. But everybody knew they weren't going to do them any good if they got into an accident. You could even use them to get a temp tag and drive off the lot, you just had to make sure you were paying cash and dealing with a crook that didn't care. Everyone knew this and nobody had a problem. My actions didn't hurt anyone or cost the state any money. I was sorta like the female Robin Hood of the hood, I didn't rob from the rich but I did help the poor.

For years, Solomon played a big part in keeping those extra ends in my pocket. He brought me more sales than I could accumulate on my own because he was everywhere all the time. Even when he came to me and said he needed some and the person would pay me later, it was cool. So of course when his brother, Ace, had his chick, Ronnie, call me at work because he needed to get his car out of impound, I was more than happy to assist. The workers at city impound could care less about the cards authenticity, all they wanted was their money. I told Ronnie to tell Ace to meet me at my crib on my break and I'd hook him up then. Of course, Ace was like family to me and it wasn't just because he was Solomon's brother. The fact that he was his brother was a plus, but I would have hooked him up regardless of our dealings.

On my morning break, I met up with Ace at my crib and he tightened me up with $25.00 for my troubles. Family discount you know… I was somewhat pressed for time and in my haste fucked up on the vehicle identification number. I fixed the typo, but pointed it out to him just the same in case he wanted a new one. He was cool because it was unnoticeable, took the card and was on his way. I made it back to work before anyone noticed I was gone, but as soon as I sat down, Ace was on the horn again telling me he needed another card. Damn!

"*Aight, I'll meet you back at my crib on my lunch at noon. Just give me the new information now, so I can have it ready for you when you get there.*"

"*You already have it,*" he said. "*Huh, I'm confused. I thought you said you needed another card.*"

"*I do, but I need another one just like the one you just did.*"

"*Okay, but why, did they notice the typo on the first one?*" I then noticed a slight chance in his voice when he replied. "*Naw, Molly, it's nothing, these mother fuckers down here just crazy that's all!*" His explanation was evasive, but I didn't make anything out of it. I dismissed it as whatever and told him to meet me back at the crib at 12:00 p.m.

Lunch hour traffic is just as bad as rush hour traffic, and by the time I reached the crib it was going on 12:30. I sped the entire way home because I didn't want to keep him waiting. My house was on the corner of a one way street so I had to glance to my right for oncoming traffic before I pulled up. That's when I spotted Ace walking away from a burgundy Corsica, with two old dudes sitting inside. I thought that was kinda odd because I didn't think he had any clientele out my way. But a fiend is a fiend, and will follow you just about anywhere in order to get their next fix.

I pulled up in front of the crib, double parked, and jumped out. Well, I didn't really jump out, because at five months, all my jumping had stopped. The more appropriate phrase would be, I made a quick exit from the car and met Ace in the middle of the street. Strangely, he had tears in his eyes, and it looked like he'd been crying. *"What's wrong, Ace? Did I take too long? Why are you crying?"*

My poor attempt to humor him failed to put a smile on his face, and it was very unusual to see one of the silliest people I knew looking so sad and serious. *"It ain't nothing, Molly, it's just cold outside that's all."* Cold, nigga it may be December but it's far from cold. Shit, I'm pregnant and I don't even have a coat on okay...

Ace, who I'd often playfully call the *Ace of Spades* handed me $40.00; two twenties with red magic marker in the corner of the bills. The red marking on the bills wasn't unusual, the hood was flooded with them. But to pay me twice for the same job was, so I questioned. *"Ace, whut's good with the $40.00? I don't need this."* I pushed the money away. He then wiped his eyes and said, *"It's just on the strength of us, Molly, you know."*

"Naw, Ace'," I pushed his hand away again, *"Ain't no charge this time, you already paid me for my troubles, we good, keep your dough."* He then dropped his head, looked down at my belly, and said, *"Well use it for the baby then."* It was strange for him to be so emotional and on top of it, I knew he didn't have it like that. If so, he wouldn't have needed me in the first place. Then again, he was family and it was lunchtime, so I took the forty and told him to meet me back at my job in

twenty minutes. I wouldn't normally have anyone come to my place of work, but considering it was Ace, it was cool. The two of us then went our separate ways and I made a bee-line to Pizza Hut. I was starving and craving some cheese!

I don't know if it was my hormones or what, but for some reason, something didn't feel right. Some may call it paranoid, but others consider it as hindsight. I've been told I over think and analyze everything. That may be so, but it's always kept me on point and out of trouble in the past.

I lived on Russling, and took Clinton Avenue all the way down. So how come once I hit Olden Avenue, the came car had been behind me the entire time. Assuming I was being followed, I was happy as hell to pull into Pizza Hut's parking lot. At least I could see who was so interested in me if they pursued.

The car kept going and I picked up my pizza and left. I headed back down Olden in route to my job, but made one more stop at Carvel, to pick up some pinwheels. When I pulled out the lot, I saw that same car again and knew it wasn't just a coincidence. But when it didn't follow me down the Blvd., I said to myself; *"Yes, Marie, you're paranoid!"* Although I didn't really need it, that extra $40.00 sure did come in handy. I was able to splurge a little and disregard my budget. I only broke one twenty. The other I stuffed in my coat pocket once I got back to work.

Once back at my desk, I completed what needed to be done, called Ace up, and told him I was ready. I told him I'd meet him downstairs in my lobby, but I assumed he had a few minutes driving time before he reached me. To my surprise, he was already there waiting for me when I stepped off the elevator.

Since Ace experienced complications with the first card, complications that he never disclosed, I did him a favor and typed up a sham insurance policy to accompany the new card. I figured this would answer any and all questions anyone asked, and I even put my cell number on the phony letter head in case they wanted to call. I could have done the same thing at home, but didn't have the time and preferred a laser printer over my ink jet.

I waddled my way over to the waiting area where Ace was standing, hands concealed inside his pockets. I reached and gave him a hug, and simultaneously handed him the policy and card, inside a plain white envelope. *"Thanks, Molly."* *"You Welcome,"* was my reply. We hugged again, said, *"Peace,"* and he was out. I took my time making my way back to the elevator, and for some reason stood and watched Ace as he walked back to the Lex. Oh did I forget to mention, he was driving Solomon's Lexus that was still registered in my name. As I took a few steps away from the glass window, I glanced over and spotted two old dudes in the opposite corner and they seemed to be watching him also. I didn't know either of them and was positive they didn't work in the building, but something about them struck me as familiar. I just couldn't put my finger on it.

As I stood in the vestibule waiting for an elevator, the two men walked over in my direction. As I got on the elevator they got on with me. They talked among themselves and I pressed the button for my floor. I over heard the two of them say they needed to go to personnel, so I took the liberty of telling them it was located on the 12th floor. Strangely, they never pressed the button. I found that kind of weird, so I pressed it for them.

As we rode up, a weird energy filled the car that made me very uncomfortable. Something wasn't right, and the bad vibe had the little hairs on the back of my neck standing straight up. Maybe it was just me, but for some reason, I'd had a bad feeling in the pit of my stomach every since Ace asked me for that second card. Maybe it was the pregnancy, maybe it was fatigue. Maybe they were an interracial gay couple and my pregnancy offended them, I don't know. I just know I was happy to reach the 11th floor and get away from them both. The way they kept gawking at me freaked me out...

I exited the elevator and marched straight to the ladies' room. The door pushed inward to enter and that always forced me to take a quick glance to my left. The weird elevator energy was still with me as I entered the bathroom and I could have sworn I saw the black dude following behind me. I felt a moment's worth of safety while in the bathroom but as soon as I walked out the door, black dude was right there!

Okay, maybe dude made an honest mistake and got off on the wrong floor. However, I was sure he wasn't blind and saw the dress bathroom door and not a pair of slacks! *"Excuse me, are you lost?"*

"Are you Marie Cook?" he asked?

That right there fucked me up, how did dude know my government name? I was hesitant to respond, but my eye's confirmed my identity. *"What happened, is my family alright, did somebody die?"* I asked? *"Who are you, what chu' looking for me for?"* He then reached for my arm asking me to step aside with him, and I flipped! I yanked my arm away and proceeded to walk away. Then, he reached behind his back and his friend from the elevator, who was actually a youthful looking Hispanic man, stood in front of me blocking my path. What the fuck was going on? I turned around to face the black guy directly and that's when he came at me with the cuffs. *"Hold up, what the fuck you doing?"* I started backing. He kept reaching for me and I kept shaking him like I was the inventor of the *Harlem Shake*. *"Don't put your hands on me,"* I yelled! That's when he said, *"Marie Cook, you're under arrest!"*

"Arrest... Excuse you... Oh no the hell I'm not!" It was now obvious they were cops but why were they trying to arrest me? I continued to back up but by now I'm almost hysterical. That's when the Hispanic one of the duo touched me on my shoulder and said, *"Shhh, Marie, calm down. We just wanna ask you a few questions."*

"Well, asking and cuffing are two different things!"

The Hispanic detective, who I'll call Manuel, gave his partner, who I'll call Detective Albert, the look to back off. Detective Albert who stood every bit of six feet some odd inches tall, with a salt and pepper beard and studious eyewear that camouflaged his deep sketched laugh lines then walked over to the double doors that lead to our main corridor while his partner and I stood by ourselves talking.

"Marie, is the baby okay"

"Yes, he's fine..." And speaking of fine, detective Manuel was fine too, just in a different aspect, with a remarkable resemblance to the Latino singer Ricky Martin.

Pointing to the chairs in the lobby, he asked if I'd like to sit down. *"No I'm fine, I'll stand,"* I replied.

"Marie, do you mind telling me what just happened down in the lobby?" Again, the question stunned me, because why would he be

asking me that? *"I don't know what the fuck you're talking about!"*

Of course my reply only confirmed I knew exactly what he was talking about, but I wasn't about to give myself up. I hadn't been read any rights and as far as I knew, they could have been talking about anything. Detective Manuel then gave me a, *"Come on, Marie"* type of look. Detective Albert, on the other hand, was still standing by the door, waiting to be buzzed in, and when he heard my reply, gave me a dirty look. As if he could intimidate me by doing so.

"Look, Mami'," Detective Manuel said, *"We know all about what just went down in the lobby between you and Rakim. All we want from you is the truth,"* he said, in his heavy Spanish accent. Detective Albert was now being let into the office and in a low voice Detective Manuel leaned in to me and whispered, *"Just make it easy on you-self, Mami, please..."*

At that point a multitude of emotions overwhelmed me, making me feel warm and flush. I zoned out for a minute but that minute seemed like an hour. As I stood there with a blank expression and no reaction I thought to myself; Is he telling me my people, my friend, my cousin, my brother just set me up? Is that why they were here to arrest me, over a mother fucking $40.00 insurance card for a piece of shit junk car that didn't even work? Naw Ace wasn't a snitch, and he'd never put me in a jam like this. I don't know how they knew his real name, but maybe they thought they could trick me into giving him up for something else, I didn't know.

After asking myself damn near a hundred questions, I finally returned to reality where Detective Manuel was still trying to convince me I'd been set up. His good-cop persona may have gotten a confession out of someone who didn't know the law, but his persuasiveness wasn't going to fly with me. I still wasn't saying shit! I don't know how he knew both of our government names, but I was pregnant with this nigga's nephew and knew he wasn't going to hand me over to the authorities just like that. We were better and bigger than that, and on top of that, I'd done too much for this nigga in the recent past for him to go out like some type of fag. Not at my job... Not over an insurance card...

"There has to be some type of mistake," I said. By now, Detective Albert was walking back out into the hall and asking, *"Where's the money Marie, where's the money?"*

"Money, what money I ain't got no money!" I tried to maintain a straight face but the emotions were killing me. Wow, I though to myself. How did he know about the money?

With a perplexed look I turned to face Detective Manuel and he dropped his head as if to say, *"I tried to tell you..."* Detective Albert then lashed out at me with his, *"Look I'm fed up with this shit"* speech, and for a third time, tried to slap those handcuffs on me. *"You not gonna put them cuffs on me"* I yelled taking two steps back. Mind you all of this was taking place in the lobby of my office. Not in the playground, not on the corner in front of the Bodega', not even at my crib, but my job. Why did this have to take place here of all places? As if waiting for me to get home would have been so hard.

Before I managed to make things worse for myself (as if that were at all possible, Detective Manuel convinced his partner to put the cuffs away. Clearly, I wasn't going to run off anywhere and even if I made the attempt, my fat ass wouldn't have got very far. I didn't know why Detective Albert had such a hard on for me, but I wasn't looking forward to fulfilling his fantasy. He was acting as if I was some type of hardened criminal or had arrested me several times in the past. That fool didn't know me! What pissed me off even more was his ability to pass judgment one me, knowing he'd just made a deal with a drug dealing snitch over a fake insurance card, and let him go... Was I missing something here? I mean damn... Guess he never heard of *Black Cop* by *KRS-1.*

Sensing Detective Manuel's sympathy for me, I asked if I could go to my desk to collect my things before we left. I was still hungry and my pizza was sitting at my desk getting cold. He didn't seem to have a problem with that but before I could move Detective Albert asked, *"What machine did you use to type the card?"* Well damn! What did he want to do, have a *Pick-a-Nigga* and hang me from the exit sign in the middle of the lobby? Why was he digging so deep for such a petty crime? He was acting like I was his biggest catch of the year! How dumb did he think I was to assist him in building a case against me? Finding out what machine I used was his job, not mine. Shit, I didn't even have any legal representation, and already he was asking for a confession. But on the other hand, having him search my desk may not have played out in my best interest.

I walked into my office on a mission to do three things; gather my shit, grab the ribbon, and remain unnoticed. I managed to do two of the three, but the nosiest of the nosiest had all eyes on me. They knew the police were on our floor to ask me some questions, and when I waddled into the office with tears flowing down my face, they knew something was terribly wrong.

Before making my exit, my colleague, friend, and ex-supervisor, Wayne, caught up to me and asked if everything was alright. Had he been anyone else I would have more than likely gone off and told them to mind their damn business, but he was different. I knew he was asking because he could see a sista was in distress. His concern was genuine, considering he too at one time had been a victim of non-justified harassment. It seemed like every time we turned around, we were hearing about another black person at the job being hounded or falsely accused. But he had no idea my shit was so deep.

I told the good brotha, who looked like a hairless Jamie Foxx *"Yeah, I'm cool, they just wanna ask me some questions,"* but he was no fool. He knew suits didn't just come to a person's job and cause a scene just to ask some questions. They would have sent uniforms to do that. However instead of bring more attention to me, he packed up the rest of my things, and told me he'd put my ice cream in the freezer. I guess that was his way of saying, "see you tomorrow." Little did we know…

When I walked back out into the hall, to my surprise, standing with the detectives were my boss, his boss, his boss' secretary and her sister-in-law, Deb. The four of them were huddled around Detective Albert like football players going over a play, but I knew the topic of their discussion was me. Detective Manuel was standing next to the elevator when he saw me approach and signaled me to come his way. I handed him the ribbon, the elevator arrived, and the three of us took the ride down. It was so quiet in that car you could hear a rat piss on cotton! Detective Manuel was cool for the most part, but Mr. Albert clearly had it out of me. His bad cop act was getting tired, and he even had the nerve to ask was I going to tell him the truth or stick to my story. In my mind I was thinking damn! He has to be one hard up mother fucker 'cause I haven't even told a story yet. I wanted so bad to bust out laughing but instead, I just stood straight, looking forward, shaking my head.

The doors opened and I had a full audience, as if the entire ordeal wasn't bad enough. Who the hell called all these people, I said out loud. Looked like everybody knew about the set up except me!

As the two detectives escorted me to the door, I heard countless familiar voices asking, *"Murf, are you alright? Murf, are you okay? Murf, what's wrong?"* All I could do was look at their inquisitive faces as if to say: DOES IT LOOK LIKE I HAVE THE LIBERTY TO SPEAK FREELY RIGHT NOW? I MEAN, SORRY FOR THE INCONVIENCE BUT IN CASE YOU HAVEN'T NOTICED, I'M KINDA UNDER ARREST!

A fourth of them may have been truly concerned but the other three fourths were just nosey spectators who wanted to be the first to spread some fresh gossip.

Before exiting the building, we were held up by the department's liaison who said she was unaware the department was assisting in a sting operation, or that city police were going to be arresting someone on state property. She went on to add that usually in a situation like this, the State Police were the ones to be called. It would have been cool had her argument been in my defense, but it wasn't. Her only concern was the State, for fear I'd pursue a lawsuit later on down the line. Detective Albert then took the liberty of stressing to her that my arrest was a direct result of an undercover buy and bust operation that originated on the streets of Trenton, and therefore gave him jurisdiction to follow up and make the arrest wherever. Regardless if I was on state property or not! In addition, he added once the city was done charging me, the state would also have the option to press charges if they so desired. I just stood there shaking my head like, damn boss, don't give them any ideas! You're not even sure if you can charge me yet!

Noticing the frustration written all over my face, Detective Manuel chose to expedite the procedure, grabbing me by the arm and walking me out of the lobby. The last word anybody heard me say was, *"DAMN!"*

While the three of us stood outside on the steps, the two of them went back and forth about which one would drive me back to the station.

I noticed a burgundy Corsica parked across the street and that's when it all hit me like a ton of bricks! No wonder they looked so familiar. They were the same two cats I saw Ace talking to across the street from my crib. And to think I thought they were fiends. Wow, so that meant the whole thing was a set up from the beginning. That dirty mother fucker, how could he! That's how Detective Albert knew about the money, he gave it to him to pass off to me. Oh, my Damn! And he had the nerve to say he was giving it to me on the strength of the baby. WOW! Now that was ill… But why bring them back to my job? Why not make the arrest on the street? Wow, Ace was a snitch! How could he do this to me? How could he set me up and why? How do you set up a woman who's pregnant? That's some ole fag shit for real!

My mind was flooded with wonder. Had I done something to Ace? Did he have malice in his heart toward me? Why not give me a signal, a sign, or some type of warning? Why hand me over like this? Shit, I would have been better off if he just would have shot me. The burn from the bullet wouldn't have felt half as bad as being betrayed like this. All I could do was shake my head in disbelief. Good thing I spent one of those twenty's at Pizza Hut and the other was hidden. Detective Albert could ask me for the money all he wanted, he couldn't prove a thing. For all he knew, it was my word against Ace, and he couldn't trust him anymore than he could trust me.

I took a sigh of relief when Detective Albert said his car was around back and it would be easier (in my condition) for me to ride with Detective Manuel. *"Thank God,"* I mumbled. At least he wasn't going to badger the shit out of me like his partner Grand-Pa'-Grump!

Detective Manuel led me to the car, opened my door, and ordered me to buckle up! *"Ha, Ha,"* I laughed, as if the belt would stretch across my belly. Once he saw I was seated, he turned around and started giving me the run-down of what had gone down and how protecting Rakim wasn't going to do me any good. *"He set you up, Mami. He set you up, he gave you the two marked twenties as bait, and he don't care about you or your baby!"* I guess he though Ace was the father of my child. I would clear that up for him later but for now I wanted to hear all he had to say while we had the opportunity to talk in private. *"We've already recovered one of the bills from Pizza Hut, so we know he gave you the money. We put a car on you and at the same time, tailed Rakim around town to make sure he didn't try to give you a head's up. We figured if he was willing to cross you, then he wouldn't hesitate to do the same to us. I didn't think it was going to work myself, and thought for sure he was going to tip you off, but as you can see, I was wrong."* Damn, I knew somebody was following me, I knew I wasn't paranoid!

I could tell dude wasn't talking just to get a confession up out of me, he was talking because he saw how loyal I was to Ace, and how fucked up he was for putting me in such a fucked up situation. All Ace would have gotten was a slap on the wrist, but me getting busted on the job took things to an entire different level. He wanted me to see the light, plus give a confession… Remember, good cop bad cop…

By now I was sick, and I don't mean sick from the pregnancy either. I was sick from the reality of what was going on. I knew once I got behind those walls at the station, I'd have to talk a lot sooner than later, but I was hoping a miracle would come my way and save me. No miracles arrived.

As soon as the two of us exited the car, several of Trenton's finest were there to meet us. Many of them knew me by face, but since I was in custody, none of them bothered to ask me any questions. They just spoke and I returned the greeting with a partial smile. Detective Manuel did do all he could to accommodate me and keep me comfortable. At the same time, he tried explaining the process and what was going to happen next. He had no idea I was all too familiar with the booking process and procedures. Once inside, Detective Manuel helped me sit down on the little narrow bench that sat off to the left as soon as you entered, then said he'd be back. I felt like I was on public display, and considering it was shift change, everyone was walking by wondering what the fat, pregnant chick had done.

Shortly after our arrival, Detective Albert walked in and the three of us proceeded on up to the second floor. Once off the elevator, we were greeted by a secretary who I could have sworn I knew from school, and I was taken to a back room off to the far left, where three other officers were sitting.

No sooner then I plopped down, two of them lashed out at me; *"Name, date of birth, and current address."* Another asked if I had any warrants; *"Thirteen to be exact,"* said Detective Albert who was fumbling through paperwork. Detective Manuel took a seat at the desk directly in front of Detective Albert and the third detective decided to fuck with me and ask about the money.

I rattled off my answers with little or no emotion at all and I refrained from making eye contact with any of them. I was alert to what was going on but all I could think about was Ace.

By now all of them, except for Detective Manuel, had gotten on my nerves with their jokes and especially about the money. So I turned to face the one closest to me and with all the sarcasm I could conjure up said, *"There is no other twenty, Ace only gave me one. If you gave him forty dollars to set me up, he kept twenty of it for his troubles."* Three of them laughed, Detective Manuel smiled and Detective Albert remained quiet. As it turned out, Detective Albert gave Ace that money out of his own pocket and was looking forward to getting it back. I even laughed to myself due to his stupidity. I mean really, how can you trust a crook to catch a crook?

Detective Albert then asked if I had any more cards. I knew he was expecting me to say no but I kept it gangsta and said, *"Yes, I have five more duplicates and the original at my house."* I figured if I gave them a little bit of what they wanted they'd fall back and leave me alone, but it wasn't going to be that easy. The two detectives running my background check discovered all thirteen of my warrants were parking violations and failure to appear, then took the liberty of calling the work house so that I could be detained. My heart dropped! I knew I should have expected as much, but damn. It's like that... For real? You gonna send a sista to jail over some parking tickets...

I don't know if anyone noticed, but I was beginning to break out in hives from the stress. I eased up off the chair slightly and pressed my back up against the wall, while at the same time cracking my toes in my shoes. I was definitely heated but had to maintain my composure. Detective Manuel then pulled his chair out in front of me and continued to tell me the story of how everything went down.

As it turned out, Ace never went to the impound. Instead, he went straight to the police station because he first needed to get his release papers to take to the impound. Had I know that from the door, I would have never given him the card in the first place. Then, while he was at the station trying to get over, he had to deal with the secretary who just so happened to go to school with both of us back in the late 80's. Once she discovered the white out on the card where I'd corrected the typo, she pointed it out to the detectives and the rest is history. Over the course of ten years I'd sold hundreds of cards and all of them past the test with city cops, troopers, and motor vehicles. So why on earth did I have to get taken down by a secretary was beyond me, and pretty ironic to say the least. Her intentions, he said, were to bust Ace, and she had no idea I was the actual source. From the sound of things, one would think Ace crossed her at one point in time as well... Damn!

Once the detectives got the card in their possession, they called the company and the company confirmed the policy number was made up. They then snatched Ace up and told him to get another card, and for his cooperation, they agreed to let him go.

I guess the explanation was supposed to make me feel better but really, it only made matters worse. I understood how things got fucked up, but he still didn't have to lead them to me. For all they knew, Ace could have gotten that card from Johnny Appleseed on the corner of Perry and Montgomery and nobody would have been the wiser. However, getting another card wasn't the kicker, it was the sale of the card that did me in. They needed me to sell Ace another card in order for the charge to stick, and that's what fucked everything up. That's why his dumb ass was crying when he gave me the money. He knew he was wrong and his guilt was getting the best of him. Wow, that cat was the Negro version of Donnie Brasco...

****

With everything seemingly out in the open, Detective Albert told Detective Manuel to take one of the other detectives with him back to my house in order to retrieve the remainder of the cards. He did as he was told and once inside the car, the two of them began asking me questions about Ace, trying to tie together the strings to our unusual relationship. It fucked them up when I told them he was my brother-in-law and I was pregnant with his nephew. *"I don't think he's gonna make a good uncle if he's putting you in situations like this,"* Detective Manuel replied. I wasn't in the mood for jokes and although he was telling the truth, his words cut because in my heart, Ace was still family.

The two of them continued to hold a conversation with me, and I pretended to listen but my mind was somewhere else. In a matter of seconds we were going to be at my house and Quan was home alone. His normal routine consisted of him arriving home by 3:30 p.m., and then calling me at work to check in. Since I got off work at 4:00 p.m., the half hour he was at the house alone was something I could live with. However, since he'd been unable to contact me for about an hour, I was worried and knew he had to have been as well. What would I do if they discovered him there unattended and decided to call DYFS? What would I do if he wasn't okay?

While the two of them went on and on about Ace and that damn insurance card, I was sitting in the back seat praying for me and my son. God forbid they found the rest of the cards I so conveniently failed to mention, or the computer I used to keep all of the info on. If they seized that, aww man... A lot of people would be in trouble.

As I turned the key to open the door, I could envision a bad situation turning worse. I climbed the stairs slowly, careful not to make any unnecessary noise, trying to listen out for my son. At the top of the stairs I hit a quick right, turned into the kitchen, and blocked the view of the computer by shutting the pantry door. I kept a straight face as I reached into the drawer and retrieved six of the cards, but my heart was pounding for fear my son would run up to me at any moment. Where was he anyway?

As I handed the cards to Detective Manuel, his side kick asked would it be okay if they searched the rest of the house. My heart dropped again and in my head I was saying, *"Hell yeah I mind!"* A search could lead to them discover more than any of us bargained for, but I felt refusing them would be just as bad. I shrugged my shoulders as if to say, *"I don't care,"* but dude said I had to give a verbal response. Verbal, shit, I was trying to keep quiet considering I now figured Quan was sleep. Luckily for me once I did say yes, Detective Manuel said, *"There's no need for that, we got what we came for lets go!"* I might have been going through hell, but dude was definitely an Angel. Though at the same time, they didn't have a warrant for the premises. Remember, good cop, bad cop...

****

267

Whoever designed my house was a genius, because each room was separate and you couldn't peep into one room from the other. This was a blessing for me because Quan had to be either in the front room, his room, or my bedroom. Considering how the boy did nothing but watch cartoons all day and night, I figured he passed out on the floor watching *Cartoon Network*. I was so thankful our presence hadn't disturbed him, so thankful he had fallen asleep before the three of us got there. Now I just had to hope he'd be okay until I got back and prayed I made it back before he woke up. Worse case scenario, I'd use my one phone call to contact my mom and tell her to go and get him.

By the time the three of us returned to the station, the Geezer [Detective Albert] had completed all of my paperwork and I was ready to send to a judge. The reality of the matter was now beginning to settle and once again I felt sick. I hadn't eaten since breakfast, and worrying about my son didn't make matters better. I realized I'd been blessed so far, and Detective Manuel had definitely cut me a few breaks. But my guard was still up because anything was possible. At this point, there was no need for me to try and hide anything, although there was a whole lot more for them to find, and wouldn't you know it, Detective Albert found it!

While the three of us were at my house, Detective Albert (who put me in the mind frame of a Black Adam West,) kept thinking of way to fry my ass. So what did he do? He returned to my job and convinced my boss to let him search my desk. As I took my seat in their office, he had the never to turn to me and say, *"You know, I'm really disappointed in you, I though you were a smart girl"!* Okay, there he goes with his bad, *"bad cop"* impression again. I was so tired of him I felt like spitting in his face. *"What the hell are you talking about,"* I asked? As if I didn't already know. I didn't catch the first part of what he said, but the bottom line was he'd found over a half of dozen additional cards (used) lying in my desk.

A statement from me now was no longer an option, it was necessary. I could have held off on it until I got legal representation but that would have delayed my release. The news of his discovery made my head spin and my baby was doing summersaults. The worse had definitely come. So, I took a deep breath and began to talk. Then half way though my story, one of the two who had been conducting the warrant search (I call them the Warrant Boys) asked about the twenty

268

dollars again. Knowing I was telling a lie, but with nothing else to loose, I stuck to my story. *"I don't have no damn twenty dollars!"* None of them believed me for a minute, not even Detective Manuel, but it was my word against their search. Detective Albert then told the third detective, (the quiet one) to take the interrogation room and have me remove my coat, shoes, and socks. With no women on duty to pat me down, they had to do the best they could. They knew they couldn't touch me, but even if they did, they wouldn't have found a thing. While one cop checked my belongings, another instructed me to pull out my pockets, lift my breast out of my bra and shake my hair. I laughed at his last request because my hair was in braids.

When the detective returned empty handed, Detective Albert was hotter then a .45, and the look of defeat on his face was so satisfying. *"Maybe she's telling the truth,"* one of them said. Laughing at him was the most fun I'd had all day.

With nothing else to hold them or me up, they read me my charge and I signed my statement. Although I implicated Ace as an accessory, I was the one who accepted the cash so I was the one hit with the felony. At the time, I didn't even know what a felony was. I though it was just some fancy name for selling fake insurance cards. I was familiar with my rights as a citizen, but not familiar with all of the terms used in the judiciary and legal system. Though the way I was feeling, they could have charged me with man one and I would have accepted it. Just as long as they let me go so I could get home to my baby. I'd always read and heard about how people were pressured into a confession once in police custody, but I could never understand why someone would give themselves up without a fight. Too bad I had to learn that lesson though first hand experience. They didn't even give me my one call.

****

Truly I was the victim in this situation, not the state, and not Ace. The room cleared after my papers were signed, but off in the other room I heard overheard someone talking about transporting me to the Mercer County Work House. I was so upset, I started to cry.

How could they even think about sending me to that place? I didn't deserve to go there in my condition. Shit, I didn't deserve to go there in any condition. That was a facility for real criminals, not someone like me. They couldn't be serious…

As my fears worsened, the one person who came to mind was Afeni Shakur and how she must have felt behind bars while carrying her unborn son. Although my situation wasn't nearly as serious as hers, the commonality was the same. Then after a few minutes, one of the Warrant Boys walked over and told me to stop crying. *"You're not going anywhere, Ms. Cook! None of the municipalities want to assume responsibility for you or your unborn. You're too far along in your pregnancy, so your release is totally up to us."* Even though city lock up wasn't the ideal place to spend the night, it was better then being shipped way out Lambertville, so I counted it as a blessing.

****

I was fingerprinted and awed by nearly every cop in the station, all who wanted me to come and talk to them when I was done. As if I were open to conversation. It was damn near 8:00 p.m., and I was sure my son had woken up by now. My stomach was in knots from worrying about him, and of course, I feared the worse. Then with no more delay, after chatting with all of the officers and detectives who were concerned about my situation, I was handed my walking papers and told I was free to go. Aww man, I was so happy and so relieved, I literally wanted to kiss them all. I was released on O.R and given instructions to report back to court first thing in the morning. However, I didn't concern myself with tomorrow or what troubles it would bring because I still had to make it through the night. Quan was my only concern at the moment. Quan and then Ace!

****

After a day of total disaster, I found it very refreshing for one of the officers to extend me the courtesy of escorting me out the door. He was as also kind enough to give me change to make that long awaited phone call I needed to make to my mom. I'm not sure if he noticed, but I was shaking nervously with anticipation, my hands were sweaty and I could barely hold on to my quarters. My face, arms, legs, and lips were all swollen, the hives had broken out full force and I'd resumed crying because my emotions were a wreck! Once the two of us reached the street, he bid me farewell but not without reminding me to show up for court in the morning. With one motion I acknowledge his reminder and said good-bye in return, never once pausing my steps. As I approached the payphone that stood out front of the police station, I talked to myself out loud. The phone only rang once and when my mom picked up, all she heard through my cries was, *"Ma, can you come and get me"*.

Luck had been on my side the entire day, good and bad. The fifty cent the officer had given to me was burning a whole in the palm of my hand, but was finally going to serve its purpose. All afternoon I'd been dying to talk to this nigga and hear what he had to say. So after hanging up with my mom, I deposited the two quarters and called Ace. (I called my mother collect) The phone rang three times and on the fourth his chick, my girl Ronnie picked up. *"Molly,"* she said, *"what happened?"* At the moment, I didn't even have the heart or the strength to tell her the details of the full story, but from what she was telling me, I could tell Ace had only given her half the truth. *"Molly, come over, Ace not here but I'll call him and tell him you on your way."* I told her I'd be there as soon as I picked up my car.

I wish Ronnie would have given me more to go on, but there was no need to fuss with her and she was innocent. If anything, she was about to be caught up in the middle of some bullshit just like me. I just hoped it wouldn't result in our friendship ending.

My mom was damn near in a panic but had already been put on notice that something was seriously wrong. My son, bless his heart, had called her a number of times, worried because I hadn't come home from work yet. My son is very well mannered and disciplined and knew not to leave the house unless he got permission from me first to do so. My mom respected my authority and never went against me. However, just this one time, she wished she would have. *"I'll be right there, Ree,"* she said, but I instructed her to go pick my son up first. By doing so, I had time to smoke a cigarette and calm down. I didn't want them or him to see me looking a mess. I also didn't want them to catch me smoking a cigarette.

Ten minutes after I hung up, they arrived. My mom, my sister, and my son! Only God knew how happy I was. The sight of my son brought a tear to my eye. Though, all three of them were a sight for sore eyes as Nana would say.

****

271

As soon as I eased my way into my mom's compact Toyota Rav 4, my son wrapped his arms around my belly and ask if me and the baby was okay. *"Yes, were okay, Quan,"* but even those few words almost broke me down again. My mom is the best when I'm in trouble because she's the first to want to go and beat the hell out of who ever offended me. Or at least she wants to see me beat the hell out of them, which ever comes first. My sister, Nette, has always been in-tune with me and could tell my troubles were deeper than I wanted to discuss at the moment. So, as we drove back into town for me to retrieve my car, I slipped back into my zone and focused on no one but Ace. After arriving at my job, we pulled into the lot and I got dropped off at my vehicle. I then asked the both of them to watch Quan till I got back, and with nothing else said, got into my ride and drove off. It would take less then five minutes to make it across town to Ace's house, but first I needed to stop at the store and cop a few loose cigarettes, aka loosies.

****

Although Ronnie and I were fly, she was till Ace's girl. I wasn't sure if he was there when I called or not, but I knew he wouldn't be there when I arrived. Ace knew he'd fucked up and that's why he told his girl that bullshit. He could run all he wanted, but he'd never be able to hide from me or the truth, and he damn sure couldn't hide from his conscience. As for myself, I was afraid. Afraid of what he might say, fearing he just wouldn't give a fuck, and afraid of how I would react. I couldn't' even think of an explanation that would justify his actions or satisfy me in the least. Yet, I still needed to look him in the eye and hear what his sorry ass had to say.

Upon arriving at Ace and Solomon's mother's crib where Ace, Ronnie, and Dee-Dee stayed, Ronnie came down to let me in. She was so curious to find out the truth and she was almost as mad as me once she found out Ace had lied to her as well. The two of us then went up stairs to continue our talk but I kept in mind she was his girl and lived with him under his roof. I didn't really expect her to take sides, I just wanted her to know what type of nigga she was truly dealing with. Deep down inside, I knew she knew I was being honest. I had no reason whatsoever to make up such an elaborate tale and pin the blame on her man. She knew I loved Ace like a brother, she knew my tears of hurt were for real...

272

About an hour passed and Ronnie continuously tried to contact her man but he wouldn't answer his phone. This only supported what I was telling her and proved he had something to hide. Ronnie stopped the phone calls and once she stopped, he decided to call her back. I knew he'd take that as a sign that I was gone, but she and I were still sitting in the kitchen smoking when she picked up and asked, *"Bae', what's going on?"* After that she got quiet, and a few seconds later, she hung up. Ronnie took a deep sigh, *"That was him,"* she said. *"He's on his way here, he forgot something."* The two of us then continued our talk, and after a while, the phone rang again. It was Ace, asking her to bring to what ever it was he forgot, down to the car. If nothing else, this was a true sign he was avoiding me because my car was parked right out front.

When Ronnie returned, her entire facial expression had changed. There was no denying he was a bitch made now. He knew I was upstairs, he knew I needed to talk to him, and he knew he should have been man enough to face be but he wasn't. He put her in the middle of our shit and told her to tell me he would be by the crib to talk to me later. *"Later, why later nigga, I'm here now, run ya mouth!"* My angry words simply evaporated into the air. *"He was crying, Molly,"* she said. *"Yeah and!"* *"He brushed me off too,"* she replied. Man, I though we were bigger than, that but obviously I was dead wrong. Ronnie couldn't give me any answers, shit she didn't even know the truth herself. My only choice now was to go see Solomon. Maybe he knew something.

****

I realized I wasn't going to see Ace that night so I left and went to my mom's to scoop up my son. I knew her and baby sis were worried out their minds by now and wanted to know the details of what happened. It was hard for me to form the words because the whole thing left a bad taste in my mouth. The two of them were shocked when I told them what Ace had done. They simply couldn't believe him, of all people, could do something like that to me. Shit, even I wanted to believe that this whole thing was one big misunderstanding and somehow Ace was just a victim of circumstance but that would have just been another lie. Even Quan was astonished when he put two and two together and realized *"Uncle Ace made mommy go to jail."* After all I'd done for him within the past year, the though of what he'd so easily done to me made gnawed at me like a itch I couldn't scratch. It was me who picked his chick up at 7:00 a.m. on Saturdays, drove her all the way to Marlton, NJ to pick him up from a drug program, then turned right back around on Sunday and dropped him back off by 6:00 p.m. every week. I did this on the strength of how tight he and I were, not because I was screwing his brother, had a car with him, or was carrying his child. I did it because Ronnie was a good chick and was trying to do right by her man. I did it because I knew she'd do the same for me. I did it 'cause Ace was my fam!

Fuck that, this nigga has to go. I wanted that nigga touched! As far as I was concerned, he'd broken all the rules and didn't deserve to be treated fair. My mom and sister were so mad, they were co-signing my vengeance. Talking to them made me feel better, but I felt Solomon should be the one to comfort me now. I left my mom's with my son, then headed across town to find the man who I thought could fix it all. I called his phone while in route, and when he answered I lost it. I was heated he hadn't come to my rescue, however Ace told him the same lie he'd told Ronnie, that he had been set up and I just happened to get caught in the middle. *"Ya brother's a snitch, Solomon, and I have the proof!"* I knew those were harsh words but just like Ronnie, Solomon knew I wasn't a liar. However, also just like Ronnie, Solomon didn't want to take sides until he knew what was what. So instead of debating, he told me to go home and he'd come by and talk to me after he spoke to Ace. Remembering that the two of us weren't really on the best of terms before this jumped off, I had no idea how this would effect us now. I was confident Solomon was still my friend and would always have me and the baby's best interest at heart. So on that note, I followed his advice and drove home. When I got there it was almost 11:00 p.m., and no sooner than I arrived he came walking through the door. (He still had his keys)

As I sat down with Solomon and explained the situation for the third time, I could see disbelief written all over his face. Not that he didn't believe me, he just didn't want to. It was sorta like trying to convince the F.O.I that Farrakhan had gotten caught eating a pig's foot or something. Yet, there was no denying that crisp twenty dollar bill I pulled from my pocket or that pretty red marking up in the corner. Solomon knew I didn't play those types of games and knew there would be no reason for me to be carrying around a marked bill. I thought I was hurt but after revealing that, Solomon looked like he was going to cry his damn self. For me it was just a tainted friendship, but for him it was much more. Ace was his brother and the mark of a snitch wasn't something that could be easily washed away. Solomon was speechless but promised he'd have answers for me in the morning. I was satisfied with his concern and felt after a good night's sleep, I could put the entire ordeal behind me and move on. Little did I know, the worst was yet to come...

When you find yourself at the bottom of the barrel, there are only two places you can go. Up or out!

ROCK BOTTOM

Ｄecember 21, 2000, a day I'll never forget. So much had happened the day before, I was still trying to mull through it all. My appearance time for court was 9:00 a.m. I figured after I made my plea and was hit with a huge fine that I'd never be able to pay, I head on into work. I dropped my son of at school as usual, then called my job and told them I'd be a little late. I figure as long as I had formal document proving I was there, they wouldn't have much to say.

As always, when anyone from the hood went to court you could always count on running into other familiar faces from the hood. So with just a slight nod of the head, I acknowledged others, who just like me, would have preferred to be somewhere, anywhere else. One must always remember to keep it tight lipped while up in the cracker's court room or you'll surely get hit with contempt on top of your charge. Luckily, I was the first one called up to the bench.

"Cool," I thought, this way I wouldn't be that late getting into work. It took less then ten minutes for the judge to read off the list of bullshit charges they were trying to pin on me, and he didn't fail to mention those thirteen outstanding warrants either. Yet, considering Christmas was just a few days away, he said he was going to let me slide until after the New Year. *"I want you to think carefully about the charges pending against you, Ms. Cook. Unlike the parking tickets I'm cutting you a break on, these charges are indictable."* Meaning, if I was found guilty, I not only faced paying a huge fine. I also faced completing long hours of community service and possibly 3-6 months in jail. I nodded my head yes in response to his statement, but how would careful thinking change any of that? Even in court, I had to be a smart ass.

Now I heard the man say 1st, 2nd, and 3rd degree, but I didn't know what that meant. Shit, I was still trying to figure out what a felony was. I felt his speech was just that, a speech. Something routine he kicked to everyone who appeared in court. I knew I'd have another opportunity to speak at a later date, but for now I was just happy he was overlooking those tickets. That in itself was a blessing.

After all was said and done, the bailiff handed me my papers and I was free to go. I got one last reminder before exiting the room though. The reminder that I was out on *"O.R..,"* and if I didn't comply with the regulations of my release, I'd be brought back in and held without bail until my court date.

Damn, dude was just like the police, talking to me as if I'd committed some hideous crime or something. I heard what he was saying, but later for all that. I had to get my ass to work and clear shit up before somebody got the wrong idea. So with papers in hand, I fled to my car and raced to my job. When I arrived, I headed straight for my desk in search for any loose cards the Geezer [Detective Albert} may have left behind. Satisfied no further evidence could be found, I made my way over to my boss's desk to show proof of my whereabouts. I also wanted to give an explanation for the past day's disturbance.

About five feet away from my boss' office, his boss' secretary informed me that, "Ron and them" wanted to see me in the large conference room. A lump formed in my throat. It was never a good sign when anyone met in the *large conference room*, but maybe it was better to talk in there than out on the open floor. I took a deep breath, opened the door, and was greeted by three individuals. Two I knew, the other I recognized from working in the building. Shocked to see these men awaiting my arrival, I hesitated before walking in. My Bureau Chief, Ron who in my opinion resembled Richard Gere was seated directly next to my boss Jim, who looked exactly like Patrick. Ron was the one to break the ice, *"Grab a seat, Marie,"* he said. Damn, this must be serious. The look on my face clearly illustrated I wasn't expecting such a reception. The gentleman I vaguely recognized introduced himself as the head of Labor Relations, then went on to explain the reason for the meeting.

As he spoke in a round about way, I casually leaned into him with my hands folded in front of me, pretending to be captivated by his every word. I wasn't beat for no cracker shit. I'd been around the block a few times and could smell something wasn't right. Regardless, I showed no emotion and gave no reaction to the bias bullshit he was spewing out of his mouth, neither did I react to "Ron and them" as they shook their heads in agreement. The bulk of his speech was nothing more then a run-down of all the department rules, regulations, and policies. Half of them I'd never even heard of in the entire ten years I worked there, but was sure someone other than me had broken.

After the small talk, they moved on to the serious stuff which was me and my arrest and how it would violate department rules if the city or state decided to press charges. Okay, here we go… In other words, if I was found guilty of anything pending against me, it could affect my position. He had my attention, but I still remained silent. He then went on to say that effective immediately, I'd be suspended with pay until the department concluded their investigation. *"Okay hold up, you all are going to suspend me? Based on what they police are trying to build against me? You can't be serious!"* That's what was running through my head, and possibly my actions showed it a little, but my lips remained sealed.

It seems that after I was done in court, Detective Albert took the liberty of notifying my job I was being charged with three felonies. In light of this Jim (The head of Labor Relations) said if I were to be found guilty of any of the charges, it would be grounds for permanent dismissal. Meaning I would no longer be able to work for the Department of Labor or the State of New Jersey ever again! Their position was very clear to me, although I didn't understand why. My crime was committed on the street, how come it had to affect my job. Why did so much fucked up shit have to happen to me!

Nana use to say I didn't know when to shut my mouth. Well, I wish she could have been a fly on the wall that day because my mouth was glued tight. What could I say? I had feelings about the matter but I wasn't about to give them the satisfaction of letting them show. I was a ten year employee with no disciplinary record whatsoever. How come at the sign of trouble they wanted to make an example out of a sista, it just wasn't fair. Jim then took it a step further by telling me he was more than positive, (more than positive) I'd be found guilty of at least one of the charges, since the second crime had been committed on state property, using state equipment. In other words, the state was going to seek dismissal regardless of the city's investigation or the outcome. The prolonging of the dismissal was just to make things look good, but they'd already made up their minds that I wasn't coming back.

Wow, they really consider me an embarrassment? Others had been caught screwing on the job, coming to work high, getting high in the parking lot, and stealing checks. None of them were let go, and they had higher titles then me. Those mother fuckers still had job, and here I'd only been arrested less then 24 hours ago and already there giving me the boot! It didn't add up, yet, despite how I was feeling, I maintained my composure. Ron then intervened by saying he'd pitched a proposition to the department and in turn they agreed to it. The proposal was simple and only an idiot would have turned it down. I could hand in a resignation instead of having it on my record that I was fired. Okay that's cool, but where's the deal? Either way, I'm out of a job. Then he went on to say if I agreed to resign immediately, I would only be forbidden to work for the Department of Labor, the band wouldn't apply to the entire state. *"I'm sorry, Marie, but it's the best we can offer."* There was nothing else to be said after that. The only thing left for me to do was leave.

I asked Ron would it be okay for me to go to my desk and collect my belongings, and with absolute consent he said yes. I rose up from my chair, extending my hand to all three gentlemen, said goodbye, and then exited the room.

Several of my colleagues were aware I was in the conference room with Ron and two other gentleman, and most were looking to hear an explosion. Those were the nosey of the nosiest I spoke about earlier, but I wasn't about to stoop to their level or give them any entertainment on that day either. I kept my cool while walking to my desk and although plenty tried to stop and question me, I kept if moving. My feelings were all tied up in knots and I not only felt betrayed but also abandoned. For the past ten years my job had been my home away from home where I was surrounded by family and friends. I worked my ass of to get to where I was at and now within a twinkling of an eye, it was all being taken away from me. Nana use to always say I needed the patience of Job, and now I was Job...

As the tears again began to flow down my face, family and dear coworkers all wanted to console me, yet, knew it was best to just let me go. This was so unfair and so unreal. My last day should have been fifteen years away. My lively hood had been stolen from me. My world had seemingly come to an end. Thank God one of the elevators was already on my floor when I reached the lobby. I damn sure wasn't in the mood for anyone to be leering at as they pondered the fate of my future. I reached the ground floor and to my surprise who was standing there waiting for me? Two uniformed State Troopers. They were waiting to escort me out, or drag me out if I refused to leave peacefully. Wow, out of all that had transpired within the past 24 hours, this right here took the cake. I mean, seriously, did they really have to go to that extreme? What the fuck did they think I was going to do, hold the cafeteria staff hostage for their mayonnaise! Did they really think I was going to risk my baby's life over them? Ha-Ha that shit really made me laugh but then again, it was probably only protocol. You know, politics and shit...

After taking one last look at my source for food, clothing, and shelter for me and my son, my only plan was to make it home safely without crashing. I succeeded, and once inside my house, I picked up the phone and called Solomon. To no surprise, he didn't answer but I wasn't beat to leave him a message. I was numb from the drama and too drained to go through the motions. I hung up and toss the phone to the side, but a minute later he called back asking why I was home from work so early. Clearly he could sense something was wrong because he had uncertainty in his voice. I didn't even bother to tell him what was said in court, I just burst out in tears and said; *"I LOST MY FUCKING JOB, BUGGA'!"* Solomon remained silent, and I let out the longest cry in my entire life.

"Aww, man, I don't believe this, what the fuck is this nigga doing?" Assuming he was talking about his brother, his tense should have been *"What the fuck has this nigga' done!"*

"Stop crying, Molly," which of course only made me cry more. Then, for lack of something else more comforting, he asked what happened in court today. Hmm, I thought, court. What the fuck does it matter what happened in court, when I just lost my damn job! *"They talked a lot about fines, community service, probation, and felony charges."* Don't worry about that he said. Then he asked what was I going to do for money? I'll get paid for about a month, but after that I'm fucked!

Solomon didn't know what to do but I do believe he was trying his best. *"Don't worry, Molly, it'll be alright."* That shit just pissed me off. He knew it wasn't going to be alright, I knew it wasn't going to be alright. We both knew I was fucked. Damn, why do people say that?

Solomon then cut our conversation short. *"I'm at B girl crib Molly and I'm on her phone."* It sounded good but I wasn't stupid. *"I'm about to go find Ace so we can get you a lawyer."* The fact that he was willing to help any way he could was a good sign, but deep down inside I felt it was just talk. Truly, there was no need to cry over spilled milk, my job was history. However, if he could help me with my charges, it would be a blessing. My cup was half empty, I couldn't see it as being half full. Life had given me lemons and I couldn't figure out how to make lemonade. I just sat dumbfounded as things unfolded.

Once me and Solomon were off the phone, I called my cousin Shantell, then Esha, followed by my baby sister Nette, and my mom. As I was talking to Shantell my sister, Nikki, called on the other line. Nikki was surprised I answered because she was under the impression I was still in jail. *"Marie, mommy and Big Kenny are on their way to the police station right now to bail you out."*

"What, where in the world did they get the idea I was in jail?"

"From the paper," she said. *"I guess you haven't seen it yet huh?"*

"No, I haven't, but stop them before they get down there!"

"Okay, I'll call and tell them now, but me and Tizmo on our way over to your house."

"Okay cool." I hung up with her then clicked back over to Shantell. *"Damn, have you seen the paper,"* I asked? *"Naw"* she replied *"but my lunch is almost here and I was gonna shoot over to your crib. "I'll pick up a paper on my way. Minnie just called and said she saw something about you in the Trenton Times."* Damn! How deep is this shit?

Once I got off the phone with Shantell, Nette called and said her and my mom were on their way too. *"Okay cool."* By now I believed everybody had seen the paper but me, so I grabbed some loose change off the kitchen counter, ran outside, and got one for myself. Then right there in the middle of page one, the caption read *"State Worker arrested on charges of Insurance Fraud"*. WOW! The media is crazy! How they just gonna take something and blow it up like that. What happened to innocent until proven guilty? They printed my picture, government name, and the whole nine, but nothing at all was said about Ace. The bad thing was the address they put on blast wasn't even mine. It was my Nana's!

I tried to read their little hyped up blog but was only able to skim through it before Shantell arrived. I could see the hurt in her eyes when I opened the door and she could see the same in mine. She knew I needed a hug and I knew I wanted someone to hug me, but Shantell and I were never able to show that typical female emotion to one another. Instead, we summed up what we had to say with two nods of the head and putting fire to the dutch. Yeah, I still puffed a little Mary Jane every now and again, and considering the circumstances, who could blame me. Chronic always helped with the stress, and after about two tokes, I thought I was good but started crying all over again. Even Shantell shed a few tears. *"Murf, what chu' gonna do?"*

"I don't know, dog, I don't know?"

Shantell is so Pro-Black she even scared me at times. *"Fuck that! Retain legal counsel and fight them crackers."* I knew her heart was in the right place but I saw the writing a lot clearer than she did. If they wanted to keep me or overlook the incident they could have. The point was they didn't want to. I was a force to be reckoned with while I was on that job and I ruffled a lot of feathers. I reached out to personnel and made sure the clerical staff were allowed to take civil service test that they had previously been denied. I went over the heads of my bosses' to their bosses to make sure the little people were treated fairly. I even passed one of their open competitive promotional exams and came out number one. That really fucked their heads up because they assumed only those with four year degrees could do so, and there I was, with my loud, ghetto ass holding the top spot!

Until that day there was nothing they could do with me, to me, or about me. So the loss of my job wasn't just about Ace and those cards, it was about silencing a voice that woke up a lot of people. A lawyer couldn't do shit to help me now. A lawyer couldn't provide me with medical insurance and quality prenatal care. A lawyer couldn't change the minds of those who looked down on me and force them to treat me fairly. The media had already ruined that for me so really, what could legal council do? True, it would have been a good civil rights case but Rosa Parks already created that awareness and look, I was still fucked!

"Don't worry, dog, God will make a way" Shant said. *"Yeah, you're right."* It was easy to say but difficult to believe. If God cared so much I thought, then why'd he let this mess happen in the first place? However, through all the clouds, Shantell still saw a silver lining, or at least wanted to believe there was one. Solomon! Shantell felt now since I was down on my luck, Solomon and I would become closer. Shant didn't care for Solomon all like that but she couldn't imagine him leaving me high and dry at a time like this. Not after all we'd been through. Not after all I'd done for him and those kids. *"I don't need that nigga's sympathy, dog, and I don't want his sympathy either."* Tough words for a tough little woman, but deep down inside, I was hoping she was right.

When my sister Nikki and her family arrived, neither of them wanted to hear shit. All they wanted to do was get their hands on Ace and beat the shit out of him. They didn't care what the police threatened him with. He should have never given them my name, or brought them back to my job. He got caught, not me, but instead of taking it like a man, he pointed them in my direction. In their eyes, you couldn't get any more *"Bitch"* then that! By now, everyone in Trenton had heard the news but none of them knew the truth. I had a house full of people and they really kept my mind occupied, but I was worried about what I would tell my Nana. However, before I could entertain that though the landlord called. DAMN! What the fuck did they want? I just paid the rent. Why are they on my back?

To my stun, they had read the paper too and were also concerned. I assured them I was fine but knew my well being wasn't their only concern. So, instead of beating around the bush I cut straight to the chase and told them I'd be moving out at the end of next month. There was no need to bullshit and no need to prolong my stay, knowing I wouldn't be able to pay the rent. *"Hold off on the move, Marie, we may be able to help you. We would hate to see you leave in the middle of your pregnancy since the apartment is so well suited for an addition to your family. I'm sure there's something we can do, just wait until we can talk."* Okay I said. I thanked her for her call and hung up.

Nikki overheard my conversation then asked, *"Why'd you tell them you were gonna move? Shit, there are too many organizations out there to help people. You need to take advantage of them, bla, bla, bla."* It sounded good, but again, I saw the writing a lot clearer then they did.

Organizations like Catholic Charities and Home Front helped people with *low income*, not *no income*! Plus, I still had a car note and insurance to worry about. There was no way I could swing both of them and take care of myself, Quan, and the baby on top of the rent. It was impossible! If anything, the move would help me put a few dollars away for when the baby arrived. Everyone was focused on what had already happened, but I was focused on how I was going to survive. The job was history and soon the apartment would be, too. I'd hold on to the car as long as I could, but there would be no guarantees. Yes, I'd done a lot of planning to better myself, move my kid up out of the hood, and provide him with a better life, but now I'd have to revise my plan. I knew all of their concern and advice was given with good intent but I couldn't hear anymore. I was tired and beginning to get frustrated. I apologized to my family and told them I didn't mean to be rude, but I wanted to be left alone. I needed to lie down. My head was spinning. It wasn't even noon and already it had been a long day. That little curly head, white girl couldn't have said it better "It's a hard knock life!"

Now that I was alone, the silence was so loud it was deafening. How the hell could all this be happening to me? I'd been set up, charged with felonies, embarrassed by the media, lost my job, I was on the verge of loosing my car and my home, and if the good Lord didn't help me, I was going to lose my mind! Then to add insult to injury, the police were protecting a snitch for his cooperation. This was some bullshit! Even worse, I was beginning to feel that Solomon's talk was just that, talk! Enough time had passed to where he should have gotten back to me by now. I believe out of everything else, him not being by my side is what hurt the most. Maybe I should have taken heed to my man Chip years ago when he stepped to me and asked why I was dealing with dude. *"Murf, you know that nigga' ain't built like that,"* he said. At first I though it was just jealousy but it also could have been a forewarning.

The entire day had passed and I hadn't got so much as a phone call from Solomon. I did get word, however, that him and Ace got into a fight because of what he'd done, but that didn't' help me or my situation. Besides, Ace was his brother and they'd eventually kiss and make up. All I had to look forward to was one month's pay from the state and after that, I had to turn to the Mercer County Board of Social Services for help. Although I was still able to work, I knew no employer would take the risk of hiring me, then turn around and have to pay for my disability four months later. There was no light at the end of my tunnel and even with welfare's help, it wouldn't be enough to take care of me and the kids. My only alternative was to withdraw my pensions, but I had to wait until my resignation was finalized before I could even do that. This was something else everyone tried to advise me against, however, none of them were in my shoes. At my age, I'd still have to work at least another twenty years before I had the age to collect full retirement so it really didn't matter. And who knew, by then, I could be dead!

****

A month passed and I was beginning to feel the burn from my losses. Not only was my money running out but Bugga' was still bullshitting me. The only thing I ever heard from him was; *"We trying to get this money up for you, Molly,"* which I knew was a crock of shit! Those niggas were sitting on cake and distribution was at their disposal. Hustling on my behalf was just an excuse to keep me off their backs. I guess they were hoping my kindness would become a weakness and eventually I'd forgive and forget. Wrong! I wanted to forgive, but instead found myself defending the lies written up about me in the paper. I needed to forget, but ended up BLACKING OUT! The hood only knew half the story, they had no idea they were all showing love to a rat! Exposing Ace was never my intentions because I knew he'd end up doing that to himself, but the fact that he kept ducking me every time I came around was beginning to piss me off.

Eventually I stooped to his level and played his game. If he was gonna run and hide, then I was gonna seek him out and put him on blast. One day I ran up in Meechy's and Happy's, where I knew him and his brother could be found, and showed people the marked money Ace used to set me up, and gave them the run of what really happened. *"This is the shit the paper ain't telling y'all. Y'all know how the Po-Po protect their informants. How come the paper don't' say anything about the nigga who set me up? Why don't they say his name? 'Cause he a snitch that's why. Y'all see it. He's a snitch!"*

Because I was cool with everyone, and I do mean everyone, it disturbed others to hear and see me act out the way I did. Everybody knew how volcanic my temper could be but they also knew I had to be

286

provoked into exploding. Tommy and Billy were two of Ace's closest friends and Tommy knew I'd never cross any of the fellas, so did Billy and Knowledge. Though, as I stood in the middle of the barber shop, telling the real story, all they could do was drop their heads. These were the same cats Ace and I both grew up with, and in thirty years, none of us had ever had any problems or beef what so ever. So why now would I decide to shit on his name, and for what reason? Ace had disgusted us all and his closest allies felt just as played as me, because up until then, they'd fell for his two bit story about how he was the victim. I knew telling my side of the story would cause people to look at him differently, but if he was grimy enough to do something like that to me, it was no telling what he'd do to them. Especially, if it came down to saving his own hide...

Everyone felt my wrath except for the one who caused it. Ace had been successful at avoiding me for over a month, but I was still hot on his bumper and wouldn't ease up. Each day my frustration grew until finally I took them out on Solomon's car by writing obscenities on it with white shoe polish. I even took it a step further by threatening everybody I saw who knew the two of them because I felt they were aiding Ace in avoiding me. It was really funny now that I think about it, because threats were all I was good for at the time. I mean really, what was I going to do in my condition? Though I will admit, there were better ways to handle the situation. Then one day I lucked up and the two of us ran into each other. *"Damn, Ace, it's been like a month, why you...?"*

"Molly, I'm sorry. I just left church and asked for forgiveness." Okay, all of that sounded good but it did nothing to help me. Sure, his guilt lead him to the altar but he hadn't offended God, he offended me!

I accepted his apology not because I felt he was sincere, but because I had too much love in my heart not to... From then on I realized that the only person who was capable or going to help me was me.

****

With criminal charges pending against me and my court date less than two weeks away. I had no choice but to follow Shantell's advice and retain a lawyer. I was ecstatic when the attorney told me he would take my case on such short notice, but damn near hit the floor when he told me his services would cost me five-thousand dollars. Five-thousand! I couldn't believe it. Apparently, the fee you paid depended on the crime committed. In my case, I was facing four charges but he was sure he could get three of them thrown out. He talked a good game and since he was my only hope, of course I told him I'd pay the retainer. I had no idea how, considering he needed a thousand up front...

I left the lawyer's office on a mission to get that five thousand by any means necessary. My first stop was the store on Spring where I was sure I'd find Solomon flirting with some hoochie. I failed to run into him face to face before he made his get away, but that didn't matter. I quickly left the block in route to his brother's house because somebody was going to give me something! Ace broke down and gave me $500 but that was it. I was still $4500 away. I returned to the attorney with the five, and dude was so cool he agreed to take small payments from me; a hundred here another hundred there, until I was able to pay him off. He understood my financial situation and felt bad that I'd fell on such hard luck while enduring a pregnancy. My perception of his kindness changed, however, once we got to court and learned I was eligible for P.T.I [Pre Trial Intervention.]

P.T.I was a program offered to the majority of first time offenders and the requirements were the same for everyone. Being I was eligible, there was no need for anyone other than a Public Defender. My expensive attorney knew that too, but being in his line of business, I guess he could spot a sucker a mile away.

I wasn't thrilled about getting into more debt, especially for a service I didn't need in the first place. But in any event, my plea of no contest was entered and accepted by the court, and the terms and conditions of that plea went into effect immediately. Meaning, I had to report to the Adult Probation Office right after leaving court and sign up for three years of probation. After that, I had to set up an arrangement to pay my fines and the Public Defenders office, even though I didn't need their help. I don't know why, but that's what I was ordered to do. In addition to that, I had three years to complete five hundred hours of community service, and last, I had to re-establish permanent employment and stay out of trouble for six months. It wasn't a bad deal but they should have known I wasn't going to be able to work until after the baby was born. So until then, I had to rely on welfare.

Welfare, now that was a hard pill to swallow because up until that day, I took pride in always being able to provide for myself and not seek the aide of government programs to get by. I hated the idea, but I had to do what I had to do. Both my attorney and former employer knew my first offense would only get me a slap on the wrist. Though, instead of working with me, they forced my hand, and mislead me into a resignation I didn't have to give. Literally, I'd never been a part of a ménage à trios, but I sure did have a lot of dicks screwing me now!

****

Leaving my home was inevitable, despite the efforts put forth by my landlord to help me stay. It was an upsetting move for me and my son, considering we'd planned to be there until he reached junior high. I had no money to rent a moving van and I couldn't think of anyone who would rent one for me. Thank God Quan's father came to our rescue. He lent us his tire truck, and his brother, "S", helped us pack and transport our things to public storage. I felt bad for leaning on them with my needs, because they'd just lost their mother a few days after I lost my job, but was grateful for their assistance. Pharaoh and I hadn't always seen eye to eye, but at least when I needed him most he was there. Prior to that day, he and I held many conversations on how loosing my job would impact me and his son. He was furious that his son had been made a victim in all of this and offered to see Ace about his dirty deed. I was somewhat flattered over his concern, but as with others, I had to turn down his offer. Causing Ace harm or doing something just as grimy to him would do nothing more than make matters worse.

****

Words are mightier than the sword. Having said, the fact that Pharaoh and others continued to tell me the same thing really made me think. The way they saw it, my misfortune was just as much Solomon's fault as it was Ace. They figured if Solomon cared anything about me, his brother would have respected his feelings, and rolled with the punches instead of kicking my back in. Solomon's actions showed everyone that he viewed me as expendable. I didn't want to see it that way, but I knew they were telling me the truth. Quan and I continued to stay on Russling until the landlord returned my deposit to me. They knew I needed that money for just about everything, so they didn't make us wait. Once that was done, we stuffed the rest of our personal belongings in the car and headed to my mother's.

Initially, I was hesitant to call on her for refuge considering her door had never been open for me in the past. But the thought of being homeless with a child and one on the way had me on the edge of insanity. I talked to my little sister first since her and my niece stayed there too, and she in turn spoke to me mom and our mother said it would be okay. For the first time in my life, she actually seemed excited to have me with her, but I knew more of it was simply her willingness to show her support. Truly, there was barely enough room for the three of them let alone me, my son and our shit. But we made the best of it. I slept on the long couch, Quan slept on the love seat, and while anticipating the arrival of yet one more mouth to feed, we settled into the belly of the beast, South Trenton, 171 Jersey Street!

****

My regiment turned into nothing more but eating, sleeping, and talking shit. Welfare gave us $322 a month plus stamps, but I had to give $100 of that up for storage and I shared the stamps with the house. In emergency situations, I ran to Meech and Chino at the store. I wasn't always in the mood to cook, and with limited space and my belly growing bigger, eating out was just more convenient. I also ran to them because I needed something to do with my time while Quan was in school. So as a fair exchange, Meech let me eat all I wanted and I watched the store for him during the day in return, till about 2:30 p.m. when Ms. Hilda (Chino's mom and Meech's wife) or Chino came in to take over. This worked out perfect since at 3:00 p.m. I had to go pick Quan up from school. Solomon would come in every now and again, lend a helping hand and try to put a smile on my face, but the smile I displayed was only to keep from crying. I was over the hate, ready to move on, and didn't want to force my feelings or emotions on someone else. Solomon didn't have to love me, but he was still the father of my child.

****

Staying with my mom was definitely and experience. Living out of crates, bags, and sleeping on the couch was rough. Though, most of the time it was just easier to sleep on the floor because I needed the extra room. In essence, we converted my mom's tiny living room into our entire house. We were packed like sardines, but we kept our area neat and clean. But cramped living conditions were the minimum to endure compared to the violence and ignorance one had to deal with from living in the neighborhood itself. No lie, living on Jersey Street was just like living in the middle of a war zone. Adults fought children, children fought adults, and the innocent always wound up caught in the middle. On most occasions, you could just sit and watch the entertainment from your porch. But there were a few times when ignoring the chaos was virtually impossible. At times, minding your business and keeping to yourself was like speaking a foreign language to the Vikings who thrived on the excitement of negativity. Sooner or later, no matter who you were, you just knew you were going to get into something with somebody; because the entire neighborhood had a chaotic vibe. One would have thought a pregnant woman would have been excluded from the shenanigans. Yet, those ignoramuses didn't value my wellbeing any more than they did their own.

It's a shame how many times me and the next door neighbors, Tito & Martina, got into it with the people across the street over our kids' right to play in front of their own house. And if we weren't fighting over the kids, we were being accused of doing or saying something that was purely a figment of their narrow imagination. Niggas were hating on me because I refused to let them get their dice games on, on the side of my mom's porch. Some even tried to pay me off but in a million years, I could never be that broke! Right is right and wrong is wrong and I wasn't about to bite my tongue, turn my head, or look the other way. My mom, on the other hand, just wanted to keep the peace, but bottom line, the drama on Jersey Street was never ending.

Adjusting to new living conditions wasn't as bas as trying to adjust to a new lifestyle. I wasn't use to being broke and I wasn't use to being that type of poor. Out of the $222 I had to work with for the month, I tried giving my mom between $80-$100 to go towards the bills. I managed to keep that up for the first two months but after that, it swindled down to like $40-$50, and sometimes just a, *"Thanks Mom. I appreciate your sacrifice."* It was unnatural for me to be so dependent and lack control over my circumstances. I hated it! At times I felt guilty, most times I felt sad, and on occasion I was just out right mad.

I was worried about my car, although Pharaoh was always nice enough to help me with the maintenance of it. I just didn't know how I was going to continue to hide it from the repo man. I hadn't made a payment in two months. And since the last car I financed listed Pharaoh's information on the loan agreement; they called him hoping he'd give them information on the car's whereabouts. Of course he looked me out, and shot them a story about me moving down south, but I still drove around looking over my shoulder. I lost my license, the car wasn't registered, and the only insurance card I possessed was out dated one. My life was in shambles and just to add insult to injury, it lacked the one thing I needed the most. Intimate companionship!

It's my theory the Creator gave us all three natural instincts that simply can not be ignored. Survival, hunger, and horny! I was doing okay at surviving and you could look at me and tell I wasn't missing any meals. But I hadn't had a piece since November 13th, 2000, which was the last time me and Droop mixed it up. Solomon was my son's father, but dealing with him was out of the question. I couldn't imagine being with anyone besides the father of my child and all of my bedroom toys were packed away. The only privacy I got was in the shower, but being pregnant made self servicing myself nearly impossible. So as a result, abstinence became my middle name.

MARIE ANTIONETTE

*THE WIND BENEATH YOUR WINGS ISN'T
ALWAYS INVISIBLE, SUCH AS THE AIR YOU BREATHE...*

SAVED BY GRACE

In order to deal with me, you have to love me. I say that because accepting me for who I am isn't something everyone can do. I'm head strong, sensitive, passionate, emotional, silly, talkative, and moody. I can switch moods twenty times a day and expect you to keep up with each and every one of them. I have a huge heart, and anyone who's a part of my life can testify that my *witty, dramatic character is* what attracts them to me the most. The towering highs and squatting lows of my personality are very alluring and to say the least, I am a handful! However, despite all of that, during a time when I thought no one understood or even cared, a handful of loyal, head strong friends just like myself simply would not let me be. I viewed these individuals as blessings. God's way of telling me that in-spite of all that had occurred and all that I'd lost; his grace and the mustarded of faith he placed inside of me was still sufficient! If only I'd learned earlier that spiritual love was the best love of all. No flesh can produce such a wonderful and lasting bliss. Such charity can only come from the heart, where love originates and resides…

****

Because I felt so alienated, I didn't extend myself to any friendships. However Tito and his wife Martina were an exception to that rule, and after all was said and done, we wound up more like family than friends. The three of us would see one another in passing, but no alliance had been formed until that one day.

It was unusually warm, early spring afternoon and I'd almost returned home from a walk to the store. For anyone else it wouldn't have taken more than five minutes to get down the street and back, and without even breaking a sweat, but in my condition and with my weight, it felt more like a half hour hike through the Sahara. My steps were as slow as a one year old learning to walk, and at about ten feet from the crib, I just stopped walking and began to cry. Tito and Martina were just getting in from picking their girls up from school when they noticed me standing alone looking sad. The two of them looked at me, then looked at each other as if to say, *"What the hell's wrong with her?"*

Embarrassed by my behavior, I sucked up my frustration, picked my steps back up, but only took a few more before self pity consumed me again. *"Fuck This!"* I was six months and already as big as a house. It was difficult to sit or stand, and walking was sometimes painful. My feet stayed swollen and my hormones had gone haywire. By now my mom had come to the door and was looking at me with the same uncertainty. Tito then asked her was I okay, and she then turned to me and asked; *"Ree, baby, why you crying, is the baby alright?"*

I took a few more steps, then a deep sigh, and sarcastically replied, *"Yeah we okay, my fat ass just tired of walking!"* Tickled by my response, Tito intervened and asked, *"Is that why you're crying?"* The look on my face said it all and the three of them busted out in heavy laughter. Tito and Martina were laughing so hard, they had tears in their eyes, which in turn, caused me to laugh as well.

From that point forward, the three of us became inseparable. We spent hot, sunny days together on the porch, hustling the products of our environment [weed], or taking long rides to wherever the road lead us. The two of them were heaven sent, and never let me spend a moment alone or allowed me to drown myself in boredom. When ever they left the neighborhood to go to dinner or the beach, they were always kind enough to take me and Quan along with them. And regardless of how much was spent on our outings, money was never an issue.

Martina and her husband became a major source of emotional support for me, and nothing cured my blues better than a good laugh. Having said, my foolhardy humor was the number one reason I got kicked out of the house (in jest) as much as I did. *"Keep it up, we gon' send you into early labor,"* is what Martina would say as she chuckled uncontrollably. Tito, on the other, hand would beckon for my mother or my son to come take me away, all while trying to catch his breath. Martina was even forced to pull over one day while driving down the highway on the way to breakfast. *"No she didn't,"* her and Tito both laughed until they cried. Then, the next thing you knew, we were on the side of the road with Tito crying, *"get the fuck out,"* while again, trying to catch his breath. We were so wrapped up in our shenanigans, we didn't notice the Pennsylvania State Trooper who pulled up along side of us. He was almost ready to put Tito in cuffs, until we told him we were just goofing around. .

We got the same response one day while chilling at Caldwalder Park. I said something off the wall and Tito pulled the bat from the back of the truck then started chasing me. Not that the two of us didn't need the exercise, and Martina was cracking up as she looked on, but to others who weren't aware Tito meant me no harm, it looked as if I were being attacked. I fell to the ground because I couldn't stop laughing and Tito fell a few yards back. Before I could stand to my feet, several good Samaritans came to my aide and were relieved to see we were just joking around.

All of our antics were always in good fun and with good intent, and I admired them for their commitment to one another, their deep family values and their humbleness.

****

The commencement of new alliances was refreshing but nothing was touched my heart like the loyalty of old friends. I was certain everyone would shy away from me due to fear of getting caught up in my mess. I figured most would back away because of embarrassment, or would fear being associated with the negativity that was surrounding me at the time. Who knew the one I fought with the most, would end up being by my side, ride or die!

Esha, my best friend for over ten years, blew me away with her loyalty and devotion. After my resignation, the heads of our department came down on her hard in an attempt to extract more information about me and my illegal activities. As if my resignation and public humiliation wasn't enough. They were smart, and figured if anyone knew anything about me it would be her. They tried intimidating and watching her like a hawk, but they had no probable cause for their harassment, except for her personal relationship with me.

Esha and I first met one another when we began working for the state and it was ironic that we ended up working so closely together. The two of us hit it off from the start, but due to our sometimes identical personalities, we often bumped heads. We'd often get into very loud and heated verbal disputes inside the office, and once, even became physical with one another. We had to straighten up our act once the state implemented the "No Work Place Violence," policy, and many thought the two of us would be the new rule's first victims. Esha was more then a friend, she was a sister, and we loved each other in our own unique way, even if others couldn't see it. .

Although a hot head and a loud mouth just like me, Esha was no dummy and smarter than most gave her credit for. The girl worked two jobs, was a home owner, and took damn good care of her kids. She'd sacrifice the tips from her part-time bartending gig, and turn them over to me, because he knew my pride wouldn't allow me to ask for help.

****

Another loyal favorite among family and friends was my God sister Nancy. She was also a co-worker who I'd grown extremely close to over the years and after my dismissal, her and her family saw me through some major rough times.

Nancy was no stranger to the trials and tribulations of life, and the kindness her and her family extended m y way was immeasurable. Nancy opened the doors of her family's home to me and my son, and their charity never had an ulterior motive. Every Sunday my son and I were invited over to her mother's house for dinner, and afterwards, sat around watching the game or playing cards and bingo. Nancy was reserved when in the office, but in the comforts of her own surroundings she was outgoing and down to earth. I respected her and her entire family for their integrity and meek mannerism, which always made me and Quan feel right at home.

Nancy, her sister Yolanda, her daughter Alexis, her niece Ty, and mother were so very receptive towards me and Quan, and spoiled him the same as Nana and Mr. James use to spoil me when I was young. Nancy and I had a lot in common with one another and she frequently compared me to her younger brother, Mikey, because trouble and mischief followed us both. The majority of her family and in-laws either worked for the state or was in law enforcement, but never did they look down on me or judge me by my mistakes and past actions. After being scorned by so many others who claimed to be as caring, being in their company restored some of my faith. Prior to our gatherings at Ma'Abuela's, Sundays were basically long, lonely, and boring. This weekly outing and outlet gave me and my son something to always look forward to and without question, Ma' Abuela's food was la bomba! In other words, the bomb!

****

Next on the list was Ms. Carol aka "Aunty Carol," and her sternness was just what I needed to keep me afloat. Aunt Carol was of co-worker of mine just like Esha and Nancy, but her tutelage in my life began many years back when I was a teenager living next door to her on Wall St. As a mother of two sons, she often directed me like I was the daughter she never had, and her love for me wouldn't depart simply because we no longer worked together. Aunt Carol was a beacon of light and wisdom during my employment at the Dept of Labor, and just like Nana, wouldn't hesitate to put my ass in check. As time progressed, her sons and I took to each other like family; just as many adopted siblings and cousin's do from hood to hood. Being as Aunt Carol came from the same old fashioned up bringing as my Nana, she felt the best way to keep me rooted was to provide me with the word of God. Hence on my 30th birthday gave me a beautiful bible and the inscription read *"To My God-Child with Love."* Ironically, it was almost identical to the one my Nana gave me when I turned twelve.

Aunt Carol knew I was no dummy, but also knew desperation and lack of necessities could cause me to do things I'd more then likely live to regret. Being as though I was no longer in arm's reach, she'd often invited me into town in order to have lunch, at which time she'd always give me a few dollars and tell me to buy Quan some ice-cream, knowing she'd given me enough to do that and much more. I guess sometimes the best way to show someone you care, is to do something for them that you know they can't do for themselves.

Aunt Carol knew that nine times out of ten, I was belligerent to get out of my own way, and constantly reminded me that, *"Pride cometh before the fall."* She knew about the hardships from my early years and always encouraged me to leave the past in the past and make amends with my mother. Not that the two of us were at each other's throats, but she knew we could do better. She knew how much I kept bottled up inside and felt if I didn't talk about it or clear the air, that one day I'd explode. However, it wasn't just past transgressions that boiled my blood and hardened my heart, it was also the present.

Living with my mother was better than the alternative, but for the life of me I still could not understand her ways or reasoning. I attempted to make myself comfortable without getting in the way. However, moms could have made things a bit easier for me, by allowing me to rest and stretch out on her fluffy king size bed, instead of locking her door every time she left the house. I knew this was learned behavior she picked up from my Nana, but in my condition, I thought or hoped she would have had a change of heart. Not only was sitting and sleeping on that pleather couch bad for my back, but by locking up everything, she made me feel as if she thought I was going to take something or rummage through her belongings. As if anything in that place was worth any street or worldly value... I tried blaming my feelings on the pregnancy, but those hurts were there long before I got pregnant.

Because I'd already lost so much, I didn't have it in me to beg anyone, not even my mother to accommodate me any further. That was the pride in me Aunt Carol said, but eventually she felt the two of us would make progress. *"You only get one mother, Marie!"* I knew where she was coming from but at the same time, *"You only get one first born too..."*

****

The select few who befriended me or remained close to me during this phase of my life were an elite bunch. All of them offered me and my son their love and support but Kenny aka Sam, offered me understanding. Sam and I were somewhat cut from the same cloth and often ventured down roads that kept leading us into trouble. And because he had been through so much and had fought similar battles, he was the ideal individual to talk to in times of distress. Sam, just like Aunt Carol, had known me and my family every since I was a little girl and he and my mother were peers. The two of them became friends long before the two of us became acquainted, and they both started their employment together at the department nearly twelve years prior to me getting hired. Aside from work, Sam and I use to run into each other frequently on the streets when I was dealing and he was slipping. However, because his character was so genuine, his non-conventional practices and choice of lifestyle didn't bother me as much as it did others. Besides, we all have our faults, Sam just didn't try to hide or sugarcoat his, and I respected him for being so real.

Sam and I were like two black sheeps; very unique, very rare, and always someone's target. So it came as no surprise when he came to me and said the department was seeking his permanent removal as well. Ironically, he was offered the same deal as me. The only difference was in exchange for his resignation, he was able to avoid going to jail. Had he refused their deal, they had enough on him to send him away for at least a year. Having already suffered my fate, it was easy for me to prepare Sam for his. So as time progressed and our finances dwindled, we resorted to taking care of each other while waiting for the Division of Pensions to release our funds. Even with a dependency, Sam made sure he put a few dollars in my pocket, dropped off a few smokes, and if he could find it, some damn good burn too... *(But this didn't occur until after I had my second son.)* It made no difference to him if it was 8:00 a.m. or 11:00 p.m., he always had me and the kids in his thoughts. A lot of people who knew Sam tended to shy away from him because they saw him as a pan handling junkie who only though of himself. To them I say, *"Judge not!"*

Sam had a heart of gold and even though he couldn't always control his demons, he did control his mouth when ever he walked into my mom's home. Sam was the only individual who actually took the time to sit and visit me on Jersey Street, everyone else asked if I could meet them elsewhere. I couldn't blame them for being cautious, but Sam had no problem venturing into the depths of the ghetto. His only issue was the way me and my son were living. He knew we were accustomed to better and couldn't wait to see us up and back on our feet again. He understood my stress and had a great deal of sympathy for me. Despite the fact of him being a user, he was a very good and loyal friend.

My guardian angles were incredible, but when my friend and ex colleague Annie came long, she put the icing on top of the cake. Everyone displayed countless, unselfish acts of kindness during my time of turmoil, but Annie went above and beyond.

As my delivery date slowly approached, so did my anxieties, and rightfully so. I was frustrated, fat, tired, and wanted to do something to lift my spirits since I had gone through my entire pregnancy alone. Having a shower seemed like the ideal thing to do, but I had been out of circulation with my peers for so long, I didn't feel anyone thought enough of me to coordinate on my behalf. Thus, I decided to throw my own. The planning of the shower would not only help boost my spirits, it created the opportunity for me to get re-acquainted with some of those whom I missed. At first the news of me planning my own shower caused some to laugh. Yet, after I explained my reasons, they all understood.

Initially my plan was to host the event at my mother's, though I feared many wouldn't show because of the location. And if they did, they'd be too afraid to stay considering Jersey Street was a round the clock war zone. I though about renting a hall but where would I get the money to do that? It was already going to cost me my entire check to throw the shower; there was no way I could incur further expenses. Saddened that my hecklers may have been right, I started to call the whole thing off. No only didn't I have a venue to host, I'd also need ample space to entertain. That's when my dear friend Annie opened her heart and the doors of her home, and told me I could have the shower at her house. My problems were now solved, and with one stone I killed two birds...

****

Because most who were invited were family and friends from the job, Annie had no problem with my guest list. This was the main reason why I wanted to be in charge of my own event. Only I knew who I wanted to attend. But aside from those we worked with like my Ti-Ti Sodi, Nancy, and my boy Bill, I invited all of my sisters, my little brother Kenny, my God brother Chino', Tito, Martina, Bill's wife Von', Amber, and Droop's girlfriend Blaque'. Von and I were both pregnant and our due dates were a day apart. Coincidentally, she was also the first cousin of Solomon's new girlfriend but that didn't bother me at all. Our history wasn't built or based around my dealings with Solomon and she had no control over who she was related to.

The shower was set for Saturday May 5th, (Cinco' de Mayo.) I asked Ma' Abuela to prepare the rice, my dad was frying the fish, Esha was making the salad, and I was taking care of the lasagna and the cake which read, *"Babies Are a Blessing"* across the top and my son's name *"Messiah"* at the bottom. I got the idea for his name from the bible because I felt he was God's way of telling me he was still in control of my life. One of the many translations of Messiah is *"The One,"* and although my bundle hadn't arrived yet, I knew the name was a perfect fit. Every major task that needed to be done had been taken care of. The only thing I had left to do was put up the decorations. Quan, Annie, and myself took on that task the Thursday before the shower, and afterwards we all sat down with her and her grandson Azur, and enjoyed a delicious home cooked meal.

On the morning of the shower, Day'Quan had a playoff game at the 6/11 field, which caused me to be out and about a lot earlier than I wanted to be. Knowing I needed all the sleep and rest I could get, I was hoping his game would end early. Lord knows I didn't want to be cranky or sleepy at my own event, but at the same time, Quan had played his heart out all year long and deserved to play in the playoffs.

Although the sun was always hot and there was never any shade, it was a beautiful day to be at the park. My son wasn't a star player, but he had good team spirit. He hit the ball for the first time that day, and I was so happy for my baby, I started to jump up and down on the bleachers. Quan, on the other hand, was so amazed at his accomplishment; he forgot to run to first base. Instead, he stood at home plate in awe, while me, his coach, and his teammates cheered him on. Our day had started out on a high note and I looked forwarded to it getting better. After the game, the two of us sat down and ate a snack, then headed back home so we could change. Walking down to the field at 9:00 a.m. seemed like good exercise, but by the end of my round trip, my feet were swollen, my back was in extreme pain, and my pelvis felt like it was going to snap! I was almost 300lbs. and the extra weight made it almost impossible to get around.

Once we arrived back at the house, my mom was standing in the door, smiling like a proud grandma. I was so happy to reach that front porch so I could sit down and rest my feet, those last few steps seemed to take forever. Knowing I had to still go to the store and pick up a few things, I needed some down time to snooze before heading out. I thought I'd at least be able to drift off while Quan showered and changed, but no sooner than I tried to get comfortable, my mom ran down the stairs and told me Annie left a message for me to call her as soon as possible! Knowing Annie, she probably forgot to ask me something about the shower and knowing my mom, it probably wasn't as urgent as she was making it sound.

Annie must have been on the phone when I called so I left her a voice message. Then as soon as I hung up she called back. I barely got a chance to say hello before she began explaining to me the mix up that had occurred. She said she was sorry for not telling me earlier or for not remembering, but she had a wedding to attend today and wouldn't be home for the shower. My heart dropped! What was I going to do? I had twenty-five people ready to show up at her door in a matter of hours. What was I going to tell everyone? I was so used to things not going my way, I couldn't even get disappointed. *"It's okay, Annie, I understand..."*

"Hold on, Murf, hold on," Annie said. I'm not calling you to tell you to cancel the shower, I just want you to come over now and pick up the key. You can still have the shower at my house, I just won't be there. I'll be at the wedding, I'm about to leave now.

1st Corinthians 13:13 says love is the greatest gift of all. Not faith, not hope, but love and love alone. Annie was a fine example of that verse and she displayed it through her actions. I was so touched. Here she was a friend, willing to leave me in her home with all of my family and friends. People she didn't even know. She wasn't even going to be there but she was still willing to extend me the comforts of her home. God is truly amazing! All my life I had been associated with lovers, family, and friends who wouldn't even lend me the keys to their car and here she was giving me the keys to her home. Now that's a friend! One would have thought it was she and I who held a thirty year friendship, instead of me and Ace. Her kindness was overwhelming.

By the time I reached Annie's house, anticipation was flowing from ever porous of my body. I was anxious and nervous all at once, but my emotions leveled out once my family and guest started to show and the celebration kicked into full swing. Not every one I invited was able to show, but those who were important to me were there, and that's all that mattered. Besides Annie and Chino, who I knew weren't going to make it, Droop nor Solomon decided to show either. Blaque' on the other hand, was there front and center and I wonder if her presence was to simply keep him away. It would have been nice to see him, since the two of us hadn't seen one another in so long.

A GIRL NAMED JOB

****

The baby got a lot of nice things; clothes, accessories, and toys. My big sister Keyda gave me $100.00 and around that time, $100.00 was more like a thousand! I was so touched I couldn't help but cry.

Nancy and Ma' Abuela gave me the Graco, olive green and cream Winnie the Pooh stroller I had my eye on from Target and Esha gave us a blue and white one made by Kolcraft. My mom and little sister gave me the matching Pooh car seat, my Nana gave me her prayers, and Blaque' gave me a little ceramic piggy bank and some ceramic booties with the June birthstone. Although my original due date was Quan's birthday, my doctor had me scheduled me for a c-section on June 4th.

My shower was a success! Everyone enjoyed themselves and I enjoyed the fellowship between my family and close friends. Each time someone took a picture, it captured my Kool-Aid grin from ear to ear, tears of joy, or hard laughter. It had been a while since I felt that good, and I had to take a moment to sit back, give thanks, and re-evaluate my situation.

Truly I was blessed! God had been by my side the entire time and sometimes carrying me. I couldn't see it at first because I was so caught up in what I no longer had. It took a reminder like this to show me that what I'd lost was nothing in comparison to what I had to gain. I though to myself if I can make it through this, I'll be okay. This is when I learned to appreciate the faith of Job and why his story has been so remarkable throughout history. Nana always said there was nothing new under the sun. So I planted that in my heart and had faith that if He did it for Job, He'd do it for me too. Hands down, the true test of friendship is hard times. Not everyone I loved or thought would be by my side was. However, they were the ones I should have never concerned myself with in the first place. Those individuals, for lack of a better term, were what one would call *"fair weather friends."* They only stuck around when things were looking up, when things were in my favor, and when I had something to offer. Though, now that I was the one in need of a shoulder to lean on, someone to lift my spirits, and restore my faith, they were no where to be found. The hand full of loved ones that were in my presence on this day, were all the friends and family I needed. They were there for me in the beginning, they were here with me now, and they'd remain with me till the end.

****

With less than a month to go for the baby's delivery, my days were laxed and my worries were few. I had all I needed for myself and my new son, and the only thing that really concerned me was my weight. I had been labeled high risk because of my excessive weight gain and at 36 weeks I was already 250lbs and growing! Doctor Murthy, my gynecologist, had become concerned about my weight as well, therefore, increased my office visits from once to twice a week. He was afraid I'd go early and I was just plain afraid.

My pelvis hurt a lot during my last month and I often called him and complained about the pressure. *"Sit still, Marie,"* he'd say. *"You still have a few weeks to go."* By now I was just simply tired of being tired, tired of being fat, and begged him to take the baby early but he wouldn't. Doc Murthy was the best gynecologist in the area and had taken real good care of me during my pregnancy. He even overlooked the fact that I no longer had the "good insurance" and kept me on as his patient even though he knew it would take welfare forever to pay for my visits.

The events that occurred in my life over the past six months would alter my life forever. At first I felt cursed. Why would such horrible things happen to me? But I grew to appreciate the valley low, or gain a respect for it in the least. Being there helped refine me and gave me time to separate the former me, from the me I was growing into. It was a humbling experience, one I'm sure not everyone could endure or pull through.

Never underestimate the strength, determination or courage of a Black Woman!

THE COMING OF MESSIAH

A s my due date approached, the further away it seemed, and I was beginning to wonder if my doctor was off with my date. Agitated use to be the best way to describe my demeanor but lately, I'd become more like the Tasmanian devil. I was so ready to deliver, I was beginning to wish Tito and Martina would have forced me into labor. Frustration was clearly written all over my face and everything anyone said to me annoyed the shit out of me.

My pension check had arrived and just in time too, I was ready to put it to good use. But I received less then half of what I expected, and that's because they deducted the balance of the loans I owed from my final check. I was looking forward to getting at least nine-grand, but ended up with about four and a half. I wasn't going to ball out like I thought but after the baby was born, at least I could move. That money would definitely secure us a new place and I'd have enough left over to pay my rent at least two months in advance. There would be no time to sit around and lounge, because I'd need to find a job as soon as possible. The beginning of the rest of my life was right around the corner, and I only had a few more steps to get there.

****

With just three weeks remaining until my scheduled c-section, there was literally nothing left for me to do but bombard Tito and Martina's house every day from dusk till dawn. Neighbors had begun to think I'd moved out from my mom's and in with them because every time you turned around, I was either walking in or out of their front door. It got to the point that when someone needed or was looking for me, they'd bypassed my mom's crib and headed straight for theirs. Tito and Martina had air-conditioning and my mom didn't, enough said! I mean seriously, there was no way I was going to sit up in that hot ass house all day sweating like a hog, when I could sit and relax comfortably in theirs. Plus, I was literally bored out of my mind. There was nothing for me to do at home, at least over their house we could sit and play spades and puff a little. Yes, I puffed a little in my last month! I know many may look down on that but the small effect the marijuana had on me and the baby was nothing compared to the sedatives and drugs I was going to intake during labor. Besides, I didn't make a habit out of it and I only took one or two tokes. I smoked not because I wanted to get high and I certainly wouldn't suggest anyone follow in my footsteps, but the chronic did help ease the pain in my lower back that was killing me day by day. I don't feel I have to justify my actions, I'm just telling my story...

****

My pregnancy became contagious, and by the time I was ready to deliver, three more were just in their first trimester. Yeap, I brought the baby bug with me to Jersey Street, and the receivers of that old wives tale weren't pleased with its timing. Martina, Stephanie, and Sonja were the victims who were touched. As for Martina and Sonja, it would be their third child, but for Stephanie it would be her first. Now I was the one with jokes, while they dealt with morning sickness and not being able to fit into their low riding jeans. For the moment we were all in the same boat, but my tour would soon be over. They hated that!

I'm glad I have those memories. Sonja and I didn't always get along, and weren't always able to agree to disagree, but in the end we ended up being cool because our misunderstandings were just that. Misunderstandings...

Chilling inside under the air all day was cool, (no pun intended) but the highlight of my days was when the sun went down. Once the sun set, we pulled out the chairs and sat out on the stoop like old timers in the south. We talked shit to and about everyone up and down the block, including ourselves and each other. We were the first ones on the scene and guaranteed to be the last ones to take it down. There were times when we called it quits early, but ended up coming back out once the kids were asleep. We even messed around and pulled a few all nighters, or pushed it till the wee hours of the morning, running back and forth to 7-Eleven for slurpees and snacks.

They say money can't buy you love and that's true, but it damn sure can help make things a lot more comfortable and stress free when it's in your possession. True, I was ready to deliver, but having a few dollars in my pocket, a commodity I'd been forced to do without for the past six months, restored my dignity if nothing else.

Now, I was able to pay my own way and not lean on my friends so much. It felt good to give a little back to those who'd been so generous to give to me, especially Tito and Martina! But it never failed, whenever we decided to do a little something, throw a little food on the grill or play cards inside the crib, we always got too loud, which resulted in Martina cursing everybody out! Even my mom would get on me the next morning and sarcastically state, *"You niggas don't think about going to bed do you!"*

Bed, shit, bed was the last place I wanted to be, considering I had to go there alone. I don't think anyone noticed but my loudness was often a cover up for my loneliness and fears. Being as Solomon had moved on with his life, (and had forgotten about me, the baby, and what his brother had put me through.) I worried about going through the delivery without his support. At least he could be there to hold my hand and see the baby once he was born. After all I'd been through on account of him and his brother, I believed he at least owed me that.

****

At 270lbs., I couldn't even lay down anymore. Instead, I used body pillows to prop myself up and sleep in an upright position. My skin felt and looked like it had run out of room to stretch, and I was so tight, I looked like I would pop if you poked me. People though I was having twins, and would always ask, *"Girl, you alright?"*

"Yeah, I'm good," but those Braxton Hicks contractions were kicking my ass. Every time I felt pain, you could see Messiah rolling, turning, and pushing my skin to the max like he was itching to get out. Martina's daughter, Ciani, was so amazed at the sight; she stayed hugging and talking to my belly, while trying to feed him her bottle. She was so curious about *"the baby,"* but didn't understand we had to wait until he actually arrived before we could give him a bottle.

The concept of pregnancy in itself was a fascinating topic, but I was more interested in the delivery. Hence, Martina and I planned to watch a cable T.V show that aired prerecorded cesarean births that took place at Mercer Hospital in Trenton. She set the timer on the digital box so it would come on even if we were watching another channel and told

Tito to remind us in case we forgot. Martina liked to watch because of the babies, but my curiosity was about the procedure itself. I delivered Quan by cesarean, but I was knocked during the procedure and had no idea of what to expect. With Messiah, I was going to be wide awake, and with a needle taped in my back, and due to my fear of needles, it goes without saying that I was scared shitless! I figured by watching the show, I could build up the strength and braveness necessary to endure the procedure without anxiety. I needed to see for myself the women do it on T.V and prove I could do the same. The "Psych" is crazy like that, you know; mind over matter...

****

On May 29th, six days away from my scheduled surgery, me, Martina, and Stephanie sat in Martina's living room with her husband and the kids and finally watched the show as planned. It was informative, scary, and emotional to say the least, however, I had a difficult time paying attention. Messiah had been giving me a hard time all day. He wouldn't sit or lay still and the pressure he was causing in my pelvic area and lower back almost had me in tears. I'd felt discomfort before but not like this, and it was so intense, I could barely sit still.

Tito was the first to notice the look on my face and nudged his wife to take notice too. *"Murf, you alright,"* she asked? I nodded my head yes, but that was just to keep down the alarm. Messiah was definitely making his presence known and Martina hit a high pitched *"Oh, my God,"* when she saw what she said looked like his elbow pressing up against my stomach. I wasn't sure if he was restless or if I needed to get some rest, but in any case, I bid my friends good night, told them I'd see them in the morning and took it down.

Before attempting to drift off to la-la land, I called my Nana as usual. Quan was already knocked out and so was my mom. Nana was resting too, but I wanted to share my day's experience with her just the same. She was always a great comfort to me no matter what I was going through. *"It ain't nothing but Braxton Hicks, Ree, you may be going in soon."*

Soon, shoot, I'd been experiencing this type of pain all month. Nana said they were contractions but who the hell contracts this long? True, Quan had me in labor for four days but this was different. Not only was I feeling the contractions and the pressure, but I felt feverish too, and by the time I settled down, it was almost midnight. Truly it had been a long and exhausting day.

In my life, the mere possibility of something unexpected occurring was pretty normal. It was exactly 2:30 a.m., when I woke up for a bathroom break, but I didn't want to move because it seemed like Messiah had finally settled down. I didn't want to tackle the stairs either, and at first was going to go next door and use Martina's bathroom because theirs was on the first floor. Although it was late, I knew they were still up and wouldn't mind.

Having great difficulty trying to get up off the couch, I started to just sit there and hold it, but noticed I was completely soaked from the waist down. Damn! Not this again. Not now. Not while I'm so sleepy and tired. I wish I could have just rolled over and gone back to sleep but it wasn't my call, it was my son's and he was ready to come out!

I made my way up off the couch up the stairs and to the bathroom. I tried to clean myself up a bit but it was futile. The water kept flowing and it was time to go. I called out to my mom but she could sleep through a war and not wake up. My little sister and niece didn't live there anymore, and with no one to help me I had to fend for myself. My bags were already packed and waiting for me by the door, and the hospital was only five minutes away. This would have been the perfect time to call Tito and Martina for help but I didn't feel it was their burden.

I made it to my bags and retrieved my keys from the table. I kissed my son on the forehead and told him to tell his Nana I'd gone to the hospital. I know he barely heard me but was sure his memory would kick in once he woke up. Normally, I would never walk out of the house looking as raggedy as I was. My hair was all over my head and uncombed. My dress looked like a tent and the towels... I had three towels wrapped around my ass to absorb my water while I continued to leak. After shutting the door behind me, I stood on the porch for a few seconds. My final thoughts before getting into the car were of Solomon. Should I call him? Should I even set myself up for the disappointment? Why bother was my after thought. I've been alone and without him for this long. No need to ask for his presence now.

****

I could no longer sit comfortably behind my steering wheel of my car and had stopped driving myself during my last three weeks. I was too afraid I'd catch a pain or go into labor while behind the wheel, lose control, and have an accident. This fear caused me to hesitate again as I entertained the thought of calling on Tito and Martina for assistance but again, changed my mind. I was too embarrassed they'd ask about Solomon and too ashamed to admit that he really didn't care. Martina use to always ask me about having a friend. I told her I wasn't interested in a relationship at the moment. My concerns were just about self and the kids. She knew it was a lie, but loved me enough not to push the envelope. I though about that and how it would all play out after the baby was born. I caught myself drifting in "what ifs." I snapped out of it and started up my vehicle.

At 2:45 a.m., I doubted very seriously if there was going to be much traffic on the roads. With that in mind, I took off down Rt. 29, destination Mercer Hospital! I passed a trooper on the highway; and if he would have known I was going in to labor, I might have gotten a police escort but I couldn't risk it. Although it would have been highly unlikely for him to ask for my license, registration, and insurance, it would have been just my luck for him to do so. Then I would have been screwed!

I arrived at the emergency room in five minutes, just as expected. I walked through the sliding doors holding my towels up with one hand, and the baby's bags in the other. The nurse on duty didn't even ask any questions. She just pointed me towards the door that lead to the elevators, but I already knew where to go. I'd already called Dr. Murthy before I left the crib and left a message that I was on my way to the E.R. After arriving in maternity, the head nurse placed a second call to him letting him know I was there. She then started a phone tree; she called my little sister Nette and my neighbors, and Nette called my dad and my lil' sister Gayle.

By the time the triage nurse had me hooked up to the monitors, Gayle, who was also pregnant and as big as a circus tent, my niece Kenijia, and Ant were walking through the door. *"You know everybody mad at you 'cause you drove yourself. I told them you were crazy..."* I laughed because her and my dad always said I was a bit touched, but what can I say, it runs in the family....

Having my little (big) sister by my side was just what I needed to remain calm. Being she would be in my shoes shortly, I knew she could read the expression on my face and see that I was a little afraid. Good thing she's a chip off the old block; silly, touched, and ignorant, just like her daddy. I say that because she stayed cracking jokes and made fun of me the whole time just in order to keep a smile on her big sister's face. By 4:00 a.m., half of my family was sitting with me in triage and by 5:00 a.m., I was being transferred up to a private room.

I asked Gayle to take my car back around to my mom's when she left. I didn't want to get any tickets parked in the wrong spot and I didn't want to risk the repo-man spotting it and towing it away. I hadn't seen nor heard from Dr. Murthy yet but, I knew the staff had spoken to him and were acting on his orders. Ironically, in the middle of my transport, I ran into my boy Bill and his wife Von, who had already been prepped for her delivery. Now according to her doctors calculations, she was right on schedule, because her due date was the 30th, but they were surprised to see me there a week early; even though by my calculations I was past due since the 22nd.

****

After being prepped and signing my life away, it was 8:00 a.m. My nurse told me to try and get some rest since I wasn't going into surgery for another twelve hours. My Nana and all my sisters were all up in my room with me now, talking and laughing away, oblivious to the pain I was in. I had that damn PIT I.V hooked up in my arm again, but I didn't really need it. Messiah was doing a fine job in encouraging his own labor quite well. I was hesitant to ask for any pain relief because I knew it would affect the baby, but I had a long way to go and needed something to take the edge off. Finally, my sister Keyda noticed my disposition and asked if I was alright. *"Yeah, I'm alright... I'm in labor but I'm alright... Y'all should go home. Ain't nothing gonna happen now and I need y'all well and rested when y'all be back."* They understood and I told them I'd call them when it was time.

With my room clear I was able to block out some of the pain by focusing on something other than all their blabbering, and I tried to resist but thoughts of Solomon crept in even though they weren't welcome. I was torn between *"what it is"* and *"what if,"* but the thought of what if, wasn't worth the energy, at least not this late in the game anyway…

At around 9:00 a.m., a different nurse came in and gave me something for pain. Almost immediately I felt relief, which only proved that prescription drugs are far worst than anything one could cop on the streets. After she shot that shit in my veins, I was out like a light and didn't wake up from my nap until 4:00 p.m., at which time the pain had returned full force. Now I know in certain cultures pain is believed to be a state of mind, but regardless of culture or belief, I doubt if you can find a woman in labor to agree with that theory. Labor hurts regardless of how high your threshold for pain may be. My nurse said my contractions were now five minutes apart but to me it felt like they were right on top of each other, non stop!

Good thing for me, my doctor was already on the floor and had just finished up with another delivery, I believe it was Bill's daughter. He came in to check on me and after seeing me in so much pain, saw no need to delay things any further. Since I was having surgery anyway, I midas well get it over with. *"Okay, Marie, I'll see you in an hour."* His words were such a relief, but even an hour seemed too far away. I tried calling my family but nobody answered their phone. *"I told them to go home and rest, not forget about me."* I left message after message but after an hour, nobody returned my call and neither Dr. Murthy nor Messiah were going to wait, I had to go. Where the hell was everybody?

Upon entering the operating room I was greeted by the anesthesiologist, a nurse, and an orderly. The anesthesiologist was Asian man, probably middle age and after introducing himself, began explaining his role. I laid attentive, listening to his every word, but was freaked about going through the delivery alone. He then asked me to sit as straight up as I could and extend my hands out to my knees. Yeah right, as if…

He then touched the small of my back where he would be injecting the two shots of novocain and then the spinal. I knew he was trying his best to keep me relaxed, but I was shaking like a leaf and begging my doctor to just please put me to sleep! I was so afraid I would flinch and suffer the same fate as my grandfather or worse. All I could think about was what Nana told me about Pop-Pop when he had to get his spinal, and how it shrunk his leg because he moved during the process. With my luck, I'd jump at the slightest pinch, even if it didn't hurt, and end up paralyzed. I said this aloud, and no one could understand my bizarre fear considering my body was covered in tattoos. I tried explaining that there was a big difference between body art and a spinal, but before I could finish my reasoning, I started to cry.

After hearing such a confession and seeing me break down, all my doctor could do was shake his head. Then, the anesthesiologist told me that in order to cause paralysis, he would have to intentionally insert the needle further into my back than necessary, which wasn't going to All I could do was pray silently and try to compose myself to conquer my fears. They didn't show this part on the baby channel!

As I sat up straight and held my breath, I noticed the orderly was about to leave. So, I stopped her and asked her to hold my hand. There was no sign of my family and I didn't think I could do it alone. I don't know what it was, but something about her put my mind at ease. She had strong Mother Land features and her accent was the same. She had survival written all over her face but at the same time, seemed very peaceful. Her touch calmed me as if she were the fragrance of lavender. She then began talking to me and before I knew it, the anesthesiologist had given me both shots and the spinal was in position and taped to my back. I became quiet as the room went silent, and moments later, I felt my lower body go numb.

"Okay, all set," said my Asian friend. I was relieved that I hadn't flinched or jumped, but how did I know I wasn't paralyzed considering I couldn't feel anything? What if the doctor cuts too deep or the medicine wears off before he sews me back up, then what? My mind was boggled again, and the orderly who was so kind to hold my hand was about to leave but I begged her to stay. *"No, no, Lady, you can't leave me, you have to stay with me please!"* My doctor nodded his head in agreement and she stayed right there by my side.

****

I entered the delivery room at 5:05 p.m., and my son was born at 5:22 p.m. He didn't come on Quan's birthday but the numbers were still there, and yet another miracle had been preformed. I was so proud of myself it took a moment for it all to register. As I laid there wondering

315

when I'd regain some feeling in my legs, I noticed something odd. I heard my doctor announce my son's time of birth and I heard the nurse call out his weight, but I didn't here him. I thought all babies cried when they were born, but I didn't hear my son and immediately feared something was wrong. In my panic I attempted to sit up, lean forward, or something, but I couldn't. *"What's wrong with my baby? What's wrong with my baby? Why isn't he crying?"* At the time my doctor was still in the middle of stitching me up and the nurse was tending to Messiah. *"Marie, nothing's wrong with your baby, just relax."*

"Well, why don't I hear him?"

"Well, maybe he doesn't want you to hear him." Doctor Murthy had a sense of humor, and knew how to get with you if necessary. *"Well, shouldn't he be crying or something?"*

"Marie," Doctor Murthy said with a grin on his face. *"Your baby is fine but not all babies cry when they are born. Your baby cleared his lungs, it just wasn't loud. Relax, you'll be able to see him in a moment."*

I trusted Dr. Murthy with my life. I knew he was as skilled as he was wise, and I was just being paranoid again. After he finished stitching me and told me he'd see me after recovery. At this point there are only four people left in the room; the orderly, the nurse, me, and my son. I reached for my African friend's hand and thanked her again for comforting me during my delivery. Her humble response made me feel like I'd gained a friend for life. She exited the room and at the same time, another nurse entered. This was the nurse who would attend to me during recovery and she was ready to wheel me out. By now I was beginning to regain feeling in my lower body, what a relief. The delivery nurse then asked was I ready to see my son, and with the greatest anticipation I said yes!

After dreaming of this moment and picturing in my mind what my son would look like, my heart was racing with excitement. Who would he take after, whose genes would run the strongest? Frequently throughout my pregnancy, I prayed for my son to come out looking just like his father. I wanted this so bad because I wanted to remove all doubt that others spoke about in silence but never to my face. In all of my dreams, my baby's face was never revealed, but I assumed he'd at least take his father's complexion or at least hoped he would. I already had one pretty boy, now I wanted a little chocolate prince!

What's taking her so long; I couldn't lie still. I kept trying to sit up so I could glance at what the nurse was doing to him but her back was turned to me. I could now hear him fret a little, and the small glance I did catch was only of him wrapped in the white receiving blanket. At least I thought it was the blanket, because it couldn't have been my child. His father was dark and the image I saw was fair. Shit.... Just as sure as my name is Marie Antionette, when that nurse brought my baby over to me he was a white as the un-driven snow! I was stunned, he wasn't dark at all, and neither were his ears or his nail beds. He was red, and as bright as the blanket he was wrapped in, with a big round face. He was nothing like I envisioned, and only characteristic that stood out from my dreams was the blonde hair. I had dreams that my baby was going to have blonde hair and sure enough, he had blonde hair and gray eyes. Amazing...

****

Eventually his color would come in and his features would change; at least that's what I wanted to believe but deep in my gut, I knew something was wrong. I immersed myself in thought and feared my greatest fear of all. I was then snapped back to reality when the nurse called my name and asked, *"Ms. Cook, don't you want to kiss your baby?"*

Not realizing what my reaction looked like to someone else, I pulled it together, smiled, then said yes, but hesitated a moment more. I was taken back by my son's expression. His lips were poked out and he had his right index finger propped up on the side of his face as if he too were in deep though. I kissed him gently on his cheek and instantly fell in love. The two of them then exited the room and I resumed thought of what I'd just witnessed. True, he was my son and I loved him with all of my heart. He was a miracle, a blessing, and I wouldn't change one thing about him. But I had to entertain the thought that maybe, regardless of how bad I wanted it to be, he may not have been... I wasn't willing to accept that fact, so in essence, I went straight into denial.

After resting in recovery for nearly two hours and regaining total feeling, I was anxious to see and hold my son again. I woke up to my attending nurse checking my dressing and asking me how did I feel?

"I'm good. I want to see my son." "Okay," she said, *"I'll be taking you to your room in a minute, do you want something for pain?"* she asked. *"Yes, please."*

When she returned, she injected something in to my IV then helped me change my garments. I only sat in recovery a little while longer getting my vitals and temperature checked and by 8:00 p.m., I was being pushed down to my new room. Once settled, I didn't want to seem rude but I could see we had different priorities. So nonchalantly I asked, *"Excuse me, is someone bringing my son down to me?"* I could tell from her reaction that I'd now offended her, but bottom line, she caught my drift. She shot me a dirty look when exiting the room, but I didn't give a damn, I wanted my child. While waiting for her to return, I called my little sister Nette, Chino, and my baby sister Gayle to first curse them out for not being up here with me when he was born, then ask them to come up and see him as soon as they could. Unsure of how they would react, I sat in tears while trying to process my emotions and confusion.

The nurse returned with my son and my heart skipped a beat. I reached out and grabbed him from her arms and caressed and cradled his chubby round body. At 9lbs even, he was the perfect bundle of joy. I wasted no time getting him dressed because I wanted him to look presentable for our visitors, family or not, it's a must we stay fly! By the time my mother, son, sister, and Nana arrived, Messiah was looking like a Baby Gap model. My family couldn't stop fussing over how cute he looked in his navy blue Baby Gap shirt, itty bitty Baby Gap jeans and tiny Timberland boots that were too big for his little feet. Once I saw the grin on their faces, my fears of what they may have though were erased. I pulled myself together and just basked in the moment.

As it turned out, my family did manage to make it up to the hospital during my delivery and managed to snap a few pictures of him on his way to the nursery. From the moment my Nana walked inside my room all I heard was *"Oh, Ree, he's beautiful,"* and both my mother and sister concurred. My oldest son's face was lit up like a Christmas tree and he couldn't wait to sit on the bed and hold his baby brother for the first time. A month before Messiah was born, Quan wrote a note on a piece of newspaper. The note read *"I Love My Baby Bubber'."* I though it was the cutest thing ever and his actions showed just how sincere his words were.

This was now the second happiest moment in my life, but my little sister could detect my worries. As she stood silent by my bedside with nothing more than a grin on her face, I could tell her thoughts were the same as mine. In my window under one of the baby's bags were two pictures; one was of Solomon, the other was of Kyron aka Droop. Although I was thrilled to have my family there with me, I wished to God they'd leave me and Nette alone long enough for me to pull them out and have her do a comparison.

With Nana and mommy content with the baby, I drew Nette's attention and asked her to grab the flicks. Then, I asked her to tell me what she though. Being she was my sister as well as my friend, I don't think she had the heart to tell me her true feelings. Therefore, instead of taking sides she said, *"He looks like you, Murthy!"* Nette played it safe and I can't really say that I blame her. She knew I wasn't ready for honesty, but she didn't tell a lie either. *"He looks like you, Quan, your dad, and your brother,"* Nana and mommy then added their two cents, agreeing with Nette that he resembled my father's side of the family more than ours. Okay, that's all well and good but they knew what I wanted to hear. I had no problem with what they were saying, but they were leaving something out. *"Don't he look like Solomon, Nana?"* The entire room went silent.

I should have known my Nana, (Moses' little sister) wasn't going to sit there and tell a lie, but I wasn't asking for one either. I just wanted them to see what I saw and confirm it. Nette knew my heart but she also knew how my emotions could take over my rational, and at the time, didn't want to see me go through the motions. So in order to save me from embarrassing myself she blurted out, *"Yes, Murthy, he looks like Solomon a little, especially around the forehead,"* but her vague description was just as bad as not saying anything at all. I saw what I wanted to see because I wanted to protect my heart, my secret, and all those who I loved; even though the truth was literally staring me in the face. Nette was being kind and didn't want to hurt me, and mommy just stood quietly, because truthfully, I don't think she had a clue because I never told her about Kyron period. Nana on the other, hand just had to be the one. *"I don't see it,"* she said.

When Nana first saw the nurse pass by her in the waiting area, she asked, *"Is that the Cook baby?"*

"Yes," she replied, and in turn, asked could she see him. When Nana saw that light bright baby, with that broad nose, light colored hair, and funny looking eyes, she closed her eyes and prayed; *"Please, God, let her find out the truth before it's too late!"* But she never expressed her feelings to me, until way later.

****

In my family's opinion, Messiah was just too damn light to have been the son of a dark skinned man, but none of that came out until damn near a year later. I knew Nette didn't think he looked like Solomon because of all the features she could have picked for comparison she picked his forehead, which just sounded like a lie. As for my mom, you could have told her the fucking sky was falling and the most she would do was nod her head. Amazing!

My nurse came so she could check on my stitching and tell my family visiting hours were over. Mommy said she would see me in the morning and Nette said she would bring Quan to see us tomorrow after school. Once the room was cleared, I was left to cuddle my son and again, wrestle with my thoughts. All I wanted to do was hold my son and adore him, but before I could get into that mode I had to get one thing out of the way. I had to make a phone call, I had to call Solomon...

"Hello."

"Hey, Bugga'."

"Hey, Mama, wassup?"

"I had the baby!"

"You had the baby, why didn't you call me?"

"I was scared, plus..."

"Aww, Molly, come on now, you know you could have called me, I would have been there for you."

"Thanks," but of course he was going to say that after the fact. *"So who he look like?"* Damn, he didn't waist any time on that note. *"He looks like me, Quan, my dad, and my brother, but he has your hair when you were a baby."* With nothing else to give him credit for, the hair was better than nothing, considering Solomon did have a slight reddish tent to his hair when he was small. *"He's handsome, but I guess my genes were stronger."* I didn't know if that was a wise thing to say but I

had to say something. At least I was honest; as honest as Nette had been with me...

I loved my son and I wasn't about to compromise him for anyone or anything, but I couldn't deny my feelings for Solomon either. I could hide them but not deny them. It was late and the two of us agreed that I needed my rest. We hung up with the promise of him coming up to see the two of us in the morning. I felt a little better after our conversation. Maybe I'd feel a lot better after he saw his son. I knew there was room for doubt, but who said he had to look just like his father. That's what I wanted, but it's not how things had to be.

Now that "the phone call" was out of the way, I could concentrate on my baby who was now fussing for a feeding. Still in awe over his presence, I held him in one arm and the two pictures in the other. I had a million signs posted all around me, but I still didn't see it. Before falling asleep together for the first time, the nurse returned once again and left me with my son's birth certificate application. She said I could fill it out later and someone would be in to pick it up in the morning. Once she left I began filling it out then realized I needed his father's signature if I was going to give him his last name as planned.

Remembering the conversation Nana and I had when Quan was born, I knew she'd object and with that in mind, decided to give him his father's last name as a second middle name. It would still read the same but it wouldn't offend my Nana, and Cook would still be his legal name. It had already crossed my mind that Solomon may not want to sign the certificate because he wanted to remain out of the system, but that wasn't going to stop me. He would be up in the morning, and if he chose, he could sign it and if not, no harm no gain. Solomon knew what I planned on naming the baby and he never voiced any objections. So I filled in all the blanks and the name given to my child was *"Messiah Anthony Hampton Cook."*

The following morning, I woke up early and giddy as ever. My stomach was killing me but I didn't care. My sister, Nikki, was the first to bless us with her presence, and she walked through the door wearing a big ole' kool-aide smile. That right there should have been the biggest eye opener of all, 'cause Nikki ain't never smiling unless she know something or she's up to something. Back in high school, the two of us use to tell people we were twins because our candid attitudes were identical. Mine was bad but hers was worst. Nikki wouldn't spare your feelings, but I would. I guess that's why I expect people to spare mine all the time, but that's not always the best route and it doesn't always play out that way.

Nikki walked in, picked up the baby, sat down in the chair, and like everyone else, awed Messiah at first sight. I knew her early morning visit had a hidden agenda, so I didn't waist any time initiating the conversation. I handed her the two pictures and said, *"Look, Nikk, look. don't he look just like Solomon!"* Nikki didn't even bother to entertain the though nor did she take her eyes off her nephew to look at either of the two pictures. She just titled her head to the side and continued to look at the baby with that half cocked smile of hers. Then, without batting an eye she said, *"Hell no, Marie, he don't look like no Solomon or no damn Bugga'. He don't look like him at all. This baby is pretty!"* I guess that meant she didn't feel Solomon was handsome…

Nikki and I have had our fare share of disagreements but nothing we couldn't settle. The two of us usually fussed with one another until we found mutual ground but this wasn't one of those times. So I asked her again, *"Nikki, don't he…"* She cut me off and wouldn't allow me to finish. I was dead serious but she thought I was playing around. Yet, just like Nette, she knew my fears were about to unfold so why make matters worse? She knew what she saw regardless of what I said and she knew her eyes weren't playing tricks on her. After realizing she wasn't going to respond, I returned to my bed and just enjoyed the visit. By the time Nikki left it was pressing mid-day, and Solomon hadn't been up to see us. The two of us took a nap and when we woke it was going on 5:00 p.m. Messiah was born on Saturday and it was damn near Monday and his father was still a no show.

I waited as long as I could, then decided to call him to see what was up. When he answered, he said he tried calling me but I wasn't in my room. Then he said his brother had the car and he was waiting for him to bring it back. Whatever! I may not have been in my room but I was still in the hospital, so there was no excuse. My family didn't want to argue with me, and I didn't want to argue with him. If he wanted to see us he knew where we were at.

It was now Monday afternoon and everyone had come to visit me and Messiah except Solomon. That right there had me feeling some kind of way. Here we are ready to go home and daddy dearest was missing in action. In my mind, nothing could justify his unexplainable and cowardly actions, but at the same time, I shouldn't have been surprised. I was anticipating going home, but my doctor decided to keep me for a few more days just to make sure all my test came back okay. So on that note, I reached out to Solomon again and told him the two of us were going to be in the hospital until Wednesday. He apologized for not coming up as promised but promised again to do so by the end of the day. I guess I grew use to accepting his lies my only reply was, "okay." Wednesday rolled around and Messiah and I still hadn't seen him. I stopped calling and gave up on it altogether. Rejection is one thing, but this was all together different. At 31, I was still kinda naïve and always wanted to see the good in people no matter what. It's a goddamn gift and a curse, and the rewards are few and far between. This was the ultimate rejection.

By Wednesday afternoon all of my test results had come back satisfactory and Messiah and I were truly going home. My baby sister, Gayle, came to the hospital to pick us up, but before dropping us off, I asked her to drive down Spring St. Here I was fresh out of the hospital with fresh stitches and a new born, and all I could focus on was Solomon's black ass! It was a nice day, very warm out, but I still had no business out in the streets.

We pulled over at the store. I left my son in the car and I went inside to speak to Chino'. Surprised to see me, he asked what was I doing out. I told him I was looking for Solomon and he said he'd just left. Solomon reminded me of "Batman," always off to the "bat cave", never staying in one spot for too long. Chino knew the two of us weren't at our best but he said he'd be sure to tell him I'd stopped by. What he didn't know was that Solomon hadn't been to see me and the baby yet, and I was in no mood to embarrass myself so I didn't bother to tell him. He was my brother but some things you just keep to yourself. I just shook my head and got back in the car. When we reached home we received a warm welcome by my mom, my oldest son and of course, Tito and Martina.

****

Soup! That's was Tito's first impression when he saw my son, because he said he looked like a hot bowl of tomato soup! Although he was cracking on my baby, I needed the damn laugh! Martina and Tito didn't come up to the hospital to see us either, but that's because they thought we'd be bombarded with visitors, and I totally understood. However, just like with Chino', I wasn't about to tell them Solomon had been a no show because I needed to save face until I figured things out. Then, no sooner than I walked through the door guess who called? Solomon...

"I just left the hospital, lady." He was five days late, and I really wasn't impressed. I guess he expected me to be grateful for the effort but it didn't faze me at all. He was stalling and I didn't know why. We talked for a while and as always, we hung up on his empty promise to come by and see us later. *"Later, why not now?"* Now would have been comforting, later was just to pacify me.

Being I was tired and just ready to chill, I grabbed both kids, loaded them up in the Lumina, and prepared to go to Nana's so we could eat, shower, and change. Unfortunately for us, my mom had been unable to pay the water bill and our water was cut off. I could have went to Martina's, but as usual, I didn't want to impose. Quan carried our bags out to the car and right before I secured Messiah in his seat, we were approached by some ignoramus who asked was Messiah Pharaoh's son. *"What! Where the fuck did you get that from?"* The way that was asked, you would have though Pharaoh was some type of celebrity. My baby was only four days old and no one but family had seen him, so how the hell did a rumor like that start so quick, and why Pharaoh of all people? He and I hadn't been together since March 29, 1995!

Keeping cool and maintaining my composure was very difficult, but those instigating trouble didn't even deserve a reply. Why was my son's father even a topic? Even Day'Quan was wondering why people were saying his daddy was Messiah's daddy, when he knew it was Solomon. "People are assholes, baby, and empty logs make the most noise!" In time he'd figure it out. Good thing I was going to Nana's, it was the perfect get away. Had I stayed on Jersey Street a minute longer, I would have ended up back in the hospital.

Later that night when the boys and I returned home, Solomon called again and apologized for not coming through. Honestly, I don't know how he expected me to take him serious and I guess he thought I was sitting at home, twiddling my thumbs waiting on him. I knew I had my fears but what was he afraid of?

Messiah was seven days old before Solomon finally came over to see us. I remember it like it was yesterday, it was a Thursday and the Sixers had just won game three of the finals against the Lakers. Their victory must have given Solomon the courage he needed to face us, but he didn't come alone. Her brought Messiah's uncle and my buddy Ace, along with him. Now, for the first time since Messiah's birth I felt completely at ease. Watching Solomon lay on the couch holding his son was a sight to behold. After seeing the two of them together, it seemed silly to doubt or compare pictures for truths. The two of them looked alike from their hair line down to their chins. Even Ace found their resemblance uncanny, despite their difference in complexion.

As the two of them drifted off to sleep, all of my fears were put to rest. Although I knew I had been with someone else, the father of my child was determined by dates and calculations, not guilt and assumption. Yes, I was an emotional individual but not a dishonest one. There was no way I could have a cycle at the end of August, get pregnant in September, and in November be 12-14 weeks. That was scientifically impossible. Solomon and Messiah napped for about an hour, then Ace woke Solomon up because he was ready to go. In truth, I knew that's why he dragged him along in the first place. Solomon needed an excuse to leave, just like he needed a reason to show up. Before the two of them left, Sol' gave me $50.00 and said he'd be over tomorrow. I felt my naïve nature return. That $50.00 was a good start I thought, but my thinking was premature, because Solomon never returned, and the kids and I continued to struggle and reside with my mom for the next two months.

Solomon's routine of all talk and no action put me in a bad position. In the past I swore I'd never take a man to court for child support but he was leaving me no choice. My baby needed more than I could provide and social services didn't cover all the expenses. I moved out of my mom's house in August 2001, and re-located to a cozy two-bedroom apartment back in the Burg. Our new home was located on Kent Street, and my landlord was some crazy ass Pakistani named Ken who didn't give two shits about anything but money and immigration.

Just as planned, I paid my rent two months in advance, which gave me plenty of time to register Quan for school, secure a sitter for Messiah, and find a job. Within two weeks I registered with a local temp agency that had a contract with the State, and was infamous for finding people permanent placement. Within a month I had my first assignment and the feeling of regaining my independence was wonderful. Finally, the ball was back in my court!

THE WORST FEAR, IS FEAR OF THE UNKNOWN...

DILEMMA

As my obstacles began to crumble my self esteem began to rise, and I no longer concerned myself with Solomon. I didn't have to fight with myself about taking him to court for child support either, because the State was going to do that anyway. I wasn't getting cash assistance anymore, but as long as we got food stamps and medical coverage, they were going to seek the father. They did this in every case, no matter what, and I tried to forewarn Solomon about it but he was always too busy to hear what I had to say. I didn't want it to be a shock or surprise to him, and I didn't want him to think I was trying to do him dirty. Me and the kids needed the help anyway, and as much as I'd done for his two girls, helping me and my boys out should have been a given. In any event, he flipped when the papers came just as I suspected, but there was nothing I could do except show up for court. Maybe we could talk it out then…

Me and Solomon weren't the only ones who had to make an appearance either, Pharaoh had to face the music too. Without a doubt, I knew he was going to flip and place all of the blame on me, for the courts being all up in his business. *(Men, let me just say this. Women are not the enemy and not all of us want to drain you dry, or put the man all up in yo' business. True, there are some scorned and hateful women in the world, but none of us make babies on our own, and shouldn't be forced to take care of them alone either. As the saying goes, you pay like you weigh!)*

Considering the number of children Pharaoh had, and the number of times he'd been to court, he knew better than I did that I had no control over the situation. It would be neglect to turn down benefits I knew I needed just to save his and Solomon's ass. I needed to take care of my kids and wasn't beat to chase either of them down for assistance. Talk is cheap! Pharaoh and I were on good terms, but he still expected me to wait until he was ready to do, before he did anything. I wasn't always cool with that. He had been out of Quan's life for seven years. He'd given him little or no support while he was away in Annadale, and less than that once he came home. Both of them knew how things worked, and yet they still wanted to fault me.

****

Messiah was four months when Solomon and I had to appear in court, but instead of seeing a judge, we met with a mediator. His role was to try and work out an agreement between the two of us that would satisfy the courts. Basically, all they wanted was for Solomon to add Messiah to his health insurance, but since he didn't have a job...

When Solomon agreed to talk, I was shocked, and again, mistook that for a good sign. The mediator wanted to talk to us separately first, and if all went well, he'd talk to us together. I told Solomon he could go first and when the two of them returned, the mediator said the state would be holding off on the child support until after the results of the DNA test returned.

"What, DNA? Where did that come from?" I looked puzzled but didn't have any objections. I didn't have anything to hide, but at the same time, didn't understand why Solomon would want to prolong things. This was something he could have said to me face to face, instead of avoiding me like a child. His request didn't come as a shock, but at the same time, he did catch me off guard. His actions already told the story that he was skeptical, but delaying things wasn't going to change anything. Solomon had pressures coming at him from every angle. He had me, the chick he was officially living with, and Dee-Dee, who by the way, was again pregnant with his child. If for no other reason, he had to satisfy them by asking for a test, but told me he just wanted to make sure.

This niggas brother cost me my job. I took care of this man's kids and in turn he allowed another woman to drive a car that was supposedly mine. He shacked up with everybody he could think of and caused me more humiliation than any person should ever have to bear. And he doesn't trust me? Now that was funny!

Tina said it best. *"What's love got to do with it?"* Yes I loved Solomon like I'd never loved anyone before, but that had nothing to do with the DNA test and I knew it. With all that had gone down between the two of us, the test was the only way to put an end to it all. Solomon had given me money to take care of Messiah and he use to talk and play with him whenever we'd run into each other. But when he looked at my boy he just didn't see himself. Shit, I didn't even see him, but the dates were on point. Before leaving the court, we were given papers on when and where to report for the test. Ironically, our date was set for November 14th, the day after I found out I was pregnant. Solomon walked me and Messiah back to our car, gave me a kiss on the cheek, and the three of us didn't see much of each other after that until it was time for the test.

****

Being back in the work force was a great feeling. Although I wasn't going to become rich bring in $1000 a month, it was a decent start, and I was in the right atmosphere for networking. The only thing I had to take care of now was the car, a sitter for Siah, and getting a piece. Yeah you heard me, I needed a piece! I'd been out of commission for so long, I was afraid to do anything with anybody. I hadn't made a car payment in over a year, and it had been longer than that since I'd had sex. Shit, even with the repo-man calling all over God's creation for me, it seemed easier to hold on to the car, then gaining my swagger back.

My problem was, I'd been with Solomon for so long, and nobody thought the two of us would part ways. On top of that, I had no immediate interest or prospects in mind. In addition to that, were my own standards. Who could prove themselves worthy, yet still get the job done? I wasn't ready to fall in love again, and I damn sure wasn't going to be somebody's jump off with two kids. I wanted to be with someone I could be comfortable with, but not someone who was going to try and tear me apart like a belated birthday gift.

****

Eventually I had to start leaving Messiah with a sitter, and it was so hard to detach from him. I wasn't ready to leave my son and was hesitant to leave him with anyone outside of family. No one close to me was able or available to care for him during the day while I worked and that deterred my thoughts of returning to work so soon. I didn't even have the money to secure a sitter and wouldn't be able to pay anyone until after I got my first check. Who the hell would be reliable and trustworthy and at the same time be willing to wait to get paid, beat the hell out of me. In the midst of my worries, God threw me a line and surprisingly, Droop's mother offered to watch Messiah until I found someone else.

Now Peaches and I had our share of ups and downs, yet peculiarly we've always helped each other out, whether directly or indirectly. The conversation of her watching my son had never taken place, though through rumor she heard my son was her grand. She got the idea from her niece, Keya, who made the same comment to me one day after seeing me and Messiah at the park. Obviously the relationship between Droop and I was no big secret, but again, according to my last cycle and the dates, Messiah would have had to either been born a preemie, or my doctor was off by 6-8 weeks in order for him to have been Droop's son.

Shit, regardless of whose son he was, I still needed a sitter and graciously accepted her offer. I told Peaches I only needed her to watch him until I could get registered with Child Care Connection and send him to a certified sitter. It wasn't that I didn't trust her, but I knew what type of buzz it would cause if the right or wrong person asked; *"Why you sending your baby to Droop's mom instead of Solomon's?"* As if it was anyone's business.

In the beginning everything was fine, but watching Messiah did conflict with Peaches work schedule. Eventually, I started splitting his day up between her and her nephew, O'Ryan. I knew Peaches was in a bad position and her health had been giving her trouble. So I stayed on my caseworker at Child Care Connection, and within less than a month, started taking Messiah to Ms. Hattie on Spring Street. Ms. Hattie was certified sitter with the state of NJ but that's not why I chose her. Ms. Hattie also use to watch me and my little sister when we were small and the two of us had a strong rapport. In addition to that, Solomon was always somewhere near and if necessary, could get to Messiah a lot quicker then I could. My baby's well being was a concern of Solomon's, even if he didn't show it the way I wanted him to. I informed him the baby would be at Ms. Hattie's during the day and he said he'd be sure to stop in and check on him. I was shocked to learn that he actually kept his word and did so. Although I no longer pursued a relationship with him, after the DNA came back, I hoped he would begin to build one with Messiah.

Between work, helping Quan adjust to a new school, Messiah, the car, and anticipating the DNA results, I had no room for surprises on my plate. Me and my family were always healthy and the most any of us had to worry about was a bad cold, allergies, hives, or nosebleeds. Meningitis was something I'd never heard of before and didn't even know existed. Messiah was five months when he began teething which meant I'd have to endure low grade fevers and constant crying for a while. Quan and I could see two pegs cutting through at the bottom of his mouth and kept Infant's Tylenol and Advil on hand. I figured aside form that, the best I could do was give him cookies or teething rings to chew on in order to soothe his gums. The Tylenol was somewhat effective with his fever, at least it put him to sleep. But my baby had no interest in that teething ring, and after a while, seemed too sluggish to even play. I was worried about his sudden decrease in activity but his doctor's office was closed until Monday. I'd have to wait the weekend out before we could make an appointment, but even then I wasn't guaranteed to get one right away.

It was a Friday afternoon and my baby's temperature was at 100° and it didn't want to break. By that evening it was up to 102° but he was quiet, so I continued to give him the meds every four hours with belief it would break by morning. I gave him a warm alcohol bath and put onions in his socks just as an extra precaution. I got that idea from my Nana, and although it wasn't conventional, it worked on us where we were small.

When I woke up the next morning and saw blood coming out of my son's nose, I panicked! I didn't understand what was happening and had no clue what to do. Quan heard me scream, came running downstairs from his room, and stopped in his tracks at the sight. *"Let's go to the hospital."* He grabbed some clothes, some bottles, the baby's binky, blanket, and bag. He got my keys off the dresser and told me to get my purse. I dressed Messiah but I could barely keep it together. What ever was wrong was a lot more serious than teething. My baby was lifeless but I could still see him breathing. When we reached the emergency room it was filled with overnighters whose primary emergency was to escape the bitter cold of outdoors. As I flew past them in a frenzy, I was hoping to God we didn't have to wait until all of them were seen before they took care of us. I approached the triage window, prepared to fill out the "why are you here card," and a nurse started asking me questions. She could see the fear in my eye as well as Messiah's lifeless body lying still in my arms. I told her he was only five months old and she told us to come right in.

Before we were assigned a room, a doctor approached and asked what's wrong. I told him my son had been running a fever since last night but this morning I saw blood running form his nose. They asked how long had he been this way, lifeless and still. I told them since last night, then they took his temp and drew blood. It took only a few minutes for the result of his blood work to return and with it came two more nurses and another doctor. Hospital staff then began to run around like crazy, bringing in all types of equipment, and hooking it up to my baby. I saw three nurses try to give my son an IV and all three of them failed. I felt helpless as I watched and wanted to rescue him but didn't know what was wrong. I wanted to take care of him but I didn't know how. He wasn't even crying but I knew he had to be in pain. I yelled, *"What's wrong with my baby?"* then slowly slid down to the floor. It felt like my ribs were cracked and my breathing was impaired.

My heart couldn't take it, what was going on? Quan stood strong as he watched in fear. He was a comfort as I watched, but it should have been the other way around. One of the doctors must have had a stroke of empathy for me. Maybe he had a child that age or just wanted to provide me with answers. He walked over to me and said my son had Meningitis and that they needed to work fast to save his life. What the fuck was Meningitis and what did he mean, save his life?

"Ms Cook, is there someone we can call for you?" I guess the blank look on my face was the indication I needed someone there with me besides my son. *"Can we get you anything?"* He was speaking to me as if I was death. All I could do was cry and shake my head no as I continued to watch them work on my child, who was still lying lifelessly. *"What the fuck is Meningitis, how did my baby get it?"* I mustered up the strength to yell it again, this time gaining the attention of one nurse. *"Ms. Cook,"* she said, *"this is not your fault. One out of every five children contract Meningitis from birth to twelve years old. It's random and there's no way to see it coming."* I appreciated her professionalism plus the fact that she was trying to prevent from blaming myself, but considering we fell into the ratio, it wasn't much comfort at all. Plus, despite her efforts she still didn't explain what Meningitis was. *"Ms.*

Cook, are you alright," she asked again. My response was yet another blank look and then I asked her to call my mom and explain to her what she just tried explaining to me because I just didn't get it.

A mother's love for her child is truly unconditional, but a mother's love for her son can't be put into words. All I could do was pray to the Lord that everything would be okay. With each new phase of my life, and every step forward, something always occurred to take me back, break me down, and rip my spirit apart. In thirty one years, I'd never prayed so hard. I hated to see my oldest son cry. He should never have to be so strong. He could see the fear in my eyes and that's what scared him the most. Now I felt helpless to help him as well. If anyone could answer his questions it was supposed to be me. I grew angry as I watched four more people poke my son repeatedly, failing to insert the IV. Crying was beginning to hurt and my legs had become numb. I lunged from the corner and begged them to let me hold him, please just let me hold him, then one of them reached to restrain me and I started having a fit. *"If you can't help him then get somebody down here who can, or just let me hold him!"*

Within seconds, a tech from the newborn nursery came down to properly administer the IV and stop the torture of the ER staff. *"Why the fuck didn't y'all do that in the first place!"* I was in bad shape, thank God my mom walked in.

My mom has never been able to deal with pressure or drama so I didn't think she'd be able to deal with this. I needed her moreso to take care of Quan, while I figured out what was what with Siah. Now that the IV was in his arm, once again, a nurse tried explaining to me what Meningitis was. They weren't sure if it was viral or bacterial, and to determine that they would need to give him a spinal. They needed me to sign consent papers before doing so and they needed me to do so right away. I gave them the okay and they rushed my son off to have the procedure done. I stayed behind for a few moments filling out his admission papers and once I was done, I was escorted up to his room. He wasn't there when I got there and I called for my mom and Quan to come wait in the room until he returned. They hadn't done the spinal yet but the nurse carrying him had to pass by his room on her way to the lab.

The three of us were standing on the outside of his room and she stopped and asked if I wanted to give him a kiss. I was trembling with fear and that kiss reminded me of when he was born. The two of us would have to spend the night so I asked my mom to take Quan to Nette's house for the evening. At the elevator, I kissed both of them then returned to my baby's empty room. In less than a minute, a doctor arrived with an intern and the two explained the dangers of Meningitis. From down the hall I could hear my son's screams. I grabbed my stomach and stumbled a few steps backwards. A nurse walked in and gave me two pills and a cup of water to drink. They were sedatives to calm me down, and I sat down on the bed and tried to pull myself together. *"Ms. Cook, would you like us to call a Priest."* A Priest, why would I want to call a Priest, I'm not Catholic? Maybe she's just trying to comfort me I thought. It took a while before her question became clear. *"A Priest, oh hell no don't call no Priest, call my dad!"*

After twelve hours, I knew no more about my son's condition than when we walked through the emergency room doors. It wasn't until 11:00 a.m. the next morning that I learned my son's spinal tap came back positive for the viral form of Meningitis. This was a good thing, they said, because it could be cured with medication. Messiah seemed to be responding to the treatments and if he continued, they had no doubt he'd make a full recovery. My immediate response was a nervous laugh followed by a huge sigh of relief and tears. The next thing I knew, they were bringing my little dude into the room and allowed me to hold him for the first time since the whole thing began. At that moment, at that very moment, I gained a new appreciation for life. I felt like God had given me a second chance amongst second chances. It felt like I was seeing my son for the very first time again. Sympatric to what I had endured, the nurse left me and Messiah alone to rest, but before leaving informed me that although Messiah seemed to be doing well. The next 24 hours were going to be the most crucial and he would have to remain hospitalized for at least a week. Hospitalized, shit! I didn't care if he had to remain hospitalized for a few days. I wouldn't have cared if she said he had to remain for a year. My baby was alive and that's all that mattered.

My baby was so handsome and I enjoyed seeing signs of life in him again. I held him in my right arm while singing songs to him. I don't know why but the hook from *'Sexy"* by "Masters of Ceremony" is what came to mind. Realizing how important the next 24 hours would be, I though seriously about calling his father. I knew if he knew the seriousness of the baby's condition he'd want to be informed and kept up to date. Then on the other hand, he may have thought I was using the baby as an excuse to get close to him again. I wasn't beat to go through that so I decided not to call. That night was rough but by the grace of God, he survived. In the morning when I woke, my son was in his crib and the nurse was taking his temp and changing his IV. At first I was mad because hospital staff wouldn't allow him to sleep in the bed with me, but I understood their policy. It was 6:00 a.m., and I had to be to work in a few hours. I wanted to speak to his doctor before I left but the nurse said he wouldn't be in until around 12:00 noon. I didn't want to go to work, I wanted to stay with my child to make sure he was okay, but I was in no position to take off. I left her my number and asked her to please call me if his condition changed for the worse. She assured me he would be okay and on that note, I kissed my son good morning and went about my way. I said my prayers as I waited for the elevator and was confident my baby was in good hands.

Thank God for little sisters! Nette was a lifesaver in my time of need. Without her help, I wouldn't have been able to stay the night at the hospital with Messiah. For the next four days, she played baby sitter for me while I ran back and forth between the hospital and work. The stress had all of us on edge, including my oldest son. There was no down time, just run, run, run. Every night after work I had to rush home and pick Quan up so the two of us could go visit the baby. Then at 8:00 p.m., had to drop him back off with Nette, only to run right back up to the hospital to stay the night with Messiah, aka Moo-Moo. In the morning I had to get up, pick Quan up, go home, change, and then drop him off to school before going to work. On average I only got about 3-4 hours sleep because I was so busy monitoring my son's temperature, for fear he would have a relapse. I even pulled an all nighter when he started acting like him self again and the cutting of his teeth made him cranky. I know most parents would complain, but I was so happy to see him fussy again. I would have never guessed I could appreciate something so draining.

My week had been demanding, and at times, I thought I would crash. Messiah was released from the hospital by the end of the week and his doctor said he wasn't concerned with the Meningitis making a return.

I was relieved, but to this day, still freak when ever he gets the slightest temp. It's a healthy paranoia, and it keeps me on point!

As the two of us were leaving the hospital, his nurse walked up to me and asked what to tell his father when he came for his afternoon visit. *"His father, when did he come up? I didn't even tell him he was here."*

"He's been coming up to sit with your little guy every afternoon; I assumed he was his dad. He looked just like him!" Looked just like him, that couldn't have been Solomon I thought, but if not then who?

"What did he look like," I asked, *"Aside from looking like my son?"*

"He was short, stocky, fair in complexion, and very well dressed."

"Oh," I replied. Just tell him to call me and that the baby is home. Funny, the people that love you the most are often too afraid to show it. I don't know if it's fear of rejection or fear of exposure, but it's definitely something. My dad never paid an ounce of attention to Messiah once he was born and that use to bother me a lot. But the fact that he would take time out of his day to sit with his grand proved he loved both of us more than I realized.

With Messiah now home, our lives could resume back to normal. Quan was thrilled to have his *"baby bubber"* back, and I was in heaven watching the two of them bond in brotherhood and friendship. Not even cartoons could hold Quan's attention over his younger sibling...

I've been told that because I chose to give my son such a powerful name, negativity would always try to attack him. I thought about how scared I was when I thought I was going to loose him and wanted to do something, anything I could, to protect him. So, I took him to church and had him dedicated to God. Trials can do one or two things, build you up or tear you down. In my case the tearing down was in the form of fear.

Messiah

Marinating me with joy

Everything I imagined and more

Second Born

Soooooo close to me

Illuminating my life

Amore'

Heaven sent…

Dedicated to My Son Messiah Anthony Hampton Cook

Mama's baby, daddy's maybe...

The Moment of Truth

They say idol hands do the work of the devil. But if the desire of companionship is evil, then I guess I stand accused. A healthy sexual appetite is just as natural as a healthy appetite for food. They're both natural instincts and I don't know too many people *(or animals)* that can ignore them for long. The same goes for one's natural behavior. Some people are naturally quiet, cautious, and don't step outside of the box. Others are natural born risk takers, like me, who live for the thrill and the challenge. I guess that's why I allowed Pharaoh back into my life. He was both a thrill and a challenge all rolled up in one.

Every since my ordeal with Ace, Pharaoh and I kept in touch with one another; good, bad, or otherwise. Although I knew he wanted to make it seem like his primary concern was his son, he had it bad for me too! He didn't sympathize, but was mad as hell because of what Ace and Solomon put me through, and told me I could call him for anything.

"Anything...?"

"Anything!"

It's funny, but Pharaoh seemed to go out of his way to frustrate me, and at the same time, would risk almost anything to be with me. Of all people, it's bizarre how close the two of us managed to remain, regardless of what he'd put me through. I confided in him when I found it difficult to talk to others. I was Pinky and he was The Brain! We were an odd pair but always managed to level one another out. I was extreme but he was an extremist! He was a good shoulder to cry on, always had a stimulating conversation to boggle my mind, and the chemistry between the two of us was a knock out recipe for good sex! Day or night, when ever I needed him, he always had time. Our ways were damn near identical, and at the same time, so very different. We shared a lot of commons, including our son, and were both attracted to the same things. Flirting with him was like taking candy from a baby, but my main reason for letting him back into my life wasn't just for the sex, it was because he was the only person I trusted to be around my children. Regardless of my needs, they were still my first priority.

Pharaoh knew things about me that I didn't have to explain and I knew things about him he couldn't deny. He was corny and transparent, but that's what I liked about him. Indeed he had grown over the years. He wasn't as hostile or haughty as he once was. He was better at expressing himself and had learned how to listen.

Pharaoh was a man of many faces, and I often thought it strange that he had so much concern for me in regards to Solomon and our DNA test. It seemed like the topic always popped up in conversation, no matter what. How could he understand what I was going through, when he had been a womanizer all his life and denied most of his, regardless of who they were by, including Quan. Though low and behold, I soon discovered I wasn't the only one going through a paternity dispute. As it turned out, a certain young lady, who I knew for a fact had the hots for him for quite some time, was claiming he was the father of her youngest child. A little girl born in February of 2002, named Mia.

Pharaoh tried hiding it from me but I put the pieces together after running into her mother Mya, at the mall while she was still pregnant. Pharaoh swore up and down the baby wasn't his but I knew better. There's a certain look a woman gives to another woman, when she wants her to be aware of something or back off, and she displayed both. She was also extremely affectionate to Day'Quan, which was totally out of the ordinary, considering the most she'd ever said to my baby in the past was hi and bye. She acted if she'd finally gained her right of passage, and I knew exactly how she felt, because dealing with Pharaoh could do that to a person.

My plans with Pharaoh were simply to have fun and enjoy myself. Neither one of us could deal with anything heavier than that; and we both knew we weren't looking for a relationship. Pharaoh eliminated the pressure of hooking up with someone I was unfamiliar with, and at times we were only an *"Oh"* away from phone sex. Because we were mature enough to appreciate romance, neither of us were in a rush and took our time wooing one another. Then finally, that day arrived. I was kinda of worried about what Quan would think if he saw me and his dad together again. I didn't want to build up any false hope or cause him to believe the two of us were getting back together.

Good thing Pharaoh worked long hours, which assured us that Quan would be sound asleep when he arrived. As for Messiah, he was too young to know anything and wouldn't remember it once he got older. All was clear on my end but Pharaoh willingly ignored his dealings with Samantha, and from the looks of thing, sacrificed it when ever he got the chance to do so. He was so bold he didn't even bother to hide his car. Our first date was very intimate and sexy, but there was no sex. Instead, we took our time and talked to each other about things too personal to talk about over the phone. Although we were familiar with each other, he smiled every time his eyes gazed over my thick, caramel hips, and giggled every time our eyes locked. After eight years of separation, it was clear a great deal of curiosity had built up between us. We composed ourselves and showed one another nothing but respect, but I knew we were both fanaticizing about ripping each other's clothes off and going hard.

Pharaoh chilled with me until about 3:00 a.m., and by then, I didn't see then need for him go home. Before leaving, we stood in my hall for another ten minutes gazing into each other's eyes and sharing a long good night kiss. I wasn't sure if the sex would still be the same, had improved or had fell off; I wasn't sure if he would be turned off by the changes to my body of if I would be turned off by his, but I was damn sure ready to find out. The crossroad between fantasy and reality was a rush in itself, and I couldn't wait to find out what lay ahead in store for us.

Pharaoh's second visit to my home was just as sexy as the first, but we didn't do much talking. Because Pharaoh couldn't be trusted, he had a hard time trusting others. I don't think he ever believed me when I told him I'd been abstinent for nearly two years, and he ended up getting more then he bargained for that night after realizing I was as tight as a jar of grandma's old jelly preserves. Our reunion with one another was just as memorable as our last time. I doubt if he'd ever been with a virgin before, but I'm quite sure he found immense pleasure in opening me up and breaking me back in. I was in ecstasy while enjoying the soft, rough strokes of his manhood inside of me and I'm more than sure he went home with my markings on his back. I was surprised I didn't wake the kids, because at times, I just couldn't hold it in. Pharaoh always knew I was a handful, but that night, I believe he got more than he bargained for. My mound was throbbing so heavily, it felt like a beating heart, and a hot, hard breathing body, beats an inanimate lifeless toy ten to one!

Having fun and enjoying one's self covered a lot of territory. I swore up and down I wasn't going to fall for Pharaoh again and I didn't. Yet, I did reap all the benefits of the attention he directed my way, including his help with taking care of Messiah. They say time flies when you're having fun. Well time sure did manage to slip away from me while I was having mine. So much that I nearly forgot about how long it had been since Solomon and I had submitted DNA for our test. It was now the beginning of March and I hadn't heard a peep out of him, or the courts. I know they say no news is good news but in this case it was just the opposite. I needed to stop pretending I could hold things together on my own and get the help I needed and deserved. This went for Pharaoh as well, but I had other ways of dealing with him for the moment. (Pussy is powerful!) Initially, I was told the results would be back in about 4-6 weeks and that I'd receive them in the mail. But it had been nearly four months, no word, no letter.

****

Just out of pure curiosity, I one day asked Pharaoh about the results of his test, but he became real tight lipped and didn't elaborate on the matter. Knowing him as well as I did, I took that as an undeniable confirmation that he was indeed the father of Mya's little girl, Mia, but I didn't push the envelope. Really I didn't care, I had my own shit to worry about, I was just being nosey. Then while sitting at work one day, I decided to give the courts a call. Maybe the results were in and they just hadn't got around to mailing it out yet, but I remember the case worker telling us we could call her if we had any questions. Well, I had a question…

I will admit, I thought I was going to have to get real ugly with someone, because not all public employees are happy to assist the public. But to my pleasant surprise, Sue, our caseworker, was the one who answered the phone and as soon as I gave her my name she knew exactly who I was. So, I told her why I was calling, and she said the results of the test wee mailed out two weeks ago. *"Two weeks ago? I've been checking*

*the mail every day for at least two months straight and I haven't gotten
any results. You sure you mailed them out to the correct address?"* I
didn't want to offend her and imply she was incompetent but mistakes do
happen.

*"32 Jersey Street, Trenton is what we have in our system and
your results were mailed to that address."*

*No, no I moved. I live at 144 Kent and I gave my new address to
my social worker as soon as I got my lease!"*

"No big deal," she said. *"I can mail them back out to you it's
not a problem."*

*"Well, since the results already went out can you tell me what
they were?"*

*"Sure, just verify your social security number, I have the file
right here in front of me."* Wow, I really didn't think it was going to be
that easy, but maybe today was my lucky day!

I recited my number to her as asked, and she confirmed my
identity. She started out by reading off a bunch of numbers that didn't
mean jack to me, and sounded more like a mathematician giving the
formula to some perplexed algebra problem instead of the actual results.
There I was at work, with my heart racing a mile a minute, and she's
talking to me as if I'm a lab technician. By the time she finished with the
list I though I'd pass out from anticipation. I wanted to interrupt her so
bad but didn't want to come off as rude. But as soon as I was about to
ask for a simpler explanation, she said it. Solomon was NOT the father
of my son, Messiah Anthony Hampton Cook.

There were absolutely no word or words in the English language,
or Ebonics for that matter, to describe what I was feeling. Unbelievable
was the only thing that came close, because I couldn't have heard her
correctly. *"Are you sure?"*

*"Yes, Ms. Cook, we're sure. The test results are indisputable.
The numbers which represent your son and the number that represent the
party in question aren't even close. I'm sorry, Ms. Cook, but there is no
way Solomon is the father of your child."*

Now on one hand her news was exactly what I needed to hear,
but not while I was at work. In about two seconds I was about to have the
breakdown of a lifetime and I didn't know what to do. Stunned, I asked
again, *"ARE YOU SURE?"* As if asking a second time would change

anything. My mouth was hung wide open, a lump formed in my throat, tears welled in my eyes, and the line became silent. I was in total disbelief!

Realizing she had been the bearer of unpleasant news, she asked the only thing she could; *"Are you okay?"* Okay, I thought to myself. Hell no I'm not okay! Okay! Basically you just told me I was a whore, a liar and slept around so much I didn't even know who fathered my child, okay, hell no I'm not okay, but I couldn't reveal that to her. *"No... I'm not okay, but I will be..."* I was disturbed by the revelation but didn't want everyone in my office to know my business. I tried my best to remain quiet and speak in a soft tone, but the tears created a crack in my voice that I was afraid others could hear. *"Ms. Cook, I need a name."*

"A name?"

"Yes a name. I need the name of the other man you were involved with so we can order a test on him now." Aww man, the shit just kept getting better. Bad enough I hadn't had the time to absorb the blow from Solomon NOT being Messiah's father and now she wanted the name of someone else. Damn! "Kyron Parker! Kyron Parker aka Droop aka little Keys is the father of my child. I don't need another test I know he's the one." I may have been in denial but I was far from being a hoe. If it wasn't "A" then it had to be "B", simple and plain!

Sue took down the information she needed, then told me I'd be notified by mail at my current address in reference to the second test. As far as me and Messiah were concerned, we didn't have to be retested. They already had our numbers and any DNA submitted becomes permanent record. She also said she'd mail the current test results out to me as soon as we got off the phone. We spoke for a few seconds longer then hung up. She told me not to be too hard on myself because I wasn't the first woman to be wrong and I wouldn't be the last. I know she was only trying to help, but her words didn't make me feel any better.

All I could do was shake my head in disbelief. Not just at the results, but at my own actions and stinking thinking! How in the world could I allow myself to get caught up in some mess like this? Even after loosing a ten year job and being dumped by someone I cared for unconditionally, this was my lowest point. I felt like the toilet paper you use to wipe the shit, not just shit! I felt like I'd disgraced myself and caused my baby to be a bastard all because I was careless, hardheaded, and refused to take the blinders off. I had no explanation for my actions and didn't know I was going to explain this to my family, friends, and more importantly, my son!

Those thoughts caused me ten gray hairs in an instant, and the ones of Solomon caused me another twenty. What was I going to say and oh my God! The results were mailed out long enough ago for him to have gotten them already. I wonder if he knew… Now that I was the one in the wrong, I felt I at least owed him an apology.

****

By now, the lines of communication between me and Solomon had been cut and his mother was the only way I knew how to get in contact with him. In the past this was something I use to enjoy until I realized I was being played for a fool. Calling Ma wasn't at the top of my list of desirables, especially since Dee-Dee was living there. Dee-Dee was now Solomon's new baby Mama and she was the last person on earth I wanted to talk to. However, since her current address was my only means of getting in touch with him, I swallowed my pride and dialed the number. Enough time had gone by and enough confusion had come about. I knew the truth, regardless if I wanted to believe or accept it or not, and it was time to put the rumors to rest, once and for all!

I closed the door to my office just a little and dialed his mom's number. At the sound of the first ring, a pit the size of a peach formed in my throat. Please let Ma pick up, please let it be Ma, I though to myself, while trembling and crying, while trying to be brave. Then the ringing stopped and someone answered. *"Hello."* I took a deep breath. *"Hi Dee-Dee, it's Murf. Before you hang up, I'm not calling you on no bullshit. I'm just calling because I have something to tell you."* I took another deep breath before continuing. *"Well, actually I have something to tell Solomon but you can relay the message for me if you don't mind. Messiah is not Solomon's son. I found out the results today on the phone so I wanted to be the first one to call the both of you and let you know."*

"Are you serious" she asked? *"Yes, I'm serious."*

"Oh my God, Murf!" Then she asked the million dollar question. *"Well, who's the father?"*

"You should know the answer to that, better than me." Then she said it herself, Droop! *"Yes, Dee-Dee, Droop! My baby is Droop's son,*

so instead of my son being your daughter's brother, he's actually her cousin." I know she had to feel relieved, even if she didn't express it. *"Well why did you call me, why didn't you wait until you saw Solomon and was able to tell him to his face?"* I knew she wasn't trying to be sarcastic but at the same time had no reason to be sympathetic. Nevertheless, I felt myself reaching the breaking point and needed to end the call so I said to her. *"Now Dee-Dee... You and I both know I wouldn't have been able to face Solomon and tell him something like this. I'm barely telling you. You live with his mother, you have his baby, and you see him more then I do."* (I really didn't believe she saw him more then I did, but it sounded good.)

"I'm not asking you to tell him in replace of what I have to say to him, but the test results are going to be mailed out to the crib. I know you're going to get them and I know you're going to open them up."

"You right about that," she said.

"Don't you want to be the one to tell him the good news?"

I wasn't really interested in getting into a conversation with chick, nor was I trying to give up a whole lot of unnecessary details. My son was her daughter's cousin and her cousin was my son's father. Although there was no official paperwork saying so, she called his name and had known about our dealings since the beginning. If you ask me, the whole thing was a set up and Solomon and I were the ones caught in the middle. But regardless, all I needed to do was humble myself long enough to say what needed to be said then hang up. I did just that and not a moment too soon either, because no sooner then my hand was off the receiver, in walked my boss wondering why my door was semi shut.

Noticing the tears running down my face, she asked was everything okay. In vulnerability I broke down and told her I'd just received some disturbing news and needed to take a break. I'm not sure if it was her concern or pure nosiness, but either way she didn't let me walk away just like that. She wanted to push the envelope and find out what was troubling me, so before I left I told her. .

"Well, Marie," she said in her Italian accent, *"things like this happen all the time, it's a part of life"* Then threw her hands up in the air as if to say "Whadda' ya gonna do?" I didn't need her two cents; I knew shit like this happened all the time but I wasn't accustomed to it

happening to me! *"If it's all the same to you,"* I said, *"I'd still like to be excused."* She must have thought I was asking for her permission. I wasn't. I needed to talk to my sister and I was going to do so with or without her consent. I walked out the office, although I knew she wouldn't take too kindly to me brushing her off, but hey, its life and things like that happen all the time. Whadda' ya gonna do!

I called my sister from the pay phone outside my office and told her I needed to see her ASAP! I didn't give her time to ask any questions, I just hung up and headed her way. Nette lived less then two blocks from my job but by the time we met each other in the middle of the block, I'd broken down like a wounded animal and was crying like a baby. Upon noticing my state, she stopped in her tracks. I guess she wasn't expecting as such. Nine times out of ten, when I placed a call like that it meant something was about to go down, so it fucked her up to see me crying as if someone had just died. *"Murthy, what's wrong?"*

"He's not his son, Nette! Messiah's not his son! He's not Solomon son!"

Baby sis just dropped her head and let out a huge sigh. *"Man... I knew it." "I knew it, Murthy, I knew it!"*

"You knew it? What chu' mean you knew it?"

"Murf, I'm sorry but my nephew don't look like no Solomon, Murf, he just don't! I've wanted to tell you but knew you wouldn't listen. I saw Solomon one day and he asked me was Messiah really his son. I told him yes because I though you knew for sure. All you kept saying was don't he look like Solomon, Nette, don't he look just like him. I told you yes because I knew that's what you wanted to hear."

She went on to say that at first you could think he was Solomon's because there were certain common similarities, but after adding Kyron to the equation, it was a no brainer! *"Murf, I cursed my best friend out over that shit because she said my nephew looked like Kyron's sister, Beauty. Then I had to think about it and realized I'd cursed her out for no reason. Murthy, that boy look just like him! I just couldn't say anything to you about it."*

By the time Nette was finished giving me her take on the matter, I'd pulled myself together and was all ears. I realized that this was just as hard for my little sister as it was for me, and the fact that she loved me so much that she'd rather please me then piss me off said a lot. The things we do for the people we love… Amazing!

"Well," I said, *"at least now I know where he got the light eyes and blond hair from!"* We then both laughed out loud and I returned to my job.

For the rest of the day I though about all the signs I chose to ignore. The dreams, the prayers, the fact that after Messiah was born I slipped up and called him little Droop. But for me, the picture was the kicker. If nothing else, that damn picture should have been the game winning point.

I kept a picture of Kyron in the glove box of my car, since it was the best place for me to hide it. Then, one day while driving down the Blvd. to pick Messiah up from Peaches', it fell out and freaked the shit out of me. I damn near crashed when I picked it up and the eyes that stared back at me looked just like my son's. I was like looking at a picture of him from the future! I was so freaked, I tore it up and threw it out the window, right in front of 682! I should have covered my tracks and told Solomon there was a possibility he could be the father instead of insisting he was. I should have never assumed anything considering my history of reproductive issues. I knew I could go an entire year without a cycle and twelve out of twelve pregnancy test would turn out negative. Leave it to me to get a menstrual during a pregnancy and calculate inaccurately. Amazing!

I was quiet for the remainder of the day. I didn't even bother to call Pharaoh. I needed a support group for this crisis. A sista needed her girls.

****

Once I got home, I wasted no time getting down to business. I fed the kids, got them bathed and situated for bed, then picked up the phone and started dialing numbers. Moe', Shantell, and Esha were my team. They were the only ones I could bring myself to talk to at the moment, and talking to them would be most difficult. The three of them arrived almost at the same time and all three already smelled trouble in the air. Just like Nette, they knew I wasn't big on calling emergency gatherings unless it was a true emergency. With everything in my life looking good, there was only one thing that could have me so unnerved. They knew it and they were going to rub it in too!

Apparently, everyone had the same feelings. They all knew Messiah wasn't Solomon's son, but felt trying to get me to see the light would have been useless. *"You hard headed, Murf, and you always have to learn things the hard way,"* were Moe's words. Esha gave an Amen, and Shantell gave an ole southern unh huh! At times, they even talked about it among themselves, but none of them wanted to be the one to face me. They all thought I was crazy for not seeing it in the first place, but now that the shit had hit the fan, they could be truthful with their thoughts.

"What's done in the dark will eventually come to the light, Marie!" Damn! Why did Nana always have to be right! Esha was right too! She told me I was going to wind up getting in trouble behind that boy or breaking his girl's heart, and I swore to her I had it all under control. *"You don't have it under control. You've been scorned by Pharaoh, scorned by Solomon, and you're about to switch roles and scorn Blaque' for no good reason! You're only looking at the now, you not looking at the outcome."*

"What outcome? How somebody gonna get hurt, if we don't get caught!"

At then end of the night, after all the preaching and I told you so. The bottom line was my girls still loved me, and could care less who Messiah was fathered by, because they loved him, too! They still though I was crazy as all hell, but that went without saying. I was now ready to take the next step. In the morning, I'd sit down with Quan and explain everything to him, emphasizing on the damage a lie can do, then I was gonna call Droop and break the news to him. That wouldn't be necessary according to Moe'. She said she was sure Kyron already knew. *"You don't' need a DNA test for him,"* she said. "You already know that it and he does, too!" True, I didn't really need a test to prove anything but I was glad the courts were going to conduct one just the same. I need the peace of mind.

I knew coming clean to Day'Quan and Droop would take some courage, and on top of them, I still had to confront Chino, Peaches and eventually Solomon. But Blaque'... Now she would be a total different story!

Pain is pain. I don't care if your best friend hurts you, your man, or your enemy or a combination of all three, pain hurts and time doesn't always heal the wound. It allows you to figure out ways to deal with it, but it doesn't always heal it. I should know. So how was I going to break this news to Blaque'? I didn't know. How was I going to tell her that the woman she trusted and considered a friend and the man she was so in love with, had an affair and made a child right up under her nose? I didn't know? What I did know was Droop and I should sit down and tell her together, and soon, before she heard it from another source. What I had to say was going to crush her either way. Not only did the love of her life and his pretend sister have a child together, there were times when she watched that child in order for me to go to work. I know she had to have seen the same thing everybody else saw. She even commented on Messiah's hair color, how it matched Droop's hair color to a "t", and how Messiah wouldn't stop crying until Droop picked him up. That right there were obvious signs both of us chose to ignore, which means I wasn't the only one in denial.

****

The next day I went to work and carried on as usual. I didn't say a word to anyone about my situation, especially my boss, and I dared her to speak of word about it to me. Considering how scary and politically correct she was, I knew the confidentiality of our conversation would forever be protected. At least in the work place it would. I'd yet to speak to Pharaoh but figured I'd call him during my break. Out of everyone else, I though he'd be the most critical, but wouldn't you know it, he wasn't the least bit surprised either.

Pharaoh said he knew Messiah wasn't Solomon's son because he looked at him every night and didn't see one trait of him anywhere. At the same time, he said he didn't feel the need to pry because it wasn't his problem, and if I wanted to keep the identity of my baby's daddy a secret, then it was my call to do so. While listening to him express his empathy, I knew there was still a catch. Pharaoh had matured but he was still Pharaoh. He never bit his tongue, never shaved his words, and could care less who he embarrassed or put on the spot. So why make an exception for me? No doubt his empathy was comforting, but if it wasn't for his situation with Mya, whose daughter he was still denying, I don't think he would have been so kind.

Now that he knew the truth, I wondered would that change the way he viewed me. Would he still give me the same respect or would he switch up? *"Girlfriend! Nothing you do could ever make me look down at you. You're the mother of my son too..."* I guess better late than never does have some truth to it, but only if he would have been thinking that way about me seven years ago! He was a man of little words but blessed with the gift of gab. He knew what to say when he was trying to get something up out of you, but what did he have to gain from this? Never before had he said something so appropriate at such an appropriate time. *"God don't make no mistakes,"* he said, and even if he was kicking his strongest game, that was still the God's honest truth!

After hanging up with Pharaoh, I still had time to spare so I went outside and had a smoke. I needed to get my head together before I made my next call. Ironically, it was March 20th, Kyron's born day and I usually called him to see what was up anyway. I laughed as I pictured his face and his reaction after I dropped the bomb on him. What the fuck was I going to say, *"Happy-Happy, Droop, I just wanted to shout you out on your Born Day, and Oh by the way, Messiah is your son!"* Yeah, that would go over real smooth, considering I'd purposely avoided him for nearly a year because I didn't want him asking any questions about the baby. I still knew how and who to go to in order to get in contact with him, but after this long, it would surely raise suspicion. I knew calling Blaque' would be risky and cocky, but I wasn't too keen on calling Peaches either. Leroy was my best chance at getting at Droop without any questions being asked. Leroy was his best friend and the two of them were like brothers, but I still had to go through Peaches or Blaque' to get his number.

Blaque' and I spoke briefly on the phone but I keep the details short and sweet. I knew she was wondering why I called her for Leroy's number and was sure she suspected I wanted to get in contact with Droop but didn't care. She couldn't prove anything and if she didn't want me to have the number, she didn't have to give it up. I waited a while after we hung before calling Leroy, because I figured she'd hang up and call him right away. When Leroy and I spoke, I tried to act as if nothing was wrong and that I just wanted to say hi to Droop for his born day. Leroy was far from stupid and knew it was more to it, but that didn't matter. Droop wasn't with him, but said he'd tell him I called, and to call him back when I got off work. *"You sure everything alright, Molly?"*

"Yeah, dog, everything cool, just keep ya phone on okay." We laughed simultaneously then hung up.

****

As a child, I hated to hear my Nana said I didn't have a daddy, and I couldn't imagine saying something like that to my child in a million years. Informing Droop about Messiah wasn't something I was looking forward to doing, but had to because it was the right thing to do. When I first found out I was pregnant, I was scared before anything else. I knew something like this was going to happen and that's why I counted on my doctor's calculations to be accurate. Apparently, I'd gotten pregnant by Droop before he went to jail, not after he came home, and that shot period I had didn't mean shit! Because I feared it would turn out to be his child, I was going to pack my things and move to Detroit. Then, I could come back and pretend I'd gotten pregnant by someone up there but things didn't work out. Nobody would have been the wiser and nobody would have gotten hurt. At times I wish I would have stuck with that plan, but in the end, I'd only be running.

Once it hit five o'clock, I was out the door like a bat out of hell and on my way to the sitter. I scooped up my son then shot down the Blvd, hoping to run into Droop before he went underground. I didn't have any luck running into him but that was okay. I was still going to call Leroy as soon as I got home.

Leroy was a funny dude, and when I called, the phone only rang once. Then I heard, *"Hold on, Murf,"* and the next thing I heard was *"What's wrong, Molly?"*

Droop was funny too, and just the sound of his voice made me want to laugh. I didn't want to tell him about the baby over the phone, so I asked him if he could come over. I told him I wanted to kick it to him about something and when we were done, I'd drop him off back around the way. Droop knew something was wrong and from then on both of us sounded nervous as hell. On top of that, I could hear Leroy laughing his ass off in the background and it only made me more nervous. Droop said he'd be right over, but then asked was I gonna give him some. I didn't answer his question, because all I could do was laugh. I swear that boy was always looking for an opportunity!

I figured it would take a while before Droop got to me since he had no idea where I lived. I was sure they'd drive past my house a few times before realizing it, but I didn't even get the chance to roll up before I heard a horn out side honking and my name being called. My phone rang too, and of course it was Droop telling me to come downstairs and unlock the door. Damn, that was quick!

Truthfully, I wasn't as nervous about telling him about the baby as I was over his last question. Now that he was my son's father, we could justify sleeping with each other and I wasn't exactly sure if I'd be able to resist if he pushed the issue.

I opened the door and pointed up to my apartment. I held one finger over my lips, indicating I wanted him to remain quiet. Messiah was asleep, but he couldn't help but snicker and crack jokes all the way up the stairs. As soon as he walked through the door, the first thing he asked was, *"Where's Quan?"* Upstairs in his room I replied. Maybe I should have told Quan first like I started to, but it was too late to think about that now.

Droop followed the light that lead to my room, then took a seat at the foot of the bed. Messiah was resting peacefully up top in the middle and I sat down to the left of him. The tension was as thick as icing on a cake but we managed to slip in a few more giggles before he asked what's up? I searched for the perfect words, but nothing came to mind. *"Molly, what's up,"* he asked again. I went to speak but my voiced cracked, tears formed in my eyes, and I started rocking back and forth. I

"Look at the baby, Kyron, look at him." Droop turned his head away from me for a minute then turned back around and asked why? *"Why you want me to look at him, Molly?"* The jovial tone in his voice was now gone and I could tell he was getting upset. *"Just look at him, Droop, look at him!"*

"Molly, I did look at him, but what does that have to do with anything?" He paused for a minute then let it out; *"Molly, I know you ain't bout to sit up here and tell me this is my baby! Is that why you want me to look at him so bad, Molly, is that why you called me over here?"*

Okay, so much for holding back the tears, but Droop hated to see me cry. *"Molly, stop crying!"*

"Droop, don't be mad at me but..."

"But what, Molly! I don't need to look at him, I know he's mine! I just can't believe you waited all this time to tell me! Why tell me now, Molly, why didn't you tell me this before? You a piece of shit, Molly!"

Now I know it sounded harsh, but calling me a piece of shit was a good thing. We always joked and played around like that, mocking Scarface as our own little way of talking to one another. But he had a lot of nerve because at the same time, he could have said something to me about Messiah, too! *"Piece of shit! I know you didn't just sit up here and call me a piece of shit and you knew all along Messiah was your son!"* I whipped the tears from my eyes and hit him with and evil look, but it didn't scare him a bit. Then I asked, *"Droop, if you knew he was your son, why didn't you say anything?"*

"You acted like you were ashamed of me, Molly. You acted like you didn't want anybody to know he was my son. You kept saying he was Solomon's son, so what was I supposed to do? What I look like arguing with you when you kept saying he wasn't mine. You wouldn't even let me see him, Molly!"

Okay, now I really did feel like a piece of shit! I though I was saving Kyron by hiding the truth about the baby, but never did I stop to think that maybe this was something he wanted. I couldn't picture him being a father, because he was so reckless and too deep in the streets to settle down. I accepted his lifestyle because it didn't put anyone at risk, but now that we had a son, I didn't know what to do.

For the next hour or so, Droop and I sat on the bed talking about the baby, trying to figure out how the hell we were going to break this news to the rest of our families. Messiah was nine months old and I wondered how everyone would accept him. How they would accept us. I asked Droop what him and Leroy discussed on the way over to my house. He smiled, then said as soon as the phone rang, Leroy handed it to him and said, *"Here go ya baby Mama!"* He said he laughed and told Leroy to stop playing. *"Damn, Droop, Leroy knew too."* *"Shit, Molly, everybody knew, you piece of shit!"* We both laughed...

The longer we sat and talked, the more things made sense. Now I knew why Peaches was so willing to watch Messiah for me and not ask any questions. She knew he was her grandbaby; so did her niece, her mother, other children, and her sisters. Even Kyron's dad, who lived upstate New York, got wind that I'd had a son by his son and without even seeing him was convinced it was his child. *"Happy Born Day,"* I said. At least this is the first gift you ever got that you can't exchange, return, or sell for cash. Droop laughed at my remark but was still somewhat fussed at me. I guess I deserved his frustration, but all in all, he was seemingly pleased about the news.

"My family is cool with it, Molly, you don't have to worry about that." But what about Blaque' I asked? *"What about her?"* he said, then laughed. *"Droop, we gonna have to tell her"* I said, but he looked at me like I was crazy. *"Droop, she gonna find out sooner or later, we midas well tell her and get it over with. I don't expect you to do it alone, I'm gonna be there with you. But if we don't hurry up, she gonna find out from the street, and that's not what you want to happen!"* Kyron continued to look at me as if I'd lost my mind, and truthfully, I wasn't up to breaking that girl's heart, but at the same time, it was the right thing to do.

I guess because I was ready to right my wrongs, I expected everyone else involved to be on the same page as me. Droop finally agreed that the two of us would sit down and talk to Blaque' together, but said he needed some time and wasn't ready to do so right away. I understood his fear but warned him not top procrastinate because the streets were talking. In nine more days, it would be my born day and he knew the three of us usually chilled together. Then the following week would be hers and if we didn't do something by then, I could see things getting worse. Droop thought it was better to wait until after our birthdays passed before we said anything, but my conscience wouldn't allow me to sit up in her face another day without her knowing the truth. The more we put it off, the more we ran the chance of her finding out from someone else. Time was definitely of the essence and our clock kept tick-tick ticking away. .

After talking, the four of us piled into the car and I dropped him off home, at Blaque's house of course. Before jumping out he said he had another confession to make. He said he was glad Messiah was his son, he loved his name, and had been trying to knock me up for the longest. I just looked at him and smiled, but I knew this was just the calm before the storm. Droop said I didn't have to worry about his family, but Droop wasn't a mom. He wasn't a mom and his son didn't have a baby by a woman eleven years older then he was. He may have been thrilled but I but I still had to face Peaches, woman to woman, mother to mother. In four more days it would also be her birthday, so I used it as my excuse to say hi, and depending on the mood, I'd tell her about the baby.

Peaches was always happy to see the kids, and was in love with Quan long before Messiah came along. When the three of us arrived at her house, I took a seat on the couch, she grabbed Messiah, and Quan went off to play with Nazi, Droop's oldest nephew. Then, Peaches handed me a picture and without knowing who it was I asked, *"Who's this?"* She then pulled one of my numbers and said, *"Just look at it and tell me who it looks like."* I wasn't sure what she was trying to get at and didn't know what she expected me to say so I asked again, *"Who is it?"* *"It's Kyron when he was about Messiah's age."* Oh, okay, I get it. No need to play the guessing game anymore, I knew what she was getting at. *"Okay, Peaches, yes, this is your baby, Messiah is your son's son!"*

Peaches grinned from ear to ear as she gave my baby a big bear hug. She acted as if I'd just given her the best news of her life, and kept yelling, *"I knew it, Murf, I knew it! I knew this was my baby!"* I was really shocked she took it so well cause had the shoe been on the other foot, I don't think I would have reacted the same. But on the other hand, it wasn't like she was in the dark about us seeing each other so why would she be surprised. She did, however, curse me out for about a half hour for hiding the truth for the past nine months. I guess I deserved her frustration...

Next Peaches wanted to know if Kyron knew about the baby and I told her yes. I told him the other day, I said and he feels the same way you do. He's happy but at the same time, mad at me for not coming forward sooner. Then she asked about Blaque', and I told her we were going to sit down and talk to her together. I was reserved about giving her too much information. She may have been my son's grandma, but she still had her ways. Plus, Peaches was fond of Blaque' and with good reason. But I could see this as her opportunity to play sides in order to save face. It's a trait all Aries possessed, and we utilized it well.

Peaches would do anything for her son as would any mother. She'd lie for him and cover up all his errors if possible. Knowing this, I knew to stay on point for what was coming next. The two of us spent half the day airing out old issues and by the end of our visit, the only thing that mattered was Messiah. Peaches said she'd do all she could to help me with the baby and she was gonna make sure Kyron did too. That was also was a relief because I really didn't want to fight with them for help, but at the same time Peaches knew she couldn't haul Kyron's load.

As for Blaque', well... If she was gonna stay with Droop she was gonna have to accept the fact that he had a baby now and needed to do the right thing. "The right thing" huh... I wasn't too sure how that scenario would play out.

Before leaving with the kids, I told Peaches I was going to have a second paternity test conducted. Peaches didn't understand why, considering everybody knew Kyron was Messiah's father, but I told her it wasn't for everybody else, it was for me. As far as the courts were concerned, Messiah's father was still unknown and that was something that didn't set well with me at all. If anything was to ever happen to Droop, the courts needed to know that Messiah was his son. DNA was the only way to prove that beyond a doubt, beyond hearsay, beyond the emotions of heart strings.

****

Like clockwork, Blaque' called me on my birthday to see what was up for later on. She wanted to stop by as usual, blaze some Piff, and maybe throw back some Seagrams Ice. Having no excuse except guilt to put her off, I tried pretending I wasn't feeling well and that I'd have to call her back later. Blaque' knew no matter how bad I felt, I was always in the mood to put something in the air, so on that note she asked *"What's wrong, Molly?"* I could barely give her a response because I knew anything I said was going to be a lie. *"Ain't nothing, Blaque', I'll call you later if I feel better."* But Blaque' being Blaque' she wasn't letting up that easy and said she was gonna stop by anyway to help me celebrate my day.

I couldn't stand to be on the line with her any longer. My voice started to crack and tears started pouring out of my eyes. I barely managed to say Thank you before hanging up, and I could hear her screaming at Droop asking, *"What chu' do to, Molly, why don't she want to chill?"* Because of our closeness, Blaque' felt either Droop knew what was wrong or was the cause of it. Damn, if only she knew how accurate her instincts were. The last thing I heard her say before hanging up was *"Y'all argue like....,"* then the line went dead. I guess Droop told her something to make her believe the two of us were mad at each other, but she was smart enough to know an argument wouldn't keep us from hanging out. She knew we'd just curse each other out until we got over it.

The guilt my emotions played on me after her call was enormous. Blaque' use to always say me and Droop argued more like husband and wife and acted nothing like sister and brother. Hmm, Nana always said hind sight was 20/20... I was beginning to feel like Droop, and that maybe even I needed more time to think of how to approach such a delicate, yet scandalous situation. Fuck it! If it's gonna go down then let it go down. I rather get it over with then live with the anxiety of when, when, when? I took my shower and got dressed, but can't remember much of that day after that. I'm not sure if I chilled with my sister, my girls or both, but I'm positive my night ended with Pharaoh right next to me in bed. The last two weeks in March were busy for me because Pharaoh celebrated his 30th born day two days after Droop celebrated his 19th.

Blaque' never stopped by at all that day and I wasn't really sure why. I was, however, prepared for her visit and wondered what happened to make her change her mind. The Sunday after my born day was Easter, and in good faith, decided to take the kids around the corner to see Peaches. As soon as we walked through the door her youngest daughter grabbed Messiah out of my arms, and Quan went off to play with Beauty's son, Nazir. Beauty wasn't Peaches biological daughter, but spoiled her son as if he were just the same. That kinda made me wonder how well Messiah would fit in, considering he was biologically her first grandson. Peaches and I took a seat on the couch, but before we could say two words to each other the phone rang. It was Blaque'.

After answering the phone, Peaches signaled for me to be quiet but I didn't understand why? Then a few seconds later she said, *"Yeah, she here,"* and handed me the phone. This was a prime example of what I was talking about when I said Peaches played sides. Why on earth would she tell that girl I was there? While the two of us made small talk, I noticed a dramatic change in her tone and strangely, she said nothing about my born day or why she never showed. She did, however, ask me about the kids and said she'd gotten them both something for Easter and wanted to bring it over. That right there sent up the red flag, because Blaque' would never ask permission to come see me or the kids. She'd just do it. Something wasn't right, but I didn't let on. I just thanked her but told her to give the gifts to her sister and brother instead because my kids were straight. Well why did I say that...?

Girlfriend flipped! *"Why don't you want me to see the kids, Molly,"* she screamed through the phone. Whoa, I wasn't expecting her to get so defensive or take things so personal. I mean, they were my kids. But considering she was feeling a little touchy, I tried a passive approach. *"It ain't nothing Blaque',"* and before she could respond, Droop's middle sister ran down the stairs and asked me to walk to the store with her.

So I caught a break, or at least that's what I thought. Yesterday, I was ready to talk because I knew Droop would be there too. But today was a different story and as promised, I didn't want to talk to her without him. Droop's sister and I walked to the store, and on our way back she asked me if she could take the boys to her aunt's house for a birthday party. Red flag number two. Nika never asked to do anything with my kids in the past, so to me that meant somebody must have confirmed to her that Messiah was Droop's son. *"Okay, Nika, you can take them, but I gotta tell you something first."* Nika then injected and said, *"Oh, Molly, I already know that's my brother's son!"* Okay, well since everybody is so cool about it, I shouldn't have a problem getting a sitter. We laughed then lit a cigarette. When the two of us reached the corner of her street, I saw Blaque's mini-van parked in front of Peaches' house. Damn, that was quick! Now I know something's wrong...

I needed to think, so instead of going straight back to the crib, I asked Nika to walk around the corner with me so I could finish my cigarette. As we crossed the street I could see someone peeking out of her screen door, and I know who ever it was saw us and was wondering where we were going. Nika wasn't oblivious to what was going on, but I couldn't figure out her role. Maybe Droop was at the house and he'd gotten up the nerve to tell Blaque' truth. But if that were the case then why not give me a heads up?

Once Nika and I turned the corner to head back to her house; I saw Blaque' walking down the street toward us. She had her poker face on but anything less than a smile was offensive in my book. As she approached, I separated myself from Nika because I didn't know what the two of them were up to. Blaque' spoke to Nika then turned her attention to me. She spoke, but at the same time, took a swing at me with what appeared to be a broken table leg. *"Whoa, bitch, is you crazy!"*

I've pulled some stupid stunts and I've put myself in harm's way plenty of times, but this was the first time I actually thought my life was in danger and that I could die. If that girl hit me in the head, I could easily bleed out. Even when Pharaoh was using me as his punching bag, I knew he didn't want to kill me. It may have felt like he wanted to kill me, but he didn't. This bitch, on the other hand, was trying to take me out and I understood why, but I couldn't let her do it. She kept saying, I was supposed to have been her friend. Okay, but he was also supposed to have been your man! Don't get it fucked up, I didn't rape the nigga!

I will admit she wore my ass out with each swing, but I blocked each attack with my arm, wrist, and hands. Making sure to protect my head and face at all cost. Before long, Peaches and Kyron's youngest brother, Anthony, Nika's twin came out and pulled Blaque' away. When the bunch of us reached Peaches' porch, Blaque' was still calling me names and talking shit, but she didn't have that table leg in her hand anymore and that's all I needed to see. I guess she though I was supposed to run away or something, but my days of running were over. She continued to throw slurs at me while being held back, but once she broke free, I shook her lil' ass up and told her to calm down! I could have laid her out but I didn't have a point to prove and most of all, definitely understood her pain. .

Someone pulled the two of us apart and Blaque' went for the table leg again. Only this time, instead of swinging at me, she took a swing at my car. *"You know this shit can go on and on"* I said. *"You bust my windows, I'll bust yours! Calm down!"* That's when the man of the house, Mr. Dave, grabbed Blaque' and carried her off crying into the house. As for me, I sat down on the neighbor's porch with my head in my hands wondering; *"How the hell did I go from Maury to the Jerry Springer Show."*

Regardless of what had gone down, I knew my kids would be okay until I got back. So I jumped in my car and sped off to go get Nette. Not to fight, but to watch the boys for me so I could go find Droop. When I pulled up to her apartment, I honked the horn and yelled for her to come down. I was so wound up, I couldn't even tell her the whole story, but she didn't even care, she just wanted to go back and tear shit up. She grabbed a bat and a knife but I told her to chill. *"The kids still there, Nette!"* She shot me a look of disapproval, put the knife in her pocket, but left the bat. When we returned to Peaches, I walked straight in without announcing myself. I didn't know what I was going to walk into but this time, I wasn't going to be caught off guard.

When I left everybody was all riled up, but when I returned things were just the opposite. Quan was still playing with Nazir and Sade was still holding Messiah, but Blaque' and Peaches were sitting on the couch next to each other crying their hearts out. I couldn't believe Peaches was consoling that girl and at the same time, acting as if she were so innocent. Just five minutes ago everybody wanted to be a killer, now they like Ralph from New Edition, all sensitive and shit! Give me a break! I was mad as hell and I was hoping one of them would come out they face so I could expose all of them. They all knew about me and Droop, they knew for years, and now they wanna act like I was the bad guy. Well I was somewhat the bad guy, but they weren't any better.

I stood in the living room floor for a few minutes but couldn't stomach the scene. I grabbed my baby from Sade and told my oldest son, *"Let's go!"*

When I got back to the car, Nette wanted to know how Blaque' found out? I told her I wasn't sure. At first she thought it may have been Dee-Dee, but I told her the two of them didn't get down like that. The only person I could think of was Droop. He must have tried to save his own ass and confessed or either cracked under the pressure, but still. Why not give me a heads up? We were better than that, so I thought and never in a million years would I have guessed he'd chose saving his own ass over loyalty. The way I saw it, he had pulled an Ace, and just thinking about it had me ready to fuck him up! Nette, on the other, hand said she didn't think he would so something like that to me, but my experience led me to believe different. *"Nette, niggas will do anything to save their own ass!"*

I told Nette I wanted to drop her and the kids off but she wasn't getting out of the car. She could be as stubborn as me at times and since I didn't want to fight with her as well, I kept her and the kids with me and made a bee-line straight for the Blvd. Droop definitely had some explaining to do but I hoped to God I wasn't going to have to fight him too! Droop had never been violent with me, except for that one time when he busted a few shots my way while I was sitting in the car, but he never raised a hand at me. I was hoping things would remain the same, but at the same time was prepared to fight. There was also a chance she found out by word on the street, and if that were the case the cool. I just needed to hear it from him that he didn't tell her and then let her loose on me without warning.

When I reached the Bully, Droop was standing front line, as if he were just waiting for me to roll up. The block was flooded with niggas as usual, most of them a part of his clique, but I didn't give a damn. My hands were bloody and swollen, so were my arms and wrist. I had bruises all over me and my rings had cut into my flesh. What more could go wrong?

As I bailed out the car, all eyes were on me. If looks could kill, Droop would have dropped dead right where he stood. *"Molly, calm down, just calm down, let me talk to you."*

"No, mother fucker, you calm down! You didn't just have to fight for you life while some deranged bitch took swings at you with a fucking table leg!" Droop's eyes lit up as if he really had no clue what I was talking about. Then, I noticed the side of his face, and it looked like he'd been burnt with a curling iron. The sight of his scar defused my anger a bit and a different emotion kicked in. *"Oh my God, Bae', what happened to your face?"*

"Nothing, Molly, what happened?"

"What happened? You tell me what happened. I though we agreed to tell her together?"

"Molly, don't come up here going off on me, why the fuck did you tell my mom?"

"Ya mom? Droop, that's ya mom, I had to tell her!"

"What!"

The two of us were going back and forth and the whole block heard our conversation. *"Droop, you mean you wanted me to hide it from your mom, too? She already knew."*

"She ain't know for sure, Molly, till you told her, so if you wanna be made at somebody, be mad at her cause she told Blaque', not me Molly!"

"Mother Fucker! That bitch set me up!"

I left Droop standing right where I found him, jumped back into my car, and headed back to his Mama's house. I told Nette it was Peaches who dropped the dime, then started adding everything up. First there was the phone call from Blaque', and Peaches' loud announcement that I was there. Then, Blaque' asking to come see the kids and Nika's perfect timing, asking me to walk to the store. It was all a set up to keep me there until Blaque' arrived. Nika was probably already on the phone with Blaque' when I walked in with the kids, but hung up and told her to call back, just to make it look good. I'm not exactly sure when Peaches spilled the beans, but I'm sure Blaque' was aware of everything when she and I were on the phone. This is exactly why I didn't fuck with Peaches like that. This is exactly why I called her shady and two faced. She was the only woman I knew who could give you a hug and at the same time slip a knife in your spine! I should have known not to trust her. I should have known she would cross me like a Judas!

I asked Nette to keep the kids with her while I went back to see Peaches but she insisted on going with me. *"I'm good, baby girl. Just keep them with you for a minute, I'll be okay, I swear."* She reluctantly agreed and I drove away. Upon my return to Peaches', Blaque' was gone but Peaches was still sitting on her couch crying like a newborn. *"What's up, Peaches? How you just gonna set me up like that?"* Peaches looked up at me. *"Murf, I swear I only told because I though I was helping. If I would have known the two of y'all were going to fight, I swear I wouldn't have said anything."* She sounded sincere but who doesn't sound convincing when they're whimpering. Just a while ago she was sitting down with Blaque' trying to save face with her. Now she using her tears to try and do the same to me. Fuck that! Peaches tried to save herself! She wanted to cover up the fact that she was aware of me and her son's dealings. She wanted to cover up that her entire family was aware of me and her son's dealings. Everybody had to know about us since nobody was surprised to find out about Messiah, and if she was trying to help, then why not tell me? Why leave me out of the loop? "

"Whatever, Peaches!" I turned around and walked out the door. Fuck that, she set me up! But what goes around comes around, this I knew for a fact!

Later that evening, after the kids and I settled in for the night, I got a knock at the door. Quan was upstairs in his room playing, and Messiah and I were lying on the bed about to take a nap. I wasn't in the mood for company and wondered who the hell was knocking at my door without calling me first. Messiah was lying on top of me and I didn't want to disturb him. I picked him up to place him down on the bed, but before I could get up, my visitors were walking in. My eyes got big because I didn't realize I'd left the door unlocked. I called Pharaoh's name because I felt he was the only person bold enough to just barge in but I was mistaken, because Blaque' and Droop were just as bold.

Dope! The two of them had to be on some serious dope to pull a stunt like that. What did she think? Did she think she was just gonna come up in my gates and have a replay of what went down earlier? I don't think so! I may have been relaxed, but I lived alone and kept protection under my pillow at all times. If anything would have happened, I would have surely gotten off on self defense.

Droop walked in the house first and at the same time, I sat up on the bed with one hand under my pillow. Blaque' followed behind him and the both of them slowly walked into my room. Droop stood along side the bed next to me and the baby, and Blaque' walked to the other side of the room and stood in front of the dresser. There was a short moment of silence then Blaque' began to apologize, but I threw my hand up and cut her off. *"I know your not here so you can apologize, so keep it real and tell me what's on your mind."*

"Well, Molly," she said. *"I did come over here to apologize but you right, it is more to it."* Blaque' wanted to know answers. She wanted to know how I knew Messiah was Kyron's son, how long we'd been dealing with each other and if we were going to continue to see one another. Ha, Ha, I couldn't help but laugh at her brazenness. I mean, was she actually standing up in my house asking me to provide her with

information about her man? What nerve. I turned to Droop and told him *"Speak up, nigga, 'cause I don't' have shit to say!"*

I will admit. There was a slight part of me that wanted to tell her everything from beginning to end, but the greater part of me said no. If she wanted to talk, she should have tried doing so earlier before she decided to swing on me. I didn't care if I fucked her man or not. I'd never violated her personally so fuck her. If she wanted answers, let her extract them from her man. I knew Droop would never tell her the truth and if he wanted to stand there and tell her lie after lie so be it. Blaque' should have asked Peaches all she wanted to know since she was her source of info. Since she was so reliable! If she thought her apology was going to hold some weight with me then she was in for a big surprise. She was an Aries like me, and should have known to appeal to my sensitive side first before attacking me. We forgive but we never forget. We can be some catty bitches and can hold a grudge for ever! My anger was still fresh and so were my wounds. I had my answers, fuck if she got hers or not...

I allowed Droop and Blaque' to remain in my presence while the two of them went back and forth with no gain. For every question Blaque' asked, Droop told two lies. His most used response was *"I don't know,"* and it was very entertaining to watch the two of them play each other out. Blaque' knew Droop was lying, but I could tell she didn't care. I wasn't the first chick he'd cheated on her with and I wouldn't be the last. I tried telling her that before but she wouldn't listen. So like Nana said, *"A hard head makes a soft behind!"* I don't why she brought him over in the first place and don't think she ever noticed he was paying more attention to me and the baby than he was her. Amazing!

****

Everything between me and Droop ended with his chick, but unbelievably, she came back the very next night still wanting to talk. Only this time, she brought along the right type of encouragement, the Piff she planned on puffing with me on my born day. Aww, now how could I resist...

Me and Blaque' sat out on my front porch blowing smoke while she expressed to me that she still wanted to be my friend. This was pretty big of her to say, but deep down inside I knew it wouldn't work. Blaque' was hurt and rightfully so. Embracing me was a way to deal with her pain, and at the same time, butter me up for info. Keep your friends close and your enemy's closer is what Nana use to say. Blaque' had the right game plan, just the wrong player. After the two of us were as high as stars, I told her, *"See me in ten years, and if you still want to be my friend then, I'll believe you."* She then tried convincing me she was sincere, but I wasn't letting down my guard.

Blaque' was good, but not that good, and I told her; *"Keeping me close, Blaque', won't do nothing but constantly remind you of the pain and betrayal you're trying so desperately to get over. True, you may not have any malice in your heart toward me and that's cool because I don't have any towards you. But you don't' want to be my friend. I'm not even sure I want to be yours..."*

We both had a lot of emotional issues to sort out, and neither of us were sure of what we really wanted.

Blaque' was as silly as me and the two of us had shared many laughs together. She couldn't do anything but laugh at me and the two of us continued to smoke and chat until the bud was gone. She was a good girl, and although I'd had a son by her man, I wasn't going to apologize for having a son by him. I apologized for hurting her, but like Pharaoh said, *"God don't make no mistakes."*

She left and I went back inside the crib. I was sure all ties would be cut after that. But I've been falsely sure of a lot of things.

****

I moved from Kent Street about two month's short of my lease because my landlord was on some straight bull shit. He wanted me to find someone to marry his so called sister who still lived in India, so she could get residency here as a citizen. He was offering me $5,000 for my help. I told him I would see what I could do but instead, made plans to get as far away from him as I possible. Five grand! What the fuck could $5,000 get me in this day and time? On top of that, why would I help his ass bring more people over here to live free and better than me and I was born here? Why help him open up another quickie-mart, dollar store, or gas station, while me and my people sell drugs just to get by?

Ken was a slum lord, and I knew he had more money and resources than I'd ever have. If he wanted his so-called sister over here so bad, let him find one of his own to be his flunky. Although he was willing to pay the first one willing to dig his own grave $20,000 in total, I wanted nothing to do with his scam. So no sooner then he propositioned me, I moved but I didn't go far. Our next stop was 28 Division Street, which was directly around the corner in front of the park, and how lucky was I to get the same landlord as I had when I lived a few blocks away on Russling. I moved in around the middle of the month and by the end of the month, Kyron's DNA results were back. The test was 99.99% positive. Kyron was, without a doubt, Messiah's natural father.

DNA is nothing more then a series of numbers. One set is from the mom, one is from the father, and the third is from the child. Someone with no common knowledge of what that really meant may have been lead to believe that Messiah was more Kyron's son than mine, since Messiah had more matching numbers with his father than with me. I say this because that's exactly what Peaches thought after reviewing the results for the first time. Peaches never seized to amaze me at how well she could twist something around, then at the same time act dumb. I knew what she was trying to say though, even if she didn't know how to say it. But she claimed she never received the test results in the mail, and instead picked a copy of it up from the courts. *"Someone must have taken them out of the mail,"* she said, but who would do a thing like that I asked.

In a round about way she tried pointing the finger at Blaque' and I believed her too. That was until Blaque' called a few weeks later asking could she come over because she needed to talk. Now what...!

With the results back and all the dirty laundry aired out, I had the slightest idea what she wanted to talk about. But I played along, because again, I didn't really have anything against the girl. She said she was coming through with some drinks and of course some Piff, so I though what the hell. What can it hurt?

Blaque' was very humble. She was fly but also meek. I liked that about her. It was one of the reasons why we got along so well in the first place. When she came over she had a six pack of Smirnoff Ice, *"Black Label"* and the Piff was already rolled. I wouldn't normally smoke anything that wasn't rolled up in front of me, but I knew her well enough to know what she did and didn't do. I was confused by her visit, and at first, she was just talking in circles. I could tell she was upset.

368

She said she wanted to know how everybody was so sure Messiah was Kyron's son, and that to her, he looked just as much like Solomon as he did Quan. She said she asked Peaches and Kyron how they could be so sure, and all they could tell her was that they were. She was confused because all anyone told her was that they were sure about the baby but couldn't give her any proof. *"How can you be sure, Molly, when all throughout your pregnancy you swore he was Solomon's? Plus, weren't you and Quan's dad messing around again...? Are you sure he's not his?"*

For whatever reason, my heart went out to Blaque'. And although I didn't owe her any explanation, I did want to ease her pain. *"Molly, I don't fell like I can trust Peaches anymore. They seem to only be concerned with saving Kyron's ass, they don't care about what's right! If Messiah is Kyron's son, I want him to take responsibility for him. He can't just walk away scot free and act like he didn't do anything."* Again, noble words from a scorned woman, but they were inspired by an agenda. I hated to play devil's advocate, but one doesn't always have the option of choosing their own weapon. So, I told Blaque' if she wanted to try and have a half way decent relationship with Kyron, she needed to cut his immediate family off. The longer she dealt with them, the longer she was going to go through the bullshit.

"You not fucking his family, girl, you fucking him, and he lives with you!" Then she went on to tell me that Peaches told her I must have tampered with the mail because they haven't received any test results yet. *"Blaque',"* I said, then laughed because by then I was feeling real right, *"why would I try to hide the results when I was the one who exposed myself in the first place?"* She couldn't give me a reply and I didn't need one. If the truth was what she wanted then I was going to give it to her because honestly, this shit was getting tired. I told her to hold on while I went upstairs and got something for her. When I returned, I had a copy of the test results in my hand.

"Here," I said, *"you can keep this copy for yourself."* I handed her the paper and took my seat. As she read the results, I inhaled the smoke from our second dutch and took a long swig of my drink. I saw the expression on her face change from confused to negative, or should I say from uncertainty to 99.99% positive! Now, nobody could bullshit

anyone anymore. The answer to her heart's most burning question was now in the palm of her hands. My hands were completely clean and I hoped she was now satisfied so she could stop pretending to be my friend. After reading the results, our conversation went flat and suddenly she had to go. She told me she'd see me later and to give the kids a kiss for her. She left behind half a dutch and four drinks. I told her to drive safe and hoped Droop would remain safe as well.

****

Rewinding the clock a little, back to about two weeks after my born day. My sister Nikki and I were riding down Spring Street looking for Solomon when I spotted him standing out in front of S*B's house. I asked her to pull over so I could get his attention even though I wasn't sure how he'd react. Nikki pulled over as I asked and once Solomon spotted us he walked over to the car. He leaned in on the passenger side, spoke to my sister first, then grabbed my hand and asked me how I was doing. I couldn't even get the words *"sorry"* out of my mouth before the tears began to fall.

Solomon grabbed my face, cuddled my cheeks, and told me not to say a word, because he understood. He said he was sorry too and had no ill feelings towards me or the kids. As kind as his words may have been, they didn't make me feel any better. How could the very best relationship of my life end up like this? True, we all make mistakes but how could he be so forgiving? Maybe it was a relief, I don't know, but what I do know is it was a lot for me to take in, considering all we'd been through. Solomon said we were too close to let anything get between us then blew me a kiss.

That right there did it. I told my sister to pull off and I balled like a baby. Nikki couldn't stand to see me so broken up and my cries called her to pull over a second time to try and console me. As we sat in front of the park waiting for me to dry my tears, my sister stated she'd never seen me or anyone cry so hard in her entire life. That much was true. Neither she nor anyone else had ever seen me cry like that, and for the record I haven't cried like that since. Sometimes a closed door is a good one. That way you know for sure there's no turning back and you have to move forward.

Solomon's willingness to forgive could have just as well been contributed to him having a baby by Dee-Dee. You know fair exchange ain't no robbery and since we were both sneaking and creeping and got caught, calling it even was the only thing either of us could do. Feelings were hurt and lives were turned upside down, but as long as it didn't affect the kids I'd be okay. I ended up being glad I had no direct choice in choosing the father of my child because God did an good job all on his own.

Nearly a year after the incident between Blaque' and myself, Peaches and I got into our own little fight. As it turned out, she didn't take to kind to me, Messiah's mother, calling her up and request my son be brought back home, after spending nearly two whole days at their house. I wasn't trying to prevent Peaches and her family from bonding with Messiah, but he was my son and when I want him to come home, I had the right to make the request. Peaches, on the other hand, felt she was the shot caller, so I had no choice but to go do to her house and get him.

Since she only lived five minutes away, I opted to walk instead of drive. Peaches felt I was being disrespectful for showing up at her door and questioning her *Nana authority*. Truly, I didn't understand her reasoning, but I wasn't about to argue with her either. I walked in her house with intentions on just getting my son and getting gout but there was a delay in my plans. Before I could get to my child, Peaches stood in my way and said, *"Don't fuck with me over, Messiah,"* all while pointing her finger in my face. I flung my head back, you know like all sister girls do when in a situation like this and replied, *"No, don't you fuck with me over Messiah!"* The next thing I knew, she had her six inch finger nails in my face, digging and scratching me up worse than any Nightmare on Elm Street you've ever seen. Blood was dripping onto my shirt, jacket, and jeans, but that didn't stop me from retrieving my son!

I guess some things never change, and although she said her frustration was due to Messiah. I knew it was more to it, I just didn't care. I told her she'd never see Messiah again, and I knew that would hurt her more than pressing charges!

HASTE MAKES WASTE, BUT PATIENCE IS TRULY A VIRTUE...

HERE WE GO AGAIN

My re-entry into the work force began a few weeks after my move onto Kent Street, at the Richard J. Hughes Justice Complex. I had a great deal of confidence about my skills, knew I'd be a valuable asset, and didn't shy away hide any facts pertaining to my felony. My employers appreciated my honesty and in turn, hired me on the spot.

For the next year and a half, I worked my ass of, slaving, making sure I did everything I was asked, even if I felt it wasn't my job to do so. I did this because on day one, I was told they were looking to fill the position permanently and I wanted to make sure I'd be their number one and top pick. The pay sucked and my days were long, but I looked beyond all of that because I had a goal to achieve. I even picked up the slack of other workers who were making triple what I was bringing home just to prove I was a *"worthy team player."*

My assignment was in Personnel, in Human Resources, therefore, I got a first hand look at how the recruitment process worked. I knew what to do, what not to do, and as long as I kept my nose clean I figured I'd make a good impression. I processed every single resume that came into that building and my work was always accurate. The only downside was deadlines, and because we accepted resumes from all over and from sources like Monster.com, we sometimes got more than we could handle.

On one occasion in particular, our deadline was approaching fast and we were only half way through with completing the job. I needed to prepare three, three inch binders for a judge, all containing at least 300 resumes, and I needed to have them to him by nine o'clock the next morning. I knew I'd never be able to complete them in time, and the person I was doing the job for was a habitual complainer. So, to keep from looking bad in front of my boss, I took the liberty of taking the resumes home, so I could put them in alphabetical order. This alone would catch me up in time to have the binders to the judge on time. I thought my efforts would be appreciated since everyone in the office always took their unfinished work home anyway.

On the evening of December 19, 2002, my boss called me up and questioned me about the resumes. I told her I brought them home with me so we could meet our morning deadline, but not to worry because I'd take good care of them. She was relieved that they hadn't been misplaced or accidentally thrown away, but shocked that I'd take such initiative. The next morning when I arrived at work, I immediately began working on the binders and that's when my boss told me to meet her in her office. With little time to spare, I wondered what could be so urgent that it couldn't wait. Four other staff members were asked to attend this unscheduled meeting also, two of them were in charge of distributing my work load.

Considering how hard they had fought to keep me when all the other temps had to leave, I wasn't expecting such a rude awakening. I was one step away from becoming permanent. Resumes had been accepted for the position I was in and I'd proven myself worthy beyond a doubt. Needless to say, it cut like a knife when boss lady told me she had to let me go. They said because I'd take the resumes home, I caused them to question my integrity. Come on man, are you serious? I'd been nothing but honest and forthcoming since day one. True, I'd gone above and beyond the call of duty, but I did it with good reason. Had the slackers been willing to carry their own load, I wouldn't have felt compelled to do so.

Here I was thinking I was on the right path to regaining my civil service status and I was thrown off track by a detour. Out of everyone in that office, I knew I was one of the hardest workers because I was the thirstiest. Never before had I heard of anyone being fired or dismissed because they did too good of a job, and just like with my resignation from the Department of Labor, I felt their actions were extremely harsh. My intuition told me their excuse was a crock of shit, but technically, there was nothing I could do. Truth be told, my actions caused those being paid $55,000.00 a year to look bad.

My boss told me I could leave if I wanted to and I'd still get paid for the day. I smiled, but said if it's all the same, I'd like to finish what I started. I wasn't in the habit of leaving things undone and since I was being fired for the resumes, I may as well get credit for the work. Plus, I had business to take care of before leaving. For starters, I'd had to notify the daycare downstairs that my son would no longer be attending since I was now out of a job. Then, I wanted to make sure I had all of my time sheets in order to show to social services since they'd have to start sending me benefits again.

Three of the Administrators I worked with were saddened to see me go, and said they'd provide me with excellent references if ever I needed their help. A nod was the only thing I was able to generate in response, because they weren't the only ones saddened by my discharge.

At three o'clock, I made my rounds and said my final good-byes to now former co-workers and new friends. Most staff just assumed my contract was over but a few suspected something more. I didn't make matters any worse and didn't see any need to give any explanation. At four o'clock, boss lady walked into my office, closed the door behind her and I rolled my eyes. *"Now what!"*

Sindy, aka boss lady, asked if there was anything she could do for me. Pissed that she'd taken away the one thing I did need, I shook my head no and continued cleaning out my desk. I told her I was going to call the agency in the morning, and she said she's already taken care of it. She said she told them, I was an excellent worker, but unfortunately, the work had run out. *"Damn, how you gonna stand in my face and admit you told a lie like that, yet, let me go because you say I can't be trusted?"*

I thanked her for her consideration, but said if she really wanted to help, she'd give me my job back. Sindy couldn't look at me and it was obvious she was uncomfortable. She should have been! She then took it a step further by asking was there anything she could do for my kids. *"What! My kids! You just fired their mom! How you gonna do something like that, then ask is there anything you can do for them! If you want to help us, give me back my job!"*

I was trying not to shout but she shouldn't have gone there. My kids were my reason for laughing at their sideway jokes and ignoring their sarcastic undertones. For two years I did this strictly for the benefit of my kids, and I was the first person to ever stay in that job for that long. I made the sacrifice for my kids and now my kids were the ones who were gong to suffer the most. They needed a mother who was employed, not one who sat at home on her ass, waiting for unemployment or welfare! *"Thank you, but NO! You can't do anything for my kids!"*

"Oh, Marie," she cried. I just brushed her aside and walked out the door. If it's on thing I can't stand, it's for someone to patronize me or pretend that they care, when really it's nothing more then an admission of their own damn guilt! The runt gets the boot and the big dogs continue to eat. That bitch had just taken food out of my kid's mouths, then had the nerve to ask if there was anything she could do. Shit, she'd done enough.

Four days after I was let go, I got a surprise visit from one of the administrators I use to work with named Pat. I liked Pat. She'd tried to land me a job at a community center before I left, but accepting the position would have meant longer travel time and I'd have to take Messiah out of the Justice Complex day care, and I couldn't afford that either.

Pat gave me a $100 gift card for Toy R' Us, and said it was from the entire unit. In my heart, I felt it was just another admission of boss lady's guilt, even if it was sincere. I say that because months later, I learned that my replacement was a former judge's intern who was in need of a job. She had her resume forwarded straight to the judge she use to work for and the rest is history. I guess boss lady felt really bad about having to let me go, but she was also in a position to fight for me too! I didn't want to be rude and offend Pat, so I accepted the card from her and gave her my thanks. The next day I gave the card to my sister for her kids because I felt some kind of way about accepting their charity. Regardless if it was a group contribution or not, trying to pacify me with a card for the kids was really irritating!

Ironically, my replacement quit six months after she took the job. Rumor had it she couldn't keep up with the work and that Diane, the habitual complainer, got all over her nerves. Diane was the cause of me getting fired and honestly, nobody could tolerate her character. I'm surprised girlfriend lasted that long, and a year after I left they were still posting vacancies for the position. I would have applied, but I was looking to go forward, not revisit my past... Next!

MARIE ANTIONETTE

****

Thirsty! Thirsty can get you in a heap of hot water, even when you have the best intentions. I say that because during my employment at the Justice Complex, I had an awful scare involving my youngest son Messiah. Because I was trying to keep my life on track, I made a habit of going to church every Sunday for spiritual guidance and support. My boy Sam and I use to both go to Friendship Baptist, downtown on Perry street, and that's where I met this guy; Charles LaDontae'.

Charles and Sam were roommates at the halfway house. Sam was there as a form of rehab and Charles said he was there because he'd assaulted his step-pop for hitting his mother. Time progressed and Charles and I became cool. Sam use to always complain about the food there and use to tease me about inviting him over for dinner. Because Sam had done so much for me while I was down on my luck, I felt preparing him a good, hot, home cooked meal was the least I could do. I even told him he could bring Charles if he liked, because I had plenty to spare. The majority of my kindness was a result of going to church and allowing the scriptures to play on my emotions. I didn't know Charles that well to invite him into my home, but since we'd met at church and he was Sam's boy, I didn't se the harm.

The Sunday Sam and Charles were supposed to come over, Sam got a call about his dad and had to take a rain check. However, I didn't want to break my promise to Charles and told him he could still come over, as long as he was willing to take a plate back for Sam when he left. I couldn't put my finger on it, but something about Charles didn't sit well with me and Shantell picked up on it too. But because he was a white boy, I chalked up my intuition up to paranoia and ignored my gut. Charles was a real talker and in conversations, told me he'd lost both of his children at birth, due to a condition they developed from their mom. He said his daughter lived for a day, but his son died moments after he was born. I felt bad for his loss, but he said he was just glad he got the chance to hold them before they went on to heaven.

Long story short, dude turned out to be a pedophile and tried to abduct my son from the daycare at my job. He found out where I worked by looking me up on NJ Direct, and recognized my car parked on the side of the building. He gained access to the building but couldn't get past the guards. His sick thirst gave him away and when the trooper because suspicious of his visit, he asked him to leave the premises. At the same time the guards at the desk called me upstairs and I freaked when they told me what he tried to do. He even tried to convince them that he was my boyfriend and that he was there to take Messiah out to the park for lunch.

It wasn't until I paid a visit to the facility he was staying at that I found out the true nature of his crimes. I was so sickened to learn he'd molested his own children, I wanted to cut the fucker's dick off and feed it to him for dinner! If he was sick enough to do something like that to his own flesh and blood, I couldn't even imagine what he'd do to mine had he gotten the chance. The fool even had the audacity to return to my house after being told to leave my job, and with crayon wrote me a love note on the hallway wall. Upon my discovery I called the police, but was frightened as to what I'd do to him if he returned before they arrived.

The next day I thanked the trooper and the guards for being so on point and for protecting my child from harm. I then made a visit to my church to warn my pastor about Charles, and about his plans to become a volunteer for our 6-12 year old youth choir. Surprisingly, I was told that there was nothing they could do or say to Charles until they got official word that he taken residence and was on a pedophile list. Furthermore, he said, *"The house of God is a place for forgiveness."*

"Oh, okay," I said. I thanked him for his time and haven't stepped foot back through those doors since. Wolves definitely disguise themselves in sheep's clothing and pastor was wrong when he said the unrighteous didn't dwell amongst the righteous. Shit, if you find people like that in church, then I'd rather take my chances in the street. At least I knew the evil I was dealing with out there.

****

As frustrating as it may have been, once again I was an "Angry Black Woman." If I didn't work I couldn't get assistance, and without assistance I couldn't pay my bills, rent, or buy food. I hadn't made enough to put anything aside for a rainy day, and just to add insult to injury, my car broke down and I had to abandon it across town. There was no way I could afford to fix it, and Pharaoh wouldn't help me because I'd cut him off from the goods. He was so fucking selfish that way and didn't care if the car benefited his son. He just wanted to punish me.

It took three months for me to receive unemployment, which meant I fell three months behind in my rent. I didn't receive my first check until April of the following year, and ironically, that's when the agency called saying they had another assignment for me. Their timing was impeccable because I was due for an evaluation from social services and had they found out I wasn't working, I really would have been up shits creek. Technically, I wasn't in the rears for the full three months, because my land lord still received half the rent from welfare. With this in mind, I didn't understand how or why they harassed me so much considering they weren't supposed to accept the funds if I wasn't paying my half as well. They used the system for their benefit and so did I.

Business is business and I understood the Hyltons' curiosity as to if I was going to pay them or not, but what I didn't understand is how they could be so demanding when the house was literally falling apart. Those glossy hard wood floors and huge rooms were just bait to lure me in, but before long, debris began to fall from the ceiling in my oldest son's room, the wall began to fall apart in mine, the roof leaked in multiple spots and the toilet kept overflowing. The Hyltons could and should have used some of that money they were getting from welfare to fix those minor issues but they didn't. Instead, all I got were broken promises, which left me with no incentive to pay them what I owed.

With money being funny and change being strange, Nette came up with what she thought was the perfect solution for both of our problems. Nette was having a time with her current landlord as well and thought if we moved in together, we'd lighten one another's load. Since I'd soon be returning to work and would need a sitter for Messiah, I accepted her offer and her and my niece moved in with me and the boys. The combination of me working and Nette chipping in provided minor relief, but in order to make ends meet, I had to work as a shampoo girl for my girl Liz at her salon E.Q Styles. I was really hard up for cash, but felt embarrassed for accepting her generosity. Had it not been for Liz and the stamps I was still getting from social services, all five of us would have damn near starved! Not to mention in a few months we'd have yet another hollering mouth to feed. Oh, did I forget to mention, lil' sis was expecting...

There was a much needed balance in my life that kept eluding me and no matter how hard I tried; it seemed as if I'd never get my life back on track. My life at this point was nothing more then a series of long showers and Dutch Masters, and ironically, that was going to be the original title of this book. Suburban families have their pills and urbanites have that good-good green. You don't have to accept my take on life, but it is what it is...

****

I don't believe in coincidences. So when I found myself spending every day and night with my across the street neighbor, who I just happen to know by way of working at the Justice Complex, I chalked it up as something that was just meant to be. I was home because I was unemployed at the time, but after going through all that I'd gone through, I vowed never to mess with an unemployed, drug dealing, sorry ass, I need a place to stay, nigga ever again! But wait, he was unemployed too, yet at the same time, was the first nigga I'd ever dated who ever had a real job! That in itself was a plus.

My new friend was different than a lot of the other guys I dated, and in a lot of ways too. For one, he had his own crib, didn't have his car registered in his baby mama's name, and use to spend half his day searching for new employment. He was cocky, but in a confident kind of way, and always made sure the kids and I were straight. He had a lot of good views on family, and took care of his children without being forced to by the courts. Maybe he was that balance I'd been missing and could provide me with the support I deserved and a few other things while he was at it. He saw how the landlord was letting the place fall apart, and used my hardship as an excuse not to do his job.

I couldn't believe these were the same people I'd rented from only a few years back. Then again, it shouldn't have surprised me because even then, the roof leaked and there was a serious rodent problem. I remember the husband telling me to plug the holes up with aluminum foil, because the mice couldn't chew threw it, instead of sending out an exterminator. Now they were acting like I was the worse tenant ever and wanted to take me to court. Slowly I felt my independence and sanity slipping away, and wondered how long it would be before I snapped from all the pressure. Now I see why so many of us spend our hard earned on lottery tickets and scratch offs, but I don't gamble unless I know it's a sure thing…

In my entire adult life, the only financial breaks I've caught were at income tax time and that third check in the month state workers get twice a year. Either that or I had to figure out a way to hustle, sweet-talk, or do something grimy to get some cash. I never caught up with my rent and in turn, the landlord never made the repairs. This was no different then the situation I'd just left on Kent, where this mother fucker had the nerve to say; *"You're black, aren't you use to roaches?"* I cursed his Dalmatian looking, Pakistanian ass out! *"Okay, first of all mother fucker! Them not roaches! They big black ass crispy waterbugs and no, me and my kids not use to no roaches!"*

It seemed like I'd gone from sugar to shit, and minor problems turned into major ones. However, I drew then line when a portion of my oldest son's roof literally collapsed over top of my son's bed! I contacted the owners and told them point blank. *"Regardless if I'm behind or not you still have to make the repairs. As long as you accept checks from the county, you have to abide by the contract and pass inspection!"* I had all the right in the world to be cocky and I wasn't bluffing about calling the inspectors. The husband wouldn't budge but after calling again and again and leaving several messages; the wife stopped by and gave me a visit. This way, she could see with her own two eyes what I was talking about.

Ms. Hylton couldn't deny work needed to be done immediately and the two of us reached a verbal agreement. I was going to pay and extra $150 a month with my current rent in order to catch up, and she was going to send her son over to start making the repairs. I wasn't thrilled that she was sending a child to do a man's job, but I wasn't going to complain. She knew I wasn't holding back to be spiteful, I just wanted to be treated fairly. As a mother, I knew she understood my situation way better than her husband ever could. I kept my end of the bargain, but the husband wasn't satisfied and wanted all the back rent at once. Now he was just being a jerk. I only brought home $800 a month and my portion of the rent was $400. I was already giving him more than half of my monthly income and not yet had he made one repair. Things got so tense up in there, I even told my lil' sister she had to go!

The Hyltons and I went back and forth with no gain until September 2003. It was then that we were able to call a truce, but I put my freedom and livelihood on the line to do so.

It was a Wednesday and I'd decided to stay home with Messiah because I didn't have any bus fair, no clean clothes, and no food to send with him to daycare. Ray had given me money to hold me down throughout the day, but I was holding on to that for dinner later on that night. Maybe I'd get a child support check today I hoped, and with that in mind, sat out on the porch and waited for the mail man with Messiah. While the summer campers played in the park, I enjoyed watching my baby play and entertain himself on the porch. Seeing him happy was one of life's simple pleasures, almost therapeutic...

When the mail main arrived, he placed my mail in my hand, and the neighbors' in the hallway. I flipped through the envelopes in search of one thing and one thing only. But instead of finding a child support check, I found a check for someone else who didn't even reside there.

At first glance I though it may have belonged to the downstairs tenants, so I threw it in the hallway with the rest of their stuff, disappointed that noting had come for me. I grabbed my baby and went inside so the two of us could nap. When we woke up, it was time for Quan to come home from school, and Messiah and I went to the store to grab something to eat for dinner. I returned home, started dinner, cleaned the house, and after sweeping down the stairs, noticed a balled envelope in the hallway. Assuming it was trash I ripped it up and threw it in the garbage. My chores were now done and so was our dinner. The kids and I ate and after doing the dishes, went back outside on the porch to chill. As soon as I stepped outside, I saw trash piled up in front of the house. The wind was whipping up something terrible that evening, so I grabbed the broom and began sweeping things up. While picking up the bigger pieces I noticed that same envelope I'd thrown in the garbage was back on the ground. Out of pure curiosity, I picked it up to take a look at it. Initially, I though it was one of those non-negotiable checks you get from a car dealership but as I looked closer I saw it was actually an insurance check for $2500!

While holding both the torn pieces of each check in both hands, I thought about all the good I could do with that money. My kids would be thrilled to see the cupboards and refrigerator filled again, instead of only having spring water and canned ravioli. I could catch up on my rent, get some necessities for the home and the family, wash clothes, and have plenty of fair for the bus and the baby's lunch.

That check could put me back on top of my game, and even with the rip straight down the middle, I was sure I could mend it back together as good as new. Quan's father use to rip money up all the time and put it in an empty water jug. Whenever my cash flow got low I'd match the serial number up and tape the bills back together, so I assumed a check wouldn't be any different. As I contemplated who I could get to cash the check, I realized all of the pawn shops and check cashing spots were closed. But in the morning I could take a walk on to Clinton and have my boy Dave hook me up. Dave worked at a check cashing joint, and had looked me out a few times in the past. Whatever the check's worth, I'd always give him 10% for hooking me up but he never asked that I do so. If he was able to do the same now, I'd be more than willing to throw in an addition $50 for his troubles.

That night, I taped the check back together and just as I though, you couldn't detect the rip. The next morning, I dropped Quan off at school and Messiah off to Peaches, (Yeap, we were back speaking again.) and headed to see my man, Dave. When I got there, Dave hadn't clocked in yet. His boy said he'd be in later on but my desperation wouldn't allow me to wait. So I propositioned him with my offer but he looked down his nose at me and declined. *"Oh no he wasn't looking at me like I was some type of junkie, and his faggot ass was working as ass boy for some Jewish cat, cashing other peoples checks. As if he was so clean he'd never had his hand in the cookie jar!"*

Making absolutely no leeway with my first attempt, I sat a few doors down on an abandoned porch thinking of my next move. Ironically, I was directly across the street from the first spot I'd rented from the Hyltons and the surprise visit the Misses paid me last night kept haunting me. I'd promised her I'd have all of her money for her by the end of the day, but maybe I shouldn't have spoken so soon and waited until I actually had the money in hand. I knew she only came by to apply more pressure and was expecting me to give her some lame excuse. I had to keep my word to her because my word was all I had, and with that in mind, I high tailed it back across town to another check cashing joint.

This second closer to my crib, but the girl there denied me too. I'd now run out of options and because of this my desperation grew. I'd already missed two days form work which meant those were two days I wouldn't be paid for. I needed to make that money up and then some and that check was my only way out.

As I walked down Hamilton Avenue back towards my house, I passed Roma Savings Bank and realized I only had one option left. Regardless of the risk or consequences, I was going to take that check to the bank!

Even though I couldn't save a buffalo nickel, I had a checking account at Commerce Bank. I needed some place to cash my checks and they were the most convenient. The closest branch was located right in town, and happened to be in the same building as my job. I knew by going into town at this time of the day, meant running the risk of being spotted by one of my co-workers, possibly even my boss, but I didn't care. Worst case scenario, I'd just tell them I was in town picking up a prescription from Rite-Aide or something.

I double endorsed the check and approached the teller, but first asked when the funds would be available. *"The money will be available by 7:00 a.m. the next morning, Ms. Cook."* I handed the teller the check, smiled, then notice to about ten cameras that I was sure got a clean, clear shot of me. I still didn't care though. Right, wrong, or indifferent, I needed that money…

Knowing I'd eventually get caught, I walked into Commerce Bank at 7:00 a.m. on the dot and withdrew $2500 of someone else's money. The money was spent before I had it in my hand and my first payment would be issued to Peaches for her assistance. Peaches lent me her car so I could run to the bank, and when I returned, I gave her $50. Then I asked her to watch Messiah a little while longer while I ran to the store. She agreed, and clutched on to that $50 like it was winning lottery ticket. In the eyes of the law I was wrong, but the way I saw it, they couldn't do anymore harm to me then what they'd already done. The landlord, on the other hand, could kick me and my kids out at a moment's notice so you tell me, what would you have done?

As I thought about my own situation, I wondered if my landlord's hands were tied as well. Everything that glitter ain't gold, and maybe they needed that money just as bad as I did.

After leaving Peaches, I went right back around to the first check cashing place I'd gone to the day before and got five separate money orders. Three were for the back rent and late fees, (they charged me a $80.00 late fee as if I had it like that) and the other two were for the current and next month's rent combined.

I spent $400 at the grocery store! That was more then I'd ever spent in one trip, but I wanted to make sure we had everything we needed and then some. After going without for so long, I felt it was okay to go just a tad bit overboard. Then I went to Wal-Mart and got everything I felt the kids needed and had unfairly gone without. I got several items for the house to make it feel more like home and even splurged and got the kids a new color TV for the front room, 'cause the only decent one we had was had was upstairs in mine. In less than an hour, I'd spent a little over $2100 without one sign of an obstacle or any questions asked. I returned home, began putting the food away, and then hooked up the TV. When Quan came home from school he was damn near speechless, and to see the happy expression in my baby's eyes meant everything in the world to me.

After sitting down and enjoying TV with the boys, I started to clean up, when I got a knock at the door. *"Who is it?"* I yelled. I heard a reply but couldn't make it out. So I yelled again and that's when I caught on to the voice. It was Ella. The crazy bitch who use to live in the apartment before me and the kids. Why was she here I wondered? She wore her welcome out a long time ago after she tried pressuring me to pay her for some raggedy ass furniture she chose to leave behind, because she didn't have anywhere to put it in her new crib. I knew she couldn't have been dumb enough to think I was going to entertain the thought of paying her more money for something I never wanted in the first place, so why was she here?

Ella knew our last conversation was on a sour note, and I was pissed she had the audacity to come to my home. My door opened outward and I could tell she was right up on it, so I gave it a good hard thrust hoping to hit her in the process. She saw nothing but attitude written all over my face and a quick, snappy *"What,"* was all she received in terms of a greeting.

"Have you seen my check" she inquired? *"Your check? Why you asking me?"* She then went on to say her insurance company made a mistake and mailed her check out to her old address instead of her new one. *"Nah, I ain't seen it,"* I said, while closing the door behind me, in order to hide the empty TV box that sat at the top of the stairs. *"Feel free to look through that mail over there if you like."*

"I looked over there already. It's not there and the insurance company said they mailed it out three days ago. It should have been here by now!" She then turned around and walked out. Normally a situation like this would make sense because mail delivered to the wrong address is common. But that wench moved out nearly two years ago, long enough for her to have changed her address with everyone she did business with, especially her insurance company. Something didn't smell right. The name on the check read Eleadora, but I never made the connection that maybe Ella wasn't her real name. In my eyes, it was only thievery if I knew the person, but now that she was putting claims on it, it put a new twist on how I viewed my actions. I didn't know if she was telling me the truth or not, but if she wasn't, how did she know about the check in the first place. Even though Ella or Eleadora had taken advantage of me in the past, I considered myself better than she was. She made a practice out of scamming people all the time. I only did it when necessary. But did that really make me better, or just a better opportunist?

I don't believe God causes anyone to feel guilt anymore than he causes us to feel sorrow or pain. Emotions are a part of our DNA and we cause our own feelings by way of our actions, because we know the difference between right and wrong. The landlord had been silenced and was now off my back. My refrigerator was full and there wasn't a chance in hell I was going to return anything to the store, not even the TV. So what was I to do? Basically, it was too late to do anything and as far as Ella, and the most she could do was call and report the check missing. Of course they'd find out the check had been cashed, but that wouldn't prevent them from reissuing another one to her. They'd just trace it back to me and I'd have to deal with the consequences at that time. It still bewildered me though, as to why she'd have them mail the check there instead of to her new address. Nobody would do something that stupid unless they had something to hide.

****

Quan assumed our good fortune came from his father paying his child support. I laughed out loud at his assumption then sat down with him and told him the truth. I knew he was too young to understand why I did what I did, but I promised him I'd never tell him another lie and I wasn't going back on my word. Quan knew what stealing was and he knew stealing was wrong. So before they came and got me I wanted him to know that although mommy was wrong, she did it for a good reason. Quan has always been a good son and he's always been able to read me. He knew I felt bad and he knew I knew I was going to get in trouble. So like any good son, he just looked at me and replied okay, then retreated back into the front room to watch TV with his brother. That night, we all went to bed on a full stomach and believe it or not, I got a good night sleep. Thursday and Friday I went to work and didn't have a complaint in the world. However, by Saturday evening things changed because Ella paid me another unpleasant, unwanted, and unannounced visit. This time I didn't answer the door because nothing was going to change. Now I was sure something was strange because instead of sweating the insurance company, she's sweating me. Little did she know her persistence only caused me to avoid her even more, though the fact that I had to avoid her at all weighed heavy on my mind.

I can ignore a lot of things but the one thing I can't ignore is my conscience. I didn't care two shits about Ella but it wasn't about her, and it never was. My son knew the truth and his thoughts were all that mattered. There was nothing left to do but wait it out until the police came looking for me, but either way I looked at it I was fucked! At times my impulsiveness cracks me up, but never once will I apologize for being me! Ella's visit on Saturday did something to me but not for her benefit. As I lay up in my bed wrestling with my thoughts, I asked myself what type of example was I setting for Day'Quan? Was I going to be a hypocrite and raise him to do as I say, not as I do? Was I telling him hard work was the plan but thievery was the back up? I mean in the end, what type of effect would this have on him, the one I was trying to do so much for. I had to make things right, and it was better to expose myself then to be exposed I said out loud to myself. I got a good night sleep that night and when I woke up Sunday morning, I knew exactly what I had to do.

It was somewhere around 10:00 a.m., and Quan noticed I was headed towards the door without him or his little brother. *"Mommy, where you going, you going to church,"* he asked. Being as it was Sunday, his question was legit. I guess he didn't pay attention that I was still wearing the same thing as the day before. *"No, baby, I'm not going to church. I'm going to tell Ms. Ella what happed to her check."* He stopped in his tracks and his little concerned voice replied back and said, *"But she gonna call the police on you!"*

"I know, baby, I know."

Then I told him to sit with his brother and I'd be right back. I could tell by the look in his eyes he was thinking he wasn't going to see me again, but I knew better. I let out a big sigh, hugged him tight, then walked out the door. Had I stood around and tried to explain myself further, I would have lost my nerve. Ella only lived across the park so the trip to her house would take me two minutes tops. Once I got there I had no intentions on making small talk. I just wanted to fess up to her about the check and be on my way. I knew she was gonna start screaming that police shit, and by all means, she could do whatever she felt necessary. Just as long as she didn't put her hand on me she wouldn't' have any problems.

As luck would have it, as soon as I reached the corner of Ella's street I saw her standing out on her porch blabbering away. At first she acted as if she didn't know who I was, but could tell she recognized me once I got closer. Her eyes got big!

I stopped about five feet away from her porch and motioned for her to come over towards me. Once the two of us were face to face she asked what's up, and I just came out and told her. *"I cashed your check!"* I waited a few seconds for her to respond, then turned to walk away. I guess she couldn't believe her ears 'cause her response was huh? So I said it again, *"Look, Ella, I cashed your check. I'm, sorry. I didn't know it was yours. I'll pay you back."*

I knew I'd never be able to pay her back, but it sounded good at the time. Then she asked me how I cashed it so I told her. Well, once girlfriend realized what I was saying and that I wasn't playing, she got right on her soap box with the, *"Oh My God! How could you do this to me? I've been so kind to you, bla, bla, bla."* Now I'm like okay, I didn't come around here for all this. I said what I had to say now it's time for me to bounce. As I was walked away, Ella stood out front with her neighbor screaming she was going to go to the bank and get her money back. *"Okay fine, do you. I just came around here to tell you what happened so you could stop coming over to my house!"* She kept going on and on and I kept it moving. Ella was a crazy bitch and if you ask me she was kind of slow. Why on earth would she go down to the bank and try to get money that was no longer there, instead of trying to contact the insurance company?

Now that I'd confessed, I needed to figure out my next move. Not sure of what to do, I called on my family. My mom and little sister were both very concerned, but Esha had no sympathy for me what so ever. She was hotter then a .45 just couldn't phantom how I could put myself in yet another fucked up situation. Being a true friend, she felt the need to remind me of all that I'd already lost and was attempting to regain. *"Your about to throw it all away, Murf; all over $2500 fucking measly dollars!"* Being the two of us were so close, she knew she could curse me out and get away with it. I know she was looking at the bigger picture, but she wasn't in my shoes. I tried explaining to her I did what I did for the sake of my kids, so they could eat, so we could continue to have a roof over our heads... Bla, bla, bla...

Esha understood the pressures of hardship, but felt I should have figured out a better solution. She said I took the easy way out. *"What's easy about going to jail, Esha,"* I screamed!" The two of us weren't getting anywhere and bottom line Esha wasn't beat. She didn't want to hear my excuse or why I did what I did. She was just pissed that I'd fucked up again and was afraid that this time, I wouldn't get off so lucky. She sat with me for a few minutes but then got up and left. *"Murf, I love you, but what you did was outright stupid."* She slammed the door behind her. Damn! She wasn't that hard on me when I told her about Messiah being Droop's son. Once she left, I went back upstairs and did the obvious. I cried.

About ten minutes after Esha left, Ella started with her harassment calls. I know I told her I'd pay her back, but even if that were true, she knew damn well I didn't have the money that quick. I told her there was nothing I could do until I got paid, then she started crying about how the bank wasn't going to reimburse her and what was she going to do? What was she going to do? How the hell did I know what she was supposed to do? I didn't even know what I was going to do!

I told Ella it would take some time for me to get that money to her and calling me all hysterical wasn't and shit wasn't going to make me get it any faster! Then she said she was going to call the police, and just as I told her when we were face to face, I said do you! All she had to do was report the check missing and have another one reissued to her at her correct address. Technically, she couldn't say it was stolen, because it never made it to her possession. She was beginning to piss me off with her *oh woe is me* sympathy act. In a few days she'd have her money if she did what she needed to do, but as for me, in a few days I could be jobless again... I hadn't thought about that until just that moment.

It was just my luck that as of May 2004, the state initiated a new hiring procedure which entailed a through background check of all new hires. Including those already employed by the state through temp agencies. So really, I didn't give a damn what she did. Just as long as she got the hell off my damn phone!

You know the worst part about waiting is not knowing how long the wait's gonna be. I knew I didn't want to go through another scene where the police came to my job and arrested me. So for two days I sat around at home, waiting for them to show, and by day three, I was at the end of my rope. If I was gonna go to jail, I was gonna need some bail. Taking off and hiding wasn't making things any better. One can't always prepare for the unexpected.

I went back to work that Wednesday and sought advice from my friend and co-worker, Berry. I trusted her counsel and knew she'd have some type of solution. I told her what I'd done and that I wanted to tell our supervisor before it was too late. Maybe if I saved them the shock and embarrassment, I'd be able to save my job. *"Hell nah, don't do that! Just chill, everything will work out. Don't get it fucked up. These people ain't cha` friend. Just wait and see what happens."* Easy for her to say, but I took her advice just the same.

I was more so embarrassed than anything. Less than two months ago another co-worker and dear friend who I looked at as a grandma gave me her assistance by giving me and the kids a full week's pay right out of her pocket. She said she hated to see a young mother struggle so hard and refused to sit back and watch me do so without lending a helping hand. I tried to be hard and refuse her gift, but she was from the old school and nothing about me frightened her except my stubbornness. Ms. Julie's kindness for me could never be put into words. So I remained quiet like Betty said, I didn't' want Ms. Julie to know.

By midday Wednesday I was shitting bricks and tried to stay off the floor as much as possible, just in case. By 3:00 I was sure they were on their way and by 4:30, thought they'd snag me as soon as I walked out the elevator doors. I was so paranoid I made myself sick. I don't know how I made it through the day, but I did. Not only did I make it through the day, I made it through the week. Thursday was just as calm as Wednesday, but on Friday the weather changed and I could tell my luck was about to run out.

When I got off work Friday afternoon, I could have hopped on the bus but opted to walk home instead. I knew the hike would take me at least a half hour but I wanted to enjoy the calm before the storm. It was a beautiful day and I wanted to take time out to enjoy my surroundings. I was so use to letting the day to day drama get to me, I didn't take time to appreciate all the beauty and preciousness around me. As I walked pass the nursing home, the sound of an elderly couple sharing a laugh caught my attention. Then I remembered what Nana said about respecting the elderly and wondered would I live long enough o experience their joy...

As I approached the intersection across the street from my house, I noticed an unmarked car parked in the middle of the park. That was nothing unusual because due to the high rise in crime, police camped out in that park all the time. But on this occasion, I knew they weren't there to deter kids from vandalism, smoking pot, or chasing vagrants off the benches. This time, I knew they were there waiting on me.

I approached my porch slowly and with caution, hoping they wouldn't jump out on me and scare the shit out of my son. I'd just picked Messiah up from school and I hoped they at least wait until I took him inside.

I walked up on the porch and went inside. Day'Quan met me and Messiah at the top of the stairs as usual, and the two of them ran off to play. I sat downstairs for a minute, then went on up into my room. I flopped down on the bed then eased up to peek out the window. The car was still parked across the street and for a moment I felt relieved. "Damn, maybe they not here for me," I thought. But no sooner then I flopped back down on the bed, I heard that infamous knock at the door and my heart dropped.

Now, I don't care where you live, or where you're from, I don't care if you're Black, White, Hispanic, or other, we all know a cop's knock when we hear it. So the moment of truth was again upon me but I was thankful it was taking place at home as opposed to my place of employment. I knew I had to answer the door but needed a few seconds to gather my thoughts and figure out what I was going to say. Though before I could do that, my baby who loved to receive company yelled, *"Who is it?"*

"Oh my God, Messiah, no!"

I flew down my stairs to try and hush him up but he'd already made it down to the door. Quan was right behind him and both of them knew not to answer. Messiah yelled again, *"Who is it"* and the voice behind the door replied *"Detectives!"* Quan stopped in his tracks and so did I, but that baby of mine didn't know what detectives meant so the fear factor escaped him.

I must admit, although I saw the car parked in the park, I was expecting them to call uniformed police to take me in. I took a deep breath, then pulled Messiah back. When I opened the door a tall, healthy Puerto Rican man stood in front of me. I was shocked because he didn't look like a cop. His face was friendly and he vaguely resembled someone I though I might know. *"Marie?*

"Yes," I replied, nodding my head then tilting it to the side with a guilty childish grin. *"I'm Detective Medina and this is my partner."* I nodded my head again. *"You know why we're here?"* he asked. Maintaining my demeanor I replied, *"Yes. Yes I know."* *"May we come in?"* he asked. Of course I said, as if no was an option, then showed them upstairs. Quan and Messiah stood curiously at the top of the staircase and greeted them with respect. Detective Medina's partner then gave the boys a few dollars and asked if it was alright for them to go get some ice-cream. Of course I didn't mind because they were on their way out the door to go play in the park anyway. You could hear the ice-cream the truck approaching and the timing was perfect.

Once the three of us were alone they went on to tell me that they weren't there to place me under arrest per say. However, they did want me to come down to the station and talk to them, *"willingly"* and give an official statement. Before the boys left, Messiah ran up to me and hugged my legs. Detective Medina looked down at him then back at me. *"Where do I know him from"* he asked. Then he said *"Kyron Parker?"* Yeap, you got it I said. Kyron Parker, this is his son. Well I'll be. Then he had asked, *"Is Kyron still in Annidale?"* I laughed, then nodded my head yes to that one too!

The fact that they were asking and not telling me to come with them, led me to believe things weren't as bad as I thought. But at the same time, knew it was serious enough for them to camp outside my house and wait for me to show up. I agreed to go with them but asked if I could make a few calls first because I needed someone to watch the boys for me. *"Make as many calls as you like. Take care of your kids first."* Funny he would say that...

I called my mom and lil' sister, then Ray. Ray was at work, but I told him to make sure he answered his phone just in case I needed bail. My mom, on the other hand, got all hysterical, but said her and Nette would be right over. When my mom arrived, I asked her to keep the kids in the park, because I didn't want Quan to see me leaving with the police and get all upset. She tried but Quan spotted me anyway, and that's when him and Messiah came running. When the detectives noticed the kids, they backed away from me. They said they didn't want to leave the kids with such a negative impression in their minds, even though they were sure, I'd be returning soon. I paused before getting in the back seat, long enough to see Day'Quan's face. Seeing him cry made me want to cry, but seeing me cry would have upset him that much more.

****

While Detective Medina signed the register, I made my way over to the elevator. I pushed the button to the third floor and Detective Medina stepped inside. There was an officer already inside the car and assuming I was a common criminal, made the smart remark, *"We can tell you've been here before."* Detective Medina then turned to the officer who was now wearing a smirk and replied, *"Ms. Cook's not under arrest. And by the way, she use to work here before she got a better job with the state."* Aside from his countless run ins with Kyron, Detective Medina remembered when I use to work for the station as a secretary. I appreciated his defense and the fact that he didn't presume my guilt before hearing what I had to say.

As soon as I exited the elevator the first person who came to mind was Detective Albert "The Geezer!" I didn't know if he was non duty, had retired, or what, I just didn't want to run into him, cause only God knew how difficult he would have made things for me had we bumped heads. Once we reached Detective Medina's desk, he offered me a seat, lit up a cigarette, then offered one to me. Both of us sparked up, took a long drag and exhaled. He then pulled out his pad and before saying a word, I blurted out *"I did it!" "I did it... I did it... I did it..."* He then leaned back in his chair, folded his arms across his chest and told me to tell my story.

"Well, basically, whatever Ella told you, I guess is true. But I didn't steal her check, it was delivered to my house. I didn't know it was hers, and I didn't recognize the name. So I deposited it into my account, and when I cleared, withdrew it and paid my bills." The good detective tried not to laugh but couldn't help himself. *"Why didn't you take it to a check cashing spot instead of depositing it in your account,"* he asked. Now I was the one trying to hold back my laughter 'cause I could tell the good detective was dead serious.

We both lit another cigarette, share a few more laughs, then I continued telling my story. *"I did try to take it to a check cashing spot, but all of 'em wanted ID and wouldn't' cash it without it. I knew right then that was my warning, but I needed the money. I knew I was going to get caught either way, so what difference did it make."* Wow you really were desperate he replied, and I can't believe you're sitting her being so forthcoming. From that point on it was smooth sailing. We talked more about general everyday shit then we did about the check and within an hour, he had a signed statement from me, detailing what happened.

Detective Medina then went off to have a few words with the judge about releasing me on O.R, and postponing my arraignment for a few weeks. This way, I'd have time to put some money aside since he was more then sure I'd have a fine to pay. The judge agreed and

Detective Medina returned wearing a smile. *"Marie,"* he said. *"I really do understand why you took such great risk and I would have probably done the same thing had I been in your shoes. The sad part is had the check been a penny less, you would have avoided a felony charge. Anything in the amount of $2500 or more is considered a "Felony Robbery" and has to be heard in Superior Court."* He then handed me his card and told me to call him if I needed anything. In the meantime, he said, he would talk to the prosecutor for the state and put in a good word or two on my behalf.

I wasn't too happy to get hit with a second felony, but looking at the bigger picture, I got off pretty easy. No, I wasn't a thief because thievery wasn't how I made my living, and I damn sure didn't deserve to have robbery on my jacket. But I was able to go back home to my kids, didn't have to post a bail, and avoided jail, so really, I couldn't complain. I still had a job, even if it was only through the temp agency, and I still had a roof over my head. I returned to work on Monday and told Betty what happened. *"You were lucky, Marie. Count that as a blessing!"* Shit, she ain't have to tell me twice. Two felonies and I was still a free woman. Fuck what you heard, somebody was looking out for me!

****

They say the truth shall set you free, but not everyone lives by that rule. I'd given the Hyltons all that was owed and then some, but they still reneged on their end of the deal. No repairs were ever made and our winter was a long and cold one. Then at the beginning of the next year, they served me with papers to go to court, calming I still owed them more money. What the fuck!

This had me beyond pissed because not only did I rob and steal just to square things off with them, I turned around and handed them nearly half of my income tax return just so I could stay ahead. I was at a loss for words when I saw that eviction notice on my front door, but I wasn't going to roll over and let them get away with their shit. The eviction notice was merely a scare tactic and they were hoping I'd just leave instead of fighting them in court. The Hyltons had been notified by the city inspectors about the violations and the crew they sent over to make repairs said we needed a new roof before they could do anything to the inside. So instead of doing things the right way, they just wanted me to move so they could do a quick patch job, then put the house back out on the market for rent.

On the day of our court appearance, I had everything in order. I had all of my receipts plus a copy of the letter inspections mailed out to both of us listing the repairs. The Hyltons were playing hard ball for sure and even had the nerve to have an attorney accompany them to the mediation. I thought that was a bit much considering this was a landlord tenant issue, but I later realized their strategy. The court room was filled with people who were behind in their rent, and all of them utilized section 8, city welfare, or some type of government subsidy. Our case was the last one and right before we were called, the Hyltons' lawyer had a few words with the judge. This is what sealed my fate because afterwards, the judge wouldn't even hear what I had to say. He wouldn't look at my receipts and he refused to look at the letter from the inspectors. All he needed to know was that I was receiving assistance from the county and that was that. He ordered me to pay the Hyltons $1700 by the end of the day or vacate the premises. All I could do was leave the court room shaking my head in disgust.

The system works for the system. I knew I didn't owe those people any money but I was tired of fighting with them. They had sucked all that they were going to suck out of me and I wasn't about to let them drain me for anything else. Ms. Hylton knew she was wrong and couldn't even look at me as I exited the courtroom. She knew her acts placed me and my babies in a homeless situation and being a mother, I wondered how she slept at night. As for me and the kids, we were use to the bullshit. That evening I began packing our things but knew I'd have alt least three days to get things together before the sheriffs could legally come and lock us out. I had not a clue as to where the three of us were going to go, but I knew something would work out before it was too late. It always did…

There's a saying about people being in your life for a reason and who ever made that on up must have known someone like my cousin Shantell. Shantell called me that Friday once I got home and asked me what happened in court. I didn't want to drop a load on her but I did need to vent. Shantell could read me like a book and knew when I was holding back. So before I could go into detail she offered me and the kids her second floor. At first, foolish pride wouldn't allow me to accept her offer because being the older of the two, I felt it was my place to assist her not the other way around. But Shantell wasn't just my cousin, she was also the kids' Godmother and wasn't about to see her kids out in the street. Her offer was my only way out but I still felt odd about putting her at an inconvenience. My money wasn't right and I had no idea how long me and the kids would have to crash there. On top of that, I wasn't sure if I would be able to assist Shant with any expenses but money wasn't an issue. She told me I could stay as long as I needed and what ever I could give would be acceptable. *"We family, Murf, and I know you would do the same for me. So stop acting stupid and come pick up the key."* There really wasn't anything else to discuss after that. Once again, I'd been saved...

Although Shantell and I grew up together, had nothing but love for each other, and lived with each other when we were younger for several years, we were now adults, and lived two very different lifestyles. Shant was a single, professional woman with no children and I was a semi-professional with a boyfriend and two kids. Ironically, Ray, had just moved out of his sister's crib into his own spot about four blocks away from Shant, but I didn't feel moving in with him would have been in the best interest of the boys. It was way too early in our relationship to make a move like that and considering he only had a one bedroom, it would have been over crowded to say the least. The boys and I made our home out of the spare bedroom on Shant's second floor, and although there wasn't room for us to do anything else but sleep, for the time being we were going to make the best of it.

It's rare to find two independent Queens who can reside up under the same roof peacefully, but our pros outweighed our cons. Since Shant lived right around the corner from my job, I no longer had to worry about getting up early to catch the bus in order to get to work, and she was even kind enough to let me use her car in the morning to drop the kids off to school. Shant was rarely home and when she was, she was in her room. Shant was an intellectual but she was also very witty. She seldom tolerated any nonsense and refused to let me sit around feeling sorry for myself. In our moments when we both needed privacy, I'd put the kids to bed early and walk up to Ray's house and spend the night. I routinely tried to stay out of her way but with two kids to tend to, that was damn near impossible.

On occasion I could tell she just wanted scream and pull her hair out, but because we were family (are family) she dealt with it like a trooper. However, there were times when our feelings couldn't be disguised or contained and words or looks were exchanged. Being I was already down on my luck and dependent, that sometimes left me with a bad taste in my mouth. There were times when I even sat alone and cried because I could tell the three of us were cramping her lifestyle, but she swore up and down that wasn't the case. In knew our family bond would forever remain intact but I was more concerned with the strain our situation would put on our friendship than anything else.

****

Once school let out, things got a little easier for me and Shantell, but not for me on a whole. Now since she no longer had to get up in the morning and go to work, she could entertain company as late as she wanted. Usually this wouldn't have been a problem because Shant had very conservative taste when it came down to her friends and associates. But regardless of how choosey she was, having more than four adults in that house at once caused the noise level to rise. I remember one night in particular when members of her band came over. It was way past 10:00 p.m. when they arrived and the kids and I were already settled in for bed. I really didn't want to have to get up and go downstairs for anything because I felt I'd be crashing their gathering. I knew Shantell waited all year to be able to chill and relax the way she wanted, and I wanted to respect her, her home, and her company. But they were loud and I felt that she should have had a little more consideration for me since they were right underneath my head. But the more I tried to ignore the bumps, loud laughter and music, the angrier I became.

I knew it was her home, but she knew I was upstairs trying to get some rest too, and she knew I had to be to work in the morning regardless if she had to or not. Eventually, the frustration got to me and I walked downstairs pretending I had to use the bathroom. I hoped my presence would cause them to quiet down a little without having to say anything, but instead, they just got louder. That's when I realized that maybe, the kids and I had worn out our welcome. I was so sleep deprived, all I could do was cry, and didn't fall asleep until about two hour later after everybody cleared out.

****

Because I didn't want to have to change my son's school, I never gave a forwarding or new address to the post office. I knew it would take a while before anyone moved in to my old spot so I continued to use that address to get my mail. Towards the end of June, I got my letter to appear in court for the robbery, and the results of my hearing landed me three years probation and a hefty fine, but no jail time. Usually with a charge like mine a judge would only allow a year's probation, but in my particular case, the judge wanted to give me enough time to pay back my debt without breaking me. She too said she understood why I did what I did, but implored me not to repeat my actions. Again I was blessed, but the prime condition of my probation was to obtain permanent employment. Huh? Say that again. How the hell was I going to obtain permanent employment now with this shit on my record? Then wouldn't you know it, no sooner then the charge was official, a position opened up at my job and they were looking to fill it immediately. Talk about bum luck!

Maybe if things moved fast enough I could get the position before anything showed up on the background check? Maybe...? Although assuming I'd be the one to get the job was a bit premature.

With the concerns of my probation weighing heavy on my mind, plus me and Ray trying to establish ground in our relationship, I really didn't have room on my plate for anything else. I knew no matter how tense things became between Shantell and I, she'd never ask me and the kids to leave. However, subtle undertones were all I needed to motivate me into looking for a place of my own. I say this because one morning, can't remember if it was a Saturday or Sunday, I woke up to the sound of Shantell spanking and cursing at Messiah, which was something I didn't even do. For whatever reason, Quan and Messiah fell asleep downstairs the night before, but I didn't think it was that big of a deal. I couldn't imagine what Messiah could have done to anger Shant so much, but I didn't waste time trying to figure it out either. I quickly jumped up and ran downstairs to stop the madness, grab my son, and find out what was wrong.

Once I hit the bottom step I heard her say to him that he was too old to be pissing on himself and she yanked him up and threw the pillows from the futon aside. Messiah was a tough little baby, and even when something hurt him he rarely cried, but the look on his face said it all. Now I knew Shant would never do anything to hurt the kids or put them in harm's way, but bottom line, Shant wasn't a mother and had no idea how a mother felt in a situation like this. We were family, true, but this time she'd crossed the line.

Shocked didn't even begin to describe my reaction to Shantell's behavior and the look on my face showed I was not pleased! Though, because I was in her house with my kids living up under her roof, I kept it cute and just took my son back upstairs with me. I didn't even bother to say two words to her but was sure she felt the vibe. After laying Siah down next to Quan, I lit a cigarette then went back downstairs to clean up her couch. That's when I made the discovery that Messiah hadn't pee'd on her couch as she claimed. Messiah had long been potty trained but at the same time, was a heavy sweater. With the heat on and a blanket over top of him, my baby left a nice wet spot on her couch but it wasn't pee. It was sweat!

Messiah is naturally warm blooded, has clammy palms and feet, and rarely needs to be covered up. Doing so can even cause him to have a nose bleed, but thank God that didn't happen 'cause I can only imagine how she would have reacted. I was hurt no doubt, but I was more upset over the fact that my child had gotten his ass whooped for something he couldn't prevent. By now I knew Shant knew it wasn't piss either, but she didn't budge to come give either of us an apology. So on that note, I lit up another C.I, [Cigarette] walked in her room, and told her that me and the kids would be out or her hair by the end of the month. I didn't even bother to tell her that the spot on the couch was sweat or ask did she realize it on her own, because at this point it didn't even matter.

Yes, the presence of two Queens under one roof can really test a relationship, but through all trials and tribulations, love truly conquers all. Shant I and got past that little ordeal just like we've gotten through countless others, and in the end, our bond was only strengthen. My focus was now directed back on my job and the fact that I felt I needed to look for employment elsewhere. Preferably, a place that didn't conduct background checks! I began submitting resumes all over the place in search for a steady jig. I applied at Doctor offices, hospitals, dentist offices, automotive dealerships, just about anyplace you can think of where clerical help was needed. Yet, even with all of my ambition, drive, determination, and skills I still ran into dead ends. Either the hours were too long, too short, or the location was too far away. Either I had money and no transportation, transportation and no home, or the home and no money. No matter how hard I tried, I just couldn't seem to have all three necessities in hand at once long enough to get back on track. Go figure...

Time was now of the essence, and with the end of the month fast approaching, I needed to find a permanent job quick so I could move. Shant, wasn't applying any pressure, but I did tell her I'd be gone by the end of the month. I became increasingly frustrated and desperate, but didn't go out and catch another felony. Instead, I sat down, exercised some patience, and drafted a letter of interest to every director, manager, department head, chief, and coordinator I could think of. I implored them all to review my resume and consider me for any position they had available regardless of range or duties. I knew I was a valuable asset, but at the same time, needed to get my foot in the door before I could prove that. For a week straight, I networked myself throughout the department, traveling from floor to floor presenting myself to everyone I thought could benefit me in my pursuit. The more I inquired, the more impatient I grew. The longer I waited, the more doubtful I became. Yet, somewhere deep inside me, way deep down inside of me, was that mustard seed of faith Nana always spoke about, and that was all I needed to stay encouraged.

Waiting was the hardest part and although I knew there were plenty of people on my side who'd speak up for me like Betty, Suzanne, and Leslie, the game of office politics still stood in my way.

It's amazing, but for some reason, things always managed to play out in my favor. There I was with two highly respected administrators on my side and the one who saved the day was a clerical support person like myself named Nikki. Nikki suggested I go talk to Ms. Sarah who worked in WIC, and it just so happened I knew Ms. Sarah from my younger years of growing up on Spring Street. Who knew twenty years later I'd end up working with her and who knew she'd be the one to get my foot in the door. Nikki said I should give my resume to

Ms. Sarah and I did. Ms. Sarah told me I should go talk to the Director of WIC, who was also a good friend of hers, Ms. Deborah.

I told Ms. Sarah I'd follow her advice but felt walking into the Director's office would have been a bit bold. So, Ms. Sarah said she'd take the resume to her for me, but instead, took me and the resume in with her during one of Ms. Deborah's meetings.

Ms. Sarah introduced me to Ms. Deborah and told her I needed a job. At first I thought she was trying to make things look good because she knew me, but as it turned out, she was earnest in her approach. Yet, even though I could tell Ms. Sarah was sincere, I felt if Ms. Deborah was interested in me, she would have contacted me earlier since she was on of the directors I'd forwarded my resume to previously.

****

Ask and you shall receive, knock and the door shall open, seek and ye shall find. In the past I thought those were just words thrown together to pacify the weak and the needy, but I believed differently. I realized now that I had to remove the fear of being rejected before I could become effective in obtaining what I desired. I'd been asking, knocking, and seeking, but doubt made my efforts useless.

After Ms. Sarah introduced me to Ms. Deborah, a tall, brown skinned, stocky built woman, Ms. Deborah said she wanted to meet with me at a later date to discuss employment opportunities. She said she had just taken a look at my resume and was pleased with my experience and qualifications, but wanted to know more about Marie the individual as opposed to Marie the employee. We agreed to meet later in the near future and in the meantime I returned to my regular duties as a temp.

Now because I was so anxious to hear something either way, it seemed like things were moving extra slow. The second meeting between me and Ms. Deborah didn't take place for another two months, but in the meantime she spoke to her MIS Coordinator about interviewing me for the position she had available in her unit. That was definitely a positive sign, but it took an additional two months before they set up the interviews, and once they were concluded, they wound up picking someone else. This was all I could take and both my hopes and spirit was crushed. But again, some type of luck was on my side because the candidate they picked declined their offer for a higher paying position elsewhere. Now they had to do the interviews all over again, at which time I was called in again, but this time, felt like a reject.

During my second meeting, the secretary, Ms. Lois, told me she felt bad about what happened because I was initially their first pick. However, since the hiring manager didn't know how to complete the paperwork for a new hire coming in off the street, she opted to take the easy way out. That made me feel a little better, but as the saying goes, *"What God has for you is for you!"*

****

Nearly a month after my second interview, I received a call from Ms. Lois, telling me I'd been selected for the position. Ms. Jones and the MIS Coordinator wanted me to come over on my break to sit down and talk to them about a hire date, and to fill out certain paperwork to get the ball on the roll. *"No problem,"* I said, and when the day arrived, I sat and told them everything I felt they needed to know, including the circumstances surrounding my separation from the state back in 2000. I was so shocked to learn they didn't care either way about my past because what they'd seen of me thus far proved my worth. With that assurance, I did a Tiger Man and walked off like champion, but I wasn't out the woods yet. I knew I should have done so in the beginning but my excitement wouldn't allow me to spoil my moment.

The next day I returned Ms. Lois and confessed that I still had something to tell them. *"I have a second felony; a robbery charge that just hit my record not too long ago..."* After admitting such foolishness I felt sick, like I'd drank some rotten milk. *"Oh my"* she said. *"This is definitely going to slow things up, but you need not worry. I have a gut feeling things are going to work in your favor regardless."* Her confidence in me kept my spirits high. R.I. P Ms. Lois...

****

Doing the right thing doesn't always feel good, but it has its reward in the end. Even though it felt like I'd just screwed up the opportunity of a lifetime, I knew telling the truth only added to my worth and good character. Ms. Lois relayed our conversation back to the MIS Coordinator and WIC Director, and they still were turned off by the news. Bottom line, they didn't care about my mistakes, all they wanted to do was present me with an opportunity to get myself back on track. By

403

law, I wasn't even required to divulge that information to them. All I had to do was inform personnel something would show up on my background check so when the report came back there wouldn't be any surprises. But me being me, I figured it best to put it all out on the table initially because they were the ones I'd be working with, not personnel.

On the flip side of things, once the MIS Coordinator, Agnes, and Ms. Deborah learned about my probation and restitution in fines, they wanted to now first hand if there was anything they could do to help *"Hiring me is all the help I need"* I responded. I was ready, willing, and able to prove myself, but refused to come off as thirsty or desperate. . (I will admit, being so forthcoming with them was a mistake, because people love to hold things over your head when they feel they've done you a favor, but that's another story, another book...)

Now you know with every blessing comes a test and my greatest test has always been patience. The department couldn't give me a set hire date until after my background check was returned and that would take 3-4 weeks. So in order to keep my mind occupied and out of trouble, I put all of my time and energy into finding a home for me and the boys. Shantell and I were cool, and there was no rush for me to leave, but I was ready to have my own space again and so were the boys.

When the report came back, my new boss was promptly notified and she immediately began doing my paperwork with a start date of May 17th 2004. You would have though it was my born day the way I celebrated, and ironically, my new start date was only two day ahead of my old start date at the Labor Building, fourteen years ago. I guess May is a good month for me. Both of my children were born in May and so is my Mama!

The best thing about my position was the fact that I didn't have to change locations or adapt to a new environment. All I had to do was take my shit from one desk to another and I'd be good to go. On my first day, my boss, who's name I happen to share in part, (Marie Antionette) called me into her office and offered to contact my P.O. and inform her that I 'd fulfilled my obligation of obtaining permanent employment. I thanked her but told her that wouldn't be necessary. Although she may have only been trying to help, I didn't feel it was her place, plus, I'd already done so.

IF I HAD TO DO IT ALL OVER AGAIN, I WOULDN'T CHANGE A THING!

LESSON LEARNED

If I've learned anything from my past, it's life doesn't discriminate when it comes to hardship and pain. Everyone is susceptible to the trials and tribulations of life. Some seemingly endure more the others, but karma usually balances things out in the end. Emotions and learned behavior can influence a person into a lifestyle that's neither beneficial nor healthy, and assuming you know it all can lead you to make decisions that you'll later regret and may not be able to fix. Life is too short to live with regrets and thankfully, I have none.

Growing up I could have had it easier but had that been the case, I don't believe I would have become so strong or wise. As I look back, I see how having a father in the home would have curbed my behavior somewhat, but Nana's constant preaching finally paid off. Besides, I was hell bent on learning things the hard way, regardless of authority.

I've learned that as you grow, you often have to leave behind a lot of people, places, and things in order to continue that growth. I've learned that mistakes do happen, but some mistakes are so foolish, you can end up torturing yourself over them, and in turn, repeating them over, and over, and over…

I've learned that some people are God sent, and some are less desirable. But if you pay attention to what's going on, you stand to learn something either way.

I've learned you should never make yourself expendable for anyone's sake, you should always view yourself as the asset, and more important, you should always recognize your own self worth. Don't expect anyone else to do it for you because you may end up disappointed!

I've learned that miracles do happen, but people have to do the work in order to receive the blessing. It's sorta like having a job, if you want the pay, the raise, or the title, you have to first put in the work to gain it. Life is not like a lottery ticket or a scratch off, even though you have to take your chances. You should always choose your battles carefully and wisely, and never invest more in something or someone, than what's being invested in you. Asking for help doesn't mean you surrender to someone else's will or give them control over your free will.

I've learned that second chances are a given, because who actually gets it 100% right the first time around?

I've learned that being in charge of one's own destiny is a gift, not an option, and you should choose a path that has many doors, instead of one the one shot road, all or nothing.

I've learned that just because you love someone, doesn't mean you won't hurt them.

I've learned even the good at heart can loose their way and submit to the temptation of doing evil deeds.

I've learned that we often loose the one's we love, but we don't loose the love.

I've learned what's most important to me is family, and then youth of our tomorrow.

I believe everybody has a calling in life, but not all of us heed the call. I believe this is why so many of us remain stagnated and stuck in time, blaming others for the outcome of our unhappy lives. I would never consider myself a role model, but at the same time, I'm sure others can learn from my mistakes as well as the good I've contributed throughout my life. As I continue to grow as a woman and a mother, I learn to appreciate the pains my mother and grandmother went through on my behalf. I've learned to forgive family for their indiscretions, and love what we have, not dwell over what we've lost. My kids are my daily source of inspiration, and without them I know I would have allowed myself to descend in a downward spiral. I've learned that people are quick to judge others, without taking the time to learn the person first.

I've learned that I was the main source of many of my own heartbreaks and misfortunes.

In the end, I got back all that I'd lost previously and more, but it seems like I went through hell in the process. Giving up and throwing in the towel were never options for me, and even if they had been, I don't believe I would have caved in permanently. Going hard is what I do and half stepping just isn't in my DNA…

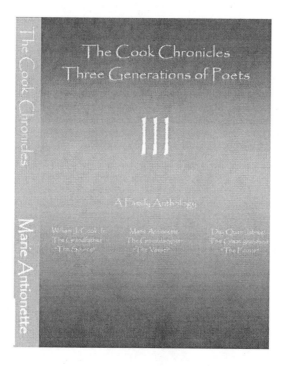

*The Cook Chronicles Thee Generations of Poets
By William J. Cook Jr., Marie Antionette
& Day'Quan Jabree
With Forward and Love Haiku by
Kicky Valentine*

Coming Soon
http://cauzingelevationpublishingllc.webs.com/index.htm
www.mzmarieantioinette.com
www.myspace.com/mzmarieantionette

The Struggle

By Marie Antionette

Coming Soon

Coming Soon

http://cauzingelevationpublishingllc.webs.com/index.htm

www.mzmarieantioinette.com

www.myspace.com/mzmarieantionette

"When you want to see a difference, you have to tell it like it is!"

Only A Jersey Girl

"A Jersey Girl is built to withstand the four seasons, which in turn, makes her well seasoned. Sunny days and warm temperatures year round is a breeze, but it takes a certain breed to endure the thunderous rain storms and deep footed snow, appreciate the fall and spring right back... ..."

Contact Author
Marie Antionette
C/O Cauzing Elevation Publishing, LLC
PO Box 159
Trenton, NJ 08601
http://cauzingelevationpublishingllc.webs.com/index.htm
Cauzinagelevation@gmail.com
mzmarieantionette1@verizon.net
www.mzmarieantionette.com